Societies and Culture in East-Central Europe
Irena Grudzińska Gross and Jan T. Gross, General Editors

Letters from Freedom

Post–Cold War Realities and Perspectives

Adam Michnik

Edited by Irena Grudzińska Gross
Foreword by Ken Jowitt

with new translations
from the Polish by Jane Cave

UNIVERSITY OF CALIFORNIA PRESS

Berkeley / Los Angeles / London

University of California Press
Berkeley and Los Angeles, California

University of California Press, Ltd.
London, England

©1998 by The Regents of the University of California

Library of Congress Cataloging-in-Publication Data
Michnik, Adam.
    Letters from freedom : post–cold war realities and perspectives /
Adam Michnik : edited by Irena Grudzińska Gross : foreword by Ken
Jowitt.
        p.   cm. — (Societies and culture in East-Central Europe : 10)
    Translated from Polish.
    Includes index.
    ISBN 0-520-21759-4 (hardcover : alk. paper).—ISBN 0-520-21760-8
(pbk. : alk paper)
    1. Poland—Politics and government—1989–.   2. Poland—Politics
and government—1980–1989.   3. Michnik, Adam—Interviews.
I. Grudzińska-Gross, Irena.   II. Title.   III. Series.
DK4449.M53   1998
947'.0009'049—dc21   98-22701
                                                                      CIP

Printed in the United States of America

This book is a print-on-demand volume. It is manufactured
using toner in place of ink. Type and images may be less
sharp than the same material seen in traditionally printed
University of California Press editions.

The paper used in this publication meets the minimum
Requirements of ANSI/NISO Z39.48-1992(R 1997)
(Permanence of Paper)

Contents

PART 2: NOTES FROM THE REVOLUTION, 1989–1990

PART 3: SPEECHES AND CONVERSATIONS

Illustrations

Editor's Note

Adam Michnik, one of the most outstanding personalities of Polish public life from the 1960s on, is a politician, writer, and journalist. This volume of his articles, speeches, and interviews follows his *Letters from Prison,* edited by me and published in 1985 in the same series by the University of California Press. Michnik was at that time in Barczewo Prison in Poland, surreptitiously writing some of the essays presented in Part I of this volume. In *Letters from Prison,* we could observe the ripening of East European democratic theory, the creation and blooming of the Solidarity movement, and its subsequent destruction by the military coup of General Wojciech Jaruzelski's police and army. This volume, which includes an interview with the now-deposed General Jaruzelski, chronicles the demise of the Communist regime, the elation that accompanied the post-1989 democratic growth of East European countries, and the slow setting in of what Michnik aptly called the velvet restoration. Michnik was an active participant at every stage of this often dangerous and always arduous journey. This very intimate involvement in public life is here reflected in the personal story of his journey from dissident intellectual to politician and then critical commentator on the new political reality. Part contemporary history, part spiritual autobiography, these writings show a country and a remarkable person in movement.

The selections presented in this volume were chosen from a rich body of Adam Michnik's writings. Most were translated by Jane Cave; a few, printed in French or previously published in English, had other translators. The author's postface was written especially for publication here. Information about events and people mentioned in this collection may be found at the back of the book.

Irena Grudzińska Gross

In Praise of the "Ordinary"

Ken Jowitt

The "Real" Poland

Adam Michnik is a partisan. He claims to be uncomfortable with the role of politician, but he does precisely what the "politician . . . must always and necessarily do, namely, fight." And he has the three "preeminent qualities" of a politician: "passion, a feeling of responsibility, and a sense of proportion." Nor can there be any doubt about Michnik's "knowledge of the tragedy with which all action, but especially political action, is truly interwoven."[1] As he says, "We live in a world of immutable dilemmas" (Chapter 19).

But what is the fight for? To define and defend the "real" Poland, which means creating a Polish civic idiom and set of civic practices and institutions. Michnik has a deep antipathy for what I call "castle politics," with its combatants, not participants, separated categorically behind ethnic moats and ideological or religious drawbridges. He recognizes that several castle constructions of the "real" Poland exist: nationalist,

---

1. A remarkable affinity exists between Weber's conception and Michnik's embodiment of political life. See Max Weber, "Politics as a Vocation," in *From Max Weber: Essays in Sociology,* translated, edited, and with an introduction by H. H. Gerth and C. Wright Mills (New York: Galaxy, 1958), 77–129. Quoted passages are from Weber, "Politics as a Vocation," 95, 115, 117.

Catholic, and Communist. He does not want to eliminate their occupants; he wants them to leave their privileged "castles" and share a "city."

For Michnik, the "real" Poland's contemporary genealogy begins with the Workers' Defense Committee, or KOR, a model "founded on the search for compromise . . . reject[ing] the revolutionary rhetoric of all or nothing." KOR was "a certain model of political reflection within a totalitarian system, a certain model of civil courage and the edification of independent institutions in a civil society" (Chapter 3). Its world-historical offspring was Solidarity. Solidarity's offspring is *Gazeta Wyborcza*. Michnik's genealogy of the "real" Poland begins with KOR, the "father," followed by Solidarity, the "son," and their "spirit," *Gazeta*.

If the nation-state is a partially conflictual amalgam of state, civic, and ethnic components, Michnik fights to ensure the primacy, not the exclusivity, of the civic. This comes out clearly in his conversation with General Wojciech Jaruzelski, whose stated concern is with Polish sovereignty and the contribution martial law made.[2] It would be very easy to dismiss Jaruzelski's claim, and it would be a mistake. Michnik knows that liberty and sovereignty are related, not mutually exclusive. He also knows that they are not identical—certainly not during martial law, which "only broadened the scope of your [Jaruzelski's] sovereignty as head of state, but dealt a crushing blow to the autonomy of the rest of society" (Chapter 23). For Michnik, civic liberty takes pride of place over state sovereignty and ethnic identity. So, as a proud Pole, he can say, "If Poland were a superpower, I would probably be . . . a gypsy," and believe that "our national interest will best be served if we become part of the world around us rather than some kind of godforsaken Slav enclave in the middle of Europe" (Chapters 3 and 24).

Michnik's fight for civic Poland, a Poland where state and ethnic dimensions are just that—dimensions, realized in the context of and relativized by the reality and centrality of a civic polity—is a fight against autarchic political, social, ideological, religious, and national fortresses animated by feelings of revenge, hatred, and "encoded animosities." Gesticulate fundamentalisms—religious, ethnic, and national—are to be fought and defeated by articulate publics. And the focal point of Polish civic heroism is *Gazeta Wyborcza*. *Gazeta*'s purpose is to overcome the

---

2. See Chapter 23. The same defense of Communist rule as having successfully preserved, prevented the diminution, or even enlarged Poland's "sovereignty" in the context of superior Soviet power is also asserted by several older members of the Polish United Workers Party (PUWP). See, for example, Jakub Berman's comments in Teresa Torańska's *"Them"* (New York: Harper & Row, 1987), 300.

Adam Michnik, September 1993. (Photo: Jerzy Gumowski)

weakness and formlessness that characterize so much of Polish life in the aftermath of the Leninist extinction. Michnik directs his efforts against an amoral urbanism, personalism, and egoism; against what Karl Mannheim described as "an inconstant, fluctuating public [that] can be reassembled only through new sensations."[3] His fight is against the "ghetto" mentality produced under Leninist rule; against rumor and dissimulation as modal *mis*representations of the population's public, or better, visible self.[4] As an intellectual, citizen, editor, historian, and politician, Michnik wants to "name things by their proper names, to articulate conflicts as conflicts" (Chapter 5). How remarkably old-fashioned this seems. How "enlightened," pre-postmodern, *tolerant*. How wonderful!

If in the early "eighteenth century the rulers of Saxony issued decrees prohibiting untruthful newspaper writings," declaring that they did not want "reasoners for subjects,"[5] *Gazeta*'s raison d'être is precisely to create reasoning and reasonable citizens. Michnik does not "know who would defend democracy if it were endangered." He does know, "however, who

3. Karl Mannheim, *Man and Society in an Age of Reconstruction* (New York: Harcourt, Brace & World, 1940), 97.

4. On the culture of dissimulation, see my chapters on "Political Culture," "Neotraditionalism," and "The Leninist Legacy" in my book *New World Disorder: The Leninist Extinction* (Berkeley: University of California Press, 1992).

5. Quoted in Reinhard Bendix, *Kings or People* (Berkeley: University of California Press, 1978), 388.

buys which newspapers [and that] for various reasons, hundreds of thousands of people in [Poland] prefer to read *Gazeta Wyborcza*" (Chapter 24).

But what will it take to sustain and enhance this civic reality? Stable democracy requires more than Michnik's courage and inspiration; even more than a civic institution like *Gazeta Wyborcza* and its attentive reading public. In contrast to mimic or facade democracy, genuine democracy has depth. It requires *three constitutions*—political, social, and moral—united by a culture of individualism. Individualism, not egoism. Not Karl Marx's civil society of "self-sufficient monads" and "Robinsinoids"; not Edward C. Banfield's "Montegrano," populated by egos absolutely obsessed with their self-interest, unrestrained by anything other than external obstacle, internal disability, or plain bad luck.[6] Rather, democracy requires that most extraordinary of cultural inventions, the individual, informed by conscience, aware of his and her independent (not derived) value and complementary (not categorical) identities.

As much as anything, Michnik's essays reveal a powerful and fallible individual painfully and continuously shaping, not deriving, his identity; asserting it, protecting it, fighting over and with it, valuing it, enjoying it. Michnik may be right to argue that the Polish Catholic Church "needs people who, like Erasmus of Rotterdam and unlike Luther, will stay in the Church" and protect it against the danger of fundamentalism (Chapter 24). Civic polities do need reasonable men like Erasmus to sustain them. As Johan Huizinga said, "In so far as people still believe in the ideal that moral education and general tolerance may make humanity happier, humanity owes much to Erasmus." But Huizinga also noted that "Erasmus is the man who is too sensible and moderate for the heroic."[7] There is a great deal of Erasmus in the editor of *Gazeta Wyborcza,* and fortunately, even more of Luther.

A Polish Luther

In the second and most fervent essay in this volume, Michnik examines Thomas Mann's exile and approvingly quotes six

6. Karl Marx, "On the Jewish Question," in *The Marx-Engels Reader,* edited by Robert C. Tucker (New York: W. W. Norton, 1972), 40; and Edward C. Banfield, *The Moral Basis of a Backward Society* (New York: Free Press, 1958).

7. Johan Huizinga, *Erasmus and the Age of Reformation* (New York: Harper & Row, 1957), 192, 188.

ideas of "this Don Quixote of the Nazi era." Among them is this: "Be one's own signpost when there are no other signposts" (Chapter 2). Michnik's individualism is his signature. "Poles," he says, "have the bad habit of justifying themselves for other people's sins. I am a revisionist, and responsible only for my own mistakes" (Chapter 3). At the core of his being Michnik is "protestant." His individualism does not exhaust his identity; or better, his individualism centers a multiplicity of identities. He is a Western individual. Listen: "I am not consistent when it comes to the order of values, knowing that conflictual values exist, but I am consistent when it comes to myself" (Chapter 3). Michnik worries about only one thing: "being right with myself. Everything else is God's affair" (Chapter 3). Sound familiar? "Unless I am convinced by the testimony of the Scriptures, or by clear reason, . . . I cannot and will not retract anything, since it is neither safe nor right to go against conscience"— Martin Luther at the Diet of Worms, 1521.[8]

Michnik's response to "Cauchon," to hierarchical and corporate authority, is the same as "Saint Joan's." Joan asserts: "My voices do not tell me to disobey the Church; but God must be served first." To which Shaw has Bishop Cauchon reply: "And you, and not the Church, are to be the judge?" Joan's reply: "What other judgment can I judge by but my own?"[9] Mieczysław Moczar did Adam Michnik a great service by attempting to impose a categorical identity on him: Jewish. A Communist Cauchon, Moczar identified himself in categorical, stereotypical, corporate terms—Communist and Polish—never in individual terms. But Michnik thought, "It wasn't up to Mieczysław Moczar . . . to decide whether I was Polish, Jewish, or Chinese. It was none of their business" (Chapter 3). In the same spirit of individualism, Michnik opposes collective guilt. Communists are not to be punished on ascriptive grounds "just because at one time or another they belonged to the Communist party." If they are punished, it will be as individuals in a court of law (Chapter 22).

Still, if Michnik's preferred identity as a civic individual is clear, he remains confused about its meaning in a Roman Catholic Polish culture. However, he knows where to search for the answer. "This is where I would look for the roots of the phenomenon that we are still unable to deal with intellectually, the phenomenon called Father Maksymilian Kolbe. We must find the courage to ask: Who really was Maksymilian

8. John Dillenberger, ed., *Martin Luther: Selections from His Writings* (Garden City, N.Y.: Anchor Books, 1961), xxiii.

9. Bernard Shaw, *Saint Joan* (Baltimore: Penguin Books, 1961), 130.

Kolbe? He was undoubtedly a saint" (Chapter 24). Saint, yes; individual, no!

Father Kolbe gave his life in place of another prisoner in Auschwitz. Michnik applauds Jan Józef Szczepański's "splendid essay" about Kolbe, an essay in which Szczepański examines this "strange combination of heroism and sainthood and parochialism, primitivism, and venomous hatred cloaked in the authority of the Catholic Church" (Chapter 24). Kolbe's saintliness and anti-Semitism are, Michnik says, "somehow closely intertwined with each other." And he shares Szczepański's justified "unease" about Kolbe. What, he asks, "is the source of this syndrome"? The answer is, traditional Polish culture and, more generally, non-Western cultures, in which identities are categorical, stereotypical, corporate, all-encompassing; like Jehovah, jealous and "greedy."

Kolbe's sacrifice was ultimate and extraordinarily courageous. But what or whom did he sacrifice himself for? I wonder if, in fact, doubt, the person (in contrast to the soul) for whom Kolbe sacrificed himself mattered as much to him as the sacrificial act itself? Kolbe's political and religious identity was that of a person immersed in one "greedy institution,"[10] the Polish Catholic nation. He could and did act in a heroic manner worthy of a martyr. But he did so neither as an individual nor for an(other) individual. *There is no discrepancy between Kolbe's saintliness and ethnic chauvinism.* Kolbe's world was composed of invidiously ordered categories: Roman Catholic, Polish, Jewish, Communist. His categorical imperative was the group, not the individual. His personal sacrifice was genuine and genuinely symbolic.

Michnik recognizes the issue is not simply Father Kolbe; it is the relation of Roman Catholicism to moral, political, and economic individualism. I do not think Michnik wants to recognize how essentially opposed to individualism the Roman Catholic Church is. He refers to Stefan Kisielewski's alliance with Catholic circles "because [Catholicism] . . . was deeply rooted in the national consciousness [and was capable of] reconciling individualism with concern for the common good" (Chapter 4). However, Michnik must confront the meaning of the common good and community in Catholic Poland. In Witold Gombrowicz, the "secular humanist," he finds a kindred spirit. Gombrowicz understood that "communism was a system that subordinated the individual

10. The concept of a greedy institution does not refer to the ethics of an institution but to its absolute claim on a person's self. See Lewis Coser, *Greedy Institutions: Patterns of Undivided Commitment* (New York: Free Press, 1974). His chapter "The Militant Collective: Jesuits and Leninists" is of particular interest in this context.

to the collective" and that the "best way to fight communism [was] to strengthen the individual against the masses" (Chapter 4). He also recognized the corporate quality of Polish Catholicism, "the danger lurking in the stereotypical anti-communism of the Polish Catholic. Thus *he called on his fellow Poles to discover the individual.*"[11] In that same spirit, Michnik describes himself as a "friend of the Church," neither member nor enemy, a friendly critic. The Church, he says, "fascinates me, and I find much in it that appeals to me." But as his girlfriend, Basia, points out, "Having few real contacts with the Church [makes] it much easier for [him] to like it" (Chapter 3).

What, then, is the answer? Can individualism be reconciled with Polish Catholicism? Michnik offers us a strikingly practical instance of "reconciliation." And the example suggests, I think correctly, that the hope for Polish individualism lies more with the growing individualism of an increasing number of "protestant" Polish Catholics than with the Church as institution: "The Church says that Catholics aren't allowed to divorce or abort, but Catholics aren't looking to the Church for answers to those questions. You could see that clearly during Solidarnosc: the same people who hung crucifixes in union premises *only listened to their consciences and not to the bishops* when it came time to decide whether or not to strike" (Chapter 3; emphasis added).

To be sure, the Church is not and will not be reconciled to even a social "protestantization" of its place and meaning in Polish life. But to the extent that Michnik's particular observation about Polish workers in 1980 is more generally true, then despite the Church's desire to absolutize its identity and stereotype its members' identity, its role is being relativized and their identity individualized.

Michnik's rejection of categorical identities and the corporate entities that "correctly" define them is most evident in his attitude toward the Communist party. The ambivalence that surrounds his attitude toward the Church disappears when he addresses the party. The party has no saving "grace." Its mortal sins were privilege and paternalism. Communist Poland was "a state organized according to the same principles as a nursery school, with its small children and teachers." In contrast, democratic Poland will be a state "designed for adults" (Chapter 23). In a civil society "people do not want to be pupils . . . ; they act as citizens" (Chapter 5).

---

11. Chapter 4 (emphasis added). Another, highly significant "other" for Michnik, Czeslaw Miłosz, says in his interview that he also "is allergic to the Polish-Catholic combination." But it is not clear how he feels about individualism.

For all their genuine, character-defining differences, both *the* party and *the* Church make "greedy" identity demands. Members of each organization ideally derive their identity from an entity that conceives of itself as corporate, superior, and exclusive. Stefan Staszewski's characterization of the party is apt: "For the Party isn't simply the Party; it is a word which replaces all known concepts and expressions; it is an absolute. . . . It is always right [infallible]."[12] All corporate groups negate the individual (some the self as well). Tactics designed by persons within such groups to devise an autonomous private space for the self may succeed; but these are ad hoc sites of personal autonomy, not principled sites of individual independence. Michnik's response to the party's corporate paternalism is intellectual, political, *and* visceral. When asked what advice he would give to the Communist party, he quotes the Polish poet Julian Tuwim, "whose words are addressed to Communists in all lands: 'Kiss my arse' " (Chapter 5). His rejection of the party is—and I'm afraid he will have to accept my characterization—part of a highly *consistent* critique of corporate political ontologies; ways of life that deny the individual's centrality and justify imperious hierarchy with paternal ideas of "false consciousness," or, in the Church's case, "invincible ignorance." His quest is for a polity, culture, society, and psychology that *relativizes* such claims and the organizations that make them. In his view democratic thought has "no place for fundamentalism of any kind," including ethnic fundamentalism (Chapter 20).

Currently, in the West, liberal intellectuals are painfully contorted in their effort to simultaneously appreciate the individual and the "particularity" of ethnic membership. In contrast, I find Michnik's take on ethnicity refreshingly conservative (as he would say à la Burke, not de Maistre) and clear. I interpret his position to be this: respect ethnic solidarity/reject solidary ethnicity.

His intolerance of anti-Semitism speaks to this distinction. "Anti-Semitism has become a code and a common language for people who are dreaming of a nationally pure and politically disciplined state . . . without people who are 'different.' . . . What characterizes this kind of anti-Semitism is a strange fascination with blood and heredity, . . . in the racial backgrounds of grandfathers and great-grandfathers" (Chapter 18). Michnik abhors this greedy, categorical, corporate conception and organization of identity. He sees it as the basis of social fragmentation, mutual hate, and violence. In such a society the civic individual can only be

12. Torańska, *"Them,"* 135.

at risk, at risk of being no more than a jester, a quixotic figure whose individualism equally offends and challenges those with opposing non-
biodegradable identities, whether they be Polish, Catholic, Communist,
or Jewish.

Michnik wants neither a Poland populated with Max Stirner's "egos"[13]
stripped of political, ethnic, and religious loyalties nor a Poland of "children" subject to the paternal direction of "greedy" corporate institutions.
He wants a Poland of civic institutions populated by individual citizens.
If I may be forgiven a Stalinist mode of formulating a point, Michnik is
saying implicitly that *either* individualism defines the meaning of group
identities in a society *or* group identity defines the meaning of personal
identity in a society. I am saying explicitly that in a civic polity group
membership resembles a banquet more than a fortress.[14] Entry to, membership in, and exit from a liberal association emphasizes individual
choice as much as group permission or certification and thereby limit the
power of permission and certification. Similarly, in a liberal modern society the individual integrates the multiplicity of his or her partial and role-
bound identities. This not only differs from but also opposes the organization of a traditional society made up of "greedy" corporate associations
separating a person's multiple identities with categorical group barricades
and imperatively coordinating them by means of an invidious status hierarchy. To create and sustain a civic, democratic, tolerant way of life, one
must relativize absolute ethnic, religious, and ideological identities.
Michnik knows one must choose to lose the solidary comfort (and intolerance) of a fortress identity if one is to gain the catholic solidarity that
comes from choosing one's identit*ies*.[15] In this regard Michnik has a
courage and insight that largely escape Ira Katznelson in his criticism of
Michnik's alleged "failure" to "[incorporate] Jewish particularity into the
Polish nation" and to adequately affirm his Jewishness.[16]

If, on the one hand, Katznelson defends liberalism (individualism)
because "for all its infirmities and hypocrisies, liberalism . . . remains the

13. See Paul Thomas, *Karl Marx and the Anarchists* (London: Routledge and Kegan
Paul, 1980), 125–75, for a concise statement of Stirner's thought.

14. I take the metaphors "banquet" and "fortress" from Stalin. See "The Proletarian
Class and the Proletarian Party," in *The Essential Stalin,* edited by Bruce Franklin (Garden
City, N.Y.: Anchor Books, 1974), 43–46.

15. I am not happy with the idea of "choosing" one's identity. It suggests a level of ease
in deciding about identity and a forgiving plasticity about the world, neither of which I accept. "Claiming identity" is both a more evocative and a more accurate formulation.

16. Ira Katznelson, *Liberalism's Crooked Circle: Letters to Adam Michnik* (Princeton:
Princeton University Press, 1996), 111, 110 fn. 16.

only great political tradition to affirm and contain moral and group pluralism," then, on the other, he criticizes it because "liberalism's universalism and individualism make it hard to find a place inside the doctrine for the recognition of groups, including cultural and national groups, as legitimate rights-bearing units of citizenship." After all, Katznelson says, "a decent liberalism does not repudiate difference."[17] True. However, a decent liberalism should not, in fact cannot, practically incorporate all difference to the same extent. Liberalism is a peculiar partisan statement. Reflecting its philosophical peculiarity, it must tolerate "differences" whose purpose is to destroy it. Reflecting its politically partisan nature, liberalism must ideologically reject and politically defend itself against certain "differences."

And what about ethnic differences? Michnik does not reject ethnicity per se. Rather, he prefers ethnic "lite"; the flourishing of multiple cultures *within* individuals, in place of and in opposition to the flourishing of multiple cultures behind categorical ethnic, religious, and political barricades.[18] He describes himself as a Pole of Jewish origin.[19] Michnik does not reject his Jewish family origins, or he would not have accepted the Shofar Award. Only if one accepts a primordial notion of ethnic and religious identity[20] can Michnik be accused of "so little affirmation of being a Jew."[21] Katznelson simply does not get it. "It" being that individual civic identities *do come at the expense of corporate identity.* They are essentially antagonistic identities: one, derived and "jealous"; the other, chosen and generous.

For those who operate with a "greedy" understanding of ethnicity and religiosity, individualism means assimilation, that is, loss of a previously corporate identity; and they are right. For the primordialist, ethnic

17. Ibid., 104, 135, 116.

18. I take the phrase "flourishing of multiple cultures within individuals" from David Hollinger, *Post-Ethnic America* (New York: Basic Books, 1995), 49, but in a spirit very different from the author who finds it exceptional that multiple cultures can not only flourish in a nation but "even [*sic*] within individual Americans." My point is that individualism provides a consistent site for the flourishing of multiple relativized cultures. My own Irish, English, Catholic, working-class cultures and my wife's Jewish, Protestant, middle-class cultures—all seem to be doing quite well precisely because they are multiple *and relative* parts of our individual American identity.

19. In a footnote, Katznelson quotes a statement of Michnik's, "by a Pole who has never hidden his Jewish origins" (*Liberalism's Crooked Circle,* 110 fn. 116).

20. Much like those who refer to "lapsed" or "nonpracticing" Catholics assume some ineradicably ascriptive quality to certain identities, some genetic impulse to resume one's "true" identity and character flaw in denying its "deep particularity."

21. Katznelson, *Liberalism's Crooked Circle,* 110.

lite isn't "real" ethnicity at all. In contrast and opposition, the individual experiences identity as a multiplicity of chosen, partial identities centered in the self, uncertified by categorical groups. Understood in this way, individualism simultaneously offers the only viable base for a civic polity and annoys, frightens, and angers the members and leaders of "greedy institutions."

In a sense the individual in contemporary Poland, and even more so in the other countries of the former Soviet empire, is a little like the character in John Le Carré's *A Small Town in Germany* "whose accent was neither wholly English nor wholly German, but a privately elected no man's land, picked and set between the two."[22] Such people presently operate in a fragile public space, with the memory of past corporate identities and the fear that as yet unnamed fortress identities will emerge with their greedy claims. Michnik's ethical, political, and individual vocation is to help recast the character of Polish identity, culture, and institutions to the point where the individual no longer lives in a "privately elected no man's land." Michnik wants a Poland where "citizens can meet and collaborate independently of their faith, nationality, or ideology"; a Poland of deep individualism, not deep cultural particularism (Postface).

However, civic individualism is not simply the sum of voting and associating. In Michnik's view, if democracy is to withstand challenge and occasional failure, individualism must have a moral constitution. By asserting and addressing the moral basis of individualism, Michnik criticizes and enriches the remarkably *stingy* discussion of democracy in Western academia—one that bears a remarkable resemblance in certain respects to Marx's definition of bourgeois civil society. The "stingy" view of democracy sees it as a collection of self-interested, instrumentally oriented, entrepreneurial politicians and selfish citizens mutually restrained by calculations about the positive utility of an electoral game that does not guarantee victory but offers the possibility of such, as well as the guarantee that the defeated can regularly challenge the victors. I recognize these features of polyarchy. And I insist that polyarchies with only these attributes are shallow, fragile, and *not* likely to develop into robust democracies. Electoral repetition will not produce civic democratic institutions. Institutionalization and addition are very different processes. In sharp contrast to the Western social scientists who believe that rational choices will magically transform egos into individuals, Michnik argues that only a sense of the moral and sacred can infuse democracy with

22. John Le Carré, *A Small Town in Germany* (New York: Dell, 1968), 6.

decency and courage. In situations in which it might be rational to run not fight, doubt not believe, punish not forgive, reject not accept or quit; in those situations morality and a sense of the sacred can be a source of courage, confidence, mercy, toleration, and endurance. Democracies with social and moral depth require Don Quixotes irrational enough to fight the odds. Which in turn raises one of life's "immutable dilemmas." Don Quixotes seek perfection, while Michnik has "always believed that a perfect society could be created only in a concentration camp" (Chapter 23).

The Moral Basis of a Democratic Society

Michnik's theory of democracy's origination and consolidation depends on "graceful," not merely rational, choices. In stark opposition to those who dismiss the idea of legitimacy, or believe that "those who make institutional changes pursue their own individual interests above all else and their interests center on furthering their own political careers,"[23] Michnik believes that "there are certain principles that we have to defend, regardless of the circumstances," even when (or especially when) our interests may seriously suffer (Chapter 24).

Listen to his location and explanation of KOR's origin: "It came out of a moral impulse. I remember attending a trial in 1976 that implicated some Ursus workers; I heard the condemnations, I saw the wives crying, and I shook with rage. I felt that it would be inadmissible to drop these people" (Chapter 3).

How (instrumentally) *ir*rational! And yet how firm a foundation moral beliefs (not abstract "values") provide new organizations, particularly when their members are surrounded by a hostile polity and society. In those circumstances, a necessary condition for success is that "those who shamelessly give priority to their interests [electoral or otherwise] without regard for moral considerations" not occupy leadership roles.[24] Michnik's appreciation of democracy's moral constitution is an invaluable complement to Joseph Schumpeter and others who address the

---

23. Barbara Geddes, "A Comparative Perspective on the Leninist Legacy in Eastern Europe," *Comparative Political Studies* 28, no. 2 (July 1995): 239.

24. Thomas Mann, quoted by Adam Michnik, Chapter 2.

strictly political component, as well as to those few and valuable formu-lations of democracy's social constitution.[25]

In part, the moral constitution of democracy concerns language. As one of his "teachers," Czesław Miłosz, says in an interview with Michnik, "Words really do have a force. Words are a serious business" (Chapter 21). And Michnik's language often has a deliberately moral cast. "Soli-darity was a confederation against evil . . . a moment of grace." How-ever, more than words are involved. "If you are defending an idea, you first have to show, by your own behavior, that you believe in it; in other words, you have to bear witness" (Chapters 23 and 3). Point: while lan-guage counts, it does not create. It contributes to an ethos; it does not bring one about. The vulgar speech at Stalin's "court" did not create a regime of terror; it did contribute to its ethos. Nor are Michnik's refer-ences to mercy and grace, his admonitions against violence, hate, and re-venge, sufficient bases for a democracy. They are symbolic parts of its moral constitution. The power of those symbols and language depends on their incorporation and expression in the graceful choices and actions of strategic actors who bear witness in nondemocratic and democratic settings—men like Andrei Sakharov, János Kis, and Václav Havel, who helped make the moral "word" *freedom* political "flesh." Moral courage substantiates moral language. Sakharov, "a great scholar, . . . named a Hero of Socialist Labor an unprecedented three times, . . . belonged to the most privileged class in Russia. And yet he rejected it all to become the defender of human rights . . . 'the conscience of Russia.' " What, Michnik asks, "gave those people the strength? . . . Why did a great physicist, a distinguished philosopher, a famous writer and essayist . . . sacrifice freedom, calm, and personal security for a seemingly hopeless battle . . . ? Not one of them ever declared himself to be a man of reli-gious calling or a politician. And yet, embroiling themselves in politics, they bore moral witness" (Chapter 15). Perhaps they bore witness out of a moral impulse. Perhaps moral—and immoral—impulses are a first and necessary, though not sufficient, cause for creating institutions. If so, what forces and settings favor moral courage as an emergent property of particular individuals and groups?

25. Joseph A. Schumpeter, *Capitalism, Socialism, and Democracy* (New York: Harper & Row, 1962), Chaps. 31, 32; Ernest Barker, ed. and trans., *The Politics of Aristotle* (New York: Oxford University Press, 1962), Bks. 2, 3, 4, 6; Harry Eckstein, *Division and Cohesion in Norway* (Princeton: Princeton University Press, 1966), Appendix B: A Theory of Stable Democracy.

Michnik identifies several. There are *institutions*, like the Roman Catholic Church, whose concern with truth, distinguishing good from evil, and belief that we are all children of God, precisely because they are moral convictions, not simply interests, carry with them not only the risk of dogmatism but also the promise of steadfast courageous defense. There are *experiences*, like jail, that underpin and increase one's moral courage (assuming, of course, one lands there in defense of principles, not illegal pursuit of interests). According to Michnik: "If I hadn't gone to jail, I might be a scoundrel like Mieczysław Rakowski or Jerzy Urban now. I thank God for my years in jail" (Chapter 3). And the longer one spends on Michnik's preferred path of living life in "truth and dignity," the greater the likelihood it will become "something truly addictive" (Chapter 2).

Inspiration — provided by those who have borne and bear witness — is a third source of moral courage and individualism. For Michnik they are his "teachers" Sakharov, Kiš, Havel, Gombrowicz, Kołakowski, Miłosz, and Mann. People you want to emulate. People you do not want to disappoint. People whose recognition you seek.[26] People you form "sacred friendships" with in jail. People who share your "fatal addiction" to living life in truth and dignity.

Moral courage is ethical in an individual, political in a group of individuals. And as Max Weber notes in *The Protestant Ethic and the Spirit of Capitalism*, "In order that a manner of life . . . should come to dominate others, it had to originate somewhere, and not in isolated individuals alone, but as a way of life common to whole groups of men." Why? Because "the spirit of capitalism . . . had to fight its way to supremacy against a whole world of hostile forces."[27] And in his conversation with Jaruzelski, Michnik makes it very clear just how hostile Poland was in 1965 to the democratic actions he and his friends undertook: "To say there was social support at that time for people like me is simply a figment of our heroic mythology. We were considered deviants, madmen who were best kept at arms' length" (Chapter 23). Like sixteenth-century Protestants, opponents of Communist regimes were deviants who on the basis of their "sacred friendships," moral beliefs, and courage sus-

---

26. Michnik tells how he once went to Paris, leaving his colleagues to face the "Power" while he drank champagne. But he also "gave interviews [and] took part in demonstrations. . . . No one had dared to do such things before me. But I felt I had to act like a live torpedo, a kamikaze, to prove to Jacek Kuroń that I wasn't a deserter" (Chapter 3).

27. Max Weber, *The Protestant Ethic and the Spirit of Capitalism* (New York: Charles Scribner's Sons, 1958), 55–56.

tained each other in their irrational fight against the odds. And won! But that isn't the whole story.

The need for democracy and the need for the sacred make up one of life's immutable dilemmas. Except for extraordinary circumstances, democracy and the sacred are conflicting imperatives. Echoing Weber, Michnik believes that "politics and ethics belong to different worlds." Though fused in the struggle against Communist power—"the politics of those totalitarian regimes was, after all, an open attack on ourselves, on our freedom, on our dignity, on truth—" in normal circumstances an ethic of responsibility and one of ultimate ends have different rationales and implications, call for different skills and virtues.[28] To make this point, Michnik contrasts the conspirator and the politician: "One becomes a conspirator for completely different reasons than one becomes a politician. Becoming a conspirator involves a moral choice, it involves choosing one's fate, whereas becoming a politician involves choosing one's profession" (Chapter 24). And yet a viable democracy must have representatives of both ethics—those with a responsible concern for the consequences of their actions and those who feel " 'responsible' only for seeing to it that the flame of pure intentions is not quenched"[29]—and representatives of each ethic must accept the value, or at least the discipline, of tolerant terms and frameworks for their continuous mutual critique.

In Weber's view a civic polity's integrity depends on the possibility of combining an ethic of responsibility with an ethic of ultimate ends. In an unusually passionate passage he declares, "It is immensely moving when a mature man . . . is aware of a responsibility for the consequences of his conduct and really feels such responsibility with heart and soul. He then acts by following an ethic of responsibility and somewhere he reaches the point where he says: 'Here I stand, I can do no other.' That is something genuinely human and moving. . . . In so far as this is true, an ethic of ultimate ends and an ethic of responsibility are not absolute contrasts, but rather supplements, which only in unison constitute a genuine man—a man who can have the calling for politics."[30]

Let me trace some of the routes and risks Michnik takes in his effort to treat the ethics of responsibility and ultimate ends as supplements. Michnik's signature effort to meld an ethic that "takes account of pre-

28. See Chapter 3; and Weber, "Politics as a Vocation," 119–28.
29. Weber, "Politics as a Vocation," 121.
30. Ibid., 127.

cisely the average deficiencies of people" and an ethic of ultimate ends that favors acts "that can and shall have only exemplary value" manifests itself in his uncompromising rejection of violence as a means to gain power.[31] "Whoever uses violence to gain power uses violence to maintain power. Whoever is taught to use violence cannot relinquish it. In our century, the struggle for freedom has been fixed on power, instead of the creation of civil society. It has therefore always ended up in the concentration camp" (Chapter 5). When Jaruzelski accuses Michnik of being "a tiger [that] was going to bite us," he replies: "Our intentions were bloodthirsty when it came to institutions but never when it came to people" (Chapter 23). Rejecting the idea that the Round Table had been a mistake, Michnik says, "I'm happy that I was able to contribute to a situation in which not a single drop of blood has been spilled during this transformation" (Chapter 23).

However, the same Michnik forthrightly states, "If the Russians ever occupied the country, they had to know that they'd be spitting blood" (Chapter 3). He tells General Jaruzelski: "If I had been in the vicinity of you, General Kiszczak, or Premier Rakowski on December 13—a moment of national upheaval—and if I'd been armed, I'm quite certain I would have taken aim" (Chapter 23). These are not the words of Jesus and the Sermon on the Mount; nor even of Gandhi. Michnik is no pacifist. However, he is absolutely removed from Frantz Fanon, for whom "violence is a royal pardon, . . . the colonized man find[ing] freedom in and through violence."[32] For Michnik, shedding blood is the last resort, the adoption of an ethic of ultimate ends to defend one's individual and national dignity and avoid the "spiritual capitulation of the terrorized." Michnik en-courages "[spitting] out the gag of fear" (Chapter 6). Courage in defense of dignity and truth is *good*. "The 1980–81 events were a revolution for dignity, a celebration of the rights of the vertebrae, a permanent victory for the straightened spine" (Chapter 5). Violence to gain and maintain power is *evil*. Violence is the antithesis of a civic political order. "Violence fractures social bonds. And, whenever society is so atomized, its intrasocial networks shattered, it becomes vulnerable to totalitarianism," to a prepolitical and antipolitical organization of power.[33]

---

31. Ibid., 121.

32. Frantz Fanon, *The Wretched of the Earth* (New York: Grove Press, 1966), 67, 117.

33. See Chapter 5. The American political theorist Sheldon Wolin makes a very similar point in "Violence and the Western Political Tradition," *American Journal of Orthopsychiatry* 33 (January 1963): 15–28.

The associated risk comes from Michnik's rather dogmatic and politically disarming, in certain circumstances, disabling, claim that violence
has never added to the emergence or development of democracy. Risk-
ing a Rabelaisian response from Michnik, things are more complicated.[34] The American Revolution and Civil War were violent acts that
made positive contributions to democracy. In this regard, Weber's appreciation of politics is more penetrating. He recognizes that "politics
operates with very special means, namely, power backed up by violence. . . . Whoever wants to engage in politics at all, and especially in
politics as a vocation, has to realize these ethical paradoxes. . . . [H]e lets
himself in for the diabolic forces lurking in all violence."[35]

A second route Michnik takes in an effort to supplement an ethic of
responsibility with one of ultimate ends is to adamantly identify with
"the Polish people, . . . with all that is weak, oppressed, and humiliated."
After all, "the ethos of the Polish intellectual . . . is the ethos of someone
who fights for freedom and is on the side of the weak . . . [not of] power
and hierarchy" (Chapters 3 and 24). Obviously, this is an ideal statement
about the appropriate calling for a civic intellectual. To side with the
weak is to deny oneself privilege and power, which Michnik argues categorically divide a people and corrupt rulers and ruled alike. Siding with
and defending the weak politically, keeps you morally humble and honest. The risk here, and Michnik recognizes it, is that unless one searches
for common ground with opponents, is both partisan and tolerant, able
to listen, not simply broadcast, one may end up absolutizing the virtues
of the weak and become intolerant and self-righteous in their defense.

A third route Michnik travels in his effort to bring morality to bear on
democracy is his personal effort to "transcend the limits of [his] own
grievances," to inject an element of mercy in political life (Chapter 24).
He even provides some evidence that his effort is appreciated, notably
by Lech Wałęsa, who on one occasion says, "You know Adam, I admire
you. In your place, if I'd had to deal with a guy like myself, I would
probably have slit his throat. You are a saint. You let me live" (Chapter
3). In a similar vein, Michnik refuses to reply to the sometimes crude
criticisms Cardinal Glemp directs at him and *Gazeta*. "I remind myself
that mercy must come before justice and I bite my tongue" (Chapter

34. To explain the risk: in response to one of many jejune comments by Daniel Cohn-
Bendit, in this particular instance, to his observation that things were more "complicated"
than Michnik made out, Michnik responded, "Complicated, yes, but only the asshole
isn't" (Chapter 3).

35. Weber, "Politics as a Vocation," 119.

24). Mercy is not weakness. "I'm the last person to pander to my fellow countrymen" (Chapter 23). Principle circumscribes popularity. When one encounters situations, organizations, or people who have "lost the capacity to distinguish good from evil, truth from falsehood," who are impervious to "reasoned persuasion," one must resort to "a sharp, piercing shout and coarse words that can disturb the internal order of the self-infatuated mind" (Chapter 2). And then one must accept the frightening risk accompanying such a stance: estrangement from one's society, culture, and nation. Can one who operates with a selfishly utilitarian understanding of democracy summon the civic courage to take that risk and pay that price? Doesn't an act of that order require a "moral impulse," a sense of the profound connection between democracy and individual dignity; one that makes acts of solitary public courage possible — and necessary! Possible and necessary for the individual who, faced with immoral alternatives that offer no real choice, for example, between Hitler and Stalin, refuses the "lesser political evil" and joins Michnik in saying, "I would pick Marlene Dietrich" (Chapter 2).

Democracy and the "Ordinary Hero"

Democracy needs Don Quixotes, with their ethic of ultimate ends, and Sancho Panzas, with their ethic of responsibility. It needs actors and institutions whose distinctly opposed moral and political competencies are at their best testy, at their worst nasty. The strategic *and* moral question is, which should predominate in a democracy? In extraordinary situations Michnik chooses Marlene Dietrich, but he regularly votes for Sancho Panza.

He says, "I don't think in utopian categories anymore. Solidarity was an anti-utopian movement, a movement without utopia. . . . Solidarity brought something completely new to European culture, and by that I mean the primacy of practical thought over utopian thought. . . . Solidarity fought for a civil society that is imperfect by nature" (Chapter 4). "We know . . . that every political order is polluted by the original sin of imperfection. We reject the belief in political utopia. We know that our future is an imperfect society, *a society of ordinary people and ordinary conflicts.*"[36]

36. Chapter 16 (emphasis added). He immediately goes on to say, "precisely for this reason, a society that must not renounce its ethical norms in the name of political illusions."

To the argument that democracies are procedural arrangements with uncertain policy outcomes, Michnik adds the observation that they are fallible and flawed entities whose deliberate lack of perfection guards against the perfection of the concentration camp. In the spirit of Gombrowicz's query, "The question that I put to Catholics is not what kind of God do they believe in, but what kind of people do they want to be?" Michnik wants a Poland of "ordinary, decent, rational people" (Chapter 24). He does not want saints, SS men, or cadres fighting for a utopia; believers for whom ideas are more real than the people in whose name and over whose bodies they are pursued. Like Arthur Koestler, he prefers the reality of men to the abstraction "mankind."

Michnik's presentation of self reflects his idea and pursuit of an "ordinary" Polish democracy. He describes himself as an "unserious" man, a reasonable man, one who says, "This role of the martyr doesn't suit me at all" (Chapter 3). He demonstrates this position in his interviews. After one of his stays in prison, Michnik went to work at the Rosa Luxemburg factory. It was, he says, "my first direct, and warm, contact with the world of workers." The ever-serious Cohn-Bendit asks Michnik, "So that phase can be seen as your forced Maoist phase?" To which he replies, "No, not Maoist. . . . The Rosa Luxemburg workforce is composed primarily of women, the most beautiful girls in Warsaw." Not to be denied, Cohn-Bendit goes on to ask, "Were the contacts between you and the workers simple from the very beginning, or was there a period of suspicion towards you?" Michnik: "Suspicion, no, never. It is I who was shy. But I never lost my way on the path leading from eroticism to politics." Later, referring to Solidarity, Michnik identified its only utopia as "the Ten Commandments and the Gospels—except for the commandment about adultery" (Chapter 3). And describing the period when every two weeks he spent forty-eight hours in jail, he complained that "the worst wasn't being in jail, but waiting to get there; we all knew full well that we would be put in jail, but we never knew when. This difficult situation ruined my sex life. I couldn't make dates anymore" (Chapter 3).

What is one to make of all this? The answer is uncomplicated. Michnik has a Rabelaisian sense of humor, an irrepressible and pointed irreverence that fits his understanding of democracy. Democracy is not the preserve of saints, cadres, and heroes. Democracy is fallible, "eternal imperfection, a mixture of sinfulness, saintliness, and monkey business."[37] Like Adam, democracy "stutters."

37. Postface. It is political science's loss that this phrase will never make the political science textbooks.

To the challenges facing new democracies, Michnik favors practical, not charismatic or philosophical, solutions. He tolerates the Kwasniewski government because it respects democratic norms, and was chosen by a citizenry acting in a democratic manner. Which is not to say that he is enthusiastic about this government. That becomes clear when he discusses the "restoration," the surprising electoral success of former Communists throughout the eastern parts of Europe. His first observations are Quixote-like, charismatic: "[The] mark of a restoration is its sterility. . . . Revolution had grandeur, hope, and danger." "I do not like restoration. I do not like its ethics or aesthetics, its shallowness or boorishness." But he concludes à la Panza: "Nevertheless one cannot simply reject this velvet restoration. One has to domesticate it. One has to negotiate with it as with an adversary and/or partner. One has to permeate it with the values of the velvet democratic revolution" (Chapter 25). Within Michnik, the ordinary democrat Panza sets the terms for the extraordinary Quixote.

Along with the "restoration" of former Communists, Michnik is apprehensive about the Leninist legacy of nearly a half century. He sees it as more than a residual stain readily dissolved by an electoral detergent.[38] For Michnik the legacy of Leninism and the interwar experience in Poland challenge and weaken the political, social, and moral constitutions of democracy. "We lack the tradition of democratic coexistence in the framework of a democratic order. . . . In Central and Eastern Europe, each of our countries has its distinct biography, its own secret knowledge about threats to democratic order" (Chapter 16). Michnik's practical response to this "lack" has been extraordinary. As editor of *Gazeta Wyborcza* he has created a strategic civic institution and the nucleus of a civic community.

In *Kings or People*, Reinhard Bendix "propose[d] to treat intellectual mobilization—the growth of a reading public and of an educated secular elite dependent on learned occupations—as an independent cause of social change."[39] And Michnik? "I say that *Gazeta Wyborcza* is playing a major role in creating a new language in which to discuss and evaluate the world around us. *For us,* Gazeta *is not just a newspaper, it's an institution of civil society, an institution of Polish democracy*" (Chapter 24; emphasis added). *Gazeta*'s role? To create and disseminate a civic idiom, an

---

38. See Adam Przeworski, *Sustainable Democracy* (New York: Cambridge University Press, 1966), 48, for a statement of the "detergent" thesis.

39. Bendix, *Kings or People*, 266.

ethos of partisan and reasoned debate; to reclaim those who belonged to Solidarity, "all those people [who] amid errors, inconsistencies, ill-considered decisions, and demoralizing arguments . . . carried out the historic task of the anti-Communist revolution in Poland" (Chapter 25). *Gazeta*'s institutional vocation? To articulate the connection between liberal proceduralism, tolerant individualism, and a "concern [with] the human condition" (Chapter 5); to permeate all of Poland with the spirit of "ordinary" democracy *and* the extraordinary courage to defend it.

Democracy is a contradiction and a paradox. Without heroism, public virtues cannot be sustained; they gradually deteriorate into egotistical calculi of social, economic, and political self-interests. The individual gets replaced by the self.[40] And yet as every liberal disciple of the Enlightenment and foe of Nietzsche knows, the charismatic hero abhors, in fact is incapable of, democratically appreciating the deficiencies of average people. Michnik responds to this "dilemma" in a Weberian spirit. All historical experience, says Weber, "confirms the truth that man would not have attained the possible unless time and again he had reached out for the impossible. But to do that a man must be a leader, and not only a leader but a hero as well, *in a very sober sense of the word.*"[41] In short, democracy needs "ordinary heroes." Adam Michnik is an ordinary hero, a genuine man whose contributions to the culture of democratic individualism and toleration in Poland and the world are fallible and invaluable.

40. See Daniel Bell's discussion of the individual and the self in his outstanding work, *The Cultural Contradictions of Capitalism* (New York: Basic Books, 1976).
41. Weber, "Politics as a Vocation," p. 128 (emphasis added).

PART ONE

Hopelessness and Hope

Cold Civil War

*Poland Ten Years after the Founding
of the Workers' Defense Committee (KOR)*

Jean Krauze: You and Bogdan Lis were both freed a month before other
well-known political prisoners, so you have had more time to assess
the political situation.

Adam Michnik: The overall situation hasn't changed much in the past
few years. The government lacks the capacity to initiate reforms and
remedies the situation by creating show institutions, fakes. And you
also have a society at large that isn't ready to engage in confrontational action, and finds that kind of action inappropriate. I agree with
that actually, since that type of confrontation could lead to deplorable
consequences. So we are in a state of cold civil war.

However, the liberation of political prisoners has created a new
and different situation, which may open the door to real dialogue and
serious reforms. Then again, I am not in the position to predict what
the leaders' response will be. Their intentions remain quite obscure to
me — they may be convinced that dialogue is necessary, or they may
be trying to throw powder into the West's eyes, to make it seem as if
the opposition had been strangled and Solidarity had ceased to exist,
which would be naive on their part. But this government has already

Interview by Jean Krauze. Reprinted by permission from *Le Monde*, September 21–22,
1986. Translated by Catherine Beltier.

engaged in what, to me, are irrational behaviors, and so often that I cannot exclude this hypothesis.

Krauze: General Kiszczak, the minister of interior, has recently said that for the most part, those now coming out of prison are not "partners in the national understanding."

Michnik: Yes, exactly. That's a very good example. Does that mean that God has granted the general the faculty to decide who is a partner and who is not? Why are people like Zbigniew Bujak, who has millions of workers supporting him, or Władysław Frasyniuk not partners, while a certain Miodowicz [president of the official unions], who was named by the government, gets to be one? This is infantile, and very dangerous, reasoning.

Krauze: From what you have seen during your month of freedom, do you not get the sense that oppositional activities in Poland have substantially diminished?

Michnik: That is a difficult question for me to answer. But can you show me just one other Communist country where the very existence of five hundred clandestine publications is imaginable? Even if we accept the notion that there has been a certain reduction in these activities because of fatigue and so on, the opposition remains the only force that can negotiate with the government.

Krauze: Are young people still joining the opposition?

Michnik: Yes, of course. I see people joining who were children during the Gdańsk accords and who are now workers.

Krauze: Workers, not just students?

Michnik: Yes, workers.

Krauze: But isn't there a certain tiredness among the Solidarity leaders? When Wałęsa is forced to repeat the same things for six years, don't his words lose their weight?

Michnik: Absolutely, and this is a problem for all movements whose leaders must maintain a certain equilibrium between the demands of the present and those of the future. And when we speak of the future, we are forced to say unpopular things. Unpopular for two reasons: because we encourage behaviors that attract repression and also because we remain believers in the notion of a dialogue, which most people do not believe in. This is a problem. But I still do not see any other possible way than that chosen by Wałęsa and the Solidarity leaders.

Krauze: KOR [Workers' Defense Committee] was born exactly ten years ago. It was founded by a group of intellectuals to aid workers who were put in prison after the riots in Radom and Ursus. And isn't the result of all these efforts and enthusiasm the fact that today, and for at least a few days, there will be no political prisoners in Poland?

Michnik: Yes, that's possible. But if I think of my life during this period, and those of my friends and all of the Polish people, I can say this: a process of social detotalitarianization has been taking place during the past ten years. It has had many phases of varying intensity, but there is no denying that this group of about fifteen people—the KOR founders—has come to represent a certain model of collective behavior. Simply put, that behavior is the combination of a relentless struggle for human rights and a refusal of violence. This has had an enormous influence on social behavior in Poland, on the society's self-education, on the appearance of a new type of social link, and on the diffusion of a new democratic model. This is all new. Those of us who had known the nationalist slogans brandished during the sixties, like anti-Semitism and everything else, were very scared that this demoralization wanted by the government would be effective. That has not been the case. The few traces of it that might remain are now purely exotic, marginal.

Krauze: Don't you fear a current of thought like that represented by the Confederation for an Independent Poland, a nationalist opposition party led by Leszek Moczulski, who himself has recently been freed from jail?

Michnik: I don't think that anyone today can fault Leszek Moczulski for the same things as ten years ago. They have changed for the better.

Krauze: Are KOR's principles still relevant?

Michnik: Not in everything. For example, KOR excludes all conspiracies and clandestinity. But conspiracy has been imposed on us by the government after December 13, 1981. KOR was the movement's beginning, its childhood. But it did build a way of thinking that remains current, a model that is founded on the search for compromise and rejects the revolutionary rhetoric of all or nothing. And especially on a certain self-limitation and a recognition of the role played by the Church. All of this remains valid. As does, above all else, the principle of the solidaristic defense of one by the other.

Krauze: You have sometimes used a contemptuous, almost insulting language toward members of the government, as in the letters you ad-

dressed to General Kiszczak from your jail cell. Isn't there a certain
contradiction between that tone and your attachment to dialogue,
your search for agreement?

Michnik: I am not a union leader. I am an intellectual, and I speak for
myself. I try to use what you call my contemptuous language only
when the government leaders deserve it. I can't be appeased by the
humanism of a government that frees me after condemning me. And
if I call for dialogue despite the nature of this government, it is because I want to avoid a civil war, from which no democratic system
has ever emerged. And after all, I am neither a psychoanalyst nor Mr.
Kiszczak's confessor. It is not he who interests me, but Poland's
affairs.

Krauze: You wrote no less than five books while in jail. Is it really so easy
to write in Polish jails?

Michnik: No, it's very difficult. But I felt that the government could steal
five years of my life, and I thought, no, I must be the one who steals
this time from them. That is why I worked so intensely. It wasn't just
about the books, it was about seeing whether I could justify my life in
captivity. Even more difficult was getting what I had written to the
outside world. The surveillance network at Barczewo [his last deten-
tion center] was very dense. There were cameras and microphones
everywhere. I was forced to undress completely so that they could try
to find what I was hiding. But they never found anything.

Every network has holes in it. I took advantage of that. I was allowed to borrow books from the library and sometimes to get books
from the outside, and I was never deprived of paper or pen, even if
my notes were stolen at the exit. And I want to be fair: as much as
guards in other prisons hounded Frasyniuk or Czesław Bielecki, I was
not mistreated. It was always a case of choosing a scapegoat, and this
time it was their turn. It had been me in 1968.

Krauze: It is quite likely that the West will react very positively to the liberation of political prisoners and will modify its attitude toward the
Polish regime. In this case, what do you expect from the West?

Michnik: We have never expected much. But certainly we hope that if we
are locked up again, public opinion in the West, understanding its
own interests, will pay attention.

2

Don Quixote and Invective

For Stanisław Barańczak

I

Fifty years have passed since a certain German emigrant published an open letter in a New York paper that put him outside the fold of official German life. His critics even claimed that he had put himself outside the German nation. They argued, what good is a writer who abandons his nation at so crucial a moment? What good is a writer who attacks the German state in a foreign, hostile press and thereby participates in anti-German propaganda financed by the enemies of Germany? Does a writer like this, who allows himself megalomaniacal aspirations to govern souls in Germany, have the right to expect his country to agree to publish his books? No! The German people will not tolerate renegades spreading slander about "brown terror" in a country they left in so mean-spirited a way. Such emigrants slander Germany in order to ingratiate themselves with their foreign sponsors. Foreigners find the national revolution and rebirth in Russia a bitter pill to swallow—that is why they attack the new order and its leaders. But they should have no illusions: the German people will be deaf to the calumny and appeals of

Reprinted by permission from *Four Decades of Polish Essays,* edited by Jan Kott (Evanston, Ill.: Northwestern University Press, 1990), 373–96. Translated by Lillian Vallee.

turncoats and subversives; the German people will not permit others to blacken the names of their most cherished sons, leaders of the National-ist Socialist party, who run a legal government and conduct a policy of stabilization. The Germany governed by Adolf Hitler does not want war—it wants order and peaceful cooperation. Germany remembers well the Weimar epoch of anarchy, upheavals, strikes, unemployment, and the specter of hunger. There will be no going back to those times. Germany is undergoing normalization. The subversives are isolated.

They, these fair-weather patriots, also say that the German state is a threat to peace. It would be hard to come by a more flagrant lie. Ger-many—the chancellor of the Reich, Adolf Hitler, has declared this on several occasions—wants peace with everyone. Thoughts of expansion are alien to Germany. This peace must, however, be a just peace, free from dictates and interferences in internal affairs. That is why it is neces-sary to break with the ideologizing of international politics, with its at-tempt to blockade Germany, with its criminal plans to support the in-ternal enemies of the German state or its traitorous emigrants. Against this background of interference in the internal affairs of Germany, no agreements are possible.

II

Thomas Mann, Nobel laureate in literature, knew the lan-guage of these arguments inside out. He couldn't stand Nazism, and much earlier, in his well-known essay "Goethe and Tolstoy," spoke of it bluntly.

I do not propose to dwell upon German fascism, nor upon the circum-stances, the quite comprehensible circumstances, of its origin. It is enough to say that it is a racial religion, with antipathy not only for international Ju-daism, but also, quite expressly, for Christianity, as a humane influence; nor do its priests behave more friendly toward the humanism of our classical lit-erature. It is a pagan folk-religion, a Wotan cult; it is, to be invidious—and I mean to be invidious—romantic barbarism. It is only consistent in the cul-tural and educational sphere, where it seeks to check the stream of classical education, to the advantage of the primitive German heritage.[1]

---

1. Thomas Mann, *Essays of Three Decades,* translated by H. T. Lowe-Porter (New York: Alfred A. Knopf, 1971), 172. Most of the subsequent excerpts from Mann's letters are taken from *Letters of Thomas Mann, 1889–1955,* selected and translated by Richard and Clara Win-

Mann did just the opposite. He defended the humanist tradition and classicism, the life of the spirit bequeathed by the past. Subsequent Nazi excesses made him realize he could not limit his reaction to a careless shrug of the shoulders. Nazi propaganda could count on being effective among the German people; it could also count on finding believers among disoriented foreigners. But these were not the only reasons for his concern. He realized that the status of an exile—especially within German tradition—was ambiguous: it meant breaking with collective national destiny and choosing a separate road. Such a decision is always difficult and always costly. Perhaps this was why he was reluctant to assume expatriate status right away?

Let us recall: he found himself in exile quite accidentally. In February 1933 he and his wife left Germany because Mann was giving a series of lectures abroad. In the course of his voyage, he stopped in Switzerland. That is where he learned of Hitler's seizure of power. He could not, nor did he want to, return to a totalitarian Germany. ("The question arises . . . whether the air there will be breathable for me," he wrote.) He did want to be present in Germany through his books, however. And thus while other refugees, including Mann's children and his brother Heinrich, engaged in anti-Nazi political activity, he, a Nobel laureate, the greatest name in modern German literature, *said nothing.*

Why did he keep silent? wondered German emigrants. He was often asked this question. One literary critic felt his silence was due to the "incapacity to make decisions and solve problems" that was so typical of liberalism when faced with "the irrational and anti-intellectual currents of the epoch." In a private letter Thomas Mann protested against this interpretation. He wrote:

I have sacrificed two thirds of my worldly possessions in order to be able to live in freedom outside the German frontiers. And even without engaging in furious polemics against the Third Reich, by being outside I am perpetually demonstrating against what is being done in Germany and to Germany today. It has seemed to me worthwhile to remain in contact with my German public, which by character and culture is in opposition to Hitler's system today and from which someday the countermovement against it can emerge. This contact would be immediately destroyed—that is, my books, which the Germans can still read, would have been banned at once—if I had

---

ston (New York: Alfred A. Knopf, 1971); the remainder (unavailable in English) have been translated from the Polish as cited by Michnik. Subsequent references, to either the *Essays* or the *Letters,* are in the text.—TRANS.

drawn my sword more plainly than I have in any case done in my statements of recent years. (*Letters,* p. 237)

When on his sixtieth birthday, in 1935, he received many letters from Germany, he was pleased. "The hundreds of letters from Germany—yes, yes, from Germany, even from labor camps—have done my heart good. The need to demonstrate an inner freedom must be strong and wide-spread if the occasion was seized upon so readily."

Nonetheless these self-interpretations were received with a dose of skepticism. Mann was accused of allowing his silence to be used by semi-official Nazi propaganda. People sneered at his concern for honoraria from German publishers, for saving his home in Munich and other ma-terial possessions. These were not completely groundless accusations. Everyone—even Thomas Mann—gives in not just to spiritual but also to completely prosaic temptations: the author of *The Magic Mountain* made no secret of this. In an April 1934 letter to another exile friend, he wrote:

My abhorrence of conditions there, and my ardent desire to see the gang in control there go to hell one way or another in the shortest possible time, has not changed in the slightest. But I see less and less why I should be excluded from Germany for the sake of these idiots, or should leave them my belong-ings, house, and property. I am continuing my efforts to wrest these things from the hands of the Munich hoodlums; and since, to the disappointment of these same hoodlums, I was not expatriated during the latest deporta-tions, there actually is some chance that I will regain possession in the fore-seeable future. To have our own furniture would mean a great saving in rent for us, and it would also be a psychic reassurance to be surrounded by the objects of our previous life. But the chief point is that recovering them would be a triumph over the present tyrants of Munich and would willy-nilly have to be accompanied by the renewal of my passport. Then I could at least travel to the Memel area to see to our house there. I claim the right of such freedom of movement; I feel their denying me that freedom is an out-rage. Isn't that a possible attitude, *too?* Do tell me whether you regard it as treasonous and unprincipled. (*Letters,* p. 216)

Thus he vacillated between temptations and desires. He deluded him-self: he got nothing back. Can one hold his calculations and illusions against him? Wouldn't holding these things "against him" conceal some ugly feature of character that allows us to demand that others live as saints and exclusively according to our expectations?

I am inclined to answer this question in the affirmative. I am inclined to believe that in the secret ease with which we believe the most repugnant slander about emigrants, and how others can be controlled by the specter of material gratifications, lies one of the chinks through which totalitarian dictatorships secrete venom into human souls. Our aroused envy of exiles is supposed to reconcile us to our torturers. How sad this is. . . .

Mann was caught in the cross fire. The newly created Union of Reich Writers demanded he declare that he served literature in the spirit of "national authority." Emigrants were waiting for him to make a clear-cut break. Everyone held Mann's indecision against him. And he kept silent; he did not want to decide one way or another. Why? His reticence concealed other, unrevealed motives. Mann feared becoming reduced by politics. For so many years he had defended his status as an "apolitical man," as a writer independent of parties and doctrines, and had protected himself with his famous irony from the vulgarity, dirt, and Manichaeanism of the world of politics that one may assume he was well aware of the dangers awaiting a writer reduced to the political medium. He was writing *Joseph and His Brothers* at the time, and he wanted to offer this book to his German readers. He could do this only at the price of silence. Did he have the right to do this?

III

He pondered the question himself. He wrote about his doubts in private letters. Taken together they make an unusual, if unplanned, literary work and a fascinating chapter in the *Bildungsroman* that was his life. In August 1934 he wrote:

Daily events in Germany so sharply irritate my moral, critical conscience that work on my third volume has come to a total halt; I am on the point of setting it aside in order to devote myself to a political credo and polemic in which I relieve my heart and take revenge for all the spiritual injury inflicted on me during this year and a half. Maybe I can deliver a blow that the regime will feel. Of course I am miserable about the novel, which in any case has been delayed, and I know very well how many arguments there are against such an investment of time and energy. Is there even any sense in neglecting finer duties to argue against this rot? On the other hand, isn't it also a duty which the world would thank me for? In short, I vacillate and don't know what to put my hand to—a horrible condition. (*Letters*, p. 225)

He also wrote:

What concern is "world history" to me, I suppose I ought to think, so long as it lets me live and work? But I cannot think that way. My moral-critical conscience is in a state of constant exacerbation, and it is becoming more and more impossible for me to continue pursuing the, it may be, sublime game of novel writing until I have "rendered an accounting" and unburdened my heart of its concern, its perceptions, its pain, as well as its freight of hatred and contempt. . . . The time seems ripe for such a statement as I have in mind, and the moment might soon come when I would repent having delayed too long in silence. (*Letters,* p. 224)

He wrote as well, and this is an important remark, that he felt the world crisis as a crisis in his own life and work; this is how the main conflict of the epoch was reflected in him. As if he were justifying himself to us. And we? We say sometimes that the duty of an intellectual is to "testify to values." And we say too that realism, efficacy, should determine all public undertakings. Undoubtedly, both of these postulates are correct. In formulating them together, however, we seem to forget rather easily that this life strategy of a "golden mean" allows harmonious existence only when democratic norms of living together function, when pluralism and the principle of dialogue are the natural environment of human words and gestures. The essence of totalitarianism is the destruction of this natural environment. When the order of pluralism dies, the rules and criteria of normal existence die with it. Whoever lives in the old way and does not accept, or pretends not to accept, the existing changes, whoever wants to live in a totalitarian system according to rules formed by the order of democratic pluralism, is either a saint ripe for martyrdom or a hypocritical conformist ready for betrayal. He is a saint if he speaks the words whose natural result are a concentration camp; he is a flunky if in making gestures that seem apolitical on the surface, he registers acquiescence to totalitarian institutions.

In Mann's letters, there is the record of his ending a friendship on these grounds. When in 1918 his youngest daughter, Elizabeth-Veronica, was baptized, the presiding pastor was Kuno Fiedler, the godfather Ernst Bertram, Mann's friend, an essayist and literary historian, the author of a well-known book on Nietzsche. After the Nazis' accession to power, Kuno Fiedler "found himself" in prison, while Ernst Bertram found himself in "the new reality." The fate of Mann's two friends was symbolic of the alternatives of the time, a prison cell or intellectual self-enslavement.

Ernst Bertram tried in November 1933 to convince Mann not to submit to the exile propaganda that was vilifying Germans in the eyes of the world, to discard the "distorting glasses" and look at the "new Germany" with faith in its future, to remember that certain painful excesses are simply the inevitable price of the "national revolution," for "you can't make an omelet without breaking eggs." Bertram tried to assure Mann that "everything was normal."

Mann answered his friend in a letter written in January 1934. He wrote with considerable respect and the same amount of resolve. He thanked Bertram for his "great epistolary effort," "that generous sacrifice of time and energy," and then he declared: "I shall not embark on a reply and an attempt at correction, for it would necessarily be endless and hopeless. We have moved too far apart, and arguing back and forth can only cause more sadness on both sides."

He assured Bertram that Hitler's propaganda was demonizing the emigrants' significance, and that his conception of their role and influence was greatly exaggerated. "If the whole world has not yet reached a proper understanding of the grace and dignity of your Germany, the wholly uninfluential exiles are not to be blamed or credited for that. The widespread notion to the contrary among your fellow countrymen is totally benighted, and it would be a good thing if you opposed it." In explaining his point of view, he wrote:

No, I do not regard the new Germany (but can it be called new? it is simply that the same forces which have oppressed and threatened us for more than ten years have now achieved absolute autocracy) through any distorting medium. Rather, I see it as I am accustomed to see things, with my own eyes. I know its thoughts and works, its style of speaking and writing, its bad—in every sense of the word—German, its base moral and intellectual level proclaimed with astonishing frankness. I know all this, and it suffices. I am sure that you too occasionally find this level an embarrassment, however fiercely you may deny it. But I use far too facile a word for things that are ultimately mortally serious. (*Letters,* p. 206)

And last he tried to talk Bertram into taking a trip to Switzerland: "We will be able to talk about the 'landslide of the century' with the requisite manly control." The meeting never came to pass, however. Bertram put his lectures on the spirit of the "new Germany" and the "national revolution" ahead of his conversations with Mann.

A few months later, in one of his letters to a friend, Mann wrote: "My old friend Bertram recently gave a speech in honor of Schiller, in which he called him 'a Doric' German-Frederickian man.' Those people have really lost their minds. It almost tempts one to warn them: 'Children, consider how this will look in a few years.' " To Bertram he wrote bluntly:

I have been reading your essays with all the response that your upright and judiciously intelligent Germanism has always aroused in me. That you are capable of confounding this Germanism with its basest travesty and taking the most repulsive scarecrow begotten by world history for the "savior" of whom your poet speaks—this is a constant grief to me, a grief that often enough all but converts into its opposite the feeling of which it ultimately is an expression. I am surely not speaking with exaggerated solemnity when I remind you that if I had followed your well-meant and insistent advice I would today—the probability is so great that it may just as well be called a certainty—no longer be alive. What would that matter, you will say, compared with the "historical creativity" now in progress? Of course it would not matter. And yet I sometimes think that this certainty, simply in view of your nature, should slightly modify your credulous support of the powers from whose grasp a merciful fate has preserved me.

"We shall see," I wrote to you a good while back, and you replied defiantly: "Of course we shall." Have you begun to see? No, for they are holding your eyes closed with bloody hands, and you accept the "protection" only too gladly. The German intellectuals—forgive the word, it is intended as a purely objective term—will in fact be the very last to begin to see, for they have too deeply, too shamefully collaborated and exposed themselves. (*Letters*, p. 222)

One must know Thomas Mann's prose and essays well, one must continually remember his cultural refinement, the reticence of his feelings, and his fascination with German spirituality and zealous World War I patriotism to truly understand how much these words must have cost him.

How differently he related good news! In a letter to his brother Heinrich written two years later, he described a miraculous meeting: "Out of the house, like a ghost, Dr. Fiedler came to meet us. He escaped from a police prison in Würzburg, jumped over two walls, he himself cannot explain how he did it; some brave Tell transported him across the lake in a boat. . . . Now we are pampering and coddling him."

But he didn't coddle the Nazis for an instant.

IV

The invective in Thomas Mann's letters of those years says the most about his mood. This paragon of impeccable manners used a gamut of unparliamentarian epithets in characterizing the Nazis. He wrote about "the ruling gang," "idiots," and "hoodlums"; about "the repulsive clown" and "the miserable wretch"; about "the excrescence" and "villains," "obscurantist cretinism," "grim farce," "base servility," and "spiritual castration." Why did he lose control of his tongue?

In simplest terms, he was enraged because his moral sense had been offended, because those closest to him had been hurt. This answer, however, is unsatisfactory. It does not explain why an inner voice told him to respond to the "landslide of the century" with the linguistic landslide of his private correspondence. Let us repeat the question: why did he write about the legal government of the German state, recognized by all foreign capitals, in the language of a barroom brawl? —he, the epitome of German patrician courtesy.

Thomas Mann had been a patriot of the German state. In contrast to his brother Heinrich, he always kept his distance from the formulas of the international left. Revolutionary criticism in the name of supranational values was alien to him. He followed in the footsteps of Luther and Goethe, which for him meant a program of loyalty to the German nation and state. This was the world of his values; if there was room here for opposition to the government, then it was only in a language of loyalty toward the law and an ironic distance to the pressure of historical events. This "apolitical man" was clearly afraid of being sucked dry by politics, with its one-dimensionality and inescapable fanaticism. And by the language of politics in which arguments are replaced with words of abuse. Why then did he reach for invective?

He was a writer who was familiar with the ambivalence of human destiny. He knew that every right has its counterright, that every conclusion is an oversimplification, that a natural and splendid feature of human existence is openness, ambiguity, and the multiplicity of values. He knew that only irony and friendly appraisal of all the formulated positions allow harmonious participation in culture. He knew this better than any other German writer. Why then did he reach for invective?

He loved his nation and his state. He knew how to look with unjaundiced eye upon the gentry, the middle class, and the rebels; the emperors and Bismarck; the generals and Social Democrats. He was able to discern the authentic values in each of these spiritual stances. It was only in regard to the Nazis that he could not. Here he gave up discursive language, friendly appraisal, dialogue in the name of understanding. Here he reached for invective. Why?

We are trying to understand why he felt it was impossible to conduct polemics with the Nazis.

To a friend he wrote: "So-called National Socialism has no place at all within any European and ethical framework. It stands in opposition not just to 'liberalism' and 'Western democracy,' but also to civilization in general" (*Letters*, p. 226).

This is how he assessed the devastation of the natural environment of pluralism. This meant that a man in Germany, subject to the pressure of terror and totalitarian propaganda, lost the capacity to distinguish good from evil, truth from falsehood; he lost the elementary power of recognizing the contours of reality and the causal ties governing it. Such a man cannot be a partner in dialogue, for dialogue is by its very nature the privilege of people who are free. A German repeating Goebbels's formulas about Jewish domination is as sensitive to arguments as the fanatic who believes two plus two is five. Self-stupefaction and self-imposed blindness result in—this was Mann's intuition—the inefficacy of reasoned persuasion. Instead one needs a sharp, piercing shout and coarse words that can disturb the internal order of the self-infatuated mind.

After all at stake was—the very soul of the German people. Thomas Mann had a clear idea of what could be lost in the struggle. He labeled Nazism barbarism and used his authority to defend democratic order and the frail humanism that was growing weaker day by day. In the essay "Goethe and Tolstoy" already mentioned above, he wrote:

The question is put today whether this Mediterranean, classic, humanistic tradition is commensurate with humanity and thus coeval with it, or whether it is only the intellectual expression and appanage of the bourgeois liberal epoch and destined to perish with its passing.

Europe seems to have answered the question already. The anti-liberal rebound is more than plain, it is palpable. It finds political expression in a disgusted turning away from democracy and parliamentary government, in a beetle-browed about-face toward dictatorship and terror. (*Essays*, pp. 170–71)

That is what he wrote during the period of the Weimar Republic. Amid the ruckus of Hitlerite *Parteitags*, humanism was losing. And with it, the German people were losing, and he, a German writer. He saw this clearly: barbarism was going to triumph for many long years. And what was worse, this triumph was not just the victory of force; it was also the introduction of *new rules*. Nazism was being recognized by Germans and by European democracies. Hitler's Reich was becoming a full-fledged member of Europe.

And he was powerless. He—a Nobel laureate, a man who talked with premiers and with presidents, the crown jewel of the most exclusive European elites—felt completely helpless. And it is this helplessness that lends the letters of this titan of German literature their unconventional ethical resonance. That is why he turned to invective: out of helplessness and the pain of clairvoyance.

V

For he saw clearly, and perhaps that is why he wrote about Germany in a way that to this day may arouse the distaste of aesthetes. He was not satisfied with distinguishing between the Nazi regime and the German people ("Germans reduced to the notion those idiots have created! What an absurdity!"); he also launched a brutal attack on German compliance with the Nazis. "This vile excrescence must first be removed, so that something decent and possible for the world and human beings can arise." He recalled the words uttered by Alexander von Villers in 1870—"I am so fed up with the gleeful and belabored platitudes of the nation that out of repugnance I have broken a thousand ties linking my soul to Germany"—and added, "Yes, yes." "Unhappy, unhappy nation! I have long ago reached the point of begging the World Spirit to liberate this nation from political life, to dissolve it and disperse it in a new world like the Jews, with whom so much kindred tragic destiny links it" (*Letters,* p. 222).

In formulating his thoughts so sharply, he had no doubt that his countrymen would accuse him of contempt for the people, of treating them "like mud." He also knew why he was so afraid of German consent to Nazism. He knew that the condition for effective Nazi terror was the spiritual capitulation of the terrorized. He was after an inner gesture of resistance (an external one would be heroism), after some psychological protest to barbarism. Every sign of resistance bolstered his faith, but he did not conceal his pessimism. In an April 1934 letter, he wrote:

But the German people are great at taking what comes, and since they do not love freedom but feel it rather as a form of neglect (for which reason it actually does become a kind of negligence for them), they will in spite of harsh disillusionments feel even better and happier under the new grimly disciplinarian constitution than under the Republic. Added to that is the regime's vast apparatus for deceiving, stupefying, and brutalizing them. The intellectual and moral level long ago sank so low that the spirit necessary for a real uprising simply cannot be summoned up. And at the same time they

have, in that debased state, the heady sense of representing a new world—
which indeed it is; a world of debasement. We are aliens in it, and ultimately
can do nothing but resign ourselves. (*Letters,* p. 217)

How could he feel like anything but an intruder when he read the
German papers brimming with the mental acrobatics of German intellectuals?

In a September 1934 letter to Ferdinand Lion he wrote:

The fact that German writers are really no smarter than they are allowed to
be there is a happiness thanks to which they do not feel how restricted they
are. . . . This is due to the concept of "the nation," which is the center and
common denominator of various philosophical and artistic directions, as
Hellpach announced at the congress of philosophers in Prague—which, of
course, outraged the congress; Swiss newspapers defend Hellpach, however, because supposedly he was always a "democrat." Can one believe such
idiocy? As if today talk about the "nation" was a manifestation of one's
"democratic leanings" and not, to a considerably greater degree—servility
and miserable renegation. I refer here to your statement that "never were we
a nation in such minute degree." This deceit, this swindle infuriates me so
much it almost kills me.

Mann looked with equal horror upon the blindness of Western
democracies. In a December 1933 letter in which he reflects on the rumors of Hitler's plans for Austria, he wrote:

But would the annexation of Austria really be tolerated internationally?
Granted, the weakness and perplexity is vast, and I fear that this gang may
put Europe into its pocket by "legal," "democratic" methods—without war,
that is. The fact is that their present propagandistic claims of pacifism are a
complete fraud—simply the counterpart in foreign policy of the pose of legality which they used on the domestic front in order to come to power. We
had better arm ourselves with the equanimity of the cynic in the event that
they succeed. (*Letters,* p. 205)

In the meantime, "they" were doing quite well: using a method that
was part request and part threat, the carrot and the stick, military blackmail and declarations of peace, Hitler's people were making a fool of Europe. They used slogans advertising neutrality and thereby gained acceptance for whatever they did. They plucked one opponent after another
and did them in individually, with the silent approval of the whole
world, which believed that each successive victim procured peace everlasting on the continent. In August 1936 Mann wrote: "The 'naive' are at
the top today, that is, those who shamelessly give priority to their own

interests without regard for moral considerations." Even Nazi brutality aroused fascination: there were more and more notables who expressed themselves on Hitler's side. "What incomprehensible crudity!" wrote Mann about Knut Hamsun's pro-Hitler declarations. Oh, yes! The Nazis were cunning and treacherous. "This is what they are like," he wrote in November 1935. "They send the half-Jew Lehwald to Zurich to give a lofty humanitarian propaganda speech on the Olympics, full of claptrap about human dignity, the brotherhood of nations . . . and so forth—in the name of the Third Reich! This is how they are. There are no baser swine under the sun!"

During Thomas Mann's visit to Vienna (in the summer of 1936), the Nazis threw stink bombs into the opera to sweeten the writer's stay. The stench was so bad the actors were vomiting during the performance: "That, too, is an experience worth having; now at least I know exactly what Nazism smells like: sweaty feet to a high power" (*Letters,* p. 252).

Poor Thomas Mann.

VI

What is so strange about having a normal European receive the news of normalization in Germany without anger? Who likes to poison his moral complacency with news of someone else's misfortune? Can it strike anyone as strange that the European gladly believed Adolf Hitler's declarations of peace? Who likes to think that war, with its cruelties and victims, is inevitable? Who does not crave everlasting peace, as long as the gates of a concentration camp do not stare him in the face?

Did Thomas Mann want war? It is impossible to answer the question put this way. Its very construction conceals a style of reasoning characteristic of people like Goebbels. No, Mann did not long for war, misfortune, slaughter, or tears. But he did understand that if the Nazis were not removed from power, war would be unavoidable. That is why he repeated that "one cannot and should not help the current rulers and destroyers of the country." One should help Germany in only one way: by helping them get rid of the Nazi dictatorship. Hence his extremely negative view of pacifism, which—often unintentionally—rendered European democracies defenseless against brown totalitarianism.

On his lips, invective became a symbol. It documented the conviction that, in relations with the Nazis, comportment based on models of democratic culture was suicide. It was a desperate warning formulated about Germany and the world. One Nazi publicist called Mann's statements "the view of one who has been overthrown." In spite of its malicious intent, this was an accurate observation. In fact, Mann was the defender of a losing humanism. From this perspective he told the Germans that the current rulers would lead them to ruin. He was of the opinion that a nation that approves the rule of bandits armed with a nationalist ideology commits an act of self-degradation.

Invective, therefore, was the way this most German of all German writers expressed his loyalty to the national environment. The German state, Thomas Mann seemed to be saying, has ceased to exist. The Nazi state—the "pitiful prison," "idiotic military camp called Germany"— does not deserve to be called a "state" in the European sense of the word (just as a gang of bandits does not deserve to be called a legal organization). People are not obliged to be loyal to gangsters. ("I am not afraid of the revolt; rather, I desire it, for anything is better than this," he wrote.) There can be no talk of compromise with Nazis. A compromise is possible only as a result of clearly delineated fields of understanding; it requires the sobering light of day. It is different with Nazism: "Hitler's stars shine only during the darkest night."

A citizen's and a German's duty, therefore, is unconditional resistance to Nazism. One must wish this "national revolution" defeat. Whosoever labels such a position betrayal of the "national cause" or "cause of peace" betrays the human cause. For this German mixture of "sentimentality and force" can bring nothing but catastrophe to Germany and the world.

For at bottom I am much too good a German for the thought of permanent exile not to weigh heavily indeed, and the breach with my country, which is almost unavoidable, fills me with depression and dread—a sign that it does not fit my nature, which has been formed by elements of the Goethean tradition of representation, so that I cannot feel I was destined for martyrdom. For me to have been forced into this role, something thoroughly wrong and evil must surely have taken place. And it is my deepest conviction that this whole "German Revolution" is indeed wrong and evil. It lacks all the characteristics which have won the sympathy of the world for genuine revolutions, however bloody they may have been. In its essence it is not a "rising," no matter how its proponents rant on, but a terrible fall into hatred, vengeance, lust for killing, and petit-bourgeois mean-spiritedness. I shall never believe that any good can come of it, for either Germany or the world. (*Letters,* p. 198)

He was aware that in proposing the candidacy of the imprisoned Carl von Ossietzky for the Nobel Peace Prize, he was throwing his writer's authority onto the political scales. When it was pointed out to him that he was discarding his writer's ethic of irony and distance, he answered that "a defender of Pure Literature seems almost pathetic to himself," and that the "political struggle in current circumstances" is at times more important, decisive, and worthy of recognition "than all of poetry."

This is what he wrote to Eduard Korrodi in the open letter mentioned at the beginning of these reflections.

VII

It was all brought on by a trifle. Korrodi had publicly attacked a German emigrant publicist for claiming that "all of contemporary literature has transferred abroad." But he did not stop at pointing out the exaggeration. He also wrote that the majority of those who found themselves abroad—with the exception of a few literary graphomaniacs or so—were Jews.

Mann agreed the claim that "all of contemporary literature" had transferred abroad was an exaggeration and overstatement. "I do not want to call anyone to the Gestapo's attention, but in many cases purely mechanical rather than intellectual reasons may be decisive, and thus the boundary between exiled and nonexiled German literature is not so easy to draw; it does not coincide so precisely with the boundaries of the Reich" (*Letters*, pp. 244–45).

By introducing the term "Gestapo" into the discussion, Thomas Mann was fixing its ideological horizons. He could also admit that the exaggerated claim about "all of German literature" could "arouse the ire of a neutral" such as Korrodi.

But neutrality remains a difficult art even for people who have such long practice in it as you Swiss! How easily the neutral, in combatting one injustice, falls into another. The moment that you raise objections to the identification of exile literature with the whole of German literature, you yourself set up an untenable equation. For, curiously, it is not the error itself that angers you, but the fact that a Jewish writer commits it; and even as you conclude from this fact that once again literature of Jewish origin is being confounded with German literature (the old complaint of the Fatherland fanatics), you yourself confound exile with Jewish literature. (*Letters*, p. 245)

In response, Mann named an entire list—"which I would never have thought of compiling"—of writers who were "pure" German. He explained that the presence of the "Jewish element" among the emigrants followed from "the sweeping nature of National Socialist racial philosophy and from the revulsion which the Jewish spirit feels for certain state institutions of our times."

But was the thesis—that the work of writers labeled "Jewish" did not belong to German literature because of its international qualities—tenable? Mann was of a different opinion:

The "international" qualities of Jews are nothing more nor less than their Mediterranean-European qualities. And these are at the same time *German;* without them, Germanism would not be Germanism, but a totally useless sluggishness. That is precisely what the Catholic Church—which today is in straits that make her revered once again even by a product of Protestant culture—is defending inside Germany when she declares that only after the Germans accepted Christianity did they enter the company of civilized nations. (*Letters,* p. 248)

Mann unveiled, with great precision and consistency, the antihumanist ground common to Nazi anti-Semitism and anti-Christianity. He also showed its anti-German edge:

Being voelkisch is not being German. But the Germans', or the German rulers', hatred of the Jews is in the higher sense not directed toward the Jews at all, or not toward them alone: it is directed against Europe and all loftier Germanism; it is directed, as becomes increasingly apparent, against the Christian and classical foundations of Western morality. It is the attempt (symbolized by the withdrawal from the League of Nations) to shake off the ties of civilization. That attempt threatens to bring about a terrible alienation, fraught with evil potentialities, between the land of Goethe and the rest of the world.

And then he concluded:

Countless human, moral, and aesthetic observations support my profound conviction that nothing good can possibly come of the present German regime, not for Germany and not for the world. This conviction has made me shun the country in whose spiritual traditions I am more deeply rooted than the present rulers who for three years have vacillated, not quite daring to deny me my Germanism before the eyes of the world.

After Mann's letter to Korrodi, the Nazis no longer vacillated—they stripped the writer of his citizenship in the German Reich.

Why had Mann pulled up his visor at this precise moment, when there had been plenty of important events before? It is impossible to answer this question. Sometimes it takes only a straw to break the proverbial camel's back. Shortly afterward Mann wrote:

Sooner or later I had to speak out, and I chose a moment when someone was insidiously attempting to draw a line between me and the exiles, and with the feeling moreover that unpleasant half-and-half notions of my relations to the Third Reich prevail in some parts of the world. But in addition, simply from inner, psychic reasons. It was in good part a temperamental act, a natural reaction to all the insults and outrages that daily come raining down upon us all. It was also the real and deep conviction that this mischief will mean the doom of the whole continent if it continues, and that I must oppose it here and now, so far as my feeble strength permits, as I have already opposed it at home. (*Letters,* p. 250)

VIII

Let us repeat nevertheless, Mann was far from being an optimist. In a Nazi world, he wanted to be Don Quixote. This was the spiritual strategy he formulated. He wanted to show solidarity with the victims; he felt that he had become one of them. In a private November 1935 letter to Korrodi, he wrote that only one thing linked him to other German exiles:

All of its members are victims of this regime (this is an honor that is not becoming to all) and . . . I cannot understand . . . the repugnance that can clearly be felt in your attitude to this category of people. Isn't there a certain mean-spiritedness concealed in the statement "A man who has quarreled with his government is a man who arouses fear in decent people" and shouldn't one correct it? What kind of government are you talking about? The label of political exile has been an honorable title in times that provided fewer moral justifications than today's! What has happened to this world!

Mann's fear was free of rhetoric; he knew that in "this world" he could only be a renegade or a Don Quixote. He looked around aghast:

Someone who himself has fascist inclinations has an easier time of maintaining calm and an attitude of repugnance to the desperate hatred of exiles. Generally speaking, the world is somehow incapable of understanding what is happening to people in Germany and this lack of understanding allows it

to maintain its phlegm and disinterest. I have observed this astounding phenomenon on several occasions. People do not understand what is happening
and even if they condemn it, they remain indifferent in their souls, because
they lack the authentic experience. Expressing this in words is truly impossible. All of this moves well beyond politics. Fascism, the government of the
proletariat, dictatorship—none of these terms render the incredible excrescence that rules there.

Only one person—an English bishop—used words that seemed appropriate. He said that he went "blind with rage" when he thought
about Germany. Mann, too, an intruder in the Nazi period who recognized himself as a "relic of a bygone cultural epoch," went blind with
rage. He kept repeating, though, that "there is nothing more beautiful
than glorious skirmishes during a retreat."

When in late spring 1934 he sailed to the United States to receive an
honorary doctoral degree from Harvard University, he took with him
Cervantes's novel. The losing Don Quixote had Mann's complete
sympathy—he became mental shorthand for Mann's own dilemmas.
The main one was, How does one make a value out of being a "relic"?
The "relic" loses, and just like Don Quixote falls under the "wheels of the
speeding vehicle of history." But so what? Is it better to forgo courage
and give up being noble? "But what would a Don Quixote at the other
extreme be like? Anti-idealistic, sinister, a pessimistic believer in force—
and yet a Don Quixote? A brutalized Don Quixote?"

No!

Agitated times like ours always tend to confound the merely epochal with
the eternal—as for instance liberalism with freedom—and to throw out the
baby with the bathwater. Thus each free and thoughtful person, each mind
which does not flicker in the wind of time, is forced back upon the foundations; driven to become once more conscious of them and to base more
solidly upon them. (*Essays*, p. 454)

One should not, he claimed, flatter an epoch whose grace one wins at
the price of trampling "reason and civilization." "To be able to look into
the future one must indeed be of the time. But not only in the sense of
actual movement, in which every donkey partakes, bursting with pride
and scorn against liberal reactionaries of a different stripe" (*Essays*,
p. 456). One must have the whole epoch in oneself, in all its complexity
and contradiction; one must know how to interpret one's own crisis as a
fragment of the world crisis. This is the only way to freedom: "Freedom
has worth, it confers rank, only when it is won from unfreedom, when it

is the process of becoming free." This kind of struggle for freedom, which "mingles cruel humiliation and moving nobility of soul," is Don Quixote-ism, a challenge made to the world.

This Don Quixote of the Nazi era has a few ideas worth noting.

First: "Do not worry about the future—this is the only possible life strategy in today's times."

Second: "Immerse yourself in innocent and internally equanimous work—this is the only thing that can help us deal with this nightmare." Create one's work calmly and persistently amid the "upheavals, coups, and threats."

Third: "Be one's own signpost when there are no other signposts."

Fourth: Know how to "wait and endure"; know how to create decent works in "sad, wicked, barrenly resistant times."

Fifth: "Maintain the bravery and the patience that Schopenhauer so beautifully associated with courage."

Sixth: Call "baseness, base."

IX

Immediately after being deprived of his citizenship, Mann wrote to a friend, "I simply do not believe this can possibly last for long." He also passed on the rumors from Germany that "the National Socialist adventure is in its final stage," that it was a matter of weeks or months. "I tell myself that either the war will come in a year and a half or two years, or conditions within this period will change so much that our books, too, will again be permitted in Germany."

The war broke out in three years—his calculations were off by just a single year.

In reading these letters after forty years, you wonder, Polish reader, if their author could have decided differently. Could he have returned to Germany and with his, even silent, presence legalized the totalitarian government? Could he have participated, as so many others did, in academic meetings and traveled to international congresses as a representative of the culture of the Third Reich? Could he have—at the price of tolerance for his books—served as an argument for the propaganda claim about "normalization in Germany"? Could he have—in the name of praiseworthy neutrality and objectivity—publicly noted his recognition of the political successes, of which there was no dearth? Could he have convinced himself that he was choosing the realism of participation against the exaggerated high-mindedness of the emigrants' refusal?

It is true that these questions have no bearing on an understanding of history. They do help, however, to get at its moral roots. We who love Mann's books and look in them for a way to face up to fate, our hearts command us to say, no, no he could not have acted differently. Reason, however, tells us to put down a question mark. The biographical adventures of twentieth-century intellectuals do not allow us to answer unequivocally.

I have called Thomas Mann's life—as recorded in his *Letters*—a *Bildungsroman*. What did I want to learn from this novel? In reconstructing one of its chapters I did not intend at all to tell the story of the author's attitude to Nazism—I am putting off this fascinating topic to another time. I was interested in only one subject. I wanted to get at the dominant feeling that dictated the most risky decisions of his life. And I think I did—it was disgust.

Mann's attitude to Nazism was saturated with an instinctive revulsion; it was only later that he wrote his penetrating analyses of the devil concealed in the legacy of German culture. It was the aesthetic abhorrence, not the intellectual afterthought, that compelled Mann to choose a position of integral opposition. It was revulsion that allowed him to see instantly and clearly everything that others would see only during the war. But let me say this differently: Mann's life was a striking microcosm of the modern history of European humanism, its isolation in the face of totalitarian forces. The helplessness of the German writer-expatriate became an augury of Europe's destiny, a Europe whose fragments were shortly to fall, one after the other, "beneath the armed feet of alien might."

Hitler's totalitarian state applied the same technique toward isolated individuals that it did toward isolated nations: the appearance of legality and paragraphs of inhuman penal codes concealed brute force. The invective and insults in Mann's letters were a desperate attempt to shatter conventions, within the framework of which Nazism was treated as an "interesting experiment." ("The scholastic apotheosis of German events without seeing reality is not just a bad joke for someone who has come to know the benefits of this 'spirit' on his own hide. This is not for me!") How quixotic Mann is in his attitude toward the Gestapo. Yet . . .

The educational value of the letters from the years 1933–36 as read today is the awareness of the *pointe* which Mann could not know when he decided to break with the German state. You, Polish reader, know the finale: Berlin in flames, the Nuremberg trials, the division of Germany. So you know that this German Don Quixote turned out to be a more farsighted realist than the devoted functionaries of brown-shirt propaganda; that this solitary exile powerlessly dispensing invective turned out to be stronger than the mighty totalitarian regime he was assailing. Can there be a more heartening argument in favor of conviction, that in being defeated—like Mann forty years ago—one might at the same time win? This is probably what you are thinking, Polish reader, and it is difficult to call this conclusion unreasonable. But this is not a story as optimistic as you and the author of this essay would like. Thomas Mann paid the highest price for his decision—the price of estrangement. The estrangement that allowed him later to speak to Germans via American radio and write *Doctor Faustus* but would not allow him to return to his homeland after the war.

For a country does not like those who were prematurely right against it, and it never forgives this premature rightness. Remember this, too, Polish reader, in reading Thomas Mann's old correspondence today. For—and this is the important moral of reading the *Letters*—a great writer is inaccessible to us only when we live with his work. Only then does he inhabit the stellar regions, off-limits to us ordinary mortals. Nevertheless, when he rises from his desk and puts down his pen he is once again one of us: weak and full of doubts, anxious and susceptible to the temptations of practicality. And, like each of us, he is reluctant to break with habits, comfort, and a feeling of safety. Yet life lived in truth and dignity, though difficult and full of complications, has something truly addictive to it. Whoever has once tasted it has a hard time getting rid of such fatal addictions.

That is why the Berlin ukase banishing Mann strengthened him. Something had ended, something was beginning, the ambivalent period was over. Now came the days in which Thomas Mann's public invective saved Germany's honor, days that testified to the conscience and sovereign dignity of a great German culture. Mann wrote: "I would be a scoundrel like the authors of that ukase if I were to regret anything. God knows, I was not born for hatred, but I hate those bloodthirsty fools and corrupters of humanity from the bottom of my heart and fervently wish them the dreadful end they deserve" (*Letters,* p. 257).

X

And you, Polish reader, remember these words well, because Thomas Mann formulated a moral obligation in them—for you as well. If you feel a bond with something like an international republic of humanists, you must be aware of the consequence of such a choice. Namely: when you read, hear, and say that on your native land Germans pronounced themselves supermen and propagated an architecture of concentration camps, pillaged and slaughtered, destroyed human bodies, and depraved human souls in the name of a millennial Reich, you, Polish reader, have the obligation to remember and repeat that there was a certain German Don Quixote, a helpless writer, who, nauseous with disgust, wished defeat to the Nazi executioners long before they invaded your country; who put human solidarity in humanist values above tribal discipline in the name of nationalist doctrines.

Thus when you remember, Polish reader, the fate of Polish writers and professors of Polish universities transported to death camps and executed in the streets, you are to repeat stubbornly, through clenched teeth, as a sign of solidarity and communion in pain: Thomas Mann, Thomas Mann, Thomas Mann . . .

Barczewo Prison, January 1986

3

Anti-authoritarian Revolt

A Conversation with Daniel Cohn-Bendit

Daniel Cohn-Bendit: Adam, when you talk about yourself, you always remind us that you are a Pole. I find that strange because it would never occur to me to attach such great importance to my nationality.

Adam Michnik: If you lived in a Germany where reading Thomas Mann, Goethe, Schiller, Heine, Hegel, and Kant was forbidden, you would feel German to an extent that you can't even imagine. I identify with the Polish people just as I identify with all that is weak, oppressed, and humiliated. If Poland were a superpower, I would probably be cosmopolitan or a gypsy. But Poland is oppressed and humiliated, and the Polish people live in misery; which is why I am in solidarity with these people and this language. For better, for worse. And the fact that some people in Poland consider me Jewish rather than Polish further strengthens my national conviction.

Cohn-Bendit: Can you tell me how you managed to politicize yourself in the Poland you've just described?

Michnik: My biography is not a typical Polish biography.

Cohn-Bendit: That doesn't matter.

Reprinted by permission from Daniel Cohn-Bendit, *Nous l'avons tant aimée, la révolution* (Paris: Editions Bernard Barrault, 1987), 200–249. Translated by Catherine Beltier. The original interview was done in May 1987 in Warsaw.

Michnik: I come from a Jewish family that Polonized itself through communism, a sort of red assimilation. So I had a particular sense of nationality, one that had little relation to present-day national symbols. For example, in Polish families, young boys generally go to church; as for me, I was brought up outside of any religious tradition. There is usually a family tradition, based on either the Polish wars of independence or on the Home Army (AK), but none of that existed in our family. My father was a known, active member of the Communist party. He spent eight years in jail, and after the war he did not want to play any political role. His entire intellectual formation rested on Marxism and communism. Even when defending extreme anti-Communist or anti-Soviet positions, his language was the Marxist language he had learned from the party.

Cohn-Bendit: How did the break occur? And when?

Michnik: Paradoxically, I belonged during the sixties to a small circle that didn't fear the Communists. I felt that Communist Poland was my Poland. So what should I be scared of? I believed then that a Communist was someone whose mission was to denounce injustice. So I did. Normal Polish families didn't raise their children that way: rather, children were taught that they lived under Soviet occupation, and that any ill-considered statement could be overheard by a spy, so one must be careful. Polish children were scared because they knew that their fear was justified. But I didn't know that, so I was brave, and I dared to speak. In school, for example, I got up and asked, "If a Communist must tell the truth, why not tell the truth about what happened in Katyń?" The professor's reaction was unbelievable! All hell broke loose—everyone was scared, and I got thrown out of class.

Cohn-Bendit: How old were you?

Michnik: Thirteen, fourteen. I've had two shocks in my life. First, when a friend of my father's, a party member, returned to Poland after spending twenty years in a camp. That's when I suddenly realized that good Communists were sent to Siberia, which I just couldn't understand. The second shock came when my cousin married a man who had spent ten years in Siberia for having served with the Home Army. Then my sky was on fire. That's the title of a famous Polish book by Jan Parandowski, about a young man's crisis of conscience. In the same way, my sky was on fire. And since then I have continued to think that it makes sense to believe, it is better to believe in God and the Holy Trinity, because I will never be so deceived by them as I was by the Communist god.

Cohn-Bendit: Oh! oh!

Michnik: I talk about God and I say: believe in God, not in the Church.

Cohn-Bendit: I haven't met him yet.

Michnik: Has God ever deceived you? But how often have the Communists?

Cohn-Bendit: His believers have often deceived me.

Michnik: I didn't say that you should believe in those who believe in God but that you should believe in God.

At the time a friend who worked for the journal *Po Prostu* took me to the Krzywe Koło, an intellectuals' club in Warsaw that had managed to keep going after 1956 (it was closed in 1962, so I still had six months ahead of me). It was an extraordinary experience, because Warsaw's most influential intellectuals, like Leszck Kołakowski, Włodzimierz Brus, Stanisław Ossowski, and Tadeusz Kotarbiński, were there. I was only fifteen, still a schoolboy.

It was thanks to this club that I met a man who played a decisive role in my life and to whom I still owe a huge debt, one of Poland's most wonderful men, Jan Józef Lipski.

I have to say that I was part of the scouts, somewhat particular ones at that, since after 1956 the scout movement died in Poland. Traditional scoutism took its place, inspired by the Baden-Powell tradition and that of the prewar scouts, especially the Gray Ranks that fought with the Home Army.

In my day, the scouts wore different colored scarves: yellow, green, white, red and white, black and white. Red was forbidden. Only one group wore red scarves, and Jacek Kuroń was their leader. That's the group I belonged to. Later, at KOR (Workers' Defense Committee) we realized that 15 percent of the members had worn the red scarf.

My political consciousness flows from these two traditions: that of rebellious communism, represented by Kuroń, and that of independent, secular intellectuals, like Lipski.

Cohn-Bendit: Was this at the same time as the *Open Letter to the Workers' Party*?

Michnik: No, it was before. Kuroń was still a member of the party and thought that the only way to change and improve things was to transform the party from inside. I am younger than he is, thank God.

There is the same age difference between us as there is between you and your brother. That is why, like you, I have never been a party member.

When I was fifteen, Jan Józef Lipski pushed me to open a discussion club with some friends. I wasn't very difficult to persuade as I was both energetic and reckless, which is still true. I contacted Professor Adam Schaff and told him, "Mr. Schaff, I would like to start a discussion group." Adam Schaff was a sort of Polish Andrei Zhdanov [Stalinist idealogue], someone who had had ideas during his youth and who had actively participated in an illegal movement before the war. When I got to know him he was already a cynical old man, but I must have touched something in him, because he said, "OK! If you want your club, you can have it! You can meet as Warsaw high schoolers, right here, at the university. If anyone gives you any trouble, call me." It was 1962 and no one in those days was brave enough to ignore Schaff. That's how the discussion club was born, with his protection. A few years later, the party organizations and the police remembered the club, which they called "the Revisionists' Kindergarten," and wondered why it hadn't been forbidden.

I was believed to have privileged relations with the Central Committee of the party and to be linked to certain factions, which wasn't true at all. I was simply lucky, because imbeciles are always lucky. That's all. There were about a hundred high schoolers in this club, many of them from Communist families.

Cohn-Bendit: What did you do at the club? What were your topics of discussion?

Michnik: We had one thing in common: we were very smart and even more naive. But this naïveté was also our strength. It's what made us so brave.

We considered ourselves Communists, so the idea that something could happen to us in a Communist country never even occurred to us. That wasn't very smart, knowing what happened to my father's friend and my brother-in-law. I should have known what communism represented.

I remember the American invasion of the Bay of Pigs. I went to a demonstration at the university and yelled anti-American slogans without any encouragement. I was very proud when I got home and told my father that I had participated in a political demonstration. He turned white as a sheet and asked me, "Who took you?" "Kuroń."

And my father said, "Tell him that you are certainly a little jerk but that he's an imbecile. With his generous ideas he should be protesting in front of the Soviet embassy against the Hungarian invasion." That was my father's communism. Mine, on the other hand, made me say, "You'll see. When the time comes, Kuroń will go and demonstrate before the Soviet embassy." In the end we were both right.

In our club, "the Revisionists' Kindergarten," which we baptized the Club for Contradiction Searchers, we discussed everything that was forbidden. But in fact nothing was really forbidden since we had Professor Schaff's protection.

Cohn-Bendit: Can you give some examples?

Michnik: Freedom in the system of the dictatorship of the proletariat; the Soviet intervention in Hungary; September 17, 1939; will there be a second proletarian revolution in Poland?

Leszek Kołakowski told me at the time, "Adam, calm down, you can't have a second revolution in a country that hasn't recovered from the first," but he couldn't convince me.

We also discussed the reasons for the dissolution of the Polish Communist party, the big Moscow trials, Trotskyism, closed and open Marxism, and so on. Stefan Kisielewski said then that all of Marxism belonged behind a locked door; I thought he was kidding. Everything progressed marvelously for six months, and then it turned out that freedom had its limits, even in the dictatorship of the proletariat. The Warsaw Socialist Youth Federation asked us to completely revise our program. We refused: shouldn't a Communist act in accord with his conscience? . . . But since *they* were the real Communists, they acted in accord with their own conscience and dissolved our club.

My political initiation took place when Gomułka personally attacked me during the Central Committee Plenum, in 1963. I was barely sixteen — certainly a record for Eastern Europe. I've asked Miklós Haraszti, János Kis, and Petr Uhl: they were all older than me. Our club was dissolved as I was entering the eleventh grade. Since I was searching for contradictions, I naturally hadn't had the time to study, and I had some catching up to do in physics or I wouldn't pass the baccalaureate. I met Kuroń in the street one day and he said, "Listen, Adaś, Comrade Gomułka mentioned you during the Central Committee meeting." And I stuttered (yes, I stutter), "Listen, Jacuś, don't bother me with such silly stuff. I have some work to do in

physics." Since then, Jacek always said, "Comrade Gomułka doesn't
have any work to do in physics, so he has time to worry about silly
stuff."

It was 1964. I passed my baccalaureate. But first there was the famous *Letter of the 34:* thirty-four personalities, intellectuals, writers,
scientists, who sent the prime minister an open letter protesting censorship. The letter caused a sensation. Gomułka's reaction was quite
violent; he acted as if NATO troops were invading Poland! He began
by punishing certain people and forbade the publication of their
names in the papers. There were university professors among them.
In response, the students organized a demonstration in support of
their professors; this was the first demonstration I saw in my life.

Cohn-Bendit: Did you just watch, or did you participate?

Michnik: I participated, of course, even though I wasn't a student there
yet. Professor Bronisław Baczko, who is now a philosophy professor
in Geneva, stopped me in the university courtyard. He knew me from
the days of the Club for Contradiction Searchers, and he also knew
my father. He caught me by the ear and took me out of the demonstration. "You have to worry about your baccalaureate now," he said.
"Then you can get into politics. Which is probably what you'll do,
since all cretins get into politics. I'm the best proof of that."

I went abroad for the first time in my life after the baccalaureate. It
was an important experience that lasted three months. I met a lot of
people, read a lot of books, talked with Polish émigrés, Italian Communists, and French Trotskyists. I returned with the firm intention of
doing something. I missed the beginning of the semester.

I met a friend, Karol Modzelewski, at the History Institute. We decided to meet again three days later. Karol warned me, "I'm not sure
it's good for you to come to my house and be seen in my company." I
didn't understand what he meant—who would see me? I liked being
seen with Karol, mostly because I was a snob. He was well liked at the
university; students appreciated him, women admired him. Uncon-
sciously, I wanted some of it to rub off on me. But he didn't let me
come to his house and suggested that we meet at the university library
instead, three days later. So three days later I went to the library: I
waited for a half hour, an hour, two hours, and finally, furious, I went
to his house, where his mother told me he had been arrested. Kuroń
and others were arrested at the same time. It was an epiphany for me:
I realized that I belonged with this type of people, despite some differences. And that's how I became a particularly zealous disciple of

Modzelewski and Kuroń. I never completely identified with their program, but I felt very close to them. They were freed after forty-eight hours and began working on their *Open Letter*. We were quite close at the time. They sent their letter to the party in 1965. They left a copy with me so that it could be disseminated to the entire world. The copy was hidden outside of my apartment so that the police wouldn't find it.

I was very shocked the first time the police visited me, when I was eighteen. I thought my arrest would last forty-eight hours, but it lasted two months. I spent two months in jail. Many years later, Antoni Słonimski said to me, "Adaś, you must understand that Poland is a country where they'll jail the guy they want to, but when they want to free someone it might not happen." I've always kept that phrase in my mind.

The *Open Letter* affair had enormous repercussions. Kuroń was already quite well known for his activities with the scouts; Modzelewski was a renowned historian; and at barely nineteen, I became famous. Everyone was talking about me, and it became a leitmotif: be famous, make a career, as long as the Communists will keep arresting me. In other words, I owe the Communists everything—I'm not sure what I would have done if they hadn't been there.

The next three years, from March 1965 to March 1968, were very important for me: I had a name at the university now.

Cohn-Bendit: Can I ask you two more questions? How did you find Kuroń and Modzelewski's *Open Letter*? What did you think of it theoretically?

Michnik: It's not very elegant to criticize after the fact. I'll answer by telling you what Kuroń wrote last year when I was in jail. It was during the Political Prisoners' Defense Week and Kuroń wrote a short article entitled "Adaś" for the review *Kos*. In it, he explained that I had had some disagreements with him and Modzelewski, over two points, basically: (1) the attitude toward Polish independence and (2) the attitude toward parliamentary democracy. I had very clearly taken a position in favor of Poland's independence and the restitution of parliamentary democracy. That it can indeed be extended to other forms of democracy but that we can't exchange parliamentary democracy for the dictatorship of the proletariat without abandoning what the French Revolution brought to Europe, namely, the Declaration of the Rights of Man and the principle of citizens' equality before the law.

Jacek recalled all of this in his article, and he was right to do so. Apart from that, this letter stands as a document that concerned me a lot: I was very close to its language, which was one of contesting communism, something that is foreign to a lot of young Poles coming out of the patriotic tradition, whereas, as I've said before, I belong to the Communist tradition. Its Marxist aspect was quite familiar to me.

Cohn-Bendit: Were those three years from 1965 to 1968 the most interesting or intense years of your life?

Michnik: My entire life has been fascinating, but I think that the most important period was the Solidarity period. I wouldn't have missed it for anything in the world. The sixteen months in prison were worth it. Those three years (1965–68) were interesting because a few friends and I managed to function as a legal opposition group within a system that didn't admit the existence of a legal opposition. It's thanks to the university that we were able to exist as such. The situation there was quite complex because many professors had liberal opinions—both neutral professors and some that were party members. Those who saw us as real Communists saw us as imbeciles, of course. For many of them communism itself was the scourge, and we were coming along and proposing a better version of it: we were clearly insane! But their honor and dignity incited them to defend us. Because we, the protesters, were nonetheless their students, the legitimation of their conformity. We represented their entrance into history. We justified their existence. That's why many of them protected us, albeit reluctantly.

The Young Communists organized evening discussions within the university, on themes like "Fifty Years of the Soviet Union's Pacifist External Policy." Each discussion was meticulously organized: we would meet beforehand and organize a seminar during which we thoroughly studied the topic and distributed the tasks: Janek, you'll talk about the Hungarian intervention; Józek, you'll talk about Katyń; Stefan, you'll talk about Finland; and you, you'll talk about the Moscow trials or Yugoslavia. The big official meeting took place in the university's Maximum Auditorium, and Walery Namiot-kiewicz, Gomułka's secretary, attended. We would come and sit all around the room. He made a speech reminding us that the Soviet Union had been fighting for peace for fifty years. Then my friend Józek got up and asked, "Is this peace a room with a kitchen?" And he answered, "This is a provocation. You are not qualified to discuss this subject." So I got up and yelled, "Yes we are! Yes we are! You have to listen!" He answered, "Contradiction does not scare the party!" And I continued, "That remains to be seen!" An uproar ensued: Janek spoke about Hungary, Józek about Finland, Stefan about Yugoslavia, and, at the end, I quoted Fidel Castro.

Cohn-Bendit: Have you no shame?

Michnik: Yes, actually I am ashamed of it. But haven't you ever done anything that you're ashamed of? Am I to tell you only the photogenic facts, or the truth? . . . So I quoted Fidel Castro, who said that the peaceful coexistence Moscow fought for consisted in keeping the bombs from falling on Moscow or Washington. But they could fall on Vietnam. How do you feel, as members of the Communist party, knowing that bombs fall on Vietnam every day? You don't do anything, and you don't want to do anything!

Walery Namiotkiewicz couldn't tell if I was pro- or anti-Soviet. In his place, I wouldn't have known either! Another time it was Mieczysław Rakowski—a liberal, now minister of foreign affairs—who participated in our meeting. We asked him if he thought of Marxism as a critical theory, and he answered, "Yes, of course." Does a Marxist believe in God? "No, never." Is Gomułka a human being or a god? "A human being, naturally." As a man, then, could he be as infallible as God? "No, that isn't possible." So then why hadn't he, Rakowski, ever found a fault to criticize in Gomułka? . . . And so on.

Cohn-Bendit: It was an anti-authoritarian revolution.

Michnik: Obviously.

Cohn-Bendit: And that's our generation's common experience.

Ewa Kulik (Bielinski's wife, who is twelve years younger than Michnik):[1] An experience that is typical only of that generation.

Michnik: That generation brought something quite specific to the Polish opposition.

Cohn-Bendit: To all contesting oppositions, even if the ideas were at opposite ends of the spectrum. Well, maybe not opposite, but different.

Michnik: Yes, Dany, that's how it is. And it is no coincidence that I supported the May 1968 movement in France. Which wasn't the case for my father. He used to say, "This Cohn-Bendit is a fascist bastard."

1. Ewa Kulik was a member of the Regional Solidarity Council, an underground resistance organization (1982–88). She was an active translator during this interview, which was also filmed—ED.

And I would say, "No, it's me. —Krivine and his band are a bunch of Stalinist morons. —No, it's me. —This Tariq Ali, this Pakistani in England, is a Soviet agent. —No, it's me. —This Tom Hayden is a KGB agent. —No, it's me." I can really say that on that occasion my father and I argued about principles.

In 1968 you gave an interview in which you called the French Communist party "Stalinist scum." I told my father, "You must like that," and he answered, "Yes, he's right for once, but his point of view is wrong. Because you are a Communist and I am not. What interests you are just points of view; what I want to know is whether people are right or wrong."

Cohn-Bendit: Let's leave anecdotes aside. What followed was the collapse that led to 1968.

Michnik: During the period between 1965 and 1968, a certain number of people in search of conflict would meet at the university. It was just a group of people, rather than an illegal organization; we never had the time to constitute ourselves as an illegal organization, but we were going in that direction. Two more years and our organization would probably have seen the light.

At the time we were looking for a formula that would help us understand the reality we lived in. We tried to establish contacts in two directions: on one hand, Catholic intellectual clubs, and on the other, French Trotskyists. I've remained faithful to that search in a sense: there's always a part of me that's marked by the Western left, while another is influenced by the Polish Catholic Church's classical current. Which means that I lack all of Kant's requirements and that I am extremely inconsistent. But I think I would die if one day I found myself consistent.

My teacher, Leszek Kołakowski, wrote a book called *In Praise of Inconsistency;* that's what I am referring to. I think that my greatest mistake at the time was to have been against the Polish bishops' initiative toward the German bishops in 1966.

Cohn-Bendit: You mean the initiative referring to the Oder-Neisse border?

Michnik: In that letter, the Polish bishops wrote to the German bishops: "We forgive and ask for forgiveness. We forgive the National Socialist crimes and ask you to forgive us the hatred with which we made you pay for those crimes." I think that it was a just, intelligent, and clear-sighted gesture. But I didn't understand it at all at the time.

With my Communist and internationalist background, I was a fierce adversary of nationalist anti-German propaganda. There are no better or worse people. There is no cursed people. The Germans are not responsible for National Socialism; the Nazis are. In the Holy Scriptures it says that ten just men are enough to save a city. And ten Germans like Thomas Mann, Heinrich Mann, Viktor Klemperer, Hermann Rauschning, and the Scholl sisters saved Germany. So I should have liked this letter the Polish bishops wrote to the German bishops, but I didn't. I had been taught that everything coming from the Catholic episcopate was inevitably reactionary, nationalist, and treacherous. When I think about my reaction now I feel guilty for not having understood. My book, *The Church and the Left*,[2] was born from this sense of guilt.

When I went to Germany, Heinrich Böll told me that reading the letter made him believe that Christ would rise again.

There was also a Catholic opposition to the letter, but I leave it to the Catholics to justify themselves. I'm only defending my point of view. Poles have the bad habit of justifying themselves for other people's sins. I am a revisionist, and responsible only for my own mistakes.

The second thing I feel guilty about is Vietnam. The first tract we distributed at the university was about Vietnam, and in it we put the American invasion of Vietnam and the Soviet intervention in Hungary at the same level. But the two are not comparable: Vietnam was a war against totalitarianism, and Hungary was a war against freedom. Or at least that's my opinion.

Cohn-Bendit: What about South Vietnam? What did General Ky represent? It's not that simple. You could say that it was a war between two totalitarianisms.

Michnik: South Vietnam was a corrupt and reactionary country, not a totalitarian one.

Cohn-Bendit: You mean to say that that kind of regime is not totalitarian?

Michnik: No, it isn't. And that's what differentiates an unbearable military dictatorship from a concentration camp. Dany, if you of all people don't understand this difference, then you don't understand communism. You should understand.

2. First published in France in 1977 by the émigré publishing house of the monthly *Kultura,* Instytut Literacki (American enlarged edition, Chicago: University of Chicago Press, 1993). — ED.

Cohn-Bendit: You are the one who should be speaking, not me.

Michnik: Yes, but you said something.

Cohn-Bendit: I asked a question.

Michnik: You can't ask questions without also saying something.

Cohn-Bendit: The problem is the following: if you were to take position today, would you, like a lot of French people, support the Americans in Vietnam? I mean ideologically.

Michnik: Yes, absolutely.

Cohn-Bendit: Explain yourself.

Michnik: I would be against the Vietcong and for the establishment of a democratic alternative in South Vietnam.

Kulik: What went wrong for the Americans is that the South Vietnamese leaders were who they were.

Michnik: That wasn't only too bad for the Americans, it was also their responsibility. Let me tell you something, Dany: if I had to choose between Hitler and Stalin, I would pick Marlene Dietrich.

Cohn-Bendit: OK . . . OK . . .

Michnik: No, it's not OK, because you pretend that Stalin represented a lesser evil. And I tell you that if Stalin had lost the war . . .

Cohn-Bendit: I didn't say that. What I say is that from a Vietnamese point of view, the Vietnam War was a national liberation war.

Michnik: Allow me to doubt that, because if that was the case the boat people wouldn't be in flight today.

Cohn-Bendit: What the National Liberation Front and many people didn't understand is that North Vietnam had other interests.

Michnik: And you don't think they understood that?

Cohn-Bendit: Not a single member of the National Liberation Front is now at the head of Vietnam.

Michnik: Well, good. That's what they deserve. And anyone who commits himself to the Communists will suffer the same fate. I am telling you this because I myself am blood of their blood and flesh of their flesh.

Cohn-Bendit: For you this is an actual historic experience. But in this case you have to consider the problem from the Vietnamese point of view.

Michnik: Well, we're in the same boat. Neither one of us knows what the Vietnamese point of view is.

Cohn-Bendit: I've talked with some Vietnamese.

Michnik: So have I.

Cohn-Bendit: But there aren't any . . . I mean there aren't any boat people in Poland.

Michnik: But there are Vietnamese students, and when they've had enough to drink they tell the truth.

Cohn-Bendit: What's true for Poland doesn't necessarily apply to Vietnam. I think that the Vietnamese experienced communism after the liberation. In 1968 most Vietnamese fought against the Americans . . .

Michnik: Spare me the speeches and tell it to me straight.

Cohn-Bendit: They weren't even pro-Communist, they were just anti-American.

Michnik: How do you know? Well, all right, there's some truth to what you say; the Americans bear some responsibility.

Cohn-Bendit: If it makes you happy, in 1967 we wrote a tract and we fought with your Trotskyist friends of that time . . .

Michnik: You didn't beat them up enough.

Cohn-Bendit: Our tract said that the Vietnamese revolution, led by the Stalinist Ho Chi Minh, had no future because he had repressed the 1947 peasant revolt with the help of the French army. The problem was always the same for me: how to defend the Vietnamese claim for independence without defending the Communists . . . But that's another discussion.

Michnik: I have another question to ask: how many windows did you break at the American embassy in support of the Vietcong, and how many for the boat people?

Cohn-Bendit: In the last few years I've demonstrated against the USSR just as often as I have against the U.S.A., and I've probably broken fewer windows at the latter's.

Michnik: But not because of Vietnam?

Cohn-Bendit: At the Soviet embassy because of Vietnam? No!

Michnik: No Soviet windows have been broken to support the boat people's cause. And only fascists have broken Soviet windows because of Afghanistan. And that's our biggest failure, Dany, our common failure. I was in Rome in 1976 for the anniversary of the Soviet intervention in Hungary, and the only flyers commemorating it were fascist flyers. The only book published in Italy about Katyń was published by a fascist publishing house. And that isn't their victory, but our defeat.

Cohn-Bendit: It's true, emotions about Vietnam ran higher. I'll give you that.

Michnik: What does "higher" mean? They existed, and now they don't.

Cohn-Bendit: It's a little more complicated.

Michnik: Complicated, yes, but only the asshole isn't.

Cohn-Bendit: Let's stop talking about Vietnam.

Michnik: OK, that's enough.

At the time, two very important events interested the Poles: one was domestic, and the other was international. The domestic one was the performance of Adam Mickiewicz's play *Dziady* (The Forefathers), and the international one was Czechoslovakia. In fact in the first two months of 1968, Poland's entire problem was conjured up on the stage of the Warsaw National Theater by the famous sentence from the Russian Bestuzhev's play: "No wonder we're doomed here. For a generation now, the country's been taken over by a legion of bandits coming from Russia."

The Prague Spring was beginning at the same time and we cried out, "Poland awaits her Dubcek!"

Those were the two most important events. We expected a new wave of democratization. The whole controversy surrounding the play had touched our national sensibility. It was a purely Polish phenomenon. We were Communists despite everything. Mickiewicz wasn't a Communist: he was a nineteenth-century romantic author. Nor was he a chauvinist. He was very anti-Russian, but in the anticzarist sense. He wrote a poem called "To My Moscovite Friends" for the Decembrists. He suited our state of mind: he allowed us to be both patriots and internationalists, to be anti-Russian while being Russophiles. And Czechoslovakia represented a new perspective for us.

When censorship forbade the play *Dziady,* we showed up at the last performance with banners calling for the play to go on again, and we yelled, "Independence without censorship!" Those words had a double meaning. It could lead the Communist leaders to believe that Poland did not need censorship since it was already independent. But they had a different meaning for the people. It meant that Polish independence should be extended, not censored.

And to go back to what we said earlier, if Goethe and Schiller were banned in Germany, I think that you would be the first German nationalist.

Cohn-Bendit: Not at all, because Goethe and Schiller mean little to me. But again that's a question of education.

Michnik: So let's take Beaumarchais, or Voltaire, or Shakespeare . . . anybody . . . Heine, Bôrne, Lessing. I am now thinking of my own education.

Cohn-Bendit: Fassbinder! As long as Fassbinder can be shown without censorship . . .

Michnik: Exactly. And suddenly you can't anymore, because the Russians forbid it. Would you then be a German patriot?

Cohn-Bendit: I would be a lover of freedom. If I wanted to put on a Sartre play in Germany and the Russians forbade me from doing so . . .

Michnik: Since Mickiewicz was a Lithuanian, I felt truly internationalist.

It was also at this time that the small group of dissident Communist protesters seized the nation's flag. Everything that had been abstract and theoretical until then was suddenly filling with Polish blood. Polish mythology isn't a scorched-earth mythology. The Poles have always lost their blood over defeats. It is not a chauvinist tradition but one of sacrifice and martyrdom. And for the first time I told myself, I'm Polish. And it is as a Pole that I could be an internationalist, or even a universalist. And it's only at that time that I understood that something was forbidden to me because I was Polish. The Communists understood this very well: they pretended that we were using Mickiewicz to hide our true face. We were called the Parachutist commandos because whenever the party organized some sort of demonstration, we would invade the place like a release of parachutists to defend our cause.

We were accused of cynically using Mickiewicz to hide our Trotskyist-Zionist interests. No one but Mieczysław Moczar could have come up with that association. Of course, I can't deny that we had something in common with the Trotskyists, but certainly not with Zionism.

I myself sent two copies of Kuroń and Modzelewski's *Open Letter* to the West (which wasn't often done at the time), one to the émigré review *Kultura,* and the other to the Ligue Communiste Révolutionnaire. The *Letter* appeared at the same time both in *Kultura* and with the Trotskyists.

The young people from the Ligue Communiste Révolutionnaire considered themselves Communists but protested the French Communist party's Stalinist orthodoxy. What was attractive about their thinking was that it gave one the space to be both an anti-Soviet rebel and a Communist Marxist. But what differentiated them from us was their doctrinal attitude toward reality.

I remember a discussion we once had: does bureaucracy represent a social layer or a class? According to the Trotskyists, it represented a social layer, whereas the Yugoslav Communist Milovan Djilas defended the theory of the bureaucracy as a class. For us, bureaucracy is a class and not a social layer, because categorizing it as a social layer means that the Communist state is a proletarian state exhibiting phenomena of bureaucratic degeneration; but if you consider it a class, you then have a totalitarian rather than a proletarian state.

We had other differences of opinion, especially with regard to the national question. The Trotskyists (like you, Dany) couldn't understand why we were so attached to the national idea; they saw us as nationalists. But the Polish nationalists saw us as cosmopolites, Zionists, or Trotskyists and internationalists. In fact, all of that was quite amusing for me.

Cohn-Bendit: Enough of the Trotskyists. Let's get back to March 1968.

Michnik: As I've told you, two events marked the month of March: the censuring of *Dziady* and the Prague Spring.

Our intervention in favor of the play and Mickiewicz left me experiencing intense national and anti-Russian feelings for the first time. It all began with *Dziady,* a classic Polish drama; I don't think there is anything comparable in French or German literature. We organized a political demonstration on learning that it had been banned. Later, I was even accused of high treason for having met with a French journalist and telling him the story. After the play was banned, a few colleagues and I were excluded from the university. The minister of secondary education had us kicked out. However, the laws of the time did not allow a minister to act that way, so the expulsion was illegal. We later organized a protest—it was a case of student solidarity—I didn't participate, since it was in my honor. But that didn't matter. I was arrested and only got my freedom a year and a half later.

The prison stay was very instructive for me. When I had a chance to read the newspapers, I discovered articles that I supposed were rigged by the police for my benefit. Until 1968 it was unusual for the Communist Polish press to use the same language as the Nazi publication *Stürmer*.

Marxism-Leninism was being extended into National Socialist anti-Semitism. I couldn't believe my eyes: the papers said that I was Jewish and that there was no more place for me in Poland! I was twenty-one years old then, and I would never have thought it possible to see such sentences written in the Polish language.

I asked myself: who am I, really? I asked myself if I wasn't, in fact, a Jew, and if I shouldn't leave Poland. And then I thought that it wasn't up to Mieczysław Moczar, a Soviet agent, to decide whether I was Polish, Jewish, or Chinese. It was none of their business, and they had no right to pick my national identity for me.

At the same time I understood the problem of my intellectual identity. The Polish Communists' anti-Semitism cut my attachment to communism once and for all: that was the first determining factor.

The second point was the Soviet invasion of Czechoslovakia; that day was the worst one in my life. I learned from the papers on August 21, 1968, that a military intervention by five different states—including Poland—had occurred. I felt like a Polish nationalist for the first time, because the Polish army's participation shamed me so greatly.

I think national identity is determined by the shame one feels for a crime committed. He who is ashamed of Polish sins is a Pole. On that day, August 21, 1968, I tasted what was like a bitter taste of national shame. This Polish morality, this Polish myth, expressed in the phrase "For freedom—ours and yours," really exists.[3] But the Communists have given it another sense: "For captivity—ours and yours."

The cross-examinations were my third experience of the time. Like Kuroń, I was one of those who never said anything during the investigation. The judges were forever repeating that I was Jewish and that I should leave Poland. "Mr. Michnik," they would say, "why don't you leave for Tel-Aviv?" And I would answer that I would love to go, but only if they went to Moscow first.

The trial took place after about a year. The main accusation was directed toward Kuroń and Modzelewski; the secondary accusation was against me. I was condemned to three years in jail. It wasn't very much; I had expected a harsher verdict.

---

3. "For freedom—ours and yours" was a password during the Polish independence wars.—ED.

Cohn-Bendit: That was in 1969?

Michnik: Yes. I remember that during my incarceration the judge was especially furious with Kuroń, who was always calling himself a Jew. It pissed him off. According to their version, Kuroń was a Pole manipulated by the Jews. But Jacek didn't like being treated like a puppet, so he would say to them, "I am a Jew, but your police works so badly that you don't even know it."

I read my name in the papers for the first time. During one of his visits, my lawyer told me that during your trial, Dany, you said that you wanted to change your name to "Kuroń-Modzelewski."

Cohn-Bendit: That isn't exactly true. I didn't say that I wanted to change my name, but when the judge asked me my name—the accused must state his name during a trial—I answered that my name was Kuroń-Modzelewski. He looked at me with big eyes and said, "What does this mean?—Yes, my name is Kuroń-Modzelewski—But your name is Cohn-Bendit!" And I answered, "Well, if you know my name, then why are you asking me?"

Michnik: What surprised me was the tone that the Polish press used to write about May 1968 in France. It was the tone that they used to write about us. Ignacy Krasicki, who was one of the worst, filthiest bastards of a journalist, wrote an article about May 1968 in France for *Życie Warszawy* in which he called you a "curse of a Jewish tenderhorn." He wrote the same thing about me.

At the time, I thought it was because we were fighting for the same cause. It took me a number of years to understand that that wasn't so. The most important thing for me was the Soviet invasion of Czechoslovakia; but for the angry students in the West, it was Vietnam. It is only when I realized that Vietnam was turned into a gigantic concentration camp after the Vietcong victory that I understood the profound difference between us. But I've always kept a soft spot in my heart for May '68. I've often fought about this with my professor, Leszek Kołakowski: he felt that one of the movements had fascist characteristics, but I felt otherwise.

Cohn-Bendit: Was he thinking of the Western student movements?

Michnik: Yes. When he was offered the Adorno chair, the members of SDS [Students for a Democratic Society] wrote him an open letter asking him not to take the post since he was a bourgeois intellectual and they wanted a Marxist intellectual. He answered with another open letter, in which he said that he had no intention of preventing the class struggle between professors and students. I think that Leszek Kołakowski was right, but nonetheless I remained sympathetic to the students.

I spent eighteen months in jail. It was a university for me. I learned a lot of things about real communism: I saw Communists in action, and it wasn't fun. Everything that I had known as theory had now become reality. I've often thought of a joke they used to tell in Warsaw when the anti-fascist movie *Mein Kampf* came out: Moczar and Gomułka are talking together. Gomułka asks Moczar, "Have you seen the movie *Mein Kampf*?" Moczar answers, "The book is better." Then Gomułka: "Movie adaptations often aren't as good as the book." Eighteen months in jail also meant a very particular practice of communism. I began to think that the fundamental reference point in communism is not class warfare, or the war between different social layers, but the relationship between prisoners and guards.

The accusation act had two chief points. According to the first, I had been a member of a clandestine organization, which was a lie. I never belonged to such an organization, and none even existed. Later, during Solidarity, having belonged to a clandestine movement would have been a positive, but in this case it was a lie. The second accusation was that I had been in contact with a foreign organization hostile to Poland, with the intent of harming the Polish state. This type of accusation justified a minimum sentence of five years in prison. The organization in question was *Le Monde,* and its representative was its correspondent, Bernard Margueritte. Because of that interview, I was good for a five-year prison sentence!

Now I am grateful to the people who instituted those proceedings against me, because it allowed me to learn a lot of things. Prison is also where my obstinacy toward the Communists originated: I swore to myself that I would never leave Poland. I felt that Poland was my native land and that I was a patriot in this country, unlike them: they dishonored it, while I defended it. I don't know if I've managed to keep that promise, but I wanted to with all my strength. I was freed in September 1969. Everything that was going on led to a sort of emigration hysteria, and many of my friends left. My parents pushed me to leave too. My father said that the Communists would never forgive me for all of the things I had said during the trial: among other things I had said that it was only my being in prison that had kept me from officially demonstrating against the intervention in Czechoslovakia. And when the judge asked me why I had refused to make a deposition during the trial, I had answered that this trial was nothing but an attempt at compiling a file against certain party leaders (I hadn't been questioned about Kuroń, but about Edward Ochab), and that I understood the mechanics of Stalinist trials, which was why I had refused to testify.

I had actually known Ochab's daughter since school, and I had helped her prepare her baccalaureate in history. During the campaign that was organized in March, during a party meeting, Ochab (then president of the State Council) was asked whether Michnik had really helped his daughter prepare her exams. Ochab and my father had been in jail together before the war, and a prison friendship is sacred. He got angry and said, "Yes, Michnik helped my daughter in history, and he did it quite well." He resigned from his post not long after that.

While in jail, I had the chance to read the speech in which Gomułka attacked me personally; after that, I figured I'd be spending at least eight years in prison. You could say that all of this was a demonstration of concrete communism. When I read the line "Blessed be jail, for jail formed me" in *The Gulag Archipelago,* I totally understood what Solzhenitsyn meant. If I hadn't gone to jail, I might be a scoundrel like Mieczysław Rakowski or Jerzy Urban now. I thank God for my years in jail. When the eighteen months were over, I became a factory worker.

Cohn-Bendit: Why? By personal choice, or because it was difficult to find anything else?

Michnik: Because I had no other choice. If I wanted to continue with my studies, I had to work for two years as a welder at the Rosa Luxemburg Factory, which produced electric lightbulbs. We used to joke that the bulbs that blew out the fastest were probably the ones I had made.

Since the working class dominates in Poland, I thought to myself: Great, I have finally come into power! This experience was also extremely important for me, since I came from an intellectual family: it was my first direct, and warm, contact with the world of workers.

Cohn-Bendit: So that phase can be seen as your forced Maoist phase?

Michnik: No, not Maoist.

Cohn-Bendit: Forced Maoist! You were sent to the factory, just as during the Cultural Revolution.

Michnik: They thought it would be a hurtful measure, but they were wrong. The Rosa Luxemburg workforce is composed primarily of women, the most beautiful girls in Warsaw. At first I was very popular with them, and I couldn't have been better anywhere else. Then I lived at the factory in December 1970: I supported those who had organized a protest. In fact, and although it certainly wasn't their intention, the government had done me a great favor by sending me to the factory. When the party press attacked me and called me an agitator, my colleagues voted on a resolution that made me an honorary member of the Rosa Luxemburg chapter of Solidarity.

There was a big demonstration at the factory in March 1981 to commemorate the events of 1968. The Grunwald Patriotic Association, which used to call me a cynical Jew who was trying to manipulate the workers, participated in it. The workers rose and ordered the Grunwald members to leave, saying, "He [Michnik] has worked here with us. For two years, he has taught us to defend ourselves and to organize protest demonstrations. He belongs to us, and we want him to represent us and to talk to us. Because unlike you he is not a Soviet agent." It's at times like those that you tell yourself, My life has not been in vain.

Cohn-Bendit: Were the contacts between you and the workers simple from the very beginning, or was there a period of suspicion toward you?

Michnik: Suspicion, no, never. It is I who was shy. But I never lost my way on the path leading from eroticism to politics.

Kuroń and Modzelewski were freed at that time. It was already December 1970. Gomułka had been replaced by Edward Gierek. I was to take up my studies again in Poznań. Gierek had decided that this was to be a period of stabilization. We tried to build an opposition movement, and we formed a lot of links with the intellectual set—which was something new.

Cohn-Bendit: Who's "we"?

Michnik: Kuroń, me, Janek Lityński, Seweryn Blumsztajn, Modzelewski. This was the first time that personal friendships were formed between intellectuals and members of this type of political opposition organization.

Cohn-Bendit: You mean the workers' opposition?

Michnik: No, the workers' opposition didn't exist yet. The workers who I considered friends listened to me; they borrowed books printed abroad, and so on; but no political action came out of it. Except, of course, the December 1970 strike for which I had written a resolution. Wałęsa still says to me, "You should have understood, you were a welder for two years . . ." The opposition during those years was by and for the intellectuals.

It was at that time that I became Antoni Słonimski's secretary—he was a great Polish poet who also had great moral authority. He was a man who tended toward liberalism and the opposition but was nevertheless respected by the government.

My contact with Słonimski was priceless for three reasons. First, he taught me everything on the traditions of the intellectual Polish class. Second, he helped me resolve the problem of being a Polish Jew. And finally, he served as a sort of screen: as long as I was his secretary, I enjoyed a certain immunity. I wasn't so scared of being arrested as I was of being arrested without it being known. My father often told me that he knew Communist Russia and that in that system a prisoner could disappear as if "swallowed up by the ground." I wanted to make sure that didn't happen to me. I didn't want to simply disappear. I wanted to get stuck in their throats. So I told my father that I would only let myself be arrested if it gave rise to a scandal. And I kept my promise.

Gierek had a pretty good image abroad during the 1970s. [Jimmy] Carter, and before him both [Richard] Nixon and [Gerald] Ford, liked him. Chancellor Helmut Schmidt liked him so much that he would have liked to take him into his own government. Even Giscard d'Estaing admired him. Everyone liked him, except for us. And we ended up being right. When I think now of Helmut Schmidt saying that he would like to make Gierek his minister of economy, I am glad for the Germans that it didn't happen.

What did our oppositional activities consist of at the time? We formed an association of people who thought about politics and organized different actions. During the first clandestine seminars we read Trotsky, Paul Sweezy, Oskar Lange, Karl Marx, and Lukács, and ten years later we were reading Miłosz, Herling-Grudziński, and Hannah Arendt. We were no longer Marxist dissidents but members of the anti-totalitarian opposition.

We were also making some of the first contacts with the Catholic circles (your friend Krzysztof [Śliwiński] was one of our links); once again we asked ourselves: Is the Church really as reactionary as we've always thought? Who is truly reactionary in Poland, the Catholic

Church or the militia? Starting with that question, I wrote my book *The Church and the Left*. I tried to bring anti-clerical, secular intellectuals and Catholics together. I am not Catholic, but I have a lot of sympathy for the Polish Church. Basia, my girlfriend, faults me for it and won't let me go to church. She thinks that having few real contacts with the Church makes it much easier for me to like it. And in that sense, she's not wrong. And neither am I.

Cohn-Bendit: How do you talk, in this secular left? When the Church denounces totalitarianism, or when it takes a stand against contraception or abortion, in other words, all of the Church's classic moral pillars, does that warrant a discussion in your eyes, or not?

Michnik: Of course we talk about it. But as long as the Church uses moderate means for these things, everything is fine.

Cohn-Bendit: What do you mean by "moderate means"?

Michnik: As long as all the Church does is say to Catholics: "You cannot divorce, or abort," and so on, there is no problem. That is its right. It would be different if it wanted to start lawsuits for all transgressions against Catholic commandments.

Cohn-Bendit: That is an open and very complex debate. In the West, for example, the Church is quite favorable toward a prison sentence in case of abortion; it practically demands that women who get abortions be prosecuted and condemned. It is still the Church that keeps that type of law from being abolished.

Michnik: That is possible. I think that here, Catholics would vote for the right to divorce or have abortions. If somebody doesn't want to divorce, no one makes them. The right to divorce doesn't mean the obligation to divorce. Saying that everything that is not forbidden is obligatory is a totalitarian philosophy. And it is idiotic.

Cohn-Bendit: I hope that you will have enough freedom to discuss moral and social questions openly with the Catholic Church.

Michnik: It isn't a topic of discussion in Poland. The Church says that Catholics aren't allowed to divorce or abort, but Catholics aren't looking to the Church for answers to those questions. You could see that very clearly during Solidarity: the same people who hung crucifixes in union premises only listened to their own consciences and not to the bishops when it was time to decide whether or not to strike. The Polish primate asked for the strikes to stop, but the Catholic workers went to mass *and* kept on striking.

In a totalitarian state, where power, not a transcendent god, is the object of the cult, the strength of the Christian religion comes from the Church teaching that one must only kneel before God and not before a temporal power. And that is why religion is fundamentally anti-totalitarian.

Cohn-Bendit: That is only the case in a secular totalitarianism. But there is also a totalitarianism that makes use of the Church, and in such a case there is a cleavage within the Church: Chile is such an example, like all of Central and Latin America and Nazi Germany. Pius VI knelt before Hitler.

Michnik: Not Pius VI, but Pius XI! No, that is a typical absurdity of the left; I am not Pius XI's advocate, but to say that he was pro-Hitler you have to have fallen on your head! . . . Who wrote *With Burning Intent?*[4]

Cohn-Bendit: Pius XI did not rail against Hitler; in no way was he an anti-totalitarian bastion like the Church can be here.

Michnik: You are very optimistic about the Polish Church. It too is divided.

Cohn-Bendit: I don't want to talk about the Polish Church now.

Michnik: As you wish . . . I still remember the first meetings with the representatives of Catholic intellectuals very well. It was very interesting. They treated us as if we were Beria and Stalin's agents, and we saw them as agents of Torquemada's Inquisition. But after a while the ice began to melt: they started reading our texts and we did the same. And we realized that we had more in common than not. That was certainly the most important element of those years. Just as National Socialism put an end to the traditional conflict between Catholics and Protestants, communism abolished the conflict between anti-clerical, secular intellectuals and the Church. The disagreements still exist, but it's not a question of having two hostile worlds anymore.

The only newspapers that published my articles in those days were Catholic papers: Tadeusz Mazowiecki published them under a pseudonym in *Więź.* And Bogdan Cywiński published Kuroń's texts in the magazine *Znak.*

We, on our side, began to discover Christian literature: reading Dietrich Bonhoeffer was essential for me because he explained how to be an anti-totalitarian Christian.

4. Pius XI's encyclical on the Church and the German Reich, published in 1937. — ED.

It is also at this time that Kuroń went to see Cardinal Stefan Wyszyński. I encouraged him to do so. During their first interview, Jacek admitted to having been an enemy of the Church for many years.

We were the instigators of the *Letter of the 59,* but half of the signatories were from the Catholic camp and half from the secular camp, which gave rise to a totally new situation. Later on, we wrote more letters, and the fight against the changing of the constitution became a matter of conscience for all Polish intellectuals.

Before that, people didn't like to show that they knew dissidents like Kuroń or me. We weren't let into people's homes, because they worried that the police would beat them up. They tried to confine us in the opposition ghetto.

Those letters proved that we were not isolated elements anymore: people like Słonimski, Andrzejewski, and Herbert participated in writing them and signed them along with us. This new psychological context is what allowed us to react the way we did to the Radom events in 1976.

As you must know, intellectuals suffered from a complex, and that is why they remained quiet in December 1970 when the workers' blood flowed. And if I spoke up it's because I wasn't an intellectual at the time but a worker-dissident hybrid. Finally, that all bore fruit. After the 1976 events at Radom and Ursus, during the worker demonstrations and the reprisals that followed, Jacek Kuroń declared that we had already betrayed the workers once and that such a thing should not be repeated. He was right, and we kept our promise.

And that's how the Workers' Defense Committee, KOR, was born. It came out of a moral impulse.

I remember attending a trial in 1976 that implicated some Ursus workers; I heard the condemnations, I saw the wives crying, and I shook with rage. I felt that it would be inadmissible to drop these people. And I started writing a protest letter on the part of the intellectuals right after. Intellectuals were taking up the workers' cause for the first time. And then Jacek Kuroń wrote an open letter, and a group to which I belonged drafted an appeal to Western intellectuals, asking them to engage in the defense of Polish workers' rights. That text appeared in the *Nouvel Observateur.* Heinrich Böll, Günter Grass, Ignazio Silone, Saul Bellow, and some others wrote a response.

With all of this going on, the psychological pressure was so great that things had to change, which is how KOR was born. It was September 1976. I wasn't in Poland at the time. It's difficult to explain why to a foreigner. I had received an invitation from Jean-Paul Sartre to come to Paris. When I went to the passport office everyone told me I was crazy and that there was no chance for me to get one. But the insane are lucky. After the Radom events, the government must have figured that I would be less dangerous in Paris than in Warsaw: they gave me the passport. Jacek was incorporated into the army. They wanted to neutralize us both. Jacek resented me a lot for that. He saw my departure as a betrayal. He may have been right, but once abroad, I did everything I could to justify it, so that it couldn't and wouldn't be taken as a desertion. Once in the West I really acted like a lunatic: no Eastern European who wanted to go home would have acted that way. And at the time no one thought I would return to Poland. Rudi Dutschke told me I was an idiot, Jiří Pelikan called me a cretin . . .

Cohn-Bendit: What did you do abroad?

Michnik: I gave interviews, I took part in demonstrations—remember, Dany, you were there too. No one had dared to do such things before me. But I felt I had to act like a live torpedo, a kamikaze, to prove to Jacek Kuroń that I wasn't a deserter. I spoke with members of the left, which was a novelty. Normally, when someone wanted to engage in anti-Communist action, they negotiated with the anti-Communist right, but I said, "I am a man of the left and I am going to speak with people of the left. And I'll demand that they take a stand."

So I spoke with Rudi, with Pelikan, with Giancarlo Pajetta, with the labor unions. I also spoke with the Italian Socialists, and I met Bettino Craxi. I only had one question for them: "Are the Italian workers ready to help the Polish workers, yes or no?"

And since my mind-set was that of a 1968 leftist, it was easy for me to talk with people like Bruno Trentin, the president of the Italian welders' union and a member of the Communist party.

I had met Cardinal Wyszyński in Rome, and I had asked him whether I should talk about Poland with the Italian Communists. "Absolutely," he'd answered. The cardinal's guarantee was, unfortunately, insufficient, and when I returned to Poland, members of the non-KOR opposition accused me of being a Communist.

My time in the West gave me a better understanding of the Western left. I felt like a leftist, but a Western leftist. At the same time, I knew that other dominant classifications existed in Poland. When I was asked whether KOR belonged to the left or right, I could give either one of two answers. The first was borrowed from Vladimir Bukovsky, who said that we didn't come from a leftist or rightist camp but from a concentration camp. And the second was from Petra Kelly: "We are not from the right or the left, we are new."

Cohn-Bendit: She said, "We are ahead."

Michnik: She also said, "We are new." Or maybe you said it, I don't remember. Anyway, the basic idea was that this was something new. I also realized at this time that there was a paradox between Western and Eastern Europe. People of my generation, those who'd been through 1968, understood me, but they weren't ready to take on the Eastern point of view; they wanted to fight American imperialism. But I got along famously with people who came from the East, like Bukovsky, Antonín Liehm, Rudi Dutschke, Wolf Biermann—who isn't very smart by the way. I don't know how things would go with him today.

Cohn-Bendit: You have a lot of things in common, like your attitude toward women.

Michnik: Does something in my attitude toward women shock you?

Cohn-Bendit: No, but the similarity is striking. I like Wolf.

Michnik: I don't mean to say that I don't like him! Since he is a man who knows what it means to be watched by the police, we got along. Which wasn't the case with the then-president of the Jusos (Young Socialists).

Cohn-Bendit: He was crypto-Communist.

Michnik: Really? I couldn't accept his point of view at all. The fundamental concepts, to him, were capitalism and socialism. For me they were totalitarianism and anti-totalitarianism. He saw me as a fierce defender of Helmut Schmidt's liberal-social coalition, whereas my main critique of it had to do with its relations with Eastern Europe. [Willy] Brandt wasn't brave enough to meet with me; he thought it would hurt his relationship with Gierek. I'm sure he was right! But his attitude gave me a lot to think about. Brandt's fear of meeting with a KOR representative made me realize that KOR could only count on itself, and that in the end the Polish people could only count on themselves.

Ever since the Poles were sold out at Yalta, no one has been ready to help them. On this subject, there is a paradoxical link between Eastern and Western European dissidents. Both sides want to undermine the post-Yalta order of things, but from completely different starting points. I think that two essential points unite us: first, to quote Che Guevara, "as long as the world is what it is, we do not want to die in our beds"; and second, we don't want Yalta.

Cohn-Bendit: But, unfortunately, for opposing reasons. A number of Western leftists want to cancel Yalta's Western conclusion without questioning its Eastern one.

Michnik: Yes, and that's the absolute opposite of what interests me. At the time I was a great believer in Finlandization. If Europe was to be Finlandized, why not start with Eastern Europe? So I suggested carrying the experience out in Poland and then instituting a parliamentary regime to replace the Communist system.

Cohn-Bendit: Self-limited independence?

Michnik: Yes, if you like. Afterward, we could talk about Western Europe. But somehow few people followed me. Giancarlo Pajetta told me that freedom was something completely relative, that freedom in England was different from freedom in Senegal. He also said that nothing has done as much damage to Poland as this desire to imitate the West.

Cohn-Bendit: Pajetta wouldn't say that anymore.

Michnik: I told him that that damage was nothing compared to that caused by the Italian Communists' fixation on the Soviet Union. And then he told us—I was at Leszek Kołakowski's home—that he had spent eight years in a fascist prison, from 1934 to 1943. Kołakowski asked him, "So you witnessed the Ribbentrop-Molotov pact in jail?" He answered, "Yes, and it was very difficult for me. But I always believed that the red flag would one day fly over Berlin. And today, it does." "Yes," I added. "It flies over the barbed-wire."

The whole trip was very exciting for me. What struck me the most was my interview with Heinrich Böll. Like all Poles, I was somewhat repulsed by Germany—after all, didn't the Germans turn Poland into a concentration camp? Although I knew intellectually that I shouldn't be anti-German, I was, emotionally. And it is thanks to Heinrich Böll that I came to like the Germans. Heinrich Böll told me, during our interview, that he would help the workers from Radom and Ursus whenever possible. No one in the West had ever been so clear. And he kept his promise. Every time we needed his help, he was there. That's why it was a great tragedy for me to be in jail when he died, and not to have had the chance to thank him for all he had done.

I returned to Poland on May 2, 1977. Exactly ten years ago today. Leszek Kołakowski called me from Oxford the night before I left: "You're leaving tomorrow? How do you feel?" "The way I did before the first night I made love." "And how was it?" "I can't remember," I answered.

When I arrived in Poland, everyone was there to welcome me: a big crowd of friends, intellectuals, and dissidents but also an impressive number of policemen and militiamen.

KOR had made me a member on the day before my return. I preferred not to be one while I was in the West: that way what I said concerned only me. But now, it was normal for me to become a member.

Kuroń had called me in Paris to ask me to find a mimeograph. I thought he'd gone crazy. Where could we hide such a thing in Poland? At his place? At mine? . . .

When I returned I didn't understand what was happening at all: although I felt it vaguely, I couldn't conceive of it. A psychological revolution had taken place. KOR was organizing meetings in Professor Edward Lipiński's apartment—he was a legendary figure in Polish socialism; in 1905, before Gierek was even born, Lipiński was already a Socialist. Gierek couldn't do anything against him. The police couldn't have entered his house. Something had changed. It was so important for Gierek to be well thought of by Helmut Schmidt, Giscard d'Estaing, President Ford, Leonid Brezhnev, and Reza Shah Pahlavi that he couldn't afford to have political prisoners anymore. This gave us a certain amount of liberty, which we took advantage of. All the people in the know told us we were dreaming: "You are doing something that is impossible. There is no opposition in communism." We answered that this opposition existed despite this impossibility. Later there was the version that branded us as agents-provocateurs, and we asked: Who and what are we provoking?

And then there was a third version, which suggested that we were in cahoots with a certain faction of the Central Committee. We would then ask the question: Which part? Then we were told that such a faction existed. When we asked how they knew this, they answered that without such a faction, we couldn't exist either. Now there is clear and Cartesian reasoning!

I had two weeks of freedom. I returned to Poland on May 2, and I was arrested two weeks later with my friends. Our arrest had to do with something that happened in Kraków. Stanisław Pyjas, a student and collaborator in KOR, had been murdered. We went to his funeral in Kraków and our car was stopped. It wasn't until July 23 that I saw the sun of freedom again. Going directly from Paris to jail was a terrible shock for me. Shortly before my return to Poland I had given an interview to Marion Grafin Dönhoff, in Hamburg. The subject was "My place is in Poland." In it, I said that I would return to Poland because it was my homeland. Dönhoff was very nice; she would ask me what kind of questions I wanted her to ask, and then I would answer the questions I had just dictated to her. It was a beautiful gesture on her part. *Die Zeit* is a very serious paper, and it was really something that the countess personally interviewed a man who is as unserious as I am!

That interview came out while I was in prison. The police were outraged. Especially since I said that political and commercial contacts should be subject to the Polish government's human rights record. During the whole investigation, that interview served as a *casus belli* against me. It was said that I wanted to starve the Polish people. "What does that mean? That I want to starve my people? When all I want is for the Polish government to respect human rights, as it has sworn to do!" The police answered, "Mr. Michnik, you know very well that that is impossible, the Polish government cannot respect human rights." And I answered, "You are the ones who said it. But if I said such a thing, I would be accused of slander against the state."

I was in jail for the third time, and I thought to myself: Never two without three. But that popular saying didn't help me since I spent another three years in prison. It was a very important event for me, because it allowed me to be fully accepted as a member of KOR. The psychological situation was quite special at the time: all year long, people would end up in jail for forty-eight hours. And meanwhile, I was drinking champagne in Paris, Rome, Hamburg, London. And no one appreciates having someone else drink champagne in his place. So, in the same way that I'd had to justify leaving Poland, I now had to justify having been abroad, drinking champagne. I'm not going to give you details about KOR, you can read all of that in Jan Józef Lipski's book.[5] I just want to tell you what KOR represented for me personally. It stood for a philosophy of political activity in a posttotali-

5. Jan Józef Lipski, *KOR: A History of the Workers' Defense Committee in Poland, 1976–1981*, translated by Olga Amsterdamska and Gene M. Moore (Berkeley: University of California Press, 1985). —ED.

tarian system. Why posttotalitarian? Because the power is still totalitarian, whereas society isn't anymore, it is already anti-totalitarian, it rebels and sets up its own independent institutions that lead to something we could call a civil society, in Tocqueville's sense. And that is what we tried to do: build a civil society.

There weren't many of us. The KOR circle was maybe two thousand strong. But that finally led to Solidarity's ten million members.

That phenomenon rested on an archetype. A certain model of political reflection within a totalitarian system, a certain model of civil courage and the edification of independent institutions in a civil society. It wasn't easy.

Every two weeks I spent forty-eight hours in jail. The worst wasn't being in jail, but waiting to get there; we all knew full well that we would be put in jail, but we never knew when. This difficult situation ruined my sex life. I couldn't make dates anymore: as soon as things would take shape, I would go spend forty-eight hours in jail. How could I possibly like the Communists in that kind of situation?

Actually, the godfather of August 1980 [Solidarity] was Jacek Kuroń. From within KOR I was taking care of the relationship with the intellectuals. I wrote a clandestine paper, and I worked in a "flying university" and for a clandestine publishing house. I wasn't in contact with the workers. Before August 1980, I had only seen Wałęsa once. I didn't like him at all—he seemed ambitious and shrewd. That's how things were at the time. But the way things are going, I'm probably going to end up asking him to marry me! . . . The aversion has changed into love.

To be truthful, Kuroń was the only KOR member to predict the events. He was always saying that we were marching toward a crisis, and I agreed with him. But when he spent three years announcing it for the following week, I didn't agree with him anymore. His predictions bored me.

And when August arrived, I didn't believe it anymore.

Kuroń decided to abolish vacations for everyone in the opposition because, he said, big things were going to happen and we needed to be there. I was convinced that this was a purely demagogic move on his part and I went to the mountains. I came back at the beginning of August. And once again, I didn't understand a thing. Let's take the Lublin strike as an example: I was hiking in the mountains and I hadn't even heard of it. I was writing an essay on the life of the opposition in a totalitarian state. For the first time in three years I had found some time to write. What I wanted to do in this essay was take eighty pages and summarize the situation: communism, the opposition, KOR, and so on. But the month of August came and my essay was a piece of garbage.

During a meeting in Warsaw, Kuroń asked who wanted to go to Gdańsk. The naval yard strikes had already begun and were organized by Bogdan Borusewicz, a friend of ours and a KOR member. I volunteered, because I felt guilty for having gone to the mountains instead of taking care of the workers' movement. Jacek accepted. He trusted me.

Like me, Jacek worried about the demands of the Gdańsk people. We found the idea of an independent and autonomous union particularly extravagant and irresponsible. We thought it was unworkable within a Communist system. So I was to go to Gdańsk to explain to the workers that they couldn't persist in those demands. Since I was popular and well known, I may have had a chance to convince them.

By a stroke of luck I was arrested, so I didn't go, I didn't convince them, and Solidarity was born. Without us and against us. But during all this time, and to this day, we've remained convinced that Solidarity is our child, albeit an illegitimate one.

Cohn-Bendit: What did those sixteen months change for you, from a political and social point of view? How did Solidarity mark your identity? It's important to know that to understand your behavior after December 13, 1981.

Michnik: Piotr Słonimski, an eminent Polish geneticist working in France, told me that he lived May '68 as a moment of grace. It's the same for me. The Solidarity era was a moment of grace. And at the same time an apprenticeship of dignity, liberty, judgment, and misfortune. I picked honey from flowers. I went to worker meetings and they applauded me. I would say that it almost marked me as much as May '68 marked you. And it was worth spending six years in prison for those sixteen months.

Cohn-Bendit: What did you say to the workers?

Michnik: We told them that for the first time in many years, Polish society was organizing itself, that they were the country's owners, that the country was theirs, that the factories and the state belonged to them, that they had to reorganize and govern this state. Do you think that's too little?

Cohn-Bendit: No.

Michnik: We also told them that we would defend Solidarity to the end, that we would never betray them, no matter what happened. And we kept our promise. The fact that I've never betrayed Solidarity is one of the few things I have to be proud of. And we will never betray it, because Poland needs it. Whoever says that Solidarity is finished may as well say that Poland is finished. The only real Poland is represented by Solidarity.

I can't speak about Solidarity objectively because I'm so close to it, and so moved by it.

Cohn-Bendit: I don't want you to talk about it objectively, but subjectively. What were your functions, other than giving the occasional big speech? In everyday life . . .

Michnik: I was in the anti-Wałęsa faction. I felt that he wanted to impose a sultanistic regime, a sort of dictatorship, on Solidarity. When I wanted to piss him off, I would read an article at the Gdańsk shipyards called "The Controversy around Stalin." This essay was built around the story of a workers' leader who had become a dictator, although he was a likable, friendly man who loved children and had many of them, who had a mustache and smoked a pipe. In other words, I would turn Wałęsa into the new Stalin.

Cohn-Bendit: How did the workers react?

Michnik: They liked my story. Wałęsa was an important man, but so was I. Wałęsa was very popular, but he was also hated and had enemies. I was a partisan of Andrzej Gwiazda. I felt that Wałęsa had compromised himself too much with the Communists and that he would sell us out in the end. After December 13 I expected to have my suspicions confirmed every day. When I realized that he hadn't sold us out, I said to Andrzej Gwiazda, who was in jail with me, "Andrzej, we'll have to buy Lech a beer."

When I got out of jail I swallowed my pride and went to Canossa to see Lech. We met in Basia's house, in Sopot. Wałęsa arrived and we embraced. I had once been his worst enemy. I told him, "Lech, the worst political mistake I ever made in my life was misreading you." Lech simply answered, "Let's not talk about it anymore." Since that day, there's been a "homosexual" love between us.

Cohn-Bendit: Let's not talk about Solidarity anymore. I can easily imagine those sixteen months. And then, on December 13, the coup d'état. Earlier, you had developed the theory of a self-limiting revolution. You said a little while ago that in 1977 you believed that Finlandization should begin with Poland. During the great Solidarity period, did you believe that this collective opposition could one day be legalized? Did you believe in a political solution?

Michnik: No, I didn't believe in anything. I'm going to tell you a joke. There's a Jew, Moses, who goes to the synagogue every Friday. He kneels . . .

Cohn-Bendit: Jews don't kneel.

Michnik: You know Jews, I know funny stories . . . So he was going to the synagogue to pray and he said, "My God, how cruel you are, I still have not won a million at lotto. My wife Rebecca won't have the money to buy a new dress. My daughter Sarah won't have money for a new bicycle. And my son David won't have money for a new car. How cruel you are!" And he would leave. Coming back the next Friday, he says, "My God, how cruel you are. I still haven't won a million at lotto. And my wife Rebecca, my daughter Sarah, my son David!" The fifth time he was still saying, "My God, how cruel you are. I still have not won a million at lotto. And my wife Rebecca, and my daughter Sarah, and my son David!" And the synagogue roof splits open and he hears a voice, "Moses, give me a chance, and at least buy a lotto ticket!"

I didn't believe, but I bought a ticket. I wanted to give God a chance, so I didn't want to be guilty of not having bought the ticket. But God is just: since I had bought the ticket, there was Solidarność.

The self-limiting revolution was a certain political philosophy; it was our only chance, we had no other. We knew that we couldn't win a fight against the Soviet Union, and that our chance lay in the Russians' fear of occupying Poland—as Poland might then become their second Afghanistan.

So I defended compromise, self-limitation, and harmony. But if the Russians ever occupied the country, they had to know that they'd be spitting blood. I recently read Colonel Ryszard Kukliński's interview and got confirmation of what I thought.

Cohn-Bendit: Who was Kukliński?

Michnik: The chief of operations when martial law was put into place. Kukliński said that the failed strike of 1981 had given Russia the signal that it could invade. And at the time, I was saying that our only chance was to accept a compromise while simultaneously worrying the government. That strike gave the Russians the idea that they could now institute martial law without any danger.

Cohn-Bendit: What kind of strike was it?

Michnik: It doesn't matter. The important thing is that it was to be a general strike, but there was only 40 percent participation.

I was being taken for an extremist because I was constantly repeating that the Russians would have to spit up blood if they invaded. I didn't know if it would happen, but I felt that things should be expressed that way. But in fact I was rather moderate, not an extremist. And, unlike Wałęsa, I thought that proposing a moderate policy did not mean entering into secret negotiations with the Communists. I believed that a policy of compromise should be understood and accepted by all of Solidarity. This compromise could only be realized if the entire movement understood the Solidarity leaders' policy and if Solidarity seriously worried the Soviets.

During the last months, basically as of August 1981, I felt like an outsider within Solidarity. I was Wałęsa's declared enemy, and Kuroń's as well. I didn't understand their politics. I thought they were searching for a compromise at all costs, whereas for me there was a price beyond which we couldn't pay for a compromise, a price that was equal to betrayal.

December 13 was like a liberation: I could finally identify with Solidarity again.

Cohn-Bendit: What, according to you, was this price?

Michnik: I feared that we would accept subjugating ourselves to the Communists, that Solidarity would become an integral part of existing structures and would become indistinguishable from the old official unions. I feared that all of the critiques Solidarity had put forth would turn into jokes. I was scared that "real Poles" would take over Solidarity—the "real Poles" was a group whose main goal was to fight KOR. They fought against us with arguments borrowed from the Nazis. They accused us of and reproached us for being Jews, Trotskyists, Zionists, and all of that scared me. I was scared because Wałęsa had still not publicly denounced this group. And I held that against him for a long time.

Cohn-Bendit: Why didn't he?

Michnik: Because he saw himself as the leader of the whole movement, to which this group belonged. Wałęsa is the leader of a movement, and I am an independent intellectual. I accept that responsibility and do so whenever possible. But I understand quite well that this sometimes poses problems for Wałęsa, especially as the government had demanded that he put some distance between himself and the rest of us. The elimination of KOR people was a precondition to an agreement with the government. But Wałęsa did not condemn us—you have to remember that—he just pushed us out.

Cohn-Bendit: Did Solidarity, or the experience of Solidarity, change something in your political utopian view of the function of the state and society?

Michnik: I don't think in utopian categories anymore. Solidarity was an anti-utopian movement, a movement without utopia. Its only utopia were the Ten Commandments and the Gospels—except for the commandment about adultery!

I think that Solidarity brought something completely new to European culture, and by that I mean the primacy of practical thought over utopian thought. Whereas the latter is based on the conviction that the single ideal society is a carceral society, Solidarity fought for a civil society that is imperfect by nature. And that is something very important to me. Everything that I wrote in prison after December 13 was written to defend that idea. We shouldn't fight for a perfect society that's free of conflicts, but for a conflictual society in which conflicts can be resolved within the rules of the democratic game.

When I ask myself now whether, as a veteran of 1968, I've remained true to myself, I can answer: yes. I've remained faithful to my anti-authoritarian ideals. That's why I was against communism. And I was against Wałęsa for the same reason, because I thought that he wanted to impose his authority on Solidarity.

During a private meeting Wałęsa said to me, "You know, Adam, I admire you. In your place, if I'd had to deal with a guy like myself, I would probably have slit his throat. You are a saint. You let me live."

Wałęsa has changed, and so have I. He's gotten better. As for me, I can't say.

Cohn-Bendit: You said earlier that you reconciled with Solidarity after December 13. I have a feeling that in your opposition, in your acts, in your inflexibility, you assimilate your political identity—to use a Christian metaphor—martyrdom. The loyal martyr, walking a straight line: that is some of what characterized your behavior after December 13, to say things a little bit harshly.

Michnik: I don't like words like *inflexibility* or *martyr*. I'm not comfortable in that role. If someone else puts shoes on my feet, they hurt. But there is still some truth in what you say. If you are defending an idea, you first have to show, by your own behavior, that you believe in it; in other words, you have to bear witness. Kant said that one has to be consistent, so one does. I am not consistent when it comes to the order of values, knowing that conflictual values exist, but I am consistent when it comes to myself. My friend and master, the great Polish poet Zbigniew Herbert, had a habit of saying, "If you have the choice between two paths, an easy one and a difficult one, you must always choose the difficult one."

Cohn-Bendit: My turn to tell a Jewish joke: "If you only have two possibilities, take the third . . ."

Michnik: I chose the second solution, the difficult path. Actually I don't know if that's the one I chose, but that's what I should have done. And I also know that I am sinning if I choose the easy way. From that starting point, it was my duty—after having proposed a policy of compromise to Solidarity the day after, December 14—to behave in such a way as to make it clear that I had not offered this proposal just to get out of jail. I became trustworthy only if I behaved like a kamikaze. This kind of thinking reflects a certain philosophy of life, and of political life also. I truly believed that a harsh confrontation would have been a tragedy for Poland. On the other hand, I wanted to persuade people that I was disinterested. So I chose confrontation for myself while calling for political compromise.

In December 1983, Minister Kiszczak, the chief of police, had Basia come to his office: he asked her to convince me to go abroad. I had the choice between spending Christmas on the Riviera and staying in jail for a few more years. In response, I wrote the minister a letter for which the entire Polish people love me, the esoteric intellectual.

From a corner in my cell, I wrote him: "I know that in my place you would have chosen the Riviera. But that's the difference between us: you are pigs, not us. I love Poland, even from my cell. I have no intention of leaving Poland. So don't count on it!"

That letter was read over Radio Free Europe on Christmas night, and in that festive mood, the Polish people could listen to the letter. Since then, no one tells me that I'm a Jew, since I've saved Poland's honor.

Cohn-Bendit: Didn't there come a moment when this attitude became a burden? How many years did you spend in jail?

Michnik: Six years.

Cohn-Bendit: And since December 13, 1981?

Michnik: Less, much less of course. Two years and eight months, plus a year and a half; a little bit over four years in all.

Cohn-Bendit: Don't you get tired every now and then? Haven't you reached your personal limits yet, I mean the limits of what is bearable, in such a situation?

Michnik: I've been lucky in my misfortune. I've written five books in prison. Prison has made me a writer—appreciated in Poland, and translated in the West. What should I complain about? Everybody gets tired every now and then. You don't necessarily have to live in a Communist system to feel it. And yes, sometimes I am tired.

Cohn-Bendit: Nowadays, do you live in fear of being arrested again, or do you have the feeling that you can settle for a little while in this freedom that is relative but quite real when compared to jail?

Michnik: You can't bargain with fate. I feel I've been lucky in life. I have a beautiful wife, I've written a few books, I feel I'm loved by those I love . . . why then make plans? There's only one thing I worry about: being right with myself. Everything else is God's affair.

Cohn-Bendit: What do you mean by "being right"?

Michnik: Being morally irreproachable. For the rest I put my faith in God; it's his affair.

Cohn-Bendit: Do you still have your lotto ticket?

Michnik: Yes, I buy one every day. It's my philosophy.

Cohn-Bendit: One last question . . .

Michnik: Why last? The more questions you ask, the more you provoke me. And that's good because I have a hard time talking about myself.

Cohn-Bendit: Yesterday, while we were talking, you said that you find it strange that all these people from 1968, who have different or even antagonistic political positions, feel sympathy for each other and display solidarity toward each other. Tom Hayden—who is now part of the Democratic establishment in the United States and used to be a militant in the reformist wing of the American student movement—as well as Rudi Dutschke and myself, Petr Uhl in Czechoslovakia, Bukovsky in the USSR . . . how do you explain it?

Michnik: And you?

Cohn-Bendit: I told you already. What you said about your behavior at the university, about this apprenticeship of an anti-authoritarian attitude, was very significant for me.

Michnik: Yes, in this context I think that "anti-authoritarian" is the key word. We rebelled against different authorities, but the sense of rebellion was the common denominator. This generation has a historic chance. We can seize it or lose it. I often have the feeling that we don't know how to seize it. We are lucky to be able to tell the Polish people about people like Dany. And Dany has a chance to help the West better understand people like Kuroń. Helping to understand doesn't mean that you have to agree with it or like it, but that you really try to understand. On top of that, you also need to translate the other's passion into your own language, your culture's own language.

If we don't manage to communicate, then totalitarianism will gain the advantage, here and in your country.

Cohn-Bendit: I can only speak for myself, but I think that a common language or passion exists through the years and through the battles. Even if we've fought those battles at different levels. I've just declared in the West that you are the member of my generation who I admire the most, but I have to say that I don't know if I'd have the courage to act the way you do in Poland. I am too in love with life to be able to consciously face the threat of prison.

Due to our life experience, starting with this anti-authoritarian revolt from the sixties to today, I think that what unites us is, on the negative side, an anti-authoritarian sensibility, and, on the positive side, a larger and passionate concept of democracy.

Michnik: I never went to jail voluntarily, I was always forced and constrained. But a gentleman must remain a gentleman, even when he's walking in shit. So, there, I remained a gentleman. Not because I wanted to, but because I had to. I am a reasonable man, by necessity rather than taste. I love life as much as you do, and this role of the martyr doesn't suit me at all. After December, when the government suggested that we go abroad, some of my friends seriously considered it; but I remained firm and from the beginning I said that I would never leave. Jacek Kuroń had no intention of leaving either, but he felt it was worth talking about. When they brought him into my cell, he asked me, "Adaś, why don't you want to think about it?" I answered, "If they put you up on General Anders's white horse and the entire country is watching you, you can't shit in your pants on the white horse. Especially not if you're Jewish."

This anti-authoritarian and anti-totalitarian movement is a chance for our generation: it's a link between East and West.

4

The Dilemma

The dilemma is inscribed in the spiritual biography of every Polish intellectual. Finding himself for years between a totalitarian Communist state and a hierarchical Catholic Church, no Polish intellectual can fail to reflect on both the opportunities and the dangers that this situation presents. He can become a loyal functionary of an official state institution, in which case he will find his dilemma reflected in the writings of Janusz Reykowski and Jan Szczepański, or he can define himself as Catholic and find the choices that confront him described in the essays of Jerzy Turowicz and Tadeusz Mazowiecki. But he may also choose to situate himself *between* these two worlds as a freethinker who has broken with the totalitarian state but who, despite some sympathy with the Church, does not define himself as a Catholic.

It is precisely this kind of intellectual who interests me and with whom I feel a kinship and a kind of intellectual bond. I also think I understand the nature of his dilemma: while some accuse him of being a renegade, others suspect him of being a dishonorable manipulator. Meanwhile, he ponders the world around him, searches for landmarks by which to orient himself, and constructs his own identity anew. In doing so, he follows attentively the words and deeds of his masters, one of whom is Leszek Kołakowski.

This essay, written in honor of Leszek Kołakowski on his sixtieth birthday, was published in Polish in *Obecność: Leszkowi Kołakowskiemu w 60-ta rocznicę urodzin* (London: Aneks, 1987), 197–219. Translated by Jane Cave.

I

I sometimes think that to understand the spiritual dilemma of our intellectual, one only has to survey the landscape that stretches between the writings of Cardinal Wyszyński and those of Witold Gombrowicz. It is here that the ideas of John Paul II, Czesław Miłosz, Zbigniew Herbert, and Leszek Kołakowski are to be found. Everything of value in Polish culture has taken shape at the intersection of its great historical paths, at the point where Christianity encounters the freethinking spirit, in the mutually enriching conflict between these two worlds. If there is even a grain of truth in this argument, it is worth listening carefully to what contemporary critics of the Polish intelligentsia have to say.

They say that the Polish intellectual is abandoning his freethinking ethos, is relinquishing his authenticity to identify with the Catholic Church, and is exchanging the red flag of the proletarian revolution for the yellow-and-white banner of the pope. These claims are accompanied by counterclaims on the part of some in the Church who argue that the turn to Catholic institutions on the part of the intellectual is motivated by the pragmatic—some would say base—desire to use the Church for his own political ends.

These accusations and suspicions are by no means absurd. Given the situation in which he finds himself, our intellectual is bound to face such temptations; frequently he succumbs. We thus share the fear that the freethinking anti-clerical who once threw in his lot with the totalitarian power apparatus might transform himself into an apologist for the clerical vision of social order. This would be a great loss for the pluralistic element of Polish culture and of dubious benefit to the cause of Christianity. On the whole, the Church has enough apologists already, and it cannot complain of a lack of enemies. On the other hand, it always has too few well-disposed, friendly critics.

By abandoning his independence and identity to throw in his lot with Catholic doctrine and the Church hierarchy, the Polish intellectual is committing a second "betrayal of the intellectuals," say his critics.[1] If support for totalitarian communism constituted the first "betrayal," as a result of the second, Poland is beginning to transform itself into a curi-

---

1. *Betrayal of the Intellectuals* is the title of a famous book written by Julien Benda in 1927.—ED.

ously two-dimensional country, where a totalitarian Communist facade is confronted by a society organized according to hierarchical orthodoxy. Culture will wither away in the grip of this dichotomy, the argument goes. Poland will succumb to a process of "Iranization": a civil society shaped by a conservative revolution will wage a cold civil war against an autocratic modernizing state. The state will be governed by a totalitarian power apparatus; and civil society, by the Catholic clergy. We are faced with the revival of the early twentieth-century National Democratic model, which combines nationalist xenophobia with a particular form of Catholicism, which combines hatred and lies in public life with the cultivation of biblical virtues in the privacy of the home. Today, no one refers to this as a "national scandal," no one perceives the potential danger for our national culture. The teachings of John Paul II have been reduced to empty phrases; and the idea of Solidarity, to a symbol tarnished by lies. Poland will sink into provincial nationalism and the depths of dark, tribal hatreds.

This is the prophecy. One hears it with increasing frequency—with such frequency that it is worth considering for a moment.

II

Let us look back and consider the commentary on the encyclical of Pope John XXIII, *Mater et Magister,* that Leszek Kołakowski wrote over a quarter of a century ago, in 1961. It was not a sympathetic commentary. Kołakowski criticized the encyclical's "philanthropic banalities," "conservative content," "misleading insinuations," "contradictions," and "lack of substance."

He analyzed the words of the Vatican from the viewpoint of an antitotalitarian socialist, an advocate of social reforms and the emancipation of labor. What did he find in the proposals of Pope John XXIII? He found—with some justification—that the encyclical provided ammunition for Catholics of every political persuasion, even those diametrically opposed to each other. The wording took account of the needs of the fundamentalist bishops in Latin America while "allowing the Church in socialist countries to engage in the appropriate political maneuvering needed to arrive at a *modus vivendi* with the state authorities." The wording was acceptable to the Christian Democratic left in Europe and to

Christians in the former colonies, to Salazar and to Adenauer; to everyone. For this reason, the encyclical, which had emerged as the result of so many contradictory pressures, turned out to be "a zero program, a nothing."

How did Kołakowski perceive the Church in 1961? He wrote:

Of all the great international institutions of social life it is . . . the most conservative, the most subject to the inertia of the past, and the most weighed down by the burden of its own doctrine. Hence it is also the institution most closely linked to extreme reactionary social structures, and it changes its position only when pressured by events to do so.

Kołakowski attributed to the Vatican "traditional aspirations to total control over social life," a refusal to cooperate with atheists on purely worldly matters, and opposition to any kind of social agreement conceived without its participation. But even these clearly formulated principles, he observed, were permeated by an ambiguity that allowed episcopates "to quote an obscure text to justify their every maneuver in changing political circumstances."

As these quotations suggest, Kołakowski wrote a scathing and derisive critique, but not one—we should emphasize—that was written "to order." On the contrary, at that time the official line was to praise Pope John XXIII and his declarations of peace and initiatives for dialogue and to contrast these with the "reactionary narrow-mindedness" of Cardinal Wyszyński. Every taunt in Kołakowski's anti-papal pamphlet reflected a genuine anti-clerical passion and accurately articulated the views of a substantial proportion of the secular intelligentsia, myself included.

This is not the place to demonstrate that Kołakowski's radical anti-clericalism was historically rooted in a major current in Polish culture. (I would add, though, that there is an increasingly urgent need for an honest history of Polish anti-clericalism. Only when we have such a history, together with an equally honest account of Catholicism, will we be able to examine seriously the changes that have taken place within both the intelligentsia and the Church in Poland.) Leszek Kołakowski contributed to, and exemplifies, these changes. It is for this reason that I have quoted the anti-clerical essay that he wrote years ago; it helps us to realize the enormous distance traveled by this Polish humanist and some of his readers.

In this review of the past, 1956 constitutes a significant turning point. From then on, Kołakowski unequivocally condemned Stalinist totalitarianism, formulated his own independent diagnosis, and pronounced his own judgment on the world that he saw around him. He became one of the theorists of the younger generation of Polish intellectuals that was in rebellion against party orthodoxy and seeking a new language and new ideas.

This generation sought antidotes to Stalinist dogma everywhere: in new interpretations of Marxism, in existentialism, in the rationalist spirit of Western democracy. The Church was viewed critically and with suspicion. Critically, because the spirit of the time demanded that every large and hierarchical organization be viewed in this light; with suspicion, because the spirit of the time demanded that all orthodoxies based on dogma and articles of faith be viewed in this way. The anti-clericalism of Western Europe, freethinking and rationalist in the spirit of Voltaire and the Jacobins, corresponded to the anti-clerical ethos of the Polish intelligentsia. Polish intellectuals, newly liberated from the spiritual constraints of Stalinism, remembered well the history of the Church, its darkest passages in particular. Kolakowski himself viewed with skepticism the Church's *aggiornamento* and Catholic declarations regarding the value of pluralism. "What do Catholics mean by pluralism?" he asked. Do they mean that "there are many ways to convert people and to exercise power," as they learned during the Counter-Reformation, or do they mean "a genuine acceptance of human diversity, open acceptance of all the values that human beings hold dear, respect for diverse ways of living, thinking, and expressing oneself, without abandoning the fight for one's own values?"

Kolakowski urged his Catholic adversaries "to reject, clearly and explicitly, the traditional totalitarian tendencies deeply rooted in the Christian world." The history of the Church, he said, could not be reduced to the formula that people are fallible and make mistakes:

The fact that Catholics themselves often fell victim to intolerance cannot justify their own intolerance in other situations. This should be constantly emphasized, particularly since the entire history of the Church itself gives rise to mistrust of Catholicism. The Church is sensitive to every attempt to restrict its own rights and aspirations but is incapable of reassessing its own past and declaring unambiguously its intention to abandon all those elements that are notoriously typical of a ruling Church and that are difficult to reconcile with the slogans frequently proclaimed by a Catholicism that finds itself in partial opposition to the social world around it.

Did Kolakowski come to change his attitude toward the Church in later years?

III

Of course he changed his attitude, just as the entire Polish intelligentsia changed its attitude toward the Church. I tried to depict these changes in a book I wrote ten years ago, *The Church and the Left,* and I shall not repeat here the conclusions I reached at that time. I will only recall that the road followed by Kołakowski, from his pamphlet on the papal encyclical and his studies of nondenominational Christianity through his memorable essays on Christ as prophet and reformer and on the presence of myth, led to his observations on the "return of the sacred," his reflections on the alleged crisis of Christianity, and to a book on religion. At the same time, this was a road of political evolution: from the attempt to reform actually existing communism from within to a merciless critique of the system, from efforts to reinterpret Marxist doctrine in the essay "Karl Marx and the Classical Definition of Truth" to *Main Currents of Marxism,* the most brilliant critical analysis of Communist totalitarian beliefs. Along the way, Kołakowski's vision of the totalitarian utopia and image of religion was transformed, and his view of both the totalitarian state and the Catholic Church acquired new contours.

In *The Presence of Myth,* Kołakowski wrote that "Christianity created the first models of the totalitarian state in Europe." Years later, this factor would be of far less significance to him. His essay "Successful Prophecies and Wishful Thinking," written immediately following the election of a Polish pope, provides a good example of the evolution of Kołakowski's view of the Church. "The Church," he wrote, "is situated, as it were, on the boundary between heaven and earth, it is both the repository of grace and the guardian of order, bringing invisible values to the visible world." What kind of Church do people need? They do not need a Church that engages in political and sexual revolutions, that "sanctifies all our cravings and extols violence." What they need is a Church that "will help them transcend the immediate pressures of life, that will show them the inescapable limits of the human condition and will enable them to accept these limits." The Christianity of such a Church "is not gold, purple, or red, but gray."

This "grayness" does not signify a flight from the real world but rather a decisive rejection of all efforts to use the Church as an instrument of any particularist political interests. I repeat: any political interests, including both liberationists and fundamentalists. Here we should recall Kołakowski's observation that if the tension between that which belongs to God and that which belongs to Caesar, between the sacred and the profane, comes to constitute a permanent feature in the existence of the Church, then liberationism and fundamentalism offer two dangerous ways of eliminating this tension.

The fundamentalists adhere to the spirit of the *Syllabus*. They long for the days when the secular power structure defended the dogmas of faith against external criticism while the Church was granted the right to exercise detailed supervision of secular affairs. This is the source of their tendency to form alliances and even to identify with political forces that promise privileges to the Church. The liberationists, on the other hand, are willing to abandon the autonomy of their faith and the Church in the world of political conflicts in order to subordinate themselves to reformist or revolutionary movements with a socialist ideology. They are ready to identify with political movements that declare themselves "on the side of the poor," without concern for the fact that, when such movements come to power, they generally initiate policies destructive of the Church.

These are two different ways in which the Church can become involved in immoral political relationships. The fundamentalists will reject totalitarian communism to the extent that it promulgates atheism and persecutes religion. In the name of defending the faith from Communist atheism they are prepared, without much scruple, to support military-police dictatorships. The liberationists, on the other hand, will ally themselves with the Communist opposition to these very dictators, without any concern for the fact that by doing so they are contributing to the triumph of a political order that, once victorious, will not only persecute and destroy religion but also trample human dignity and human rights on a scale far beyond anything practiced by obtuse reactionary generals. Fundamentalists happily agree to human rights violations in anti-Communist dictatorships, while liberationists, by supporting communism, fuel the engine of totalitarian tyranny. Fundamentalism and liberationism constitute two variants whereby the Church abandons the position of consistent anti-totalitarianism. Liberationism simply renounces resistance to totalitarianism in favor of the mirage of institutionalized brotherhood, which inevitably turns into yet another variant of totalitarian prison civilization. The fundamentalist critique of communism focuses, as I have already said, on its atheism. Since it is simply a continuation of the Church's nineteenth-century dispute with liberalism, it makes a doctrinal dispute the core of its critique. This mode of thinking makes it impossible to draw a distinction between liberal democracy and a total-itarian state like Soviet Russia.

As Kołakowski argued, "Despotic government, and in particular the persecution of religion, derives not from the fact that communism is *atheistic* but from the fact that it is *totalitarian,* that it is inherently driven to destroy all forms of collective life and all forms of culture save those imposed by the state." This is a crucial distinction. It is not atheism as a philosophy but totalitarianism as a system, "without regard to its ideo-logical coloration—racist, communist, or religious—that now poses the gravest danger to Christian culture and values."

This has two obvious consequences for Christians. While struggling for their own rights under a totalitarian state, they condemn themselves to a situation of moral ambiguity "if they do not base their claims on an explicit acceptance of pluralism as the basis of social life, in other words, on a radical rejection of totalitarianism, regardless of ideology, which may be atheistic or religious."

The conviction that atheism constitutes the essential defect of com-munism always leads one to false conclusions. The liberationists, who lend their approval to the Communist project, are satisfied with the right to loyally affirm Communist beliefs in the language of Christian doc-trine. For their part, the fundamentalists, by attacking atheism while re-maining silent on the totalitarian context, "lead people to believe—or at least do not clearly deny—that totalitarianism would not be repugnant if its dogma were based on the Nicene Creed rather than the *Collected Works* of Lenin." This can lead to a paradoxical convergence: the loyal liberationist and the steadfast fundamentalist are united by their belief that their mission is to convert the ruling Communists to the true faith, rather than to resist the destructive practices of the totalitarian state.

Leszek Kołakowski was the first to formulate clearly these dilemmas that have troubled the Polish intellectual for years. The precise expres-sion of what had previously been only a vague intuition seems to have been the result of changes taking place in intellectual circles. The Church was also changing. Both these processes gave rise to Solidarity—an independent, self-governing organization of millions of Poles that emerged out of a workers' rebellion and combined the traditions of our movements for national liberation with the ethos of Christianity.

Solidarity frequently demonstrated its connection with the Church as the guardian of Christ's moral teachings, but it resisted the liberationist or fundamentalist temptation to treat the Church as an instrument. It offered to meet the Church in truth and in resistance to totalitarianism, but it also offered a pluralistic vision of civil society, and it jealously guarded its own independence. Can this particular arrangement be maintained for long? Will it prove amenable to efforts to continue it? The answer to these questions will determine the shape of Polish spirituality.

Here we should note that Leszek Kołakowski was one of the chief intellectual architects of this phenomenon.

IV

The encounter between the Polish intellectual and the Church has become fact. So let us repeat our question: Is it completely absurd to say that, by making his way toward the Church, the Polish intellectual is committing a second "betrayal"? Let us try to answer this question by trying to understand the current situation. We shall ignore the broad range of collaborationist positions cloaked in Catholic credentials; they belong not so much to the history of Polish ideas as to the history of Polish playacting.

At a time when Solidarity has been delegalized, some people expect the Church to assume the leadership of the political opposition and lead us Poles to the barricades to recapture the gains of August 1980. One result is that the episcopate has been criticized for its unwillingness to assume this role. The bishops have been accused of cowardly opportunism, of faintheartedly abandoning Solidarity in its distress, and of seeking to satisfy the Church's own narrow interests at the expense of the interests of the nation. In other words, there have been expressions of regret that our Catholic bishops do not wish to identify the interests of the Church with the short-term interests of the opposition to totalitarianism. Here we are faced with a specifically Polish version of the liberationist orientation.

There exists, however, an opposite tendency. Its adherents take as their starting point the thesis that Solidarity is dead. In this situation, they say, the Church represents the Poles' only opportunity to achieve independence. It is only in the Church that Poles can come together; only the Church's pastoral programs provide people with opportunities for social activity. Support for Solidarity is being replaced by ostentatious solidarity with the episcopate, while the episcopate's pronouncements are interpreted as political declarations of an opposition party. Moreover, there are attempts to regenerate within the framework of Catholicism all the rotten baggage of a reactionary heritage: provincial chauvinism, aggressive xenophobia, and a conspiracy theory of history. The fundamentals of human rights are being abandoned in favor of nationalistic egoism. The encyclicals of John Paul II are being replaced by old *endecja* brochures, articulating a most peculiar version of Polish political theology. Declarations of total support for the episcopate have become the chief determinant of political identity and simultaneously serve to promote our bishops to the ranks of political leaders of Polish society. What else might we expect? Well, the universal democratic demand for civil rights could turn into the particularist demand for rights for the Catholic community, the struggle for social autonomy could be reduced to a campaign aimed at guaranteeing the Catholic hierarchy a privileged influence over public life, while the conflict between the totalitarian state and a pluralist society could start to become expressed as a dispute between an atheistic government and a Catholic nation. The shadow of the Iranian syndrome lurks on the horizon of public life in Poland. This would be the final outcome of the Polish version of fundamentalism.

Reality is actually far richer, teeming with diverse viewpoints that cannot possibly be fitted into the model outlined above. Let us just say that this same reality offers the Polish intellectual two ways in which to commit the second "betrayal." Some of us have already chosen, and all of us face such a choice. Anyone who does not recognize this will inevitably fall victim to self-delusion.

V

Here we should point out that party commentators are also using the specter of Iranian theocracy to frighten us Poles. From their point of view, the entire Solidarity movement is simply an East European version of Iran's conservative-religious revolution against modernity. They portray Solidarity supporters as "narrow-minded traditionalists feeding on a fanatical spiritual mishmash that combines a perverted version of Catholicism with chauvinistic forms of the romantic tradition." The union's supporters are said to foster the belief that "the nation's martyrdom will be rewarded by benevolent supernatural powers" and "the miraculous intervention of mystical forces." They engage in "the magical rituals of burning candles, erecting crosses, and undertak-

ing pilgrimages to fight off evil forces." They generate "collective irrationality, steadfast in their belief that an act of faith can reverse relations
of power, laws of economics, and all the rules governing political life."
Solidarity supporters are the latter-day offspring of the Counter-
Reformation's triumph over the Renaissance. In August 1980, just as in
centuries past, the Catholic Counter-Reformation transformed the
thinking, Renaissance brain of the Pole into a "Stone Age head, moved
only by greed and superstition, closed to the world of progress." It has
made the Pole a fanatical believer in Polish messianism, an exterminator
of heresy, a nationalist megalomaniac "enclosed in self-congratulatory
bigotry as though in a coffin."

Once again, official commentators argue, Polish Catholicism has become the source of the nation's misfortunes. Catholicism has replaced
"the culture of labor, rationalism, and practical skills" with the philosophy of Poland as the bulwark of Christianity, with "the cult of the sword,
Providence, and the spoils of war." The spirits summoned at gatherings
around the graves of the fallen on All Soul's Day return to haunt us, "patriotic religious celebrations become hysterical mystery plays," and the
spirit of "the irrational crusade of martyrs" is triumphant.

How terrible those Catholic priests are! "Swept away by the spirit of
the Counter-Reformation, their voices full of such celestial bliss that it
seems to elevate them to heaven, they engage in miracles of interpretation, finding in the Gospels passages that were clearly written with
modern-day Poland in mind, about the satanic forces that have enslaved
her and the Way of the Cross that leads to her resurrection." It is they
who perpetuate, according to the party, the "parochial paradigm of a
politicized Church and political customs permeated by the cult of religious ritual, by obsession with the nation's mission, and a worshipful attitude toward myths and symbols."

Hence, modern-day Polish mythology, the spiritual petrification of
bygone ages, "is a half-secular, half-religious mixture of belief in miracle
and mission. The sense of mission arouses people to even the most absurd forms of activism, while the belief in miracles allows them to assume that somehow everything will work out."

Naturally, the process of recovering the nation's memory, the work of
the uncensored mind, has been defined by party writers as "a crime
against the Polish mentality," and the notion of "Sovietization" as nothing other than "the subterfuge of a delusional mind which sees the world
in archaic stereotypes and maintains its sense of self by blaming external
forces for its own helplessness."

"It is strange," one party journalist concludes, "that the Polish intelligentsia, which always considered itself the guardian of progress, by its very nature opposed to fanaticism, superstition, and prejudice, has not yet perceived the threatening wave of obscurantism, flecked with the deceptive gold dust of romanticism."

VI

We can deal with these arguments in one of two ways. We can reject them as a manifestation of a hypocritical and servile mentality whose intentions are dishonest and whose purpose is to curry favor. However, we can try to interpret these arguments as a malicious caricature of genuine dangers, and as a distorted image of our own real concerns. We can also see them as a warning, for these arguments constitute a logical development of the anti-clerical stereotype held by the Polish intelligentsia, a tendentious and highly one-sided extrapolation, but one that is legitimate and consistent. They illustrate the trap that awaits the intellectual who today takes issue with the clericalization of Polish political thought. It is all too easy to slide into superficial stereotypes and to point to Catholic obscurantism while forgetting those times of Catholic witnessing to faith and hope; it is all too easy to be shocked by acts of intolerance on the part of Catholics while forgetting their acts of love and brotherly solidarity; it is all too easy to dwell on the burnings of the Inquisition while erasing from memory images of Catholic martyrs. After all, we ourselves have witnessed such stereotyping.

This problem has a long and complex history in which we can find the prototype of the vision promulgated by party writers and the outline of the dilemmas that confront us today. One only has to leaf through old issues of *Kuźnica,* probably the most interesting Marxist journal published in postwar Poland, which represents an important, albeit sad, chapter in the history of the Polish intelligentsia. There one finds numerous articles in which the enthusiasts of the early years of the Leading System pronounced that Catholicism was struggling "to retard social progress," that it was "a moribund ideology." In so writing, they noted with some irritation that there had emerged around the journal *Tygodnik Powszechny* "a paradoxical sect of intellectual friends of the Church." *Kuźnica* argued that members of this sect believed the concept of God to be "the most embarrassing tenet of Catholicism" but the Church itself to be the sole defender of human rights and Catholic morality "the only hope for the salvation of human dignity." They considered Stefan Kisielewski the enfant terrible of the entire sect. "How many new Catholics do we have today," they needled him on the pages of *Kuźnica,* "who yesterday might have been suspected of everything, save adherence to the morality of the Gospels?"

Kisielewski did not appear to be put out by these malicious attacks. He had decided to ally himself with Catholic circles because he considered Catholicism a universalist idea, and one that was deeply rooted in the national consciousness. It would withstand the test of modernity, and had two thousand years of history to its credit; it would withstand the test of war and revolution, reconciling individualism with concern for the common good. For that reason, he saw Catholicism as the right idea in a time of struggle with totalitarianism.

Kisielewski realized that this formula might be considered controversial by some Catholics, for whom Catholicism was a religion, not a way of thinking about politics, culture, or the economy. It is true, he admitted, that "Catholicism is, first and foremost, a question of belief, revelation, and grace." Nevertheless, "not every member of the Catholic community knows how to avail himself of this grace, not every Catholic consciously practices his faith." For many people it is enough to have been formed by Catholicism: "The Church has followers and adherents among nonpracticing Catholics. Secular writers have the right to appeal to these people in the effort to promulgate the Catholic worldview and its political lessons."

For Kisielewski, Catholicism provided the only base on which it would be possible to develop Polish political thought. "People flock to the Church," he wrote, "at times of change and cataclysm, when traditions crumble, when the future appears dark and menacing and the very continuity of national life seems endangered." This was the source of the growing authority of the Church. Catholicism had offered shelter to all those "who in difficult and complicated times want to preserve a clear view of the world around them, who want to keep their calm and self-control in the face of events, who want to retain respect and admiration for the past while adapting to the demands of new times, and who, finally, feel the need for authority, for hierarchy, and a stable reference point." Catholicism also offers refuge to adherents of "secular humanist liberation movements whose main goal is to defend human rights and dignity." After all, European humanism has its roots in Christian morality. "Although many secular humanist activists find some religious dogma and ritual alien or meaningless, the core of Christian morality contained in the Ten Commandments is and will always be the most perfect and concise expression of the moral achievements of the Europeans."

It is indeed worth reading the old books of Stefan Kisielewski. They help us to understand the friendly coexistence of the Polish intellectual and the Catholic Church in the face of totalitarian dictatorship.

A turn to Catholicism was also to be found, we should add, among the intellectuals associated with *Wiadomości Literackie,* an important group who found themselves in exile after the war. A variety of people perceived the Church as the main pillar of Polishness and the main basis for resistance to Sovietization. Nevertheless, Kisielewski's example was hard to replicate. He was an inimitable mixture of the conservative and the freethinker, and he injected into Catholic cultural circles the full force of his heretical personality. He aroused conflicts and provoked scandals, but they continued to tolerate him. The circle of "catechumens" around *Tygodnik Powszechny* (Zbigniew Herbert, Jan Józef Szczepański, and Leopold Tyrmand) followed Kisielewski only part of the way, choosing to branch out along paths of their own. We should reflect on these paths—and on Jerzy Turowicz's tolerance for the "nonconfessors" who wrote for his periodical—when reflecting on the dilemmas of today.

However, an equally important task is to consider the biting comments of Witold Gombrowicz. With whom was Gombrowicz quarreling?

VII

Catholic spires still loomed above Sovietized Poland. And above the Catholic Church loomed the great figure of Cardinal Stefan Wyszyński. What did he think of communism?

For him, the essence of Polish misfortune was the conflict between "Christianity and godlessness." "If we are to be prepared for this conflict," he wrote in his diary, "we need time in order to strengthen our forces in defense of God." This, no doubt, was how every Catholic bishop reasoned, but the Polish primate went further; he considered "the transformation of the socioeconomic structure" a necessity. He was prepared to support the official reform program but considered that the government's "program of narrow-minded atheism constitutes an obstacle." He was aware, of course, of other obstacles, such as "repressive political trials, the destruction of social life, and the liquidation of political parties and free trade unions." Nevertheless, the atheism professed by Marxists seemed to him the chief obstacle. The primate's biographer, Andrzej Micewski, summarizes as follows the arguments voiced by Cardinal Wyszyński during a conversation (in January 1953) with government representative Franciszek Mazur:

In the primate's opinion, Marxism had arisen on Protestant-Anglican soil and had been applied on Orthodox soil. This was the reason why Marxism was, among other things, hostile to Catholicism. If there was to be a Polish road, Marxists would have to revise their attitude toward Catholicism. On the other hand, such a revision would be difficult, given the legacy of the nineteenth century, when struggles between Masons and the Church and between individualism and religion were fashionable. There was no necessary connection between atheism and Marxism, and even less so between atheism and the new system. . . . The atheism of Marxism was retarding social transformation and the achievement of prosperity. The struggle against the Church was alienating the best people and was promoting rigid thinking and spiritual sterility.

Thus spake the primate to the representative of Communist power. There is no reason to doubt Cardinal Wyszyński's sincerity. Nevertheless, a certain tactical consideration also lay behind these words: he wanted to halt the government's destructive policy of repression toward the Church. As he watched the progressive Sovietization of Poland, the primate became convinced that there existed "a special bond between the Church and the nation." In this extraordinary situation, the Church, as the only independent institution in the country, had to take on the function of representing the nation and defending the national identity. Millions of Poles saw the primate as the leader of the nation. In this time of *interregnum,* he was a kind of *interrex.* He was a symbol of Polish resistance.

And it was in this role that he told the Polish people: Defend your endangered national tradition, remain true to the Catholic faith of your fathers, and gather together around the Church. Only in this way, he believed, would Poles be able to preserve their identity. And he prayed for Poland, recalling its historical fate:

On this day of thanks for the victory at Chocim,[2] only one church in Poland offers its prayers to the God who defended us with his mighty hand. Do any

2. At the Battle of Chocim, in 1621, Poles defeated Turkish forces that far outnumbered them. — ED.

of the great patriots of today even think about this event? And yet perhaps it was decisive for the further development of culture in central Europe.

I thank Thee for the power of faith that overcame the power of arms. I thank Thee for the noble idealism that summoned whole lineages to the battlefields and sacrificed virtually all the sons of more than one family. I thank Thee for the strength Thou instilled in the hussars. I hear their song and I see them galloping to victory. May all this sing to Thee, Father of Nations. And while I thank Thee for the past, I beg Thee to remember the battle that we are waging today, for a Poland that is not overcome by foreign perfidy, materialist brutality, semieducated conceit and insolence. This terrible force is gathering strength, terrorizing even the good and the brave. Defend Thy people, our Father and Lord.

Writing these words while in prison, Cardinal Wyszyński expressed the emotions of the tormented Polish people. The primate's fears notwithstanding, a substantial proportion of the population thought precisely this way about God and Fatherland.

Witold Gombrowicz, on the other hand, was highly critical of precisely this way of thinking about captive Poland and Catholicism.

VIII

"Today's Poland," observed Gombrowicz in 1953, "is like a piece of stale bread which breaks into two halves with a snap: the believing and the nonbelieving." Nevertheless, the dividing line is actually one's attitude toward communism rather than issues of faith. Polish thought has come to a standstill, paralyzed by communism. "Thus," writes Gombrowicz,

we are allowed to think about Catholicism only as a force capable of resistance, and God has become the pistol with which we would like to shoot Marx. This is a holy secret, which bows the heads of the exquisite Masons, drives the anti-clerical wit out of lay commentaries, dictates moving stanzas to the Virgin Mother to the poet Lechoń, restores a touching First Communion innocence to socialist-atheist professors, and, in general, is the miracle worker of which philosophers have long dreamed. (*Diary*, 1:27)[3]

A prayer of thanks for the victory at Chocim? For Gombrowicz, this

3. Witold Gombrowicz, *Diary*, vol. 1, translated by Lillian Vallee (Evanston, Ill.: Northwestern University Press, 1988). This and all subsequent quotations are somewhat amended. —TRANS.

was simply a symbol of our impoverishment. With passion he described an anniversary celebration among émigrés, where, "having sung the Rota and danced the Krakowiaczek," the participants performed their patriotic duty by extolling the former superiority of Polish arms and the great poets, and praising Wawel Castle and Chopin, Copernicus and the May 3 Constitution. "But I," wrote Gombrowicz, "felt this ritual as if it were born of hell, this national mass became something satanically sneering and maliciously grotesque. For they, in elevating Mickiewicz, were denigrating themselves, with their praise of Chopin they showed themselves insufficiently mature to appreciate him, and by basking in their own culture, they were simply revealing their own primitiveness" (1:5).

"What," Gombrowicz peevishly asks, "does Mr. Kowalski have in common with Chopin? Does the fact that Chopin composed ballads raise the specific weight of Mr. Kowalski by even one iota? Can the Siege of Vienna add even an ounce of glory to Mr. Ziębicki from Radom?" (1:7). Of course not. Everyone is responsible for himself, and everyone should be either proud or ashamed of himself. Nobody is going to judge the Poles on the basis of Sobieski and Chopin, but on the basis of what they themselves are doing today. And what are they doing? They are locked in a paralysis of Polish Catholicism, which is a sign of their immaturity, a symbol of their impoverishment, and a way of escaping from a creative existence. This is why Polish émigré life is imbued with the atmosphere of the hospital—the patients are offered only dietetic meals.

What is the point of scratching our wounds? Why should we inflame the wound that life has already inflicted on us? Shouldn't we behave ourselves now that we have been spanked? . . . All the Christian virtues reign here— kindness, humanity, compassion, respect for the individual, moderation, modesty, decency, and common sense, and everything that we write is nothing if not charitable. So many virtues! We were not this virtuous when we were more sure of our ground. I do not trust the virtue of those who have failed, virtue born of poverty. (1:4)

Gombrowicz's harsh judgment did not mean he had declared spiritual war on Catholicism. The kind of campaign that Boy-Żeleński waged against "the black occupation" was foreign to Gombrowicz, as he himself stressed. He argued against a particular version of Catholicism that "has caused great harm to Polish development because it has been reduced in us to a too easy and serene philosophy in the service of life and its immediate needs" (1:30). This was the side of Catholicism traditionally represented by the Church hierarchy in Poland, and the side of Catholicism that was completely alien to the author of *Ferdydurke*. Nevertheless, historical events also revealed other sides of Catholicism to Gombrowicz. Amid wars and revolutions, amid political mysticisms and totalitarian faiths, the ideal of a progressive, enlightened, humanistic, and rational humanity had been drastically relativized. Of course, these values were worthy of respect, but what was most important, observed Gombrowicz, was "that the other man not bite me, spit on me, or torture me to death." Here the encounter with Catholicism took place: in "the acute sense of hell" inherent in human nature, in the "fear of man's excessive dynamism." Gombrowicz was alienated from the Church by the view that the ideal Catholic is someone "who believes, who wants to believe, and who will entertain no thought other than that which dogma has not prohibited." Gombrowicz tried to reverse this perspective: "The question that I put to Catholics is not what kind of God do they believe in but what kind of people do they want to be?"

So what had happened?

We were horrified to see that we were surrounded by countless millions of ignorant minds which were stealing our truths in order to pervert, belittle, and transform them into instruments of their fervor. We discovered that the number of people is far more significant than the quality of our truths. Hence our burning need for a language so simple and basic that it can unite the philosopher and the illiterate. And hence our admiration for Christianity, which is wisdom tailored to all minds, a song for all voices from the highest to the lowest, a wisdom that does not have to turn itself into stupidity at any level of consciousness. But, if somebody told me that it is nevertheless impossible for a person who is spiritually free to achieve genuine understanding with a dogmatist, I would answer: Take a look at the Catholics. They also exist in time and are subject to its influence. (1:31)

For this secular humanist, this student of Rabelais and Montaigne, had unexpectedly perceived a Catholicism that was "profound and tragic," that responded to the totalitarian order and the crisis of culture with an evolution similar to that of humanism. And thus Christian "teaching, which was the undoing of the Roman Empire, is our ally in the struggle to demolish all those too lofty edifices that we are constructing today, in the struggle to achieve a state of nakedness and simplicity, of ordinary, elementary virtue" (1:30 –31).

Was Gombrowicz right? And what precisely did his proposal signify? For Cardinal Wyszyński it was obvious that, in the conflict with Communist atheism, it was necessary to strengthen the cohesion of the resisting nation. For him, communism was a system that undermined the national will, a system of violence and persecution by an alien force, a system in which Poles "continually live like cattle." For Gombrowicz, communism was a system that subordinated the individual to the collective, hence, he argued, "the best way to fight communism is to strengthen the individual against the masses."

These differences are neither superficial nor insignificant. Cardinal Wyszyński wanted to preserve the Polish model of culture, which he saw as a source of Poland's strength. Gombrowicz wanted to lay bare and destroy this model, which he saw as a source of weakness. For Cardinal Wyszyński, Henryk Sienkiewicz was the Polish "hetman without a post," teaching the nation to serve "God and country." For Gombrowicz, Sienkiewicz constituted the negation of all that was profound in Catholicism; he was "like a woman who maintains purity in thought and deed not in order to please God, but because instinct assures her that this is the way to please men." For Cardinal Wyszyński, Sienkiewicz was the first "general" to mobilize Polish youth around the struggle for freedom and the person who aroused the conscience of the nation. For Gombrowicz, Sienkiewicz was the person who "embellished history," "simplified people," "fed the Poles a mass of naive illusions," and "numbed our conscience, stifled thought, and hindered progress."

Today, then, when we refer to Cardinal Wyszyński as our Thousand-Year Primate, and when Gombrowicz's leading position in the pantheon of Polish literature is unchallenged, let us ask: Which of them was right?

IX

Aleksander Wat, poet and author of perhaps the most profound of all Polish settling of accounts with communism, considered Gombrowicz of no use whatsoever in the struggle against totalitarianism. The nation had found its strength not in rebellion but in "separating itself from the enemy," said Wat.

Its strength lay precisely in this mass Catholicism, this obscurantist, parochial, and so often shabby Polish Catholicism, which had purified and strengthened itself "in the catacombs" and found its true shepherd in the person of Cardinal Wyszyński. This Catholicism rendered the Polish soul immune to the magic of "ideology" and the whip of *praxis*. The Polish October was brought about not by rebellious writers and revisionists but, together with the crumbling strength and cohesion of Stalinism, by the stubborn, unremitting, and relentless psychological resistance of the Catholic nation.

Wat voiced this opinion in 1965 or shortly thereafter. This was the culmination of his long and difficult journey from communism to the truths of the Catholic faith. Was it, however, an accurate depiction of the situation?

Cardinal Wyszyński attached the utmost significance to the concept of the "national community." He wrote that this community had arisen "from the blood shed by the sons of Polish soil," that the nation was strengthened not by divisions but by "a single, common love for the Motherland, which has nurtured us at her breast, and which we at times are obliged to nurture . . . *with our own blood.*"

Gombrowicz, however, asked Poles: "If you were told that, in order to remain Poles, you must abandon part of your humanity, in other words, that you will be able to remain Poles only on condition that you become worse human beings—a little less talented, less rational, less dignified—would you agree to this sacrifice to retain Poland?" After all, he continued, these values "are absolute and cannot be made dependent on anything. Anyone who says that only Poland can ensure him reason or dignity abandons his own reason and his own dignity."

In other words, in the conflict with communism, Gombrowicz did not consider it sufficient to withdraw intellectually into national-religious tradition. He found this framework too restrictive, and the model of the Catholic Pole culturally sterile, incapable of comprehending reality, incapable of providing an uncompromising defense of fundamental values. While Cardinal Wyszyński was commemorating the tenacity of the national community threatened by Communist atheism and Aleksander Wat was praising the parochial and obscurantist spirit of the nation that had survived the Communist crucible, Witold Gombrowicz was citing with approval the following diagnosis of Polish psychology provided by one of his Polish correspondents:

My God, this Poland is the dismal dream of a madman! What gloom, what suffocation, uncertainty, and boredom. . . . I find this new Poland so ridiculous because, with God and the truth, the Saxon epoch has stayed with us the longest and has left the deepest imprint. The nation is ignorant, National Democratic, truculent, boorish, lazy, belligerent and half-baked, sanctimonious and infantile. And they have grafted onto all this a Kremlin-style communism. Now they must really be as merry as hell!

Gombrowicz wrote these words in 1958. The events of ten years later, of March 1968, oblige us to interpret them with great care. The spirit of obscurantism proved to be a highly ambiguous ally of the Polish cause.

Witold Gombrowicz pointed early on to the danger lurking in the stereotypical anti-communism of the Polish Catholic. Thus he called on his fellow Poles to discover the individual, to free themselves of restrictive national-religious forms, to replace the moribund conservatism of their fathers with faith in themselves and in the liberating youth of their sons, to replace the fatherland with the "sonland."

When we read today the blasphemies of Gombrowicz, we need to keep in mind the context in which they were uttered. Gombrowicz's lampooning of the Polish intelligentsia was, above all, an act of defiance in the face of totalitarianism and its destructive consequences. The struggle for Poland seemed to him to be a conflict between those who had opted for shameful servitude to communism and those who, in desperation, had chosen to remain in sterile opposition as mindless servants of national-religious stereotypes.

X

Let us disregard the fact that this was a simplified diagnosis and focus instead on Gombrowicz's conclusions. At the height of Stalinism, he issued this characteristic appeal to his fellow intellectuals:

Pharisees! If you need your Catholicism, you should acquire a little more dignity and try to become Catholics in all sincerity. This should not be just a political maneuver. I believe that whatever happens in our spiritual life should happen in the deepest and most honest way possible. The moment has come for atheists to seek a new understanding with the Church.

And how did Cardinal Wyszyński perceive the attitude of the intelligentsia at this time? He believed, to quote Micewski, "that Poland has not, in fact, yet had a genuinely Catholic intelligentsia. Educated circles have always succumbed to intellectual and moral relativism. This has been particularly apparent at key moments, when the intelligentsia has deserted the fight for Catholic ideals."

The intelligentsia, declared the primate, places great demands on the clergy but is itself absent. Its antipathy toward communism does not prevent it from carrying out ideological orders, from writing pamphlets attacking the Church. The intelligentsia senses that "only the Church" can save Poland but is not itself to be found in the Church. The intellectual comes to the Church for "political thrills," but he does not live in grace. Yet grace is the main strength of the Church.

What an unexpected coincidence of opinion! Both Cardinal Wyszyński, the architect of the Catholic order in Poland, and Witold Gombrowicz, the iconoclast, reproached Polish intellectuals for their spiritually shallow and politically superficial attitude toward the Church. Today, when the dispute over the relationship between the intelligentsia and the Church has reemerged, we should bear in mind these two kinds of criticism. Is it possible that each of them formulates in a different way the same accusation regarding "a second betrayal of the intellectuals"?

In raising the question of such a betrayal, we are not, of course, referring to religious conversion. We know perfectly well that a practicing Catholic—a layperson or a member of the clergy—need not adhere to a clerical vision of the social order. The encounter with God does not signify the abandonment of one's humanistic identity. By "betrayal," we are referring only to a particular kind of conversion, one that is political rather than religious. Such a conversion involves abandoning the elementary notion of truth in favor of political tactics, abandoning the principles of pluralism and inalienable human rights.

One may turn to the Church for a variety of reasons. I may do so because I perceive the Church as a force that plays a key role on Poland's political stage. But the Church is not, and does not seek to be, a political force. My intention thus puts me in an ambiguous position: I must disguise my motives, pretend to be a Catholic, and use a language that imparts to Catholicism the spirit of a political sect. I must then repeat that the specter of the Iranian syndrome is just the invention of "the secular left," that every criticism of the Church is empirical proof of the existence of a conspiracy of atheists and Masons, that warnings of the danger posed to Polish spirituality by narrow xenophobia are voiced only by cosmopolitans and Bolshevik agents.

I can, however, turn to the Church for other reasons. I might seek there an ally for the view that the world needs truth, because only the truth can set us free, that we need a climate of tolerance and compromise, because this provides the only basis for a democratic order, that we need to distinguish good from evil, because only then can we salvage the moral norms of my culture. Turning to the Church for these reasons, I am decisively rejecting the kind of relativism that renders one's moral judgment of the real world dependent on the political interests of a party, class, nation, or whatever. There are, of course, various kinds of relativism: the relativism of Gombrowicz, which constitutes a spiritual search, and the relativism of the nihilist, which constitutes moral capitulation. To quote Leszek Kołakowski:

If we really abandon the idea that there is a difference between good and evil—a difference that does not depend on our decisions, that we are powerless to determine as we please, and that therefore confronts us as a ready-made thing, irrespective of whether it originates in religious belief or an imperative of Kantian practical reason—then we are under no moral constraints. We can do anything as long as we believe that we shall thus contribute to the victory of some tendency or other, whose victory by definition will be morally justified, even if it bears the name of Hitler or Stalin.

I repeat, also quoting Leszek Kołakowski, that the world needs the realm of the sacred, for perfect rationality is a suicidal ideal. So I turn to the Church—even if I am led there by Kant's moral imperative—not in order to be on the side of force, but to be on the side of truth. Thus I must bear witness to the truth, including the truth about the Church.

I should now say something about my own attitude to the blasphemies of Gombrowicz and the patriotic-moral teachings of Cardinal Wyszyński. It is easier for me to talk about Gombrowicz. I do not share Aleksander Wat's opinion that people like Gombrowicz "can only nip in the bud" the independent culture reemerging in the grip of totalitarian communism. Quite the opposite: Gombrowicz, to quote Jerzy Jarzębski, "is the patron of the generation that has defended itself against the omnipotence of Doctrine and its Institutions. He is a catalyst of rebellion." Gombrowicz aroused resistance to the fiction of official cultural life. It was he who fought the good fight against what Czesław Miłosz called "the Polish rituals of nationalist backwardness." It was Gombrowicz who constantly called on us to be honest and to display spiritual courage, to transcend our own limitations, and to live authentically and creatively, rejecting the Polish "mug" and the Polish "fanny."[4]

What would Polish culture be without Gombrowicz? What would it be without his diabolical wit and his infernally penetrating intelligence? It would be a crippled, mutilated culture, with only half a brain and half a heart. For while questioning everything around him, Gombrowicz "never," wrote Miłosz, "doubted one thing: pain, and this wonderful pain made the world real again."

But could Gombrowicz's intellectual project have become the universally accepted project? Could his "interpersonal church" have replaced the universal Church? Such a question—obviously formulated incorrectly— leads us to ask about the function of iconoclastic Don Quixotes within an endangered Polish culture. Does this culture need such people?

4. "Mug" and "fanny" are terms from Gombrowicz's novel. —ED.

I think it highly likely that the Catholic Church had to be the way it was: somewhat parochial, somewhat obscurantist. Not only could it not have been a Gombrowiczian church, but even a Jerzy Turowicz was bound to seem a dangerous innovator. And perhaps it was precisely this Church, unchanging and hidebound, that could save Polish society from spiritual Sovietization. But if this is the case, what are the consequences for the Polish intellectual?

An intellectual must retain an elementary loyalty toward his subjugated nation. He is not allowed to retreat into theorizing while a crime is being committed; nor may he content himself with a display of basic high-mindedness alone. Witold Gombrowicz displayed solidarity with his nation in its opposition to totalitarian oppression, always calling a crime a crime. Nevertheless, he had to rebel against the cultural form of Polish resistance if he wanted to remain true to his own artistic conscience. Gombrowicz was ambivalent toward the Polish and Catholic archetypes of national consciousness. Could it have been otherwise?

Here we face the most troubling questions, questions about the ambiguities present in the Catholic tradition. When we observe the evolution of the language of the Church over the last fifty years, we see that the idea of human rights, previously anathema, has acquired its own civil rights and is now to be found at the center of Christian thought. A similar process has taken place in Polish Catholicism. A certain Franciscan who gave his life for another in Auschwitz, the quintessential institution of totalitarian civilization, has been canonized and surrounded by a cult. This fact has its symbolic dimension. Professor Father Józef Tischner, a distinguished figure of Polish Catholicism, sees in this Auschwitz martyr "the living embodiment of a Polish philosophy of man, a philosophy that runs deep in our blood but has never been fully described!" It is the saint Maksymilian Kolbe, says Tischner, who "discovered the Polish way out of the Polish crisis of hope."

I think Cardinal Wyszyński would have subscribed to this statement. I doubt, however, that Witold Gombrowicz would have done so; or Czesław Miłosz, Leszek Kołakowski, and Jan Józef Szczepański, for that matter; or our intellectual, who turns to the Church in search of the truth. It is not that Father Tischner is not telling the truth but that it is a truth tainted by what it leaves unsaid. "The modern secular world," wrote Jan Józef Szczepański in his essay on Maksymilian Kolbe, "probably needs sainthood more than at any other time in history. I suspect, however, that what it needs less than at any other time is hagiography."

Maksymilian Kolbe's heroic choice of martyrdom was an extraordinary act, and no torturer's dialectic or cunning "demystification" can invalidate it. Nor is anything changed by what we know about Father Maksymilian's political record. And this record—whether we like it or not—is part of our most recent history. Jan Józef Szczepański situates the prewar activity of Father Maksymilian within what he calls "a fairly disturbing tendency" in Polish Catholicism, one associated with "the excesses of Counter-Reformationist bigotry, with Sarmatism, political activities of the extreme right, with . . . various chauvinist and anti-intellectual movements." Szczepański goes on to note that these facts "do not in the slightest detract from the boundless respect" that Father Kolbe deserves. "But," he adds, "I cannot ignore the fact that I feel uneasy, that something here makes me feel uncomfortable."

I share Szczepański's opinion. If Father Kolbe is a symbol—as Father Tischner claims—"of the Polish horizon of hope," then our Polish conscience dictates that we undertake an honest accounting of the legacy of Polish Catholicism's links with nationalistic doctrines. Times have changed, and so has the Church since Vatican II, and the former way of thinking now constitutes so much troublesome baggage for contemporary hagiographers of the saintly Franciscan. The Church has yet to include a critical analysis of that way of thinking in its teaching.

I am full of ambivalence about Father Tischner's observations. His silence on the baggage of chauvinism and intolerance is striking. He finds it easier to disregard my fears of obscurantism than to judge, from a Catholic perspective, the former appeals to boycott Jewish stores, to segregate Jews in the classroom, and to "pacify" Ukrainian villages. It is much easier to repeat that "we did not kill our kings" than to recall the murder of President Gabriel Narutowicz; it is much easier to say that "we never finished off our wounded enemies" than to recall the pogroms in Przytyk and Kielce; it is much easier to condemn former Marxists than to examine critically the difficult truths about our own roots.

I can understand—although I do not accept—this kind of selectivity in the teaching of Cardinal Wyszyński. However, I am unable to fathom the reason why Father Józef Tischner avoids these questions, which are so important to the examination of our national conscience. Does he really want to sacrifice truth in favor of hagiography? In polemicizing with Father Tischner, I am not making my life any easier. My questions are addressed to a distinguished philosopher and celebrated preacher whom I admire and respect. Nevertheless, I wonder whether some small part of the responsibility for the wrong roads taken and the wrong choices made by many young people cannot be attributed to the silence of such indisputable moral and intellectual authorities as Father Tischner.

And again I wonder what Polish culture would have been without the Quixotic truth-telling of Witold Gombrowicz.

XI

I am afraid of intellectual betrayals, both the first and the second kind. May the spirit of Cardinal Wyszyński protect us from the first and the biting sarcasm of Witold Gombrowicz protect us from the second. In the space between these two great spirits exists modern Polish culture. And we too, we indomitable intellectuals, also live between the prayers of Cardinal Wyszyński and the irreverence of Witold Gombrowicz, between the truth of the priest and the truth of the jester. We need both these truths, because each of them, in its own way, teaches us modesty and humility. What kind of intellectual strategy should be adopted by today's Polish intellectual who rebels against the totalitarian government and looks sympathetically and hopefully to the Church, in the search for a way to be present in the anti-totalitarian resistance movement?

Both Cardinal Wyszyński and Witold Gombrowicz would have said, I think, that first and foremost one should maintain one's modesty. Leszek Kołakowski, who wrote a wonderful synthesis of the virtues of the priest and the jester, could have said the same. Our intellectual should, above all, remember all those periods of history when European intellectuals joined forces with totalitarian movements. He should keep before him the image of all those who donned red or black shirts whether out of ideological fascination or pragmatic reasoning. He should, as Kołakowski wrote, remember that when "intellectuals try to become popular leaders or professional politicians, the results are usually not encouraging. The market square with all its dangers is, in the end, a more suitable place for them than the royal court." This remains the rule even in the case of leaders elevated to power through revolutionary movements and even in the case of the princes of the Church.

So what are you, you homeless, insubordinate intellectual? You can follow Cardinal Wyszyński in proclaiming the people's need for the sacred and Witold Gombrowicz in proclaiming the importance of mocking the sacred, but does this mean that you are one of those who say that simple folk need reverence while intellectuals need freethinking skepticism? Are you one of the "born again," inspired by what Kołakowski calls "an inconsistent desire to manipulate"? He writes:

There is something disturbingly crass about intellectuals who themselves have no religious loyalties or faith, but who emphasize the irreplaceable moral and educational role of religion and bemoan its tenuousness, to which they themselves conspicuously bear witness. I am not criticizing them because they are not religious, nor because they talk about the value of religious experiences. I am simply not convinced that they can help to bring about the changes that they want. To inspire faith one needs to have faith, not intellectual conviction regarding its social utility.

So here is your dilemma, you wandering intellectual. You will read into these words a call to religious conversion, and it is indeed hard to read them any other way. However, you know how fatal and treacherous some kinds of conversion can be, and you also know that an act of religious conversion will not automatically resolve your dilemma. Be happy if you find God. Be happy also in the very grace of the quest. And tell Leszek Kołakowski, in the words of Thomas Mann, that for you, religious belief is "both attentiveness and obedience. Attentiveness to the inner changes in the world, the transformation of the ideals of truth and justice; obedience to the call to make life and reality conform to these changes in order to satisfy the spirit." The point, you should explain to him, is not to flatter your own epoch, whose favors you can obtain only at the cost of lies. It is a question of "not living in sin," since, as Mann stated, "to live in sin means to live against the spirit, through inattention and disobedience to hold fast to things that are outdated and backward."

Thomas Mann was an ironic skeptic, so you know that his words are not without danger. After all, skepticism and irony can lead either to base capitulation or to a heroic duel with the world. Deaf to the appeal of God, the ironic skeptic may find within himself that Kantian imperative and make of it a weapon against the contemptible might of totalitarian civilization. Such skepticism is born of both pride and humility. It is also Mann's "piety, that is a kind of wisdom."

So be pious and humble, you proud intellectual, but do not renounce skepticism, at least not in the world of political involvement. Participate in the anti-totalitarian community, but maintain your homelessness. Remain faithful to your national roots, but cultivate your permanent rootlessness. Bring the clear simplicity of the commands of the Gospel (where yes means yes and no means no) into a world of unstable moral norms, but fill the bland world of officially codified values with the laughter of the jester and the doubts of the skeptic. For your destiny does not lie in celebrating political victories or in flattering your own nation. You are to remain faithful to lost causes, to speak unpleasant truths, and to arouse opposition.

You are destined to receive blows from friends and foes alike, "because only in this way will you attain the good that you will not attain."

5

Towards a Civil Society: Hopes for Polish Democracy

Interview with Erica Blair (John Keane)

Erica Blair (John Keane): In a recent essay you describe Gorbachev as "the great Counter-Reformer," who is effecting changes which are as unavoidable as they are risky. What exactly do you mean? What is Gorbachev trying to achieve in the Soviet Union?

Adam Michnik: All the changes taking place from above in the Soviet Union are designed to maintain or modernize its empire. Gorbachev is not a man fighting for freedom. He instead wishes to make the Soviet Union more powerful. He is responding to three developments. First, the economic forces of Soviet communism have collapsed. The Soviet economy resembles a large old house built on marshland. Each day it sinks a millimeter or two deeper into the mire. The house still remains upright. It does not experience revolutions or catastrophes. Everything appears to go well. But after twenty-five years of subsidence, the whole ground floor of the house has been destroyed. This is Gorbachev's peculiar problem. He isn't facing a workers' revolution or nationalist resistance. He is confronted by a new type of revolt—a revolt of inanimate things—which cannot be quelled by the usual methods. When people revolt against our system, the police or army can be sent in against them. But a subsiding house is unafraid of the

Reprinted by permission from *Times Literary Supplement,* February 19–25, 1988. © John Keane / The Times Literary Supplement, 1988. "Erica Blair" is a pseudonym used by John Keane.

police or army. It doesn't acknowledge the leading role of the Communist party. And it cannot be explained by any Marxist-Leninist formula. Gorbachev is thus searching for a method of crushing the anonymous revolt of the economy—of propping it up as it slowly disappears into a quagmire.

Gorbachev is also faced with a cluster of international problems. The Soviet Union has two great world competitors, the United States and China. After the breakdown of détente, the United States assumed the position of leading superpower. The Reagan administration declared the Soviet Union to be the evil empire, and in so doing confronted the present leadership with fundamental problems. President Reagan is undoubtedly one of the fathers of the Gorbachev reforms. He forced the Soviets to abandon their strategy of détente based on bilateral relations and attack the West on its periphery. The Kremlin was faced with the real risk of open confrontation with the whole Western world. Gorbachev's foreign policy seeks to address this risk of a new arms race by reversing the dangerous geopolitical trends confronting the Soviet Union in the global arena. This strategy has been reinforced by the extensive political and economic reforms in China in recent years. These reforms have been doubly effective: they have produced considerable material benefits, as well as altered the geopolitical position of China. Particularly important are the improved relations between China and the United States, which have forced the present Soviet leadership to recognize the possibility of its isolation at the international level.

Poland is a third consideration for Gorbachev. The Polish events have taught the Soviet leadership certain lessons about what will happen in the Soviet Union unless they pursue their own internal reforms. If Solidarity is viewed as a reform movement capable of destroying the totalitarian system, then Gorbachev is a counter-reformer. He wants to defend the system by reforming it. The imposition of martial law in Poland on December 13, 1981, was something quite different. It was a counterrevolution. It supposed that the Polish crisis is caused by a complex of specifically Polish mistakes, and that their correction is possible by enforcing the peace and quiet of the Soviet Union or Czechoslovakia, where there is no crisis. Every action of Jaruzelski's team after December 13 aimed to create similar conditions of peace and quiet in Poland. But Gorbachev has responded: "No! There is no specifically Polish crisis. This is the crisis of the whole Communist system." In this sense, Gorbachev has shattered the ideology of the Jaruzelski group, which is now under pressure from the reforms emanating from Moscow. The Gorbachev counterreformation has had a restraining influence on the Jaruzelski counterrevolution. Jaruzelski has been forced to return to the rhetoric of reform. He cannot pursue policies based on repression, because they would be contrary to Gorbachev's policies.

Blair: In Western Europe and North America there is considerable discussion about the links between this "peace offensive" of Jaruzelski and the desperate need for economic reform in Poland. Many believe that Gorbachev has privately urged Jaruzelski to move in the direction of economic reforms, thereby forcing him to cultivate the social support crucial for their successful implementation. Hence the talk of democracy, national reconciliation, the amnesty of September 1986, a second phase of economic reform, and the November 1987 referendum. Would you accept this Western interpretation of current Polish events? Has Jaruzelski embarked upon a "peace offensive" and serious economic reforms?

Michnik: Talk of Jaruzelski's peace initiative is a joke—as misplaced as if it had come from General Pinochet or the South African president. General Jaruzelski could make a genuine peace initiative by seeking a peaceful rapprochement with his own nation. But so far he hasn't done so. No doubt he needs social support, not only to facilitate economic reforms but also just to be able to run the country. Every dictator from Pinochet to Castro requires social support. However, the crucial problem of Jaruzelski is that his efforts during the past six years to remedy the Polish economic crisis have collapsed. And today his grandly announced "second stage" of economic reforms, translated into ordinary language, means nothing more than a violent attack on the standard of living of ordinary Polish people. Jaruzelski knows that he is standing on a live volcano. All his declarations and reform initiatives therefore have a double meaning: to deceive his own nation and to lie to the Western world in order to win credits.

Blair: What are your reasons for thinking that these pseudoreforms are unworkable and unlikely to lead to a "liberalization" of the Polish system, as many Western observers hope?

Michnik: The ingenious scheme of Jaruzelski is to build communism in Poland on the American dollar. His "liberal" gestures are all geared to this objective. It is important to understand what "liberalism" actually means in this context. Communism is a system based on a specific form of apartheid. Under the apartheid system in South Africa, a whole category of citizens is discriminated against because of the color of their skin. Within Communist systems, a whole category of citizens is similarly discriminated against because of their political views, religion, or party affiliation. The important question for me is whether or not General Jaruzelski intends to abolish our apartheid system by fostering equality among our citizens. This would require the destruction of the power of the *nomenklatura,* which is comparable to the white population in South Africa. So far, Jaruzelski shows no signs of wanting to abolish our form of apartheid. Everything he does preserves the power of the ruling groups called *nomenklatura.* In so doing, he undermines any possibility of economic reforms. For the unchecked power of this ruling *nomenklatura* is the source of the present irrationality and crisis of the Communist economy. Our whole economy is subject to stiff and arbitrary planning measures introduced and guided by this small ruling group, which is not subject to legal constraints, market forces, or democratic procedures.

Blair: The Polish "neoliberals," followers of Milton Friedman, make a similar complaint. They argue for the introduction of market mechanisms into the command economy as a means of improving its productivity, output, and distributional effectiveness. Why are you critical of their views?

Michnik: The proposals of the neoliberals are unrealistic. They dream of transforming General Jaruzelski into a General Pinochet. They want him to retain dictatorial political powers and to guarantee full economic freedoms. This is impossible. The *nomenklatura* will not relinquish their grip on the economy because this is their source of power. Besides, the economic achievements of General Pinochet are unimpressive. In Chile a free market coexists with poverty and a permanent economic crisis.

Blair: What if some strange turn of events confronted Poland with the possibility of replacing General Jaruzelski with a General Pinochet?

Michnik: If forced to choose between General Jaruzelski and General Pinochet, I would choose Marlene Dietrich. The alternative is absurd and irrational. It offers me the choice, as I fight for democracy in a dictatorial system, of sitting in prison either as a Communist or as an anti-Communist. In Chile I would be imprisoned as a Communist, whereas in Poland I have already served six years as an anti-Communist. I am not interested in this kind of "pluralism." The point is that economic reform in Poland is impossible without basic political reform. Political reform is impossible without a long-term—if gradual—program of abolishing our apartheid system. The precondition of such reforms is the recognition of Solidarity as a partner in the dialogue about the future of Poland. Without this, all Jaruzelski's talk of reform through dialogue will remain nonsense.

Blair: To what extent must economic and political reforms also address the deteriorating ecological situation in Poland? The situation appears desperate. Poland's waters are mostly undrinkable; cities such as Łódź and Warsaw do not have a single water-purification plant—one of the many reasons for the generally poor health of the population. Everywhere one travels, the air smells toxic. About 10 percent of Poland's territory, inhabited by one-third of the population, has been officially designated as "ecologically endangered terrain." Is this picture accurate?

Michnik: I am no expert on ecology. But I am convinced that these problems are linked with the conflicting interests of social groups. The problem faced by Polish society is that from the official point of view a civil society doesn't exist. Society is not recognized as capable of organizing itself to defend its particular interests and points of view. So the key to solving our ecological problems is the same as that for solving our economic problems. We need institutions capable of defending the environment. Certainly, ecological concerns may conflict with economic issues. What is beneficial for the economy may be ecologically harmful; more automobiles for society, for example, would result in further environmental degradation. Our world is full of contradictory values, and I cannot imagine a social order in which all of them were equally and harmoniously realized. But conflicts are genuine only when they are genuinely expressed. This is what our society is fighting for: to name things by their proper names, to articulate conflicts as conflicts.

Blair: I am curious to know how Polish society is reacting to the present situation. Compared with Czechoslovakia and Hungary—countries with which I am more familiar—the level of publicly expressed confidence and dignity among Polish people seems much higher. Is my impression correct? Or since the events of 1980–81 has this social confidence been slowly whittled away? Is Polish society in danger of feeling defeated?

Michnik: The changes you observe are absolutely irreversible. The 1980–81 events were a revolution for dignity, a celebration of the rights of the vertebrae, a permanent victory for the straightened spine. Whatever happens, one fact cannot be erased from the twentieth-century history of this nation: that the downfall of the totalitarian Communist order began here in Poland. I am convinced that while the events of 1917 signaled the rise of the Communist system, the meeting at the Gdańsk shipyards in August 1980 began its destruction. Six years after the Hungarian Revolution there was no trace of the revolution. And six years after the invasion of Czechoslovakia there was no trace of the Prague Spring. But six years after the declaration of martial law in this country Solidarity exists along with a civil society. There is an underground press, an underground culture, underground science, as well as other underground structures. The people are relaxed, unafraid, and their backs are straight. We have educated our Communists, and this is the greatest achievement of Solidarity. But this is now history, and we need to talk about the future.

Blair: In the West it is frequently remarked that Solidarity is no longer a serious threat to Jaruzelski. The disappearance of large demonstrations from the streets is cited as supporting evidence for this view. Is Solidarity being forced on to the defensive?

Michnik: If we consider Solidarity as a movement of ten million people, as it was in the days before martial law, then of course at present it is weaker. Movements involving millions of people are normally active only in important revolutionary moments. Solidarity is no exception, and in this sense it has come to resemble Western social movements. But I cannot treat seriously remarks that Solidarity has ceased to be a problem for General Jaruzelski. If this were the case, why doesn't he permit Solidarity to operate normally?

Blair: But are there fewer demonstrations in the streets? Why is the struggle of Solidarity against the state much less visible?

Michnik: One reason is that society is tired of demonstrations and struggles which lead only to an escalation of confrontation with the government, and thus reduce the chances of concessions from it. Poles cannot win a war against the Soviet Union with stones and their bare hands. There is another reason. The worst actions today would be those which blocked changes in the Soviet Union. There is a nineteenth-century precedent for this in Poland, where in 1863 the January Uprising blocked the reforms of Alexander II in Russia, thus allowing the soul of Russia to pass from Aleksandr Herzen to the archpriest and prophet of nationalism, Mikhail Katkov. In 1956, the Khrushchev reforms were also blocked by the Hungarian Revolution. Current developments in the Soviet Union offer a real possibility of changes for the better throughout the Communist bloc. Since we have helped stimulate these changes, and since their deepening is impossible without Solidarity, we do not want to frustrate them. We therefore work through our underground press, plays, and films, and not through violence in the streets. Solidarity has two methods of fighting the totalitarian state. It can rely on strikes and demonstrations, and it can turn its back on this state by confronting it, as Maciej Poleski says, with the silence of the sea. A society which remains silent seems easy to control. In fact, it is very difficult to rule, precisely because it is insensitive to the impulses of the state. Lech Wałęsa likes to ask the question: "What is the difference between fish in an aquarium and fish soup?" His answer: "The fish in the aquarium can be converted into fish soup, whereas the fish soup cannot be converted back into aquarium fish." This subtle joke summarizes Jaruzelski's problem today. As long as he refuses to recognize Solidarity, he must suppose that society resembles fish soup. But if he wants society to resemble an aquarium of live fish, as he must do if his reforms are to be successful, then he must recognize that it is Solidarity that gives real life to our society. Without Solidarity, Jaruzelski's hands are tied, even though Solidarity is unable to call a general strike at a day's notice. This is the secret of the Polish situation. For six years Jaruzelski has been paralyzed by his insistence that Solidarity does not exist. His actions against Solidarity resemble the attempt of Xerxes to defeat the sea by doing battle with it. Jaruzelski is faced with a painful choice: either he is realistic and acknowledges the crucial importance of Solidarity in a society independent of the state, or he believes—as Marxist-Leninists sometimes do—in the miracle of Solidarity's disappearance.

Blair: Since the imposition of martial law, there has been a debate among Western politicians about how best to react to the Polish regime. How do you assess these official Western reactions to Poland, especially from the United States government?

Michnik: American policies towards Poland and Eastern Europe in general have been unclear during the Gorbachev era. During the first years of martial law, I was strongly in favor of the Reagan administration's tough policies towards the Polish regime. More recently, I was most impressed with the remarks of Vice President Bush on Polish television. Bush reported that he had met Wałęsa and other Solidarity leaders (I also had the honor of being among them), and that he thought it inappropriate to advise Polish society on what it should do. But he expressed the view that in other countries the source of a rising standard of living is respect for human rights and pluralism. And Bush stated quite explicitly that the partner of the United States is not the Polish state but the independent Polish society. Of course, these sentiments constitute only the barest outlines of a coherent policy. But the fact that this meeting took place and these remarks were made is extremely important. Vice President Bush achieved something which is to a large extent the result of Mrs. Thatcher's earlier remarks to the Soviet people on Moscow television. Ten years ago, all this would have been unthinkable. President Carter's letter to Sakharov resulted in great tension between the United States and the Soviet Union. Nowadays, it is impossible for the vice president of the United States to visit Moscow without meeting Sakharov. This is a new and important precedent. The principle of Soviet policy used to be that states can only discuss weapons, armies, and military problems. Now even the Soviet Union has to discuss human rights. For me it is shameful that what Margaret Thatcher was brave enough to do is not done by the British Labour Party or the Trades Union Congress. The problem of human rights and independent trade unions should be central to their policies as well. It is not merely a problem for conservatives. Western citizens and states must not turn their backs on us. It would destroy the possibility of democracy, not just in Poland, but throughout Eastern Europe.

Blair: Poland is a peculiar country, the writer Antoni Słonimski once remarked. The Polish system today contains many peculiar features—a powerful and respected Church, agriculture under private ownership, extensive cultural freedoms—once considered impossible in a Communist system. Despite this, you continue to speak of the Polish regime as totalitarian. What precisely do you mean by totalitarianism in this context?

Michnik: I was last in the West eleven years ago, during the last phase of the Franco dictatorship in Spain. Trade unions and political parties were operating semilegally, there were wide cultural freedoms, an independent Church, independent agriculture, even a market. Even so, nobody called this fascism with a human face. Everybody claimed that this was fascism in a state of disintegration. What we experience in Poland today is not socialism with a human face but totalitarian communism with broken teeth. Ours is a disintegrating totalitarian system, whose "liberalism" is symptomatic of its weakness. The classical analysis of the totalitarian order presented by Hannah Arendt no longer describes our situation accurately; it applies only to state institutions themselves. The Polish system consists of a totalitarian state coexisting with a society which cannot be controlled through totalitarian methods. The state wants to exercise totalitarian power but is unable to do so. It is forced to compromise with life, and this results in a provisional equilibrium between society and the state. Since the death of Stalin, the totalitarian doctrine has not changed. The state still wants collectivization, and, since religion is the people's opium, it still wants to abolish the Church. But the state doesn't know how to achieve such goals. It nevertheless emphasizes one fundamental rule of totalitarianism: the leading role of the party.

Blair: There is a potential confusion here. In the West, the term "totalitarianism" is still normally used to describe a type of brutal and delirious regime which requires the population's fanatical devotion—a regime such as Hitler's or Stalin's. Your remarks suggest that this sense of the term "totalitarianism" is inapplicable to the present Polish regime, precisely because its power is less delirious and more calculated and subtle—if often ineffective. Would you therefore say that this regime is totalitarian in the revised sense that it is mobilized constantly to prevent the formation of a civil society independent of the party-dominated political order?

Michnik: Undoubtedly. This state simply requires everybody—Catholic and non-Catholic, party members and nonparty members alike—to praise the glory of General Jaruzelski and his group, and to attribute their failures to hard luck.

Blair: The idea of a civil society figures prominently in your criticisms of this new form of totalitarianism. In *Letters from Prison* you say that the birth of Solidarity was synonymous with the restoration, for the first time in the history of Communist rule, of a civil society capable of reaching a compromise with the state. What do you mean when you speak of a civil society? How can this old-fashioned eighteenth-century term be of relevance today?

Michnik: Václav Havel, one of the fathers of the recent renaissance of the term, and one of the most penetrating writers in Europe, has shown that totalitarianism is essentially paternalistic. In the totalitarian order, the state is the teacher and society is the pupil in the classroom, which is sometimes converted into a prison or a military camp. In a civil society, by contrast, people do not want to be pupils, soldiers, or slaves; they act as citizens. The idea of a civil society was born at the end of the eighteenth century as a reaction against the feudal system. The Communist system is a late-twentieth-century, more barbaric form of feudalism. It is therefore not surprising that the anti-totalitarian opposition draws on the classical forms of struggle for a democratic order. The point is that, as citizens, we in the democratic opposition don't want to be treated any longer as children or slaves. The basic principle of the anti-feudal movement was human rights, the idea that everyone has rights equal to those of the monarch. That's what we also want. We want everybody to enjoy the same rights as Jaruzelski, secured by the rule of law.

Blair: Your activities display a deep commitment to democracy—a term which is many-sided and much-abused these days. Exactly what do you mean by democracy? Is there anything specifically Polish about your understanding of the term?

Michnik: I am a child of a specifically Polish democratic tradition. Four of its most important contemporary representatives—the writer Czesław Miłosz, the poet Zbigniew Herbert, the philosopher Leszek Kołakowski, and a priest from Kraków, Father Karol Wojtyła—have greatly influenced my understanding of democracy. Among these figures there are no politicians or political activists, and that is probably why I think democracy is not based on exclusively political principles. For me, democracy concerns the human condition and human rights. It entails a vision of tolerance, an understanding of the importance of cultural traditions, and the realization that cherished human values can conflict with each other. Political democracy, by contrast, is an order based on majority rule. It can and often does conflict with human rights, which can be realized only within an order guaranteeing the point of view of all citizens, including that of minorities. The essence of democracy as I understand it is freedom—the freedom which belongs to citizens endowed with a conscience. So understood, freedom implies pluralism, which is essential because conflict is a constant factor within a democratic social order. But, as Kołakowski has pointed out, freedom gives us power over ourselves. It thereby enables us to do good and evil, as we choose. Although this freedom is God-given, it enables us to relinquish truth and good. We have the freedom to reject two thousand years of Christian civilization. But we also have the freedom to ask ourselves why we should do so, and which other values allow us to reject it. And so if I hear I should reject something which is part of my cultural tradition, I must ask: what is to replace what I am rejecting? Cardinal Wojtyła taught me to ask this question. The principle of freedom also raises questions—posed clearly for me by Czesław Miłosz—about the need for tolerance. Should the strength of my culture rest upon pluralism or upon uniformity (*Gleichschaltung*)? Should Poland be a country for Catholics only? Should it become a military dump? Or should Poland instead comprise a wealth of cultures? Should it not be a place for all the people who live within its borders—a country for not only Polish Catholics but also Ukrainians, Byelorussians, Lithuanians, Jews, Gypsies, Baptists, and others? Finally, democratic freedom as I understand it requires citizens to ask themselves the question posed by Zbigniew Herbert: if the majority of people had succumbed to a victorious totalitarian system, like that of Hitler or Stalin, should I go along with them? Or in the name of democracy should I choose instead to go it alone and to be defeated by embracing my belief in freedom and tolerance, my cultural tradition, and my human dignity? I consider all these questions central to democracy.

Blair: Among the important consequences of this view of democracy is a disavowal of both violence and revolutionary politics. You have been a strong supporter of the Polish opposition's remarkable capacity to avoid the use of violence. "To believe in overthrowing the dictatorship of the party by revolution," you write in *Letters from Prison*, "is both unrealistic and dangerous." Elsewhere you point out that those who use force to storm present-day Bastilles are likely to build bigger and worse Bastilles. Why in your view are calls for violent revolution so dangerous, and a major threat to democracy?

Michnik: My reflections on violence and revolution were sparked by my puzzlement about the origins of totalitarianism. I searched for clues in the writings of George Orwell, Hannah Arendt, Osip Mandelstam, and Albert Camus, and I came to the conclusion that the genesis of the totalitarian system is traceable to the use of revolutionary violence. My father was a Communist. He believed that revolutionary violence would produce social justice. This earned him eight years in prison, at the time of the Moscow trials of the 1930s. He must have posed the question: Do I want a repetition of the trials of Stalin's time? I repeated this question to myself, and I answered that violence consumes and demoralizes the person who uses it. Castro wanted a free Cuba. But in the revolutionary struggle against Batista, he was corrupted by power. Whoever uses violence to gain power uses violence to maintain power. Whoever is taught to use violence cannot relinquish it. In our century, the struggle for freedom has been fixed on power, instead of the creation of civil society. It has therefore always ended up in the concentration camp.

Blair: It is a commonplace observation that revolution is a transformative experience, an adventure of the heart and soul, as Ryszard Kapuściński says. Citizens initially feel strengthened by it. Their inner feelings of emptiness momentarily disappear. Astonished, they discover boundless energies within themselves. They experience joy in their determination to act and to change the world. Participation in the revolution becomes a giddy exploration of the unknown. Your writings cross-examine such experiences and highlight their unintended outcomes, such as terror and vengeance. For you, revolution is certainly a giddy experience—which most often produces sobering outcomes. Revolution is the child of liberty, but the parent of despotism.

Michnik: Exactly. This is a problem in every revolution. Just as the English revolutionaries yearned for freedom and produced Oliver Cromwell, the struggle of the French revolutionaries for the *droits de l'homme* led to the guillotine. In the twentieth century, the Russian, Chinese, and Cuban revolutions are not exceptions to this rule. Nor is the Iranian revolution, which is a conservative revolution against a modernizing dictatorship. The child of this revolution is Khomeini, who is worse than the shah. I wouldn't like this sort of outcome in Poland. Violence fractures social bonds. And, whenever society is so atomized, its intrasocial networks shattered, it becomes vulnerable to totalitarianism. Hypothetically speaking, if Jaruzelski were to be replaced tomorrow by Wałęsa or Kuroń, nothing would change. The crucial problem is therefore to build a democratic society which renders totalitarianism impossible by altering the social mechanisms of power along the lines attempted by Solidarity.

Blair: You mentioned that democracy is sometimes nurtured by cultural tradition. An obvious example is Polish Catholicism. The far-reaching effects of the Catholic Church on the political system—as well as its support for the Polish opposition—have often been underestimated in the West, especially on the left, because of certain misgivings about Catholicism. The possibility that a Church might defend democratic liberties seems as implausible to some people as the sight of striking workers reciting Hail Marys. This skepticism is fueled by the belief that the theology of the Church is reactionary. In *The Church and the Left* you attempted to explain that Catholicism means something rather special under Polish conditions. What is it about Polish Catholicism that makes it a driving force—a motor of social resistance, a powerful institution which is independent of the state apparatus and enjoys deep respect in civil society?

Michnik: People in the West who do not understand the specific nature of the Polish Church should consider honestly the history of Ireland. This would help them grasp the crucial protective role of the Catholic Church in a poor country at war with a powerful empire. The Church in Poland plays a similar role. It is the guardian of Polish national identity. During the most difficult years of totalitarian oppression, it defended human dignity and cultural identity, including freedom of worship. In the Stalin era, the Church was the only institution from which people did not hear lies. This is one reason why Poles remain faithful to it. Another reason is that the present totalitarian system insists that every person is state property. The Church's view is that the human being is a child of God, to whom God has granted natural liberty. This God-given dignity is so great that the individual can admire only God and not the state. It follows from this that in Poland and other Communist countries religion is the natural antidote to the totalitarian claims of the state authorities, especially given that the Church relies not upon power but upon dialogue. Of course there are dangers associated with Polish Catholicism, and Catholic intellectuals here are aware of them. The Polish Church is tempted to renew the alliance between the altar and the throne. All the impulses coming from the Vatican are nevertheless opposed strongly to an alliance between Church and state. The Church of Pope John Paul II rests upon a philosophical defense of human rights—not just of Catholics but of everyone.

Blair: Nevertheless many people in the West, including some Catholics, complain about the lack of universalism of some teachings of the Church. They question the restrictive definition of "natural liberty" which it lays down. The prohibition on divorce and the sexist rulings on contraception are cases in point.

Michnik: Precisely because I am not a Catholic, I am surprised that people in the West are concerned much more with the sexual ethics of the Catholic Church than with the violation of human rights in Soviet-type systems. And I have observed that nobody is more concerned with the ethics of the Catholic Church than non-Catholics. Let us consider the Church's position on divorce. The Church says: If you want to live in agreement with the Church, then you should not divorce. It does not use the police or the army to impose its point of view. Besides, the Church expects much more from people than sexual ethics. It summons people to love their enemies—a command much more difficult to live up to than the prohibition on divorce. It reminds the world that truth is truth and that good is good. It understands that we may not achieve the truth, but it emphasizes the necessity of acknowledging our failure to do so. The sexual theology of the Church is understandable in this respect. The world has no need of a Church which instantly proclaims everything people want. Nowadays the world needs a Church which speaks the truth, even if the truth is difficult and unpleasant. No doubt, the Church is a conservative institution. And of course if there were only conservative institutions of this type within a society—we are not faced with this threatening possibility in Poland—then the Church would function as either a cemetery or a prison. I would nevertheless be very afraid to live in a world without conservative institutions and values. A world devoid of tradition would be nonsensical and anarchic. The human world should be constructed from a permanent conflict between conservatism and contestation; if either is absent from a society, pluralism is destroyed. This is why I'd like to live in a country whose laws concerning sexual ethics were very liberal but in which the Church's teachings were very strict.

Blair: In the essay on Gorbachev, you remark that the Moscow reforms could consolidate a new philosophy of political compromise—compromise understood as a method of regulating domestic conflicts within the socialist bloc, and of constructing new international agreements, for example, between Poland and the Soviet Union. For many Western readers, your emphasis on the need for compromise is surprising—especially since it comes from someone with such sharp democratic impulses. The theme of compromise after all has its roots in the early modern conservative tradition. "All government, indeed every human benefit and enjoyment, every virtue, and every prudent act," said Burke, "is founded on compromise and barter." How do you reconcile your commitments to both democracy and compromise? Doesn't talk of compromise make sense only if both sides in a conflict take seriously the need for compromise? What evidence is there that the Polish state is capable of conciliation, or that it is prepared to compromise with an organization it has done its best to destroy? Aren't you saying, to speak plainly, that the Soviet-type system is here to stay in Poland, and that a free Poland is impossible?

Michnik: My vision of compromise certainly adopts realism as a starting point. The geopolitical reality is that we are not strong enough to drive the Red Army out of Poland. But my vision of compromise has another starting point. It is based on my conviction that pluralist democracy necessitates compromises in the face of complex realities. The philosophy of compromise is a philosophy which recognizes quandaries. The philosophy of radicalism, revolution, demagogy, and violence, by contrast, takes an easier path, although, as I've explained, it produces the guillotine and not democracy. From its inception the left failed to recognize this. It lacked an understanding of the conservative perspective.

Blair: In Europe the conventional distinction between left and right is actually founded on this disagreement with conservatives. Traditionally, the right was recognizable by its cautiousness about the future and its deference to the past, whereas the left, intent on overthrowing the past and building upon the present, usually looked towards the future with an unbridled optimism. Doesn't your emphasis on the need for democratic social change through compromise cut across this traditional distinction?

Michnik: Yes. Revolutionaries always wanted to identify conservatism with Joseph de Maistre. They failed to take account of the quite different perspectives of Edmund Burke. There are in fact two conservative traditions emanating from the French Revolution. De Maistre was a counterrevolutionary. He was the White Guard who worked to erase all traces of the French Revolution and to restore the Bourbon dynasty. Burke was a counterreformer. Following in the footsteps of Montesquieu, he recognized clearly the complex problems posed by the Revolution. He argued that the values of the Revolution should be assimilated by working for change by means of compromise. *Reflections on the Revolution in France* cleverly analyzes the paradoxes of freedom and revolution. Unfortunately it is today banned in Poland.

If I were proficient in English I would translate this book and present Gorbachev and others with a complimentary copy—to teach them the philosophy of compromise.

Blair: How would you apply this originally Burkean idea of reform through compromise to the current situation? What is the basis of your hopes for a new compromise in the Gorbachev era? In broad outlines what would this new compromise look like?

Michnik: I regard Gorbachev's telephone call to Sakharov as a symbol of the possibility of a new compromise within the Soviet empire. Gorbachev is confronted by a fundamental choice. Either he acknowledges that there are irremovable conflicts within Soviet society and, accordingly, works to build a social order based on compromise—among Tatars, Lithuanians, Estonians, Latvians, Georgians, and other minorities such as the intelligentsia—or he attempts to resolve all conflicts by using the police and the army. I urge him to rely upon methods of compromise. There is no other choice for the Soviet Union: either there will be compromise or there will be Stalinism. To avoid the latter, Gorbachev must find agreement with the natural leaders of the national minorities. He must develop a program which encourages them to remain within a Soviet commonwealth of nations.

Blair: What are the chances of reaching a new compromise within Poland? Is the Jaruzelski group at all capable of conciliation?

Michnik: This question must be answered by Jaruzelski. He must decide whether he will enter into a dialogue with Solidarity or be pushed aside like Gomułka or Gierek. I can see no other alternative, though he may last another two or three years. The Polish nation can wait this long, but I'm not certain whether Jaruzelski has this much time. The authorities think that so long as they have a gun at our heads they can do as they please. This is untrue, as the example of Gierek shows. Jaruzelski must also make a decision: to be recognized by history as the man who introduced martial law or as the joint architect of a new compromise. All signs indicate that Jaruzelski's policies are premised upon the collapse of perestroika in the Soviet Union, that he is the prisoner of his own history, and that he is incapable of compromise— and that a new compromise in Poland therefore requires his removal from power. Yet Lech Wałęsa has said that someone must be held responsible in this country. This is why Solidarity's hand will always be outstretched to compromise. We are ready for compromise, but we shall never agree to capitulation. We shall continue to call for solutions by compromise, but in a wholly uncompromising way. Perhaps we will have to take to the streets once more. But if that were necessary I would feel that an opportunity had been squandered. My duty as an intellectual is to tell the truth, even when the truth is unpalatable for both my friends and the authorities. The truth is that if we were again forced onto the street, then there would be bloodshed. I want to do everything to avert this possibility. And I want to have the feeling that, having done everything to avoid bloodshed, only the stupidity of Jaruzelski made it possible.

Blair: More than two decades ago you were arrested for the first time for involvement in the writing and distribution of *An Open Letter to the Party.* This document, signed by Jacek Kuroń and Karol Modzelewski, openly criticized the regime in the name of the emancipation of the working class. What do you think of this document today? What would you write if you were to draft another open letter to the party?

Michnik: Jacek Kuroń and Karol Modzelewski are today ashamed of that letter. They consider it an intellectual mistake. I have a better opinion of it. It is a highly interesting historical document, which signals the end of a certain mode of political thinking. Its starting point was the thesis that the Russian Revolution was a leap from the kingdom of necessity into the kingdom of freedom. And it repeated the Trotskyist call for a revolution of workers against the deformed bureaucracy. Its authors rejected the Church but respected the Scriptures. Many groups in the West still use this language of Bolshevik criticizing Bolshevik. In our part of the world, this language is now dead. It belongs to a closed chapter of history. It is as incapable of expressing our reality as the controversy between the Jacobins and Girondists. The debate about how to improve socialism has become irrelevant because nobody in Poland knows any longer what socialism means. Our discussions now concentrate instead upon how to achieve freedom. Seen in this way, the letter of Kuroń and Modzelewski is important. It is a requiem for Marxist revisionism. The observation of Engels that revolutions usually achieve something quite different from what they intend certainly applies to this letter. This is the first document in Poland to reject completely the ruling system. It argued for a genuine workers' revolution, but in fact signaled the beginning of a genuine civil society.

Blair: So what kind of advice would you include in an open letter to the party today?

Michnik: There could only be one piece of advice. I would repeat some words in *From the History of Honor in Poland*. I wrote this book in prison, and I concluded it by quoting the Polish poet Julian Tuwim, whose words are addressed to Communists in all lands: "Kiss my arse!"

PART TWO

Notes from the Revolution, 1989–1990

6

A Specter Is Haunting Europe

Yes, it looks like this really is the end of totalitarian communism. Nothing can be done to revive the system that promised a glorious future and brought terror and poverty, lies and depravity, a system that stripped people of their national culture and violated human conscience. We are looking around suspiciously and uncertainly. Is it really possible? Is it just wishful thinking on our part? Is it just another trick on the part of the ruling group? Are they lying to us yet again as they so often have in the past? Let us consider the following: in politics, facts count. The most significant facts of this spring were the Round Table negotiations and the relegalization of Solidarity. What is the underlying meaning of these two events?

The Round Table signified a willingness to transform what had been a policeman's monologue into a political dialogue. It also called into question the entire philosophy and practice of martial law, which had brought about a situation in which Solidarity members were able to speak out only from the underground, from prison, or from the dock. This reorientation, which encountered substantial resistance within the ruling group, was not easy to bring about, since it had been preceded by years of propaganda defaming Solidarity. We had been offered the possibility of capitulation, emigration, or resocialization through prison. They had assured us that never again would they engage in political dialogue with Wałęsa and the people of Solidarity.

Translated by Jane Cave from *Gazeta Wyborcza*, May 9, 1989.

Things turned out rather differently. What were the reasons for this? First, the economic bankruptcy of martial law. If the military action of December 1981 had resulted in full wallets and full shelves in the stores, the ruling group would not have needed the Round Table. However, any improvement in economic performance turned out to be dependent on political changes. Their aspirations blocked, people just turned their backs on the authorities.

Second, the international context. The Soviet leadership, facing similar dangers at home, opted for glasnost, for a great political opening. At the same time, the broad campaign aimed at unmasking Stalinism became a major source of pressure. Genuine changes took place.

In every Polish crisis to date we have heard the same complaint: everything can be blamed on the Polish national character, Polish laziness and quarrelsomeness, the Polish tendency to anarchy. The political turnabout in the Soviet Union and the clear diagnosis of the crisis in that country made nonsense of these traditional explanations. The Polish crisis was clearly seen to be a part of a more general crisis of totalitarian communism.

People's efforts to achieve freedom take various forms. In Russia, the intelligentsia rebelled; in the Baltic republics, National Fronts have been set up; in Hungary, a multiparty system is being re-created. In Poland, the key issue was the relegalization of Solidarity. This was the only way to break out of the conflict between the power apparatus and the broad opposition movement that had been pushed underground. For this reason, I think it misleading and inappropriate for General Jaruzelski to refer—as he did several days ago—to the possibility of "pardoning" people persecuted for political reasons in recent years. Rather, it is these people who should be asked for their pardon.

By persecuting people who chose to participate in the anti-totalitarian resistance movement, the Stalinist *nomenklatura* tried to defend itself against the democratic transformation of the state. This transformation could take place only thanks to those people who spat out the gag of fear, who stood up against the all-powerful apparatus of power, and who made from the truth of their conscience what Václav Havel calls the power of the powerless.

From time to time we are asked: Do you want to improve the system or overthrow it? At one time we used to be asked this question by public prosecutors; today we hear this question at numerous public meetings. We reply: The totalitarian system is our enemy. We don't want to improve or correct it. We want to replace it with a system of parliamentary democracy. But we reject the path of revolution and violence, since we know how easy it is to replace one dictatorship with another. We believe that the changes taking place in other countries, especially the USSR, are opening up new perspectives from which to consider the Polish road—from a totalitarian system to one based on democracy and independence.

A specter is haunting Europe, the specter of the end of communism. This is why the elections to the Sejm and Senate are so important. We must show that we Poles want democratic change and can manage to bring it about with our votes. By voting for the candidates of Lech Wałęsa, we shall be voting for Poland to set out on the road to democracy and independence.

7

After the Round Table

Anna Husarska: In June there will be elections to the restructured Polish Parliament—consisting of the Sejm, or Lower House, and a restored Senate, or Upper House. At the Round Table negotiations, in which you participated, the government agreed to submit 161 of the Sejm's 460 seats [35 percent] and all 100 Senate seats to free competition. You just came from a hectic meeting of Solidarity's National Citizens' Committee, where the 261 candidates were designated and an election platform was approved. What are Solidarity's chances of winning this partially free ballot?

Adam Michnik: Of course, it is difficult to predict the outcome. But for my generation it is the first opportunity to elect people we really want to representative bodies—at least, formally representative. We have to do everything we can to take advantage of this opening. For over forty years the government in Poland was undemocratic and uncontrolled. Although these elections will not make it democratic, they offer a chance for society to control the governing of the country through its independent representatives.

Husarska: You yourself will be a candidate for the Sejm from the Katowice district (in Silesia) . . .

Interview by Anna Husarska. Reprinted by permission from *The New Leader,* April 3–17, 1989. Copyright © the American Labor Conference on International Affairs, Inc.

Michnik: I do not feel that I am fit to be a Parliament member. But I think those of us who are well known, whose names might attract many votes, should run to strengthen the Solidarity ticket.

Husarska: Why have [the Solidarity leaders] Zbigniew Bujak and Władysław Frasyniuk refused to run?

Michnik: They explained their decision at the Citizens' Committee meeting, and we have to respect it. They feel there is a greater need for them now in the union than in the Parliament. Both support the Solidarity platform and its candidates, and I know that Bujak will campaign with me and with others. Lech Wałęsa left the matter up to the individual union leaders while suggesting that it would be desirable for them to participate. At the same meeting Bronisław Geremek finally agreed to run.

Husarska: The dates for the elections are very close [June 4, with runoffs on June 18]. Is there time to prepare the campaign?

Michnik: No, there is not enough time, and the government knew this when it set the dates and would not budge on them at the Round Table. It was conscious of the fact that the sooner the elections were held, the worse for us, given that we have no experience, no electoral structures. But we have to do the impossible.

Husarska: Opposition in Poland is now much more diversified than it was a few years ago and certainly not limited to Solidarity. Other organizations, political parties, and groupings such as the right-wing Confederation for Independent Poland and the pacifist-oriented Freedom and Peace movement want to present their own candidates. This might split the vote of the opposition and lead to its defeat by the people who—although not members of the party—agree to run as its "covert candidates." What is the position of Solidarity on this problem?

Michnik: Well, that is the price of democracy. We cannot forbid other opposition groups to put up their candidates, but we will not withdraw ours either. As for the covert candidates, we have to present a program to the voters that is more attractive than theirs—which won't be difficult. We have to play fair and then watch that the other side does not falsify the results.

Husarska: At the Citizens' Committee meeting one delegate raised the point that several Solidarity candidates are at the same time members of Catholic groups of some sort, and that once in Parliament they might create their separate club. Does this represent a danger in your view?

Michnik: We need a united team, so it would be a pity if such divisions were to appear. We must try to prevent them, but again this is the price of democracy.

Husarska: The 35:65 arrangement in the Sejm is valid only for the coming elections. Will subsequent elections be really democratic?

Michnik: I want to believe that they will.

Husarska: But in the past, more often than not, the authorities have broken the agreements they signed with the opposition—for example, those at the Gdańsk shipyard in 1980 [creating Solidarity, which was then outlawed sixteen months later]. Why trust them this time?

Michnik: We have to take the risk. The Round Table talks were achieved without the threat of strikes. By entering the negotiations the government accepted that Solidarity's presence on the public scene is a necessary stage in the political development of our country, and this acceptance should not be underestimated.

Husarska: Don't you expect that the regime will now try every possible trick to prevent Solidarity from using the rights it acquired at the Round Table?

Michnik: Of course I expect it, but we have to see the wood behind the individual trees.

Husarska: There are indications of what I interpret as a dangerous comeback of anti-Semitism in Poland. For instance, I've seen graffiti in the street of Warsaw saying, "Don't vote for Jews," or "Don't vote for Jews-Communists [*zydokomuna*]."

Michnik: If someone says not to vote for Jews-Communists, it is obvious he does not mean Jews but something else. The Warsaw list was prepared by people close to Wałęsa, who has the support of the pope, and a candidate for the Senate is the president of the Catholic primate's Social Council, Professor [Władysław] Findeisen. If such a list can be called Jews-Communists, then this is Gombrowicz [i.e., surrealism]. If you want to call it anti-Semitism, then it is an anti-Semitism so special that it does not refer to Jews.

Husarska: The legalization of Solidarity has in a way undercut the raison d'être of the clandestine publishing industry. Almost the entire editorial board of the main union underground weekly, *Tygodnik Mazowsze,* is moving to the new official union daily . . .

Michnik: Yes, together with Ernest Skalski and Helena Łuczywo [editor of *Tygodnik Mazowsze*] and a dozen other journalists we will put out this paper whose name is *Gazeta Wyborcza*. We have an agreement allowing us to print 500,000 copies, and we will fight for more.

Husarska: What about the other union or political opposition publications? Should they now come aboveground?

Michnik: In my opinion not all should abandon the clandestine network. Let us wait for the censorship law to be liberalized. Underground publications in Poland were for the last seven and a half years the living symbol of the opposition's survival. They have established important new values, and we should avoid doing anything that could be interpreted as the liquidation of these values.

Husarska: You follow the Soviet press regularly and are known to be one of the keenest observers of the changes going on in the Soviet Union. What is their relation with the new developments in Poland?

Michnik: The relation is very direct. What is happening now in the USSR has also determined our situation, for the Soviet reforms have an international dimension. Until Gorbachev took over it was widely thought that the Polish crisis was due to our country's specific conditions. Glasnost and perestroika are crucial here because they deal with Stalinism, and now the authorities readily admit that what is going on in Poland is part of the general upheaval of the Stalinist system. The same is true of the latest developments in Hungary, by the way, although the difference is that Solidarity started under Brezhnev.

Husarska: Some time ago, Timothy Garton Ash of the London *Spectator* compared the present changes in the Soviet bloc with the fall of the Ottoman Empire and came up with the term "ottomanization," meaning something like "emancipation amid decay." Do you agree with his analogy?

Michnik: Garton Ash is the most outstanding observer of the political scene in Eastern Europe, and his formula is very brilliant, but the analogy is not a direct one. What we face here at the moment is a choice between a revolution with the price in bloodshed or a peaceful evolution. I personally hope that evolution is possible. One thing is obvious: This system is doomed.

I do not want to speculate on how Stalinist communism will crumble. That is a job for a prophet or a swindler. The only thing I can say is that this system lost whatever power it had to develop; it stopped being attractive to anyone except the narrow class of *nomenklatura* that seeks to preserve its own privileges.

Now this system can either reform itself to the point of becoming something else or it will have to step down and make room for another system. There are examples in other countries . . .

Husarska: You don't mean "Finlandization"? That metaphor is somewhat confusing and old-fashioned, isn't it?

Michnik: It is still used. I even heard it mentioned recently by a government official. But Finlandization happened in a particular situation: on the one hand, there was an aggressive, totalitarian empire; on the other, a small country. Finlandization was an art of sovereign coexistence, of the Finns with Stalin. It is not apropos in the sense that Stalin is no more and the Soviet Union is changing both internally and in its foreign policy. No, I don't think the Finlandization metaphor suits today's conditions. I prefer to see our situation as evolving in a way similar to what happened in Spain.

Husarska: But Spain did not have a powerful, aggressive, and totalitarian neighbor. It was not part of any empire.

Michnik: True, you are right. I have to admit that there is a difference. But Spain was a dictatorship that somehow reformed itself without revolution. The awareness of the need for changes appeared on both sides, and this is the main thing that interests us here. In a recent issue of the weekly *Przegląd Tygodniowy* there was an interview with the Hungarian Politburo member Imre Pozsgay, who uses the very same analogy with Spain. When I first suggested it [in an essay entitled "The New Evolutionism," written twelve years ago], it was shocking. Today it is banal.

Husarska: Granted, but the end of the Franco era brought a change from right-wing dictatorship to democracy, while here . . .

Michnik: Anna, don't you sometimes get confused where is the left and where is the right?

Husarska: I do, touché.

Michnik: I wouldn't attach too much importance to that. For me what matters is that it was a dictatorship, that the Spaniards fought for the human rights the dictatorship denied them. Spain had gone through a bloody civil war, so bloody that it seemed impossible the two sides would ever sit down and talk to each other. And yet it turned out to be possible. I believe that in Poland it will also turn out to be possible. Let us call it the Spanish way to democracy in Communist countries.

8

Joy . . . and a Moment of Reflection

We thank you, friends. We thank all of you who helped Solidarity during the election campaign. Thanks to you, thanks to thousands of nameless friends in every corner of Poland, we won the campaign and the elections.

First, the campaign. For the first time since December 13, 1981, Solidarity openly reached every district and factory, every town and city. People who for seven long years had been told that it makes no sense to stick with Solidarity now had the opportunity to assess the meaning and value of their stubbornness. We have returned. We are here. We shall remain.

We had very little time and few resources, but we had enough hope that we would be able to organize ourselves quickly enough to meet the test. Although there were some slipups and some disagreements, the day of June 4 will be commemorated as a Polish national holiday. The Poles voted for their hopes. They believed in Solidarity. They believed in Lech Wałęsa.

A number of thoughts come to mind at this point. The election results constitute a commitment for the future. During the next four years, Solidarity must work to show that it deserves people's trust. Consequently, this is a time for reflection rather than euphoria. We must proceed in such a way that we meet people's expectations. On the one hand, we must not allow ourselves to become incorporated into the *nomen-*

Translated by Jane Cave from *Gazeta Wyborcza*, June 6, 1989.

klatura, and, on the other, we must not allow ourselves to engage in triumphalist, confrontational rhetoric.

The success of Solidarity relative to the candidates of other opposition groups is a sign that people are not now interested in any form of extremism. It signifies that, together with our colleagues from the opposition, we need to search for a common language and understanding. The elections to the Sejm and Senate were made possible by the agreement reached at the Round Table. We should remember this.

Now that the elections are over, we should construct an institutional order based on the ideas of dialogue and compromise. Poland's geopolitical situation remains, after all, unchanged; the repressive apparatus remains in the hands of the same people as before. We are entering a time of hope, but also a time of danger. The fatal shots recently fired in Tbilisi and Beijing show the dangers that we need to avoid. Solidarity will adhere to the Round Table agreements, and we expect the authorities to do the same. We must cast off the straitjacket of the totalitarian system together.

We should also take account of the relatively low election turnout. Millions of Poles did not participate in the elections. Why? This was not because of the propaganda campaign launched by the extreme, radical wing of the opposition. It indicates a lack of faith in the Round Table agreements, a lack of faith in the future; it is a sign of continuing apathy and discouragement. We have to win these millions of people over to the cause of building democracy in Poland.

This is how I see the task that awaits all those who advocate an evolutionary path from Stalinist communism to parliamentary democracy. These elections are a vital step on what will be a long and winding road, but this is the only road that is open to us.

9

Nothing Will Ever Be
the Way It Was

The results of the first round of elections to the Sejm and Senate have created a new situation in Poland. From this moment on, nothing will ever be the way it was. We are presented with a great opportunity, which spells danger to many others.

Poland must be governed differently. Poles must plan their future differently, since citizens claim their rights differently from slaves. We have to become a civil society. This means that we must come to feel responsible for the state. Some in the ruling apparatus have responded to the election results with panic.

We have received information that a "state of alert" is in force in various parts of the country. So we need to call on the competent authorities to react in a way that will not exacerbate social tensions. Fear has big eyes and is a bad counselor.

Instead of developing this train of thought, let's quote yesterday's statement by the government's deputy press spokesman regarding the situation in China. "We believe," he declared, "that the conflict will be resolved by the Chinese themselves through political means, without the use of force, and that, as was the case in the past, reason and realism will triumph and the reform process will continue."

We quote this statement with absolute approval, something that we rarely do on these pages. This is how things ought to be, now and in the future, especially in our country. The use of force, as well as the threat to

Translated by Jane Cave from *Gazeta Wyborcza*, June 8, 1989.

use force, is a means of wielding power that belongs to the repertoire of Stalinist domestic and foreign policy. We condemned the use of force in the past (Hungary 1956, Czechoslovakia 1968, Afghanistan 1979, Poland 1981) and will continue to condemn all such use of force in the future.

We well know that in the process of straightening their spines, people also raise their social aspirations. We hear this in the telephone calls and letters that we receive. At the moment, most of the queries we receive are concerned with the outcome of the vote for the national list. This has caused a number of Solidarity representatives to declare that the Round Table agreement will be respected and that the governing coalition will therefore obtain, after the second round, 65 percent of the seats in the Sejm. Our readers consider this a breach of the law (the electoral law and the constitution) and a violation of the will of the electorate. This issue has to be addressed candidly.

As a result of the Round Table agreement, Polish citizens can elect 35 percent of the Sejm deputies and 100 percent of the Senate members according to democratic procedures. This is our first step toward parliamentary democracy, but it does not mean that Poles can elect their legislature and executive as they think fit. Those who believe that deleting the names of all candidates on the national list will enable us to change the balance of power in Poland are deluding themselves.

There remains only one question: How can we get out of this mess? We think that the next few days will provide a sensible answer.

10

Your President,
Our Prime Minister

In the very near future, the shape of the political order in
Poland will be decided. So far, it is the question of who will be a candidate for president that has aroused the strongest emotions. It is unfortunate that, in such a situation, memory and rhetoric dominate. Let us try
to examine the situation calmly and answer the question, what kind of
political arrangement will Poland need during the coming months and
years?

The economic situation is disastrous. The country is threatened with
social upheaval and unrest. Solidarity's overwhelming victory in the elections proves that the Poles want fundamental change. So do the widespread demands that Lech Wałęsa should be a candidate for president.
What does the Solidarity chairman say to this? He points to the realities
of the international and domestic situation. He points to our neighbors
to the east, the west, and the south. He points to those who control the
repressive apparatus (the Ministry of Internal Affairs, the Ministry of
Defense) in Poland. Let us consider these circumstances.

In our part of the world, the opponents of totalitarian communism
are engaged in a bitter conflict with its defenders. It is a significant sign
of the times that de-Stalinization is under way in the Soviet Union. The
changes taking place there as a result of pressure from anti-totalitarian
forces can only mean that the Polish nation and the peoples of the USSR
have the common goal of overcoming their Stalinist heritage and build-

Translated by Jane Cave from *Gazeta Wyborcza*, July 3, 1989.

ing a democratic order. In the USSR, efforts are under way to introduce market mechanisms and to decollectivize agriculture. National cultures are coming to life, as are people's aspirations for freedom and dignity.

Isn't this just what we are trying to do in Poland? And doesn't this mean that we have common interests? This is why the changes taking place in Poland threaten not the national interests of Russia or those of any other nation of the Soviet Union but the interests of the totalitarian Stalinist Communist system. The current widespread anti-Russian phobia—so carefully noted by observers—is either an expression of disorientation or simply a provocation organized by the opponents of change.

The situation is different in the German Democratic Republic and Czechoslovakia. There, Soviet newspapers are confiscated, and demands for reform are stifled. How is Poland perceived in Moscow? As a great and important experiment in the transition from totalitarianism to parliamentary democracy. Our success or failure will ruin or strengthen those in Moscow who hope for a return to Stalinism.

How can the democratic movement defeat the Stalinist *nomenklatura* without resorting to revolution and violence? In my opinion, only by an alliance between the democratic opposition and the reformist wing of the ruling group. Poland now has the possibility of forming such an alliance. Let us consider: it is not easy to abandon totalitarian communism. To date, no one has succeeded. The task before us is thus unprecedented.

Poland now needs a strong and credible political arrangement. We need more than superficial changes such as replacing one candidate for the post of president or prime minister with another. For this reason, discussion about the relative merits of our two generals, Jaruzelski and Kiszczak, is futile. For many years, I publicly attacked both of these gentlemen, and I could now find many positive things to say about them. But now it is a question not of individuals but of political mechanisms.

We need a new arrangement, one that will be approved by all the main political forces. A new arrangement, but one that will ensure continuity. Such an arrangement could be constructed on the basis of an agreement whereby the president will be elected from among candidates from the Polish United Workers Party, while the post of prime minister and the task of forming a government will go to a candidate from within Solidarity.

Such a president will guarantee continuity of our international agreements and military alliances. Such a government will have the support of the overwhelming majority of Poles and will guarantee the thoroughgoing transformation of our political and economic system. Only such an arrangement will allow us to implement the demand for a "grand coalition" and obtain the assistance we need to rebuild the economy. And it will be an arrangement that has credibility in Poland and in the outside world.

II

Farewell to the Brezhnev Doctrine

In Mikhail Gorbachev's television appearance last Saturday, one can detect some important new emphases. Analyzing the current state of relations between nationalities in the USSR, Gorbachev stated, "Today, we are reaping the fruits of the abuses of power that were committed during previous decades—the expulsion of entire nations from their land, the disregard for the interests of numerous nationalities." He condemned the use of force and coercion in relations between the peoples of the USSR. He stated clearly that we can "count on changes for the better only if each nationality, each nation feels secure in its own home, in its own land." His argument implied the need for far-reaching reform of the federal structure.

What implications does this have for us Poles and our view of the world? We must think seriously and logically about de-Stalinization and about transforming relations between our countries. Now that the Soviet leadership has abandoned the Brezhnev doctrine of "limited sovereignty," we must try to achieve a new agreement between peoples who are free and equal, an agreement between sovereign states and nations.

It will soon be twenty-one years since the Prague Spring was crushed by force. A wave of neo-Stalinism then engulfed Czechoslovakia for many years. We would like to believe that Polish forces will never again be used to offer this kind of " fraternal assistance," that the Brezhnev doctrine is gone forever. Gorbachev is right when he says that the well-being

Translated by Jane Cave from *Gazeta Wyborcza*, July 4, 1989.

of one nation can never be achieved at the cost of limiting the rights and freedoms of other nations.

We appreciate the evolution that has taken place and that continues to take place in the relations between our eastern neighbor and the countries of the Warsaw Pact. In contrast with the military interventions in Hungary, Czechoslovakia, and Afghanistan, which aroused helpless anger and moral repugnance, today's policies are characterized by tolerance and imagination.

Further evidence of this evolution is provided by the recent statement by Vadim Zagladin. After all, we can remember the summer of 1981. We can remember the daily fear we experienced when reading the aggressive, lying commentaries in Soviet newspapers. And we can remember our even greater fear of military intervention. Today, Moscow newspapers express friendly interest, which evokes an appropriate Polish response on the pages of our papers.

We must try to think, speak, and write about Polish-Soviet relations that are no longer dominated by tanks, with a realistic sense of the state and national interests of all those involved. We must try to rid ourselves once and for all of our Stalinist inheritance. This should be the essence of our efforts to build a democratic and sovereign Poland.

12

If the President of Poland . . .

If the president of Poland had been elected by popular vote, Lech Wałęsa would have become president. On this question, none of the Sejm deputies or members of the Senate, who actually elected the president, has any doubt.

General Jaruzelski was elected by a majority of one vote, but the decisive vote was cast by the absent Lech Wałęsa, who declared that the president should be elected speedily from among the candidates of the coalition. President Jaruzelski was elected by the smallest possible majority. This means that an enormous number of those in the National Assembly, which was elected in a less than completely democratic fashion, considered it appropriate to vote against this candidate.

The election was by open ballot. I am not, then, revealing any secrets when I say that a certain number of coalition deputies did not vote for the general and a certain number of Solidarity deputies did not vote against him. Everyone voted as his conscience and sense of civic duty dictated. In this sense, it was an honest election. This is a major innovation in our public life.

The Poles demonstrated their negative attitude toward the policies implemented since December 13, 1981, which the general had come to symbolize. Simultaneously, they demonstrated their concern for the stability of the state.

Translated by Jane Cave from *Gazeta Wyborcza,* July 20, 1989.

This imposes a particular responsibility on General Jaruzelski. I don't think it is a distortion of the truth to say that the vast majority of members of the National Assembly have declared themselves in favor of evolutionary change, in favor of a completely free vote in the next elections, for both the presidency and the assembly itself.

This time, they had only one candidate to vote for. He was a politician with a complicated biography, the author of martial law in December 1981 but also the coauthor of the Round Table agreement. His future actions will determine whether he finds a place in history as a person responsible for the intervention in Czechoslovakia and the killing of Polish workers or as the person who was capable of a major political reorientation and who became one of the architects of the Polish road from totalitarian communism to democracy.

What next? All of us have the duty to do what we can to bring about democratic change. Poland finds itself in a favorable international constellation, and we Poles have the possibility of building a democratic state. The presidential elections have shown that Poles can achieve an understanding between themselves, but this can only come about as a result of an alliance for democracy against the conservative structures of the *nomenklatura*.

What do these elections mean for the ordinary citizens of Poland, for those who stand in line, fearfully contemplating the prospect of massive price increases? Nothing. But these people will call our deputies and senators, our generals and ministers, as well as our president to account if they do not take steps to save the country from ruin. Much of the power to bring about change is in the hands of the president.

13

Poland's Fate Is Being Decided

Today, Poland's fate is being decided in the lines outside the stores rather than in the corridors of the Sejm. People are horrified by unbelievable prices, and the empty shelves only increase their bitterness. It has become obvious to everyone that something has to be done—and quickly.

Poland needs a sign that the system has begun to change. A new government could be such a sign. It is no secret that there is considerable opposition to the candidacy of General Kiszczak. This is not really opposition to the general personally: the people of Solidarity—many of whom were imprisoned during martial law—well remember that it was General Kiszczak who was the architect of the Round Table, that his level-headedness and realism led him to become a coauthor of the process of political transformation. It is not a question of exacting revenge on the minister of internal affairs. The point is that people are convinced that no prime minister from the ranks of the Polish United Workers party (PZPR) is capable of forming a government that will end the country's crisis. Similar sentiments have been voiced by deputies belonging to the United Peasant party and the Democratic party as well as the PZWP.

Does this mean we are facing a real crisis? Possibly, but not necessarily. Lech Wałęsa's offer remains open. The opposition, which was victorious in the election, may proceed to form a government. This govern-

Translated by Jane Cave from *Gazeta Wyborcza*, August 2, 1989.

ment would have the task of transforming Poland into a country with a normal economy, normal wages and prices, a normal life. Such a government—in cooperation with all the main political forces—would have credibility with our allies. It could obtain qualitatively new and effective economic assistance from the West.

We are in a truly exceptional situation. Poland has not found itself in such a favorable international constellation for many years. Soviet leaders are engaged in a process of far-reaching state reforms. From their point of view, Poland is an experiment in the transition from totalitarianism to democracy. For this reason, they view Poland's efforts not with hostility but with interest and goodwill.

Lech Wałęsa has an enormous reserve of public trust. This capital should not be wasted. Invested wisely, it may allow us to refer to this period in the future as a turning point rather than a crisis. A turning point signifies a return to health. A continuing crisis leads to death. This is why it is so important to ask, who will finally be entrusted to form a government? And let us remember, in the final analysis, everything will be decided by the people standing in line.

14

What Next in Russia?

At the invitation of the editors of *Moscow News,* I wrote an article for the most recent edition. Among other things, I wrote the following:

We have finally learned how the opponents of democratic change think. Two speeches during the recent plenum of the CPSU [Communist Party of the Soviet Union] Central Committee caught my attention. V. Anufriev, the second secretary of the Kazakhstan Central Committee, openly stated that the current Politburo under the leadership of Gorbachev has to be changed since it does not have enough authority to decide the fate of the state. Why? Because someone has to take responsibility for events in Eastern Europe. "Our buffer zone has collapsed," Anufriev complained, "and now they are raising territorial and material demands, attacking our consulates, desecrating the graves of our soldiers and national heroes, and humiliating our great country. And we are again handing out hundreds of millions of rubles, stealing from our own people. We are welcoming with open arms assorted "mazowieckis."

This nonsense does not deserve a response. The desecration of soldiers' graves is a hooligan act regardless of whether they are Red Army graves in Poland or the graves of Polish soldiers in the USSR. On this we are all agreed. However, this mishmash of half-truths and outright lies indicates nothing but ignorance and ill will. Ignorance—so I was taught at home—should never be praised. To reduce the processes taking place in Europe to anti-Soviet excesses is tantamount to demonstrating lamentable incompe-

Translated by Jane Cave from *Gazeta Wyborcza,* February 20, 1990.

tence. To refer to sovereign European states as a "buffer zone" is tantamount to demonstrating one's own imperialist psychology. As a deputy to the Polish Sejm, I wish to declare that, while respecting the national dignity of the Russians and all the other nationalities of the USSR, I demand respect for the national dignity of the Poles. We shall never allow anyone to refer to our country as the "buffer zone" of another state. And one more thing: writing the name of my prime minister in the plural reminds me of the Stalinist trials and shows exceptional boorishness. Apart from anything else, we Poles write the names of people (and not just prime ministers) with a capital letter. The secretaries of the Kazakhstan Central Committee evidently follow different rules of orthography.

I will say one thing clearly: I take an extremely positive view of recent Soviet policy on Poland. It has been marked by considerable thought, goodwill, and desire for dialogue based on a partnership of equals. I found confirmation of this policy in the speeches by Foreign Minister Shevardnadze and Aleksander Yakovlev. I think we have many common interests and that we shall be able to build a strong, genuine bond between our two countries. I am, therefore, far from willing to interfere in the internal affairs of the Soviet Union. If I refer, then, to the speech by Vladimir Brovikov, the Soviet ambassador to Poland, it is not to defend Gorbachev, whose policies were directly attacked by Brovikov. I will only note that referring to tolerance for "dissidents" as a sign of "indecisiveness and helplessness in countering antistate activities" raises the question of what positive proposals you might have, Mr. Ambassador. We are personally acquainted, so I can ask you directly and publicly: What do you want? Instead of tolerance, trials and labor camps? Do you want to send Sakharov back to Gorki? What are you hoping for, Mr. Ambassador? Do you have anything to offer apart from nostalgia for the age of terror? You ridicule criticism of Stalinism, saying that "it has become fashionable to attribute all our misfortunes to our 'accursed past.' " Do you really think that democratic change is more deserving of condemnation than Stalinist genocide? And if you do think so, do you think you can be a good ambassador for your country in Poland? I assure you that we Poles will not accept such language. It is a good thing that the majority of speakers at this plenum used different language.

So much for what I wrote in *Moscow News*. What can we learn from all this? In the violent social and national conflicts occurring in the Soviet Union we can see a dispute about the future of this state. The totalitarian order is being destroyed before our very eyes. The explosion of the Asiatic republics has been interpreted in a number of ways: as the work of the mafia within the ruling apparatus, as the result of Islamic fundamentalism, and as a national liberation movement. However, everyone is agreed that the old model of the state is dying on the streets of Uzbekistan, Tadzhikistan, and Azerbaijan.

What will happen next? What will become of the Baltic republics, Moldavia, Armenia, and Georgia? When asked what Moscow would do if any of the republics declared its secession from the Soviet Union, one of the leaders of the Russian democratic movement told me, "Nothing. Not because Moscow understands the situation, but because it has run out of reserves." He then recounted the following anecdote: "A policeman brought to the police station a citizen who had been taking a piss in the middle of Red Square. The policeman said to his colleagues, 'I take a look and see that this citizen is taking a piss. I told him to stop pissing, so he did, but not because he understood me, but because he had run out of reserves.' " This anecdote illustrates the viewpoint from which the leaders of the Inter-Regional Group of Deputies look at the future. But perhaps it suggests an excessively one-sided view of the weakness of the power apparatus.

The following questions are of fundamental importance for Poland: Which road will Russia take? Will it work out a new model of a multinational state, or will individual republics become independent states? What kind of relations will Russia have with the states of Central and Eastern Europe?

One thing appears to be indisputable for relations between Warsaw and Moscow: the search for a new kind of relationship between states and between nations must be conducted within the framework of a dialogue between equals and a shared belief that our common, overriding goal is to build a democratic order in this part of the world. Any attempt to return to the principles of superpower diktat or to shift political debate to the realm of demagoguery and cheap emotions may lead to hatred and intolerance, to military intervention, to violence and bloodshed. Whether this can be avoided depends on all of us.

15

Notes from the Revolution

The final days of 1989 brought with them the end of the Communist era. The system that had proclaimed itself the future of the world was buried in the ashes of burning Romanian towns. No doubt there will still be police and military relapses, no doubt various epigones of communism will still tantalize with their baubles and sow dissension with their calumnies. But the idea has died. For communism, it is the end. At last.

In August 1986, I was released from the prison at Barczewo, Poland. I left behind me notebooks with thoughts for a book about Nazism and, in the cell adjacent to mine, Erich Koch, a Nazi who had been *Gauleiter* of eastern Prussia during the war and who was living out his remaining days in a Polish prison.

I had been jailed on December 13, 1981, when the Communist regime of General Wojciech Jaruzelski declared martial law and struck at Solidarity, and, apart from a brief interval of several months, had spent the years since behind bars. The years in prison were not a bad time for me. I wrote several books, which were translated into several languages, and I received several international prizes. So I was leaving prison without hatred in my heart and full of goodwill toward the world. And full of curiosity.

I found that something momentous was happening in my country. The government's mechanism of repression was weakening, but so were

Reprinted by permission from *The New York Times Magazine,* March 11, 1990. Copyright © 1990 by The New York Times Company.

the underground structures that Solidarity had built. In the Soviet Union, the system was beginning to twitch and slowly transform itself; the sharp anti-Communist, anti-Soviet rhetoric that had served Solidarity during the martial law era no longer sufficed to describe the world.

I remember clearly the discussions from this period, discussions about the very existence of Solidarity. It was clear that the political changes made by the Jaruzelski government were purely cosmetic, yet was it worth taking advantage of those changes to legalize certain elements of Solidarity and try to institute real change? Was it worth even keeping Solidarity alive when it was growing weaker by the day, turning into a caricature of the multimillion-strong mass movement of 1980–81?

Some were publicly abandoning the Solidarity banner, others were stubbornly clinging to it, insisting that it remain hidden underground. Still others—and they turned out to be right—were loudly chanting during street demonstrations that "there is no freedom without Solidarity." It was the eventual recognition of Solidarity's legal right to exist that led to the end of the military dictatorship and the opening of the road to democratic transformation. These people sensed that Solidarity could survive only as a living movement, visible to the eye of public opinion, not as an underground cult.

In the end, Solidarity, under the leadership of Lech Wałęsa, was able to fashion an open structure. This structure allowed Solidarity to confer a national political dimension on the workers' strikes of May and August 1988; to hold out until the Round Table discussions with the government the following February; and to find a compromise that eventually made possible the election of a non-Communist government. Thanks to that, Poland today is a different country. The breakthrough was possible because Solidarity leaders were able to interpret the meaning and scope of the changes taking place in the Soviet Union. They understood that these changes, far from cosmetic, were reflections of the deepest of all crises. The world has grown accustomed to associating these changes with Mikhail S. Gorbachev. For us, however, the proof of their authenticity was the return from exile of Andrei Sakharov.

I spoke only once with Sakharov. It was late evening, October 16, 1989. I remember it well; at midnight, I turned forty-three years old. Sakharov and his wife, Elena Bonner, were hospitable and warm. Sitting in their Moscow apartment, I felt I was speaking with old friends; we understood one another in half a word, half a smile. I felt that in a sense we had lived the last twenty years together, feeling the same hopes and disappointments, the same despair and determination.

· Elena Bonner, Lech Wałęsa, and Adam Michnik at the funeral of Andrei
Sakharov in Moscow, December 1989. (Photo: Sławomir Sierzputowski)

I thought about this two months later as I stood, Lech Wałęsa at my
side, over Sakharov's freshly dug grave. I thought about the role
Sakharov played in the history of the twentieth century and in my own
life. A great scholar, a renowned physicist who was named Hero of Socialist Labor an unprecedented three times, Sakharov belonged to the
most privileged class in Russia.

And yet he rejected it all to become the defender of human rights—
the defender of the man enslaved and humiliated by totalitarian dictatorship, of the free man who is clapped into prison, of the healthy man
who is thrown into a mental hospital, of the man hungry for truth who
is fed only the lies of official propaganda.

Sakharov taught us that human rights are the foundation of the civilized world, that the readiness to fight for those rights is the gauge of the
human worth of each one of us. The great anti-totalitarian revolution,
which inscribed on its banners the rights of man and engulfed like a fire
the countries of my native Europe, began with Andrei Sakharov.

Sakharov was consistent—he defended everyone. Workers and farmers, army deserters and emigrants, writers and painters, Jews and Tatars. He defended all those who needed defending. They called him "the conscience of Russia." And they were correct.

For Sakharov also personified another Russia: the noble Russia, free of chauvinism; the Russia of magnificent intelligence and great courage; the Russia friendly to the world, and to my country as well. That is why it was not only those who defended the totalitarian order—the apparatchik, the policeman, the lying propagandist—who criticized Sakharov in his own country. Certain anti-Communists also criticized him—those who wanted to replace the Communist ideology with the ideology of Greater Russian imperialism. He was denounced as a Western liberal, a naive humanist, a countryless cosmopolitan. Sakharov did not approve of any form of dictatorship—not the one fitted out in Communist ideology, or the one cloaked in anti-communism. He was a man of European democracy who wanted to disseminate European and democratic values in his own country.

One might say that Sakharov had placed himself firmly on one side of the great nineteenth-century Russian dispute between the Occidentalists and the Slavophiles, the dispute over whether Russia would follow the road of European democracy or evolve its own autocratic system, built on nationalist ideology and bolstered by the rites of the Orthodox Church. This dispute has been resurrected in contemporary Russia; indeed, it has become the country's most momentous struggle, and there are echoes of it to be found elsewhere in Eastern and Central Europe.

I believe it was in December 1979 that a group of Hungarians visited Warsaw, among them a tall, dark, slender philosopher with whom I talked the night away. We were more or less peers: readers of the same books, children of a similar system of values, both among the "illegitimate offspring" of the Twentieth Party Congress in 1956, when Khrushchev exposed Stalin's crimes and began the first attempt to reform the system he had built.

János Kis and I next met in 1989, this time in Budapest, at the ceremonial funeral of Imre Nagy and his assassinated comrades, the leaders of Hungary who had been executed after the 1956 uprising and were now, thirty-three years later, being honored at last. By then, Kis already had behind him years of work in underground publishing houses, and many excellent essays about politics and philosophy to his credit. He had become one of the most distinguished actors on the Hungarian intellectual and political scene and a leader of the Hungarian Alliance of Free Democrats.

Kis passed through all the stages typical of the Central European intellectual who in his youth had identified himself with the left. Leftist values—a rationalist and universalist perspective, a sensitivity to social injustice, opposition to xenophobia, spiritual nonconformism—have remained central to his thinking. Those values led him to join the Hungarian opposition and risk arrest.

It is not surprising that for the officials of the Communist party, including its "reform wing," Kis and his friends were the most dangerous of foes. Their Alliance of Free Democrats represents the political culture of liberal Europe. The Hungarian "constructive" opposition, by contrast, which came together in the Hungarian Democratic Forum, sought its roots in Hungary's national traditions, taking as a starting point the perilous situation of the Hungarian minority in neighboring Romania. By draping itself in the rhetoric of nationalism, the forum could find common ground with the reformers in the bosom of the Communist party itself.

The dispute between the Democratic Forum and Kis's Alliance of Free Democrats—which has become a central political rivalry in Hungary—is often described as a conflict between the left and the right. But it makes more sense to see it as the latest version of the struggle between the two great Hungarian historical traditions: the urbanists and the ruralists, the city and the countryside. We can see in these two parties two distinct sensibilities, two intellectual cultures, two spiritual identities.

We the people of Central Europe are rejecting communism for two broad reasons: because it is totalitarian and violates elementary human rights; and because it is foreign, brought here on Soviet bayonets, and thus is at odds with our sense of national tradition.

The second of these reasons has brought with it strong feelings of nationalism. Nationalism is the articulation of provincialism and particularism, a basis for xenophobia and intolerance. Nationalism is not only a political doctrine but also a technique of self-justification, a means to rid oneself of the suffocating feeling of responsibility for the years of cowardice, for all the indignities and humiliations.

Nationalism always leads to egoism and self-deception. To egoism, because it allows one to ignore the injuries suffered by other nations and disregard other peoples' values and ways of seeing. To self-deception, because by focusing on one's own injuries, nursing the memory of those injuries, nationalism allows one to ignore the injuries one has also inflicted.

Thus a member of the Hungarian Democratic Forum will take as the starting point of his political thought the misfortune the Hungarian nation has suffered. A man from the Alliance of Free Democrats, on the other hand, will try to view this misfortune in the wider context of Central Europe and infuse his concern for the fate of Hungarians with his belief in the right of every national community, every national minority, to a dignified and free life carried on within the standards of European democracy and in accordance with the Declaration of the Rights of Man.

Of course, the rejection of totalitarian communism must entail, to some extent, a return to the roots of national identity. This is precisely why one must ask what sort of roots they are and what sort of identity it is. For his part, Kis reaches for variants of liberal ideas and sets them against the various incarnations of the conservative right, who cloak themselves in religious-national traditions—presented as native traditions (as distinct from foreign ones, which deserve rejection). This inevitably leads to the cult of the strong state, governed by the elite.

Against this, János Kis strongly emphasizes his democratic option. He does not desire a return to the institutions and spiritual atmosphere of the interwar period. I think he simply desires, like so many of us, the return of his country to Europe.

For a long time, this idea of "a return to Europe" seemed to me somewhat exotic. For what does it mean? Europe is not only parliamentarism, civil liberties, the free market; it is also conflict over the shape of the welfare state and the scope of self-government. Europe is not only Mitterrand but also Le Pen; not only Weizsäcker but also the German Republican party. The idea of a return to Europe may carry with it a radical anti-Russian rhetoric (as it does for Milan Kundera, for example), but it can also stand for faith in the Europeanization of the entire eastern part of our continent, including Russia itself.

One can put it differently. The East European idea of a return to Europe means a commitment to certain attributes of European culture. It means replacing the totalitarian dogmas of communism with an attitude that presupposes a critical distance toward oneself, and it means respecting tolerance in public life and skepticism in intellectual endeavors.

Yet this does not mean that the Eastern European countries should simply copy the political and economic order of Western Europe. Indeed, they cannot. The Western European political arena was the product of bourgeois democracy, from the French Revolution to the present day. In Poland, that tradition was destroyed by the polymorphous Bolshevik Revolution, which also demolished the country's traditional social structure and economy. It is unclear what will arise in its place. It may be that the new Polish political arena will be a cross between Western Europe and the United States—two great parties or, rather, civil movements and all the riches of pluralism.

Václav Havel and I became acquainted during the summer of 1978 on White Mountain, in the Sudetenland of Czechoslovakia. We met illegally—the members of the Workers' Defense Committee and the members of Charter 77. I see clearly that sunny day, a table with a bench on a mountain path, Jacek Kuroń deep in conversation with Havel. We made a joint declaration then, on the tenth anniversary of the invasion of Czechoslovakia. We talked of starting some sort of joint publishing house.

Then Havel and other Czechoslovak friends were jailed, and we in Poland organized a church hunger strike in solidarity with them. Next came the Polish August of 1980, when the Solidarity mass movement reached its peak. During that time we took every opportunity to protest publicly about Havel and his imprisoned countrymen—until, on December 13, 1981, we found ourselves imprisoned.

It was years later that news of Havel's first press interview after his release filtered through to my prison cell. In it, he protested about his jailed Polish friends from the Workers' Defense Committee and Solidarity. And so it continued, by turns: arrests, protests, meetings in the mountains.

In Poland, everything happened more quickly. At the time the Round Table deliberations between Solidarity and the Communist regime were starting in Warsaw in February 1989, Havel was again on trial in Prague. A great wave of protests swept Poland, and no less than Mieczysław Rakowski, Poland's prime minister, made a point of attending the Warsaw premiere of Havel's play *Audience*. On that occasion, I myself climbed up on the stage and read a few thunderous words.

By August, we could travel to Czechoslovakia, not only as members of a legal Solidarity but as elected deputies to the Polish Parliament. Though the security services were still shadowing our friends, the police were by then afraid to come near us. We visited Havel in his beautiful little mountain home in Hradec.

Now we meet him as president of Czechoslovakia. He is a writer, a playwright, a man of ideas, author of the most penetrating diagnoses of the anti-totalitarian opposition of the last dozen or so years. His memorable essay, "The Power of the Powerless," was the best-formulated philosophy of the movement that succeeded in building a civil society in Central and Eastern Europe.

Judging by his biography, Havel has always been a man of political moderation. He never succumbed to the narcotic of Communist ideology, but neither did he shut himself up in a doctrinal anti-communism. The most precious values of Czechoslovak culture find expression in Havel's writings—the love of freedom and the respect for tradition, the humor and self-irony, the tolerance and unswayable integrity. He never resorted to anachronistic divisions of the left-right variety. In building the community of Charter 77, he was able to formulate his ideas in a new language that created a common ground for yesterday's antagonists. On that ground, an anti-totalitarian community was painstakingly constructed, a democratic polis in the world of oppressive dictatorship.

Today I can't help wondering: what gave those people the strength? What made it possible for Sakharov, Kis, Havel, to live for years the way they did live? Why did a great physicist, a distinguished philosopher, a famous writer and essayist abandon academic careers and sacrifice freedom, calm, and personal security for a seemingly hopeless battle against the Communist leviathan? Not one of them ever declared himself to be a man of religious calling or a politician. And yet, embroiling themselves in politics, they bore moral witness. And they prevailed over the political professionals of police dictatorships. How was that possible?

A striking characteristic of the totalitarian system is its peculiar coupling of human demoralization and mass depoliticizing. Consequently, battling this system requires a conscious appeal to morality and an inevitable involvement in politics. This is how the singular anti-political political movement emerged in Central and Eastern Europe—the Ten Commandments as political program, the backbone of a struggle led by a scientist, a man of letters, a philosopher.

In Poland it was the same, and yet different. For a long time it was the Church that voiced resistance to the state of bondage: Cardinal Stefan Wyszyński and, later, Pope John Paul II. And it was writers and philosophers who articulated the anti-totalitarian opposition: Miłosz and Herbert, Kołakowski and Konwicki. Among the principal leaders and creators of the politics of Solidarity were people of precisely that background: Geremek and Mazowiecki, Kuroń and Modzelewski.

And yet in Poland—from 1956 on—the fundamental lever of transformation was the workers' revolts. The product of the most important of those revolts—that of August 1980—was Lech Wałęsa. Wałęsa is a truly extraordinary product of Poland's plebeian history, the working-class leader of a millions-strong labor union, encompassing the entire nation. In him the cleverness of a peasant is combined with deep faith, a tough unyieldingness mixed with the balance and elasticity of a tightrope walker.

In Poland, too, the European spirit is struggling with the narrowly nationalist one. Wałęsa is a figure firmly in the middle of this struggle. He symbolizes a fusion of religious and nationalist sentiment and a rebellious, contentious spirituality, typical also of the milieu of the intellectual opposition. That is where his strength comes from, and he is using it to help create the new shape of Europe.

It is truly difficult to foresee what sort of Europe this will be. The process of reunifying Germany is already under way. For the Poles, this process will constitute a sort of test: Are they prepared to accept all the consequences that flow from the right of Germans to live in their own united country?

But it is also a test for the Germans: Are they ready to deal with their concerns over Poland in Warsaw and not in Moscow? German resistance to Polish participation in the two-plus-four conference that will arrange for reunification suggests that Chancellor Helmut Kohl yearns nostalgically for grand diplomacy in the style of Rapallo or Yalta. But Poles remember that from Rapallo a straight road led to the Ribbentrop-Molotov pact and the invasion and occupation of their country. That is why the Poles must be present when their case is negotiated. Their presence is also in the interest of European democracy.

But German reunification is only one question mark hanging over the future of Europe. The other is the Soviet Union. Who knows what will happen there now? Gorbachev and his team are facing new challenges: beyond the collapse of communism in Central Europe, there is the deep conflict of nationalities within the Soviet Union itself, the conservative apparatchiks' attack upon glasnost, the increasingly vehement criticism of Gorbachev's policies by the democratic sector, some of it now within the Soviet legislature—all this adds up to a crisis of dramatic proportions.

Already, there are many indications that Gorbachev's reform from above has reached its limit. The three fundamental tasks—reforming the economy, developing a new relationship with the nationalities, and transforming the system into a pluralistic democracy—seem impossible to achieve by those methods. As the tradition of Great Russian nationalism is increasingly consolidated, it is becoming ever clearer that the Soviet Union is facing enormous convulsions. It is difficult to foresee the consequence of these for Central Europe.

This is only one of the many unknowns facing our countries as they cast off the corset of totalitarianism. Among the many traps lying in wait, nationalist conflict is especially dangerous. It is easy to see Yugoslavia, with its proliferating internal conflicts, as a posttotalitarian Central Europe in miniature.

This European mosaic of nationalities could be swept by a conflagration of border conflicts. These are unhappy nations, nations that have lived for years in bondage and humiliation. Complexes and resentments can easily explode. Hatred breeds hatred, force breeds force. And that way lies the path of Balkanization of our "native Europe."

Spending some time recently in Toronto, at the invitation of Canada's Ukrainian community, I couldn't help observing the neighborhoods of that city—Ukrainian and Jewish neighborhoods, Polish and Chinese ones, which together made up a sort of precious alloy of differing nationalities and religions.

For me, a man from Central Europe in the last decade of the twentieth century, this was a valuable lesson. For now two roads lie open before my country and our newly freed neighbors: one road leads to border wars, the other to minimizing borders, reducing them to little more than road signs; one road leads to new barbed-wire fences, the other to a new order based on pluralism and tolerance; one road leads to nationalism and isolation, the other to a return to our "native Europe."

Sakharov, Havel, and Kis are signposts for the democratic camp in Central Europe, for those who did not accept the order of totalitarian communism and do not want to replace it with a new order based on tribal hatreds.

Every part of Central Europe has produced people who think this way. Now is the time for them to meet with one another and to talk. About what? About our common European home.

16

After the Revolution

Politics is the art of achieving political goals—of achieving what is possible in a given situation, that is, in a situation that has its conditions and its limits. In this respect, the ethical point of view, the consideration of what is good and what is bad, what is fair and what is unfair, what is honest and what is dishonest, is external to politics. An ethical action, like an unethical action, is usually analyzed by politicians purely in pragmatic terms. Does it lead toward the goal or does it lead away from it? Montaigne observed, in his famous polemic against Machiavelli, that if a politician rejects ethical norms it can make him untrustworthy, and sometimes deprive his political actions of effectiveness.

Politics and ethics belong to different worlds. Yet we, the men and the women of the anti-totalitarian opposition movements, have a different view of politics, and of our participation in it. The politics of those totalitarian regimes was, after all, an open attack on ourselves, on our freedom, on our dignity, on truth. The elementary reflex of defending those elementary values entangled us in politics, transformed people of culture into people of politics. Thus there was born the phenomenon of an artist or a humanist occupying the center of the political stage in our part of Europe. Thus there was created the political idea of building civil societies outside the totalitarian state (for example, the Workers' Defense Committee, or KOR), what György Konrád has called anti-political politics, what Václav Havel has described as politics based on the power of the powerless.

Reprinted by permission from *The New Republic,* July 2, 1990.

Now we are leaving totalitarianism behind. Our nations are shedding the fetters of dictatorship, spitting the gag of censorship. We are engaged in a great experiment of confrontation between the idea of politics based on the power of the powerless and a social reality that was shaped when politics was based on the power of the powerful. We have always announced that our politics will be carried out without violence, without hatred, without revenge. True to the Christian message of our culture, we have always distinguished between the sin and the sinners. We have always tried to behave according to this difference, and we are trying to behave like this now.

But we are encountering the resistance of the social fabric. We see acts of violence, we hear shouts of hatred, we come upon calls for revenge. Sometimes we feel like the sorcerer's apprentice, who released forces that he could not control. These aroused ambitions, these displays of belated courage, these intrigues and personal conflicts, these slanders, these accusations of embezzlements against any adversary, or of being secret agents or crypto-Communists—where do they come from? We look around and ask, Where does this taste for kicking those who are down come from, this ever-growing area of intolerance, this urge to imprison people of the ancien régime, this dream of vengeance, this chauvinism, this xenophobia, this egalitarian demagoguery proper to populism that conceals simple envy? Where does this return to the idea of a nationalist state come from? This explosion of hatred for everyone—for gypsies, for AIDS patients, for all who are different?

What is the mechanism behind this revival of hatred for adversaries in public life? we wonder with concern. And we wonder, after all, whether we are not all children of totalitarian communism, whether we do not all carry inside ourselves the habits, the customs, and the flaws of that system. The death of the Communist system does not mean the end of totalitarian habits. The carefully bred slave of communism did not die with the end of the Communist party's reign. Even the enemy of communism was often formed in the likeness of the system he was fighting.

We must reflect on what these new developments mean. The hateful chauvinism is a degenerate reaction to the human need for national identity and national sovereignty, a need that was beaten down by communism. The envious populism is a degenerate reaction to the human longing for a just social order. Into the place left empty by Communist ideology, these two fiends steal. Like a cancer attacking the fragile human organism, they attack the tender emerging organism of our pluralist European democracy and our normal market economy.

Let us recall that historically, in our region, nationalism mixed with populism produced fascism. The central contest of this period of transition from totalitarianism to democracy is not mainly a contest of parties or political programs but a contest of two cultures. It is best symbolized by the names of two outstanding Russian activists of the anti-Communist opposition, Andrei Sakharov and Igor Shafarevich. Sakharov was an exponent of the European tendency within Russian culture; he rejected communism because it trampled on human freedom and human dignity, because it was the dictatorship of the minority *nomenklatura* over the majority of society, and at the same time it persecuted all minorities in the Soviet Union. Shafarevich rejected communism because it was a system foreign to Russia, because he perceived it as a European creation brought to the Russian land by foreigners, and because it preached a godless ideology. So we are returned again to the fundamental dilemma that was formulated by Leszek Kołakowski many years ago. Is communism evil because it is atheist or because it is totalitarian? Do the Communists sin by not adhering to a doctrine, or did they stifle the very essence of human and national freedom?

The present period of transition from dictatorship to democracy must consist of a compromise among the main political forces. There must be a pact for democracy. The breaking of this pact makes public life brutal and introduces anarchy, and eventually chaos. And chaos cannot be reformed. Chaos leads inevitably to dictatorship.

Every revolution, bloody or not, has two phases. The first phase is defined by the struggle for freedom, the second by the struggle for power and revenge on the votaries of the ancien régime. The struggle for freedom is beautiful. Anyone who has taken part in this struggle has felt, almost physically, how everything that is best and most precious within him was awakened. Revenge has a different psychology. Its logic is implacable. First there is a purge of yesterday's adversaries, the partisans of the old regime. Then comes the purge of yesterday's fellow oppositionists, who now oppose the idea of revenge. Finally there is a purge of those who defend them. A psychology of vengeance and hatred develops. The mechanics of retaliation become unappeasable: witness the Jacobin terror and the Iranian revolution.

We inherited from the totalitarian era, like a birthmark, the conviction that wisdom is the same as permanent suspicion. Józef Tischner is right in saying that this is one of the most serious threats to democratic order in Poland. And yet contemporary Europe provides examples of countries that were able to stop after the first phase of the anti-dictatorial revolution, and thanks to that, they may now enjoy democratic order and wealth. Take Spain. Its transition from dictatorship to democracy demonstrates that a state can be built in which yesterday's political adversaries, the prisoners and their guards, do not lose their political identity, but can, and wish to, live next to each other in a common state, in a state in which they are able to respect the rules of pluralism, tolerance, and honest political struggle.

But we know, if only from looking into the mirror, or deep into our own hearts, how perverted we are by totalitarian communism. We lack democratic culture and democratic institutions. We lack the tradition of democratic coexistence in the framework of a democratic order. In Central and Eastern Europe, each of our countries has its distinct biography, its own secret knowledge about threats to democratic order.

I think of Poland. The Polish experience is well symbolized by Józef Piłsudski. Piłsudski was, in my view, the incarnation of the best Polish traditions of struggle for freedom and for independence. He was, after 1918, the first chief of the independent state, the guarantor of the first free parliamentary elections and of the passage of the most democratic constitution in Europe. He was also the guarantor of the first democratic election of the president of Poland, Gabriel Narutowicz. And he was witness to the moment when Poles suddenly lacked the sense of compromise, the moment when this first democratically elected president was murdered following a brutal campaign of hatred in the press and in the streets. Piłsudski retreated to Sulejówek, and the Polish Parliament proved incapable of creating a stable government. Three years later, in 1926, he returned to power at the point of a bayonet. The long and painful agony of Polish parliamentary democracy began.

In sum, the man who fought and won freedom for Poland, the father of Polish independence, also laid the foundation for dictatorship in Poland. He hurled abuses at parliamentarians and at Parliament; he offended political adversaries and was responsible for the shameful Brześć trials, in which some of his parliamentary opponents, on the left and the right, were imprisoned. The dramatic story of Piłsudski holds a dramatic warning for us. We must always bear in mind this fragment of our heritage of independence, this time when, without Communists and without Soviet advisers, we squandered our opportunity to build a democratic and lawful state.

An intellectual is pretty helpless in the face of these dangers: as a political man he must be efficient; as a man faithful to the ethical origin of his commitment he knows that he must abide by the truth. That is how we are, divided in two. We know how fragile are the bases of democratic order in Poland, and we know that to denounce continuously the slippages in our democracy will make it even more fragile. We face, in these circumstances, a peculiar conflict of loyalties. What is more important we ask ourselves, the fragile democratic order or the defenseless truth? None of us has a ready answer to the question of which of these two loyalties should prevail. We are doomed to inconsistency. We are doomed to live in a state of tension, uncertainty, permanent risk.

Still, it is not true that we know nothing. We are children of a certain tradition. And we know that this tradition does not permit us to renounce the truth with impunity. We are the children of our Judeo-Christian culture, and we know that this culture, which recommends loyalty toward the state, commands us to bend our knees only before God. We know, therefore, that we should put faithfulness to truth above participation in power. We know, by reaching for our roots, that the truth of politics resides, in the end, in the politics of truth; that every political order is polluted by the original sin of imperfection. We reject the belief in political utopia. We know that our future is an imperfect society, a society of ordinary people and ordinary conflicts—but, precisely for this reason, a society that must not renounce its ethical norms in the name of political illusions.

Yes, it is true that we are helpless before the many ethical traps of contemporary politics. It is then that we reach out for the truth of our own roots, for the ethics of the power of the powerless, or simply for the Ten Commandments. The rest is lies, and has the bitter taste of hypocrisy.

17

My Vote against Wałęsa

This is a strictly personal reflection.

I feel obliged to publish it for the sake of all those who do not understand what has happened, and whose message of anxiety and solidarity has been reaching me over the last few months.[1]

My primary feeling is one of embarrassment. The divorce within Solidarity was an ugly event. Instead of an open discussion of ideas, we got opaque insinuations and arguments about symbols.

The conflict over the Solidarność logo epitomized a more general disagreement concerning the shape of Polish public life, the kind of political culture we should adopt, and the future of our country. Principles, rather than details, were the issue, and the split within Solidarity became unavoidable. The process, which had started with the annexation of the right to use the Solidarność logo, ended with the transformation of union structures into vehicles for Lech Wałęsa's election. One can hardly help feeling bitter about this.

The Solidarność logo is of great emotional value to people who were faithful to Solidarity for the last ten years, and who now find it difficult to part with it. These people printed the logo in underground pam-

Reprinted by permission from *The New York Review of Books*, December 20, 1990. Copyright © 1990 Nyrev, Inc.

1. Michnik refers here to the demand in spring 1990 by Lech Wałęsa that *Gazeta Wyborcza* no longer use the Solidarność logo. This demand was made after *Gazeta Wyborcza* failed to give full support to Wałęsa. Michnik and his fellow editors acceded to the demand after it was endorsed by Solidarity's National Committee in September 1990.

phlets, scrawled it on city walls, and chanted the word in street demonstrations. Many Solidarność badges have been torn out of lapels and sweaters by the riot police and the secret police, but people who wore them remained faithful to those familiar letters, despite persecution and prison sentences. For them, it meant the logo of hope and trust in a better, democratic, independent, and just Poland.

This logo has now been transformed by the majority of the Solidarity Trade Union's leadership into an instrument of blackmail and a censor's stamp. From now on, editors of all newspapers that display the logo in their masthead will know what articles they should avoid. When I realized this, I was relieved at my colleagues' decision to remove the slogan "There is no freedom without Solidarity" from *Gazeta Wyborcza*'s masthead. I feel no solidarity whatsoever with those who will turn a symbol of freedom and hope into a sign of opportunism and a tool for silencing people.

What was the charge against us? The resolution of Solidarity's National Committee defined it all too clearly: we criticized Lech Wałęsa.

I may not have met all those who voted in favor of the resolution, but I pity them all. Impoverishment of the mind and spirit will always surface, sooner or later. I also congratulate Lech Wałęsa on such allies in his struggle for the Belvedere Palace [the president's office]. He is getting what he asked for.

Campaigning at the Warsaw Steelworks, Wałęsa answered a question concerning the future of the newspapers that criticize him today: "Let them make these newspapers flourish," he said, "and then you will come in and take them over." The statement was later interpreted by Wałęsa's press spokesman to mean: "Yes, democracy will take them over. New political forces will emerge from the election, and they will need their own press and media, which leaves them with one option: either they set up new ones, or they take over the existing ones from those who have been politically defeated."

I never expected Wałęsa and his spokesman to utter such a compact definition of the Bolshevik line of reasoning.

I have always openly admired Wałęsa's political acumen. I truly respected his strategy during the difficult martial law period. And I supported that strategy of persistence and common sense by being one of Wałęsa's collaborators. His policy was both cautious and courageous. And, above all else, it was effective, and enriched by a remarkable instinct.

Our roads have since parted. We now represent diverse points of view. But I would still like to believe that an argument about ideas, rather than an exchange of insinuations, is possible between us. It would be very bad if what was once a friendship turned into venomous hatred.

Lech Wałęsa, my political opponent of today, is an outstanding politician. I believe that if you cannot pay due respect to your opponent, you will never be able to win respect for yourself.

I like many things about Wałęsa. I like his sense of humor, I admire his intuition and political savvy, and I admit that he played an outstanding role in our war with the Communist order. Therefore, it saddens me to see the chairman of the Solidarity Trade Union and Nobel Prize laureate waste the unique Polish opportunity, destroy his own good image and that of our country in the eyes of the world. It is painful for me to observe Wałęsa's evolution from the symbol of Polish democracy to its present grotesque caricature. The decision to deprive *Gazeta Wyborcza* of the Solidarność logo for criticizing Wałęsa was the first shibboleth of what will happen to Polish democracy when these people reach for state power. It also summarized Wałęsa's own concept of democracy.

Wałęsa wants to be president, and I do not blame him for this ambition. It worries me, however, that he wants to be an "axe-wielding" president who rules by decree and who likens democracy to a driver's control over a car. "Now that we are changing the system, we need a president with an axe: a firm, shrewd, and simple man, who does not beat around the bush." These are Wałęsa's words. What worries me more than his words, however, is that he treats Solidarity as an instrument for the fulfillment of his own personal ambitions. It is also the confidence with which he announces that he will win at least 80 percent of the votes in the compulsory, open election that he demands. And his threats of a street revolt. It also worries me that he always speaks about himself, and never mentions his program. In conclusion: it worries me that Wałęsa will use any means to get into the Belvedere Palace.

As Solidarity chairman, he has proposed no program for the trade union in periods of austerity. During the last year, we have not heard a single word from Wałęsa on the union's role or activity in the process of transition to a market economy, on methods for defending the interests of the working class, or on ways to deal with unemployment.

Instead, we have repeatedly been told that Solidarity had to split. Eventually, Wałęsa came and split it. He got rid of all those capable of opposing him and barring his way. In order to remove them, he considered it useful to describe them publicly as "eggheads" and "Jews."

I can understand Lech Wałęsa's motivation. His ambitions have not been fulfilled. Twice, he refused to compete for high political posts; he would not run for either house of the Parliament; nor did he attempt to become prime minister. In my opinion, he has always been driven by one motive: a certain vision of himself in public life. Wałęsa's political ideal is that of a special place: ultimate power without responsibility. His concept of the presidency is to rule, and to defer all responsibility to the prime minister, the cabinet, and all the other government elite.

This concept is far from surprising: Wałęsa has always been a charismatic leader who would not respect a statute or a program, acting as if he did not understand the rules of democratic procedures. In August 1980, his ignorance was justified. Later, during martial law, Wałęsa decided that he did not need any understanding of those procedures. It may have been this decision, and his charisma, that made Wałęsa such a good leader during that period.

What is the nature of charismatic power? Charisma is the ability to control people's emotions. Emotional subordination and the acknowledgment of a leader's special abilities and talents create a special relationship between the leader and the ordinary man. The ordinary man's blind trust in his leader makes him obedient. In the ordinary man's opinion, the leader knows best what to do in any situation. The leader's power is subject to no restrictions or regulations. His qualifications and competence become unimportant. So does the law. What becomes important are the random decisions of the charismatic leader.

This leader emerges from the void of a destroyed political stage, marked by the lack of, or the sudden surge of, hope; he is the result of a collective dream and of the desire for a new myth. He may be a prophet, a popular leader, or a street demagogue. He epitomizes the myth of the just, invincible leader. He evokes admiration and awe.

Charismatic authority is inherent in the most revolutionary historical processes: it helps to overcome fear and apathy, to destroy traditional order, and to overthrow old governments, whether monarchies or foreign occupations. Once victorious, this authority becomes domineering and anti-democratic; it towers above the people. Born out of collective hope for a free, dignified life, it leads toward a new dictatorship. The faith in the charismatic leader's infallibility becomes the subject's duty. The leader and his team demand that the faith be completed with voluntary acts of submission. A refusal to perform them is subsequently treated as a felony, a crime, and as high treason.

This is when a charismatic authority begins to wane. Such a leader, endowed with "divine grace," proves unable to work wonders. But it is too late for the people to change anything: the leader has lost his charisma but has kept the police. His team, chosen according to the principle of obedience rather than for professional qualifications, will not hesitate to use force to defend its power. The history of revolutions confirms this pattern, from Cromwell, through Lenin, down to Khomeini.

The myth of a charismatic leader collapses as soon as people lose faith in his supernatural power and denounce their own blind obedience. This history of revolutions teaches that the sooner the light dawns, the greater a nation's chance to save its freedom and stability of order.

A victorious charismatic leader becomes pathologically jealous of his power and popularity. He also becomes suspicious, sensing enemies and plots all around him. In order to get rid of rivals, that is, of ordinary democratic mechanisms, he will promise anything to one and all, and he will not discuss political programs: he himself becomes his own program. He always talks about himself, his merits and congenial achievements, describing his plans in the most scant and general terms. He promises accelerations: fast improvement for everyone.

Lech Wałęsa will not be president of a democratic Poland.

He may lose in the general presidential election. Judging by his boastful declarations, the Solidarity Trade Union chairman may have too little to offer, apart from himself and a flood of contradictory promises. How does the "just division of Polish property" he promises agree with the demand he makes for "accelerated privatization"? Or the promised, instantaneous end to unemployment with the necessity to launch market mechanisms? And can his promise of doling out millions of złoty to individual people be taken seriously?

Wałęsa may also win the presidential election, but even if he does, he will not be president of a democratic Poland. Rather, he will become a destabilizing factor, creating chaos and isolating Poland from the rest of the world. Wałęsa said:

I do not favor classic concepts of the presidency, neither the French, the Italian, nor the American models. I will do it my way. I want to surprise everyone. My model is not wine drinking and dinners; it is a "flying Dutchman" who travels around the country and intervenes wherever necessary. There will be too much of Wałęsa, and this is why so many are afraid.

Wałęsa may win the election if he manages to maintain his image of "the father of the nation." A father is free to get drunk and beat up his wife, but his children are not allowed to raise their voices or hands against him. If this myth paralyzes Polish minds and hearts, Wałęsa will win. He will win, even though he openly declares that he needs democracy only as a tool that allows him to grab the rudder of rule. I am afraid that once he grabs hold of it, all that will remain of democracy will be his own decrees.

Wałęsa's merits and virtues are unquestionable: as a politician, he is wonderfully sensitive to public feelings and extremely gifted in the game of politics. Millions of people associate his name with the end of communism. However, this excellent politician apparently ignores the fact that the era of charismatic leaders is past. Today, charisma can only serve destruction.

Some features of Wałęsa's character that made him a great leader of the several-million-strong Solidarity movement disqualify him as a president of a democratic state. Wałęsa is unpredictable. Wałęsa is irresponsible. He is incompetent. And he is also incapable of reform.

Wałęsa's unpredictability was an asset in the struggle against totalitarian communism. But it spells disaster in the democratic structures of a modern state. His irresponsibility was a by-product of opposition and underground activity: if you cannot influence the state, you take no responsibility for it.

Wałęsa cannot learn from his own errors because he is deeply convinced that he commits none.

Finally, Wałęsa's opinions on the economy and foreign policy are paralyzing and horrific in their absurdity. Not only to Poles. Some foreigners who have met with him feel the same.

Lech was once a Polish and an international myth. The memory of the U.S. Congress applauding the Solidarity leader is vivid in my mind. Wałęsa's speech in front of Congress was an excellent, inspired lecture on the Polish effort toward freedom. He has destroyed this myth through his own appearances over the last few months.

A leader's personality is his own business. Lech Wałęsa has always been egocentric, but we learned to live with it. But now, the situation has completely changed.

Wałęsa believes that whatever is good for him is also good for Poland. And for a time, I agreed with him. And for a time, it probably was true. But not any longer. Wałęsa's presidential ambitions have had a catastrophic influence on Poland. He has introduced a new, brutal language into the public debate. Wałęsa said:

This is a scandal! This government will be brought to trial, I am saying it even now: it will be brought to trial for destroying documents, for helping the Communists make themselves comfortable, for robbing Poland—it must be prosecuted, and prosecuted it will be, in due time. Because it has failed in its duty.

This kind of language is a magnet for all those who are frustrated, who are driven by personal ambitions, and who lust after power. Toward his critics, Wałęsa adopts a patronizing, supercilious tone. He promises them that "Warsaw will be aired out." He promises to become the springboard for truly Napoleonic careers. He has already started to distribute ministerial posts and other public offices. Promises, promises. To each man according to his ambitions—is this not the true meaning of Wałęsa's "personal revolution"?

Lech Wałęsa—and I am saying this on the basis of a close personal acquaintance—has never been a populist or an anti-Semite. Populism and anti-Semitism were both idiotic doctrines to him. However, by preaching nonsense about "eggheads," and by dividing people according to a racial criterion into Jews and non-Jews, he has appealed to followers of anti-intellectual populism and anti-Semitic phobias. These people will now support Wałęsa's ascent to the presidency.

Wałęsa says, "I am a pure Pole, born here," by which he implies that some other Poles are "not pure," and were born elsewhere.

Criticizing some unfavorable opinions of the Western press, Wałęsa says that "some people's tentacles reach far." Doesn't this lingo of obsessions and insinuations sound familiar?

Poland is not the only issue here. Poland is the most developed example of the process that we see in all post-Communist countries. Democratic institutions are not deeply rooted, the economic situation is very difficult, great expectations have been aroused, and the procedures used for resolving conflicts have not been really tested. So stabilization is fragile.

The evolution from a totalitarian system to a democratic order is unprecedented and unprecedentedly painful. Great hopes generate enormous frustration. Many people do not understand that the reconstruction of a democratic state and a market economy must have its own consequence in the form of new work standards, new prices, and the bankruptcy of unprofitable businesses. The breakdown of the standards and ideas characteristic of the era of communism and anti-Communist opposition has not been accompanied by the swift approval of new ideas typical of democratic systems. The picture of the world becomes dim and shaky. This is the ideal time for demogogy. Demagogy that aggressively attacks the government may be successful, which must lead to

Meeting on the Czechoslovak-Polish border, March 1990. Seated, from left:
Lech Wałęsa, Jan Stachowski (translator), and Václav Havel; standing:
Adam Michnik and Zbigniew Bujak. (Photo: Krzysztof Miller)

destabilization. Destabilization in turn elicits chaos. Chaos generates a
new poverty and a new dictatorship.

Make no mistake: all post-Communist countries will have to face this.
Everywhere, in Russia and in Czechoslovakia, in Hungary and Romania,
the phantoms from the past awaken: movements that combine populism, xenophobia, personality cults, and a vision of the world ruled by
a conspiracy of Freemasons and Jews. A great danger to the democratic
order comes from this direction.

We all must take care of democracy. This is what democracy's success
is based on in Portugal, Spain, Greece, and Chile. And it seemed to be
the basis for the success of Poland's democracy after the creation of
Tadeusz Mazowiecki's government. It seemed that all major political
forces would unite in support—even critical support—of the government of national hope; that the period of this interim government,
which would end with parliamentary and presidential elections, would
be a time of compromise and concord. It was a condition and a chance
for political and economic reforms, as well as for a new foreign policy.

The reality was different. Wałęsa broke up Solidarity's camp and declared "war on the top," and that upset the internal compromise among

Poles. A substantial debate was replaced by noisy rhetoric typical of an election campaign. Now, we face another choice: What kind of Poland do we want?

Observers from Western Europe and the United States have adopted a wait-and-see policy toward post-Communist Europe. The initial euphoria has been replaced with concern. Where are these countries heading? Are they really returning to Europe, or to the old world of populistic dictatorships, intertribal conflicts, and permanent destabilization? The harm done by Wałęsa to the Polish cause through his utterances is based on this: on giving the impression of a country which is not stable, which is torn by constant conflicts.

I think—and I tell Western journalists—that this picture is false and simplistic; that the small, noisy, and aggressive minority is not typical of Poland. To prove that, however, it is not enough to repeat that Poles are by nature tolerant and are the victims of nasty slander coming from an internationally hatched plot. We must speak out loudly about this sick marginal group; we must oppose this syndrome of populism, authoritarianism, and xenophobia that produces terror.

What path do we wish to follow? Is it a path to the Europe of contemporary, democratic standards, or, on the contrary, a path of return to bygone traditions symbolized by authoritarian regimes, the hell of national conflicts, and extreme cases of religious intolerance? The position of Poles in Europe depends on the answer to this question.

I have given a good deal of thought to whether I should write this text. I must make the assumption that I will be misunderstood and that the meanest of intentions will be ascribed to me.

I have the feeling, however, that I must not be silent any longer. Readers may claim that I am wrong, but I must be sure that I have written everything that I have come to believe by honest reasoning. This leads me to say that Lech Wałęsa's presidency may be catastrophic for Poland. It may be the first case of a Peronist-type presidency in Central Europe, where only the shreds of a beautiful pennant, sacrificed to the absolute thirst for power by Solidarity's leader, remain from the hopes for a national revival. If I had left this warning unstated, I would have felt like a participant in a lie dictated by my own personal comfort.

I do not attribute any ill will to Wałęsa. I do accuse him, however, of a complete lack of imagination and knowledge of a democratic state ruled by law. Wałęsa's style of political action, which was his power during strikes and in the setting of covert activity, has become a dangerous trap in the era of building a democratic order. The same behavior that used to destabilize a totalitarian order must now lead to the destruction of the political culture of the young democracy. A charismatic leader will suppress all independent reactions with an appalling intuition, until he breaks the fragile Polish democracy.

We must listen very carefully to what Solidarity's leader says today. We must listen to his threats and promises. Because, perhaps unintentionally, Lech Wałęsa clearly promises neglect of the law and democratic procedures, revenge on his political opponents, unprofessional ideas, and rule by incompetent people. I believe that television should show each one of Wałęsa's public speeches several times, with no cuts. Everyone must know what he is choosing when he casts his vote in the presidential elections, so he will not be able to excuse himself later on with a lack of information.

Lech Wałęsa is a politician with a great talent for setting people at odds, and that is why he is so dangerous. His great merits will change into their opposites. They will become a curse for Poland. That is why I will not vote for Lech Wałęsa.

The expropriation of the Solidarność logo by Lech Wałęsa is a sign. A sign of the end of Solidarity. Solidarity used to be the essence of my life. I believed that the path to an independent Poland led through it. I would ask myself a single question: What is Poland going to be? And I would answer, in November 1980:

A self-governing, tolerant, colorful Poland, based on Christian values, and socially just. A Poland that is friendly toward its neighbors; a Poland, let us repeat this, that is able to compromise and act with restraint, to be realistic and loyal in partnership, but unable to tolerate slavery, unable to accept spiritual subordination. A Poland full of conflicts, which are natural for modern societies, but also full of the principle of solidarity. A Poland where intellectuals protect persecuted workers, and workers' strikes demand freedom for the culture. A Poland that speaks of itself with pathos and derision; that has been conquered many times but never subdued, defeated many times but never crushed. A Poland that has regained its identity, its language, its face. . . .

I believed that Solidarity, in spite of its internal differences, would be able to remain united in the name of all that was universal and essential. Today, I feel defeated.

The idea of Solidarity has entered its final stage. For its death Lech Wałęsa is responsible. I will remain a Solidarity man until the end of my days. But the logo that was with me for ten years I now lay beside my most personal mementos. Next to copies of court sentences, or the books I wrote in prison. I do not want to hide the pain I feel. I do not wish, and have never wished, to support myself with the symbol that now stands for power and authority. I wore this emblem when it brought prison sentences; I do not want to wear it when it promises privilege. I sense this as a moment of trial—now we will find out what each of us is worth—without a symbol.

PART THREE

Speeches and Conversations

18

Poland and the Jews

I would like to confess to having a certain problem. What should a Pole who has never hidden his Jewish origins say to express his gratitude, and his reasons for accepting this great distinction?

During my entire life, I was, and I wanted to be, a Pole in the eyes of foreigners. That is how I always presented myself, here in the States, in Europe, and in Israel. In all the documents I have had to fill out, in the space for nationality I have always put down "Polish." At the same time, whenever the malignant shadow of anti-Semitism loomed over Polish public life, I clearly and unequivocally acknowledged my Jewish origins and my grandparents' membership in the Jewish nation. As a Pole, so far as anti-Semites were concerned, I always wanted to be a Jew. And I believe that I will have sufficient courage always to be a Jew for the anti-Semites.

I think about how to be a Pole of Jewish origin today, after the Holocaust was carried out on Polish land — the land that the Nazi executioners selected to be the cemetery of the Jewish nation. How can one be a Pole of Jewish origin in the country that lived through the pogrom against Jews at Kielce in 1946, the anti-Semitic excesses in 1956, the anti-Semitic campaign orchestrated by the Communist government in 1968,

Reprinted by permission from *The New York Review of Books,* May 30, 1991. Copyright © 1991 Nyrev, Inc. Given as an address in April 1991 at Central Synagogue in New York, on receiving the Shofar Award "for leadership on behalf of justice, equality, and commitment to the rights of the individual according to the finest tradition of Judaism and the Jewish people."

and, finally, the wounding anti-Semitic rhetoric of the last presidential campaign?

This is not the place to analyze the complexity of Polish-Jewish relations. Nor is it the place to remember that Poland sheltered multitudes of Jews for centuries. Or the place for a subtle analysis of the awakening of the national consciousness of both Poles and Jews, and the nationalism and chauvinism that were the pathologies of this consciousness and led to the transformation from coexistence between Poles and Jews to conflict.

Finally, this is not the place to remember the sad facts of the Second Polish Republic between 1918 and 1939, when so many Polish citizens of Jewish origin were mistreated and humiliated in the so-called classroom ghettos of the universities and the hate-filled campaign conducted by anti-Semitic factions of the Polish public.

However, it must be remembered that already then, during that noisy campaign, what was at stake was not merely Polish-Jewish relations. The brutal campaign against the first president of the Second Republic, Gabriel Narutowicz, accused him of relying on the support of Jewish political parties. It ended in his murder in 1922, revealing that the organized anti-Semites, who blamed Jews for every Polish misery and incited hatred and xenophobia, were in fact making an assault on Polish democracy and its representatives.

The murder of President Narutowicz was the Polish equivalent of the Dreyfus affair. What was at stake here, as in France at the turn of the century, was not only relations between the two nationalities but the shape of the state and the nation. In both France and Poland the question was whether the nation was to be open and the state tolerant and multicultural, or whether the state was to be based on authoritarian principles and nationalistic doctrine. And I think this has been the central question ever since. Whenever the shadow of anti-Semitism arose in Polish public life, it was an unmistakable signal that people with antidemocratic, intolerant views were on the political offensive.

Today Poland is a country without Jews; and when anti-Semitic opinions are expressed in Poland, Jews are not the issue, whatever the authors of the opinions themselves may think. The question is whether there will or will not be a Polish democracy.

Last year, two prominent Poles, heroes of the Polish wartime resistance movement, Jan Nowak-Jeziorański and Jan Karski, publicly opposed the common Polish practice of digging into people's family history and classifying them by racial criteria. Their strong statement had far-reaching implications, and not only for Polish-Jewish relations. Theirs

was the mature voice of that most beautiful of Polish historical traditions—the tradition of an open, tolerant society, a multinational commonwealth which did not burn its heretics.

What is anti-Semitism in today's Poland? First of all, it is not unique.
Aggressive anti-Semitic slogans can be heard today in Prague and
Bratislava, in Russia and the Ukraine, in Hungary and in Romania. All
these voices have a double edge. Each is a manifestation not merely of
hatred of Jews but simply of hostility toward the fundamental standards
of European democracy. Anti-Semitism has become a code and a common language for people who are dreaming of a nationally pure and politically disciplined state—a state without people who are "different" and
without a free opposition.

The explosions of anti-Semitic xenophobia in my country have recently provoked uneasiness and protest on the part of the most respected
and distinguished representatives of Polish culture as well as the Catholic
Church episcopate and the president of the republic. The episcopate issued a special bishops' letter in which—for the first time in the history of
the Catholic Church in Poland—anti-Semitism was unequivocally condemned. President Lech Wałęsa established a special council for Polish-
Jewish relations. Clearly, these acts and initiatives, deserving as they are
of support, do not solve the problem. For—I will repeat—the issue at
this late date is not Polish-Jewish relations; the issue is the plague of anti-
Semitism, which, though it only touches the margins of Polish public
life, has, as we know from history, the tendency to spread.

Anti-Semitism is like a malignant virus which first implants itself in
one cell in order to poison and kill the entire organism. What characterizes this kind of anti-Semitism is a strange fascination with blood and
heredity, a morbid interest in the racial background of grandfathers and
great-grandfathers. The attempt is, once again, independently of historical truth and the demands of logic, to divide Polish citizens, or citizens
of any country, into the better, the "real" ones, and the worse—those infected by Jewish blood.

That is why the habit of ascribing Jewish forebears to political enemies has become a grotesque and tragic part of the political debate in
post-Communist countries. One must discuss all this with utter openness and have the courage to call the disease by its proper name. I can assure you that in Poland there are many people who have such courage—
there are in fact large numbers of them. I'll say more: these are the
people who create the authentic cultural values of Polish democracy and
make up its spiritual core.

Relations between Poles and Jews are still burdened by two stereotypes—one Polish and the other Jewish. According to the Polish stereotype, there has never been any anti-Semitism in Poland, and the Jews were never so well-off as they were there. In this stereotype, each critical voice condemning anti-Semitism is considered an expression of the anti-Polish conspiracy on the part of international forces who are filled with hatred for Poland. There is also a Jewish stereotype, which says that each Pole imbibes anti-Semitism with his mother's milk; that Poles share the responsibility for the Holocaust; that the only thing worth knowing about Poland is just that—that Poles hate Jews.

The Polish stereotype produces among Jews, even Jews well disposed toward Poland, an instinctive dislike of Poles. This stereotype makes any calm and clarifying debate on the history of Polish anti-Semitism impossible. On the other hand, the Jewish stereotype immediately arouses a sort of "secondary anti-Semitism" among Poles, because people who are completely free of anti-Semitic phobias feel accused of sins they've never committed. And having been accused of being natural anti-Semites, they feel hurt and perceive ill will on the part of Jews; and such feelings tend to preclude an honest dialogue with Jews about the past and the future.

It isn't easy for me to talk about all this, because my judgment is far from impartial. Because of my own past—as a Pole of Jewish origin, engaged from early youth in the democratic opposition, fighting for the freedom of Poland and of each human being—I have always perceived anti-Semitism as a form of anti-Polonism; and, listening to Jewish accusations of Polish anti-Semitism, I've always felt solidarity with the great part of Polish public opinion that in every historical period was capable of opposing clearly, bravely, and unambiguously the successive campaigns of hatred.

Among my friends one thing was always clear: anti-Semitism is the name of hatred. But it was also clear to us that the stubborn categorization of Poland as an anti-Semitic nation was used in Europe and America as an alibi for the betrayal of Poland at Yalta. The nation so categorized was seen as unworthy of sympathy, or of help, or of compassion. That is why, for years and decades, we have stubbornly explained that anti-Semitic pathology doesn't define Poland, just as Le Pen doesn't define France, the John Birch Society doesn't define America, the Black Hundreds don't define Russia, and extreme Israeli chauvinism doesn't define the state of Israel.

In the history of the relations between Poles and Jews, there have been better and worse phases. People have been injured and crimes have occurred. One must speak and write about all this honestly, and today, in a Poland free of censorship and police rule, we have every possibility of doing so. Such public debate will in my view contribute to creating a more real picture and to breaking through the stereotypes on both sides. I'll never reconcile myself to the use of the label of anti-Semitism in order to smear the nation that, in 1939, was the first to say "no" to Nazism, the nation that, squeezed between two bandits, Hitler and Stalin, chose to make a tenacious fight for freedom; the nation whose citizens have had so many trees planted in the Holocaust Memorial in Yad Vashem in Jerusalem. That is why I perceive labels of this kind as a personal insult. And it is why I'll never reconcile myself to Polish anti-Semites gaining legitimacy by claiming to defend the honor of all Poles, whereas it is precisely they, the Polish anti-Semites, who besmirch Poland's good name.

For I am convinced that the practice of assigning collective national responsibility for the sins or crimes committed by individuals or political groups always serves to justify those very groups and individuals. Whoever says that all Poles are anti-Semites helps to justify actual anti-Semitism. It is well known, after all, that wherever everyone is guilty, no one is guilty.

I am a Pole. I must explain now why I accepted an award created for Jews. I accepted it in the name of solidarity—solidarity with the ashes of the murdered millions, among them my entire family. Those people weren't asked about their national background or identity. They were killed as Jews, because that is how they were categorized in the headquarters of Nazi anti-Semites. And this I must not forget. If I denied my origins, I'd feel like a person spitting on the ashes of the murdered.

And yet, I feel solidarity with something more than just the ashes of my murdered grandparents. I am not speaking of solidarity with Jewish history or with the Jewish religion, or Jewish traditions or customs, or with the Jewish nation, or the state of Israel. With what then? When I look for words to describe this complicated and intimate feeling, what comes to my mind is solidarity with the Jewish fate. The Jewish fate is the fate of a threatened people who have suffered many blows, who know the taste of humiliation, of defeat, and who have always faced hard choices. It is finally the fate of people who have been rejected and persecuted.

In other words, the Jewish fate is a certain condition, and if that condition is not understood, contemporary civilization, contemporary spiritual life, and contemporary ethics would be poorer in something essential. And it is just from this perspective, the perspective of a descendant of Holocaust victims, that I look at my country, at Poland. The Polish nation has built into its history the idea of a tolerant country—and it also has in its history the idea of itself as a wholly Catholic state. Today, these two ideas are set against each other. Right now, the argument about the shape of Poland cuts across all the political camps, all milieus, generations, and social classes. It also cuts across the members of the Catholic Church and the members of Solidarity. In its essence, it is an argument about the meaning of Polishness and of a democratic order.

I accept this award as one of those who are for a tolerant state, a state in which there is room for many cultures, many different personal histories, and many points of view. I am for a country that will create a stable democracy; for an open society that will be able to protect itself against the invasion of barbaric hatred. Anti-Semitism is always the language of such hatred.

I speak for a therapy that will emerge from the effort to understand the disease. Such therapy, a permanent therapy, is what all countries need today. Hatred of another nation is always the sign of barbaric intolerance. Whoever mouths judgments that justify a general hatred of Jews or Poles, of Russians or Lithuanians, of Arabs or Kurds, is constructing the world on the model of hatred. And such a person will certainly fulfill the paradoxical biblical prophecy of Saint Paul: "The good that I would, I do not: but the evil that I would not, that I do." A great Polish poet noted somewhere during the dark days of the Nazi occupation that just when a man thinks he can do nothing is when he can do the most.

I have a feeling that we can challenge hatred; and I accept this award as an encouragement to have the courage to oppose hatred.

19

Poland and Germany

Relations between Poland and Germany will determine the shape of a sizable segment of the future map of Europe. Various opinions about these relations and the future of Europe in the context of these relations will be forthcoming. A diplomat will have one opinion, a politician another, and an economist yet another. The diplomat will talk about the new architecture of the European continent. He will ask whether a coalition has become possible on the Continent now that the Berlin wall has come down, now that communism has collapsed and the Warsaw Pact has been dissolved, now that the cold war is really over. The politician will consider the dynamics of relations between states and the search for the common ground where mutual interests undergo a qualitative transformation into a political partnership. The economist will be concerned with reciprocal economic relations.

I want to appear in a different role. I am a Pole, a historian, and a journalist, and as such I am interested in Polish-German problems concerning memory. I want to consider what I remember as a Pole, what I have in the back of my mind when I find myself in a German city and, together with you, think about the future. My memory is selective; above all, I remember the occupation. Of course, I have no personal recollection, because I was born after the end of the war. From my early childhood, however, I was taught what fascism was and at every step I encountered its victims. As a Polish historian and journalist I must also ask

Speech given in Munich, July 1991.

myself what I don't remember even though I have a duty to do so. Here, in a German city, I have a duty to remember the Scholl family and all those other Germans who mounted a heroic resistance to fascism; to remember the few who risked their lives and the lives of their loved ones to express their opposition to the inhuman Hitlerite dictatorship. It so happened that I, living under a dictatorship, albeit one that was incomparably milder and less oppressive, in observing my surroundings began to understand the drama of German anti-fascists like Dietrich Bonhoeffer, Thomas Mann, and Hermann Rauschning. Also, the drama of resistance carried out in isolation, against one's own people at a time when the oppressive regime enjoyed full recognition from the international community.

I tried to look at the situation of a German oppositionist from a German perspective, and it still seems to me that this situation constitutes an existential challenge for every contemporary European—for fascism, its barbaric aggression against other countries, and the dreadful result of this aggression, the Holocaust, will never be eradicated from the history of contemporary European freedom. We shall continue to live with the Holocaust, and we shall continue to return to it in every serious conversation between ourselves. Every attempt to consign it to oblivion, to my mind, opens the way to new hatreds and a new dictatorship.

Nevertheless, it seems to me that the German lesson is interesting for yet another reason. Namely, the people of post-Communist Europe are interested in how the Germans coped with building a democratic order and with the whole complex issue of German guilt. Today, although the scale and situation are different, we face similar problems, and we want to learn from your experience of building democracy.

As a Pole, the offspring of victims of the Holocaust, a citizen of a country that was horribly and irreparably wronged by German fascism, I also have a duty to remember the suffering that occurred in my country after the end of the war. For decades, my generation was protected from this knowledge. Every reference to the suffering of the Germans forced out of Poland was defined as fascist propaganda. I remember the psychological shock I experienced when reading Günter Grass's *The Tin Drum,* where I learned for the first time, from a credible witness, what it had really been like. I felt that in some way I was guilty for my ignorance about the fate of those people who were punished collectively, who were ordered to pack the possessions accumulated over generations into two suitcases and were transported out of their native land. I don't feel guilty about the fact that they were deported, because I had no influence over that; that resulted from decisions taken by the powerful of the world. It was not my nation or my government that determined the basic shape of the Yalta conference. Poland was a victim of this agreement, and a change in the structure of the Polish state was a consequence. And while a German could see this agreement as a punishment for fascism handed out by the international community, a Pole could only have a sense of an undeserved wrong. But nevertheless, while reading Grass's book, I felt a shame that I still feel today. I would like to believe that this shame is an integral component of the world in which we live. This shame allows the guilty to approach the dilemmas of this world more honestly.

We live in a world of immutable dilemmas: between the need for democracy and the need for the sacred; between concern for European universalism and the building of national identity; between the need for order and concern for an order based on pluralism and freedom of expression; between the rules of the free market and the day-to-day hunger for Christian compassion. It seems to me that these dilemmas are common to all contemporary European spiritual life. I have studied these dilemmas in the books of great German writers, Thomas Mann and Carl Jaspers, Heinrich Böll, Günter Grass, and others. I would like to talk about this with you, and I will gladly tell you about my fears when I observe the changes taking place in Poland and other post-Communist countries and what I fear when I hear about the growth of aggressive xenophobia and fascist tendencies in the eastern *Lander* of your state, the territory of the former GDR. I think we need a frank discussion. I promise you frankness on my part and I urge you to reciprocate.

20

Three Kinds of Fundamentalism

For Jonathan Schell

We are facing an urgent political problem: the historical consciousness of the Poles. There is no need to explain that interpretations of Polish history have had an enormous influence in shaping our attitudes toward, and involvement in, politics. It would seem that the time has come when these Polish stereotypes of the past—especially stereotypes of the Second Republic—need to be subjected to calm analysis. Hitherto, the entire history of the Second Republic has, to a large extent, fallen victim to mythology and stereotyping, which yields either the dark legend of official Communist propaganda or the shining legend of those who tried to defend themselves against Communist falsification of history. It would seem that we need to ask new questions of our past.

Above all, it seems, we need to consider what happened in 1922, when Gabriel Narutowicz was murdered. What kind of process was then set in motion? In what kind of atmosphere did the assassination take place? What were its historical consequences? Why did this date not become a landmark in Polish historical consciousness? Why was this event so readily forgotten?

It would seem that we also need to look afresh at the conduct of the major political forces. We need to examine afresh the political stage as an arena of conflict over the shape of the state and the shape of democ-

Translated by Jane Cave from *Krytyka,* no. 36 (1991):9–14.

racy—and ask ourselves the following question: What twists and turns marked the anti-democratic evolution of Piłsudski and his followers, of the *endecja* and the Polish Socialist party? We also need to analyze the history of the Catholic Church during the interwar period. Without such a reassessment, we are doomed to idealize our past, we are doomed to a sense of history burdened with myths rather than sober judgments, and we are doomed to be defenseless against what might be called the revenge of memory, a memory that was for years relegated to our subconscious.

If I had to define the new phenomena that are now appearing, with greater or lesser force, on or below the surface of current political debate, I would point to the reemerging danger of fundamentalism. Fundamentalism consists of nothing other than the conviction that one possesses a prescription for the organization of the world, a world free of conflicts other than the conflict between good and evil; free, for example, of the conflicts between interests or different points of view that are an integral component of a democratic order. In my opinion, we can speak of three kinds of fundamentalist threat.

First, national fundamentalism. There is a temptation to subordinate all spheres of public life to what is referred to as the national interest. This interest is always defined in terms of a fairly specific political perspective. According to this perspective, it is the duty of a good Pole to be in solidarity with the Polish minority in Lithuania regardless of how it behaves itself—whether it is wise or foolish, pro-Soviet or pro-Lithuanian. One must be in solidarity with this group for the simple reason that they are Poles—nothing more. Any attempt to criticize the actions of the leaders of the Polish minority in Lithuania is treated as an anti-Polish act. This kind of thinking presents, to ourselves and to our neighbors, an image of Poland free of conflicts except for that between the "correct, Catholic" interpretation of our national interest and nihilist-cosmopolitan-leftist tendencies. Within the framework of this definition of the national interest, it is considered anti-Polish to point to the anti-Semitic tendencies to be found in Polish political debates or to argue that we in Poland should not remain silent about the pogroms carried out against the Gypsies.

I am referring here to the fundamentalism that is characteristic of certain kinds of nationalist movements and doctrines, which—it would seem—are now playing a major role not only in Poland but in other post-Communist countries also. In the modern world, this type of fundamentalism is reviving, in the Arab countries, for example; it is to be found in Israel as well as—on the right—in the countries of Western Europe. In the discussions taking place in France on the subject of Le Pen and his followers, or in the German historical debate about Nazism, we can observe a fear of the revival of this type of fundamentalism. For this reason, it is worth examining it, not just as a Polish but as an international phenomenon.

Second, there is religious fundamentalism. This phenomenon is connected with the new situation in which the Polish Church now finds itself and the new situation in which the sacred everywhere finds itself. It is no revelation that one of the sicknesses of the modern world is the disappearance of the sacred, the disappearance of the sphere of values that are common to society and to which the entire community can appeal. This can be compared to the Stone Tablets, whose destruction signifies perhaps the collapse of the foundation in which are rooted all our common values.

The churches have yet to give a definitive response to this trend. We may doubt whether it is actually possible to formulate a response. Attempts to respond have, nevertheless, been made. One of them was Vatican II, which involved an opening up to the world and the recognition that certain authentic values may emerge outside the Church or even outside one's own faith or culture. A quite different response is provided by fundamentalism, which, in this case, involves the renewed attempt to blur the boundary between the sacred and the profane, between natural law and penal law, between moral principles and the legal norms of the state. On these issues, we are facing the most fundamental debate and one no less significant than, say, the debate over returning to Europe. When talking about returning to Europe, different people are referring to completely different things. It seems, for example, that when some representatives of the Catholic hierarchy talk about returning to Europe, they are talking about Europe before the French Revolution, a Europe that no longer exists.

Finally, in today's Poland there exists a third kind of fundamentalism. The people most susceptible to this danger are likely to be people from the pre-Solidarity and the Solidarity era democratic opposition, this writer among them. What I have in mind is the blurring of the distinction between moral norms and the rules of political struggle. Underground activity gave rise to a scale of values on which this distinction is virtually nonexistent, on which every political act is translated into the language of moral values. This is not the case in a democratic order, and this fundamentalist—let's call it moralistic—mentality may generate considerable confusion. This does not mean that I think there is no room for morality in politics or in normal political discourse. Nor do I think—since we are talking about religious fundamentalism—that there is no place for the Church in politics. Obviously, there is a place, but it is a specific place. Just as the Church should not become a political party, just as religious norms should not become legal norms, so the moral norms formed in the politics of the anti-Communist underground—which were Manichaean norms—should not be applied automatically in a democracy. They may prove to be fatal for democracy and for ourselves. Morality can easily turn into fanaticism and become an instrument with which to achieve goals that are far from noble.

Another threat that we ought to consider is populism. Populism is not a new phenomenon, but it is worth examining anew. For example, it is worth reexamining the lesson of Peronism. What was Peronism? What language did it use? What were its preferred procedures? What were the mechanisms that brought it to power, the mechanisms that removed it from power, and the mechanisms that guaranteed its existence?

In Poland, populism was the language of worker revolt against the to-talitarian state—this must be clearly stated. This was, of course, a revolt in the name of freedom and dignity, but these values were expressed in the language of populism. The famous term "them" was a typical for-mulation taken from populist discourse and not from any analysis of po-litical or social interests. It can be argued that this rebellion was based on an egalitarian consciousness that had legitimized Communist power for decades. In this sense, we can say that this was a revolt against commu-nism in the name of the egalitarian values espoused by communism. So it was a revolt in the name of values that were not altogether consistent, although social justice was one of its key ideas.

The market that is currently being constructed in Poland has no place for social justice as one of its key ideas. The role of the market is not to ensure justice but to force people to be efficient and creative. Justice may be served by a redistribution of goods but not by market mechanisms. Nevertheless, this egalitarianism—encoded by communism and by Sol-idarity's anti-Communist revolt—lives on and is to be found in the pop-ulist discourse of each trade union, whether state unions (the OPZZ) or Solidarity. It is fascinating to compare the language that the OPZZ and Solidarity have been using during the past year. It is a new phenomenon, and we have to relate to it in a new way.

We also have to tell ourselves finally that the revolt against commu-nism in Poland—and what a successful revolt—was the revolt of the crowd. As long as the Communists only had to deal with the elites, they could afford to ignore their demands. They could afford to ignore them as long as it was a question of democratic-legal procedures. The Communists began to take account of the opposition only when it was backed by the crowd—and with the crowd the Communists were obliged to talk. This situation gave rise to the feeling that in a crowd we are effective—or rather, we are effective when we speak the language of the crowd.

The language of the crowd is the language of populist discourse. Today, it would seem that we are witnessing a reversion to this language of the crowd, in other words, to modes of conduct acquired during the period of resistance to communism; modes of conduct that used to be rational within the framework of a nonrational system because they provided the only means of delegitimizing the political system. Today, these same modes of conduct are delegitimizing parliamentary democracy and opening the door to authoritarianism. We have reached democracy without the political culture appropriate to a democratic order. It is a little as though a bush savage had been placed in front of a computer. This does not mean that the savage is a less worthy human being—he manages in the bush a thousand times better than the civilized American. It is just that a computer is of little use in the bush.

There is a great danger that people will become disappointed with democracy, as has been the case several times in the history of Europe. There is a danger that we shall again hear a language that we have heard before: when people spoke about "Sejmocracy," it was the language of the Sanacja; when they spoke about "parliamentary cretinism," it was the language of communism; and when they spoke about rotten "demoliberalism," it was the language of fascism.

There is a danger that democratic procedures will become associated with crisis, with anarchy in public life, with the declining quality of life and the growing sense of insecurity. There is a possibility that we shall hear increasingly vociferous arguments that it is time to put an end to chaos and corruption, that we need someone with a strong hand to restore order. These ideas may be packaged as the idea of presidential rule or as the idea of a stable democracy; this packaging may be accompanied by historiographical analysis to the effect that Poland collapsed in the eighteenth century through anarchy, squabbling, and the *liberum veto,* and that, consequently, we now need to put an end to this situation. In other words, there is a risk—which is also familiar to us from our history—that at a time of profound crisis, people will emerge who are somehow an answer to this crisis. When traditional procedures and cultural models break down, when channels of communication lose their credibility, a savior appears who embodies our hopes for an end to chaos and for salvation.

Again, this is not a specifically Polish phenomenon. Nor is it new. Nevertheless, we need to examine it afresh; we need to consider the mechanisms that give birth to this authoritarian temptation and their results; we need to ask which problems authoritarian regimes can solve and which they certainly cannot.

The answer to this question will determine not only the state of mind of the Polish intelligentsia—which seems to be as far astray as it was during the worst of times, as though it has lost its ethos, its vision of itself and its place in society. If we broaden the process of reflection that I am talking about here, we may increase our chances of counteracting fundamentalism with democratic thought in which there is no place for fundamentalism of any kind, whether nationalistic, religious, or moralistic. According to democratic thought, there are no people who are, by their nature, privileged. Within the framework of democratic discourse, there is a place for authority. If, however, someone argues that a certain state of affairs ought to exist because of natural law or the national interest and that this state of affairs may not, for example, be the subject of a referendum, he violates the fundamental principle of this discourse.[1] Democratic order depends on the possibility of subjecting everything that concerns everyone to a referendum.

This may determine whether populism—the language of revolt—will be met with the language appropriate to parliamentary democracy and the rule of law. This may also determine whether the totalitarian temptation—the cult of the strong hand—will be met with rational democracy—the cult of the strong head.

---

1. This was the attitude of the Church on the issue of abortion. — ED.

21

One Has to Rise
Early in the Morning

A Conversation with Czesław Miłosz

Adam Michnik: You are, as you have frequently said, a child of the Grand Duchy of Lithuania. What exactly was the Grand Duchy?

Czesław Miłosz: In my youth I was surrounded by people who were very attached to the traditions of the Grand Duchy, although they differed from each other enormously in other respects. For example, Father Walerian Meysztowicz, an ultraconservative, glorified the duchy as the creation of the Lithuanian aristocracy and the Boyars. He considered himself a member of this class and was exceedingly proud of its distinctive character. He and his contemporaries were proud that they spoke Lithuanian, but God forbid that anyone should talk to them about a Lithuanian state created by the peasantry.

But as a young man I really didn't pay much attention to all this. I was a member of the gentry, full of complexes, aware of national and class conflicts. I was concerned about such issues but not to the point of asking myself whether I should choose Poland or Lithuania. I was mainly concerned with poetry, French poetry, the avant-garde, things of that nature.

Michnik: But you lived among people of different nationalities. There were Lithuanians, Byelorussians, and Jews. You had the specific expe-

Translated by Jane Cave from *Gazeta Wyborcza*, June 8, 1991.

rience of living among, or alongside, Poles who refused to accept the fact that different nationalities lived in this region as equals.

Miłosz: The group of writers to which I belonged, the Żagary group, was strongly anti-nationalist and aware of living in a multinational city. I invented a fictitious poet whom I called Aron Pirmas. Aron is a Jewish name, and Pirmas means "first" in Lithuanian. He was a poet whose verses we published in *Żagary*. Perhaps we were inspired by a similar invention—Kuźma Prutkov—in Russian literature. But we created an original figure who corresponded to the local national mix.

Michnik: Polish thought contains two great figures, Piłsudski and Dmowski. Two different sensibilities, two value systems, two different ways of thinking about the state and the Polish nation. What can you say, from the perspective of the Grand Duchy of Lithuania, about the opportunities and pitfalls to be found in a multinational, multicultural, and multireligious region?

Miłosz: Opportunities and pitfalls . . . As a young boy, a student, I already had a different perspective. I became friends with a native Lithuanian who naturally had a different view of national and political issues.

Michnik: In what language did you talk to each other?

Miłosz: In Polish, of course. He was a student at our university, although when he first started coming to seminars he spoke a mixture of Russian and German.

Michnik: Are you referring to Ancevicius, the Lithuanian activist?

Miłosz: Yes, yes, my friend Franas. I always had a highly negative opinion of Dmowski. On the other hand, there were moments when I strongly supported Piłsudski. Actually, I think these attitudes were handed down in families. Our family never had the slightest sympathy for Dmowski and his supporters. But the dangers, the pitfalls are obviously enormous, because if you understand the point of view of others, this tends to lessen your fervor on behalf of your own nationality.

Now, for example, I understand that [Professor Michał] Romer's position was correct. Romer was one of those Poles who considered Lithuania his fatherland. He considered himself a Polish-speaking Lithuanian. The same was true of my professor, Wiktor Sukiennicki, who recently died in California. This was, as I see it now, a correct position, but one that was extremely difficult to maintain. And today I

Adam Michnik (right) and Czesław Miłosz at a book promotion, Kraków, May 1995. (Photo: Jerzy Szot)

realize that Piłsudski's idea of a federation was bound to fail because nobody supported it—not the Poles, not the Lithuanians, not the Byelorussians. The Lithuanians had a very simple argument: they felt themselves extremely threatened by the Polish language and Polish culture. They were being gradually Polonized, albeit in a noncompulsory fashion. They were being absorbed by Polish culture and were gradually being deprived of their language.

But I would like to explain that I never pretended to be a Lithuanian, because if someone who spoke Lithuanian was a Lithuanian, and someone who spoke Polish a Pole, it was very difficult to maintain a position like Romer's. Lithuania wasn't like Finland, where Swedish and Finnish continue to coexist: Mannerheim was a national hero, but he didn't speak Finnish. When [the poet] Tomas Venclova and I spoke at Jagiellonian University, he spoke as a pro-Polish Lithuanian and I as a pro-Lithuanian Pole.

Michnik: Someone who was close to you, both emotionally and in terms of family relationship, was Oskar Miłosz, who was in his own way something of a phenomenon. An outstanding French poet who spoke Polish, he decided to become Lithuania's ambassador to France.

Miłosz: We must remember the circumstances in which he decided to become a Lithuanian. Before the First World War, he belonged to the Society of Polish Artists in Paris. His autobiography has a Polish, not a Lithuanian, perspective. He made his decision during the war. What prompted him? Unless I am mistaken, in 1917 Dmowski was in the United States and there he laid out his credo. This evoked a great deal of mistrust toward Poland on the part of a sizable segment of American public opinion. Dmowski considered that everything in the East was effectively Poland. Lithuanians, Byelorussians, and Ukrainians simply didn't exist. So when Oskar Miłosz heard about this, he said, "If Poland doesn't want to recognize an independent Lithuanian state, I will become a Lithuanian."

Michnik: But wasn't there something more to this? Wasn't it a question of identity for Oskar Miłosz?

Miłosz: In our family there were very strong conflicts. Oskar's grandfather, Artur Miłosz, fought at Ostrołęka [against the Russians, 1831], where he lost a leg, was awarded the Virtuti Militari medal, and was forced to flee abroad. In Italy, he married Natalia Tasistro, a singer and daughter of the concert master at La Scala. The family considered this a terrible match. They were horrified that he'd married some Italian. Then the couple went to live in Vilnius.

Oskar Miłosz thought they were a wonderful pair, loving and heroic. He was very proud of them. His father, Władysław Miłosz, grew up as an orphan in the care of relatives, because his parents died prematurely. These relatives persecuted him because of this marriage. Oskar Miłosz used to say that his father had instilled in him a mistrust of Poland. Oskar's father, Władysław, married a Jew, and the family continued its campaign. Hence this constant gravitation to our family, which came from Lithuania.

Michnik: How should we judge the Second Republic? This is a question that has recently reemerged after years when the issue was taboo.

Miłosz: Everything that is now being said is untrue. It's an idealization, a complete untruth. It was a poor state burdened with terrible problems. And the political issues are well known.

Michnik: What do you have in mind when you say "political"?

Miłosz: I have in mind the extremely sad history of those twenty years [1918–39]. It began with the murder of the first president. Then the rule of the Sejm, a bunch of apes. Then the rule of the colonels and their degeneration. And all of this against the background of the world economic crisis, dreadful poverty, lack of resources.

Michnik: But what could Poland have done, caught between Hitler and Stalin?

Miłosz: I don't know, but it was a country whose main failing was small-mindedness, the pettiness of the dunghill as evidenced in the suicides of people who came from the outside world. Professor Petrażycki committed suicide. Lednicki, the great Polish activist in Russia, committed suicide; the *endecja* hounded him to death.

Michnik: But this was also a culturally rich period. Great talents emerged, and there were some fine journals. Basically, my generation owes a great deal to this period in our culture: Żeromski, Dąbrowska, the Skamander group, Strug, Gombrowicz, Witkacy, Czechowicz.

Miłosz: I don't know, it's difficult to say. For my generation, which grew up in conditions of crisis, this entire reality was impermanent, fictitious. It was Aleksander Wat, after all, who wrote in *My Century* that we suddenly realized we were living in a house of cards.

Michnik: The Vilnius in which you lived, your circle of friends, turned out to be amazingly fertile and immensely significant for Polish intellectual life—Cat-Mackiewicz, Paweł Jasienica, Stanisław Stomma, Henryk Dembiński, Stefan Jędrychowski, Antoni Gołubiew, Teodor Bujnicki. Were all of you able to be friends all of the time, or were there incidents that made this impossible? You were all together, then Gołubiew and Stomma became enlightened Catholics and Dembiński and Jędrychowski became Communists. You were on the left, although you didn't become a Communist. What was it like? I'm trying to understand whether the animosity that we see between people today is somehow encoded in the culture of our social life.

Miłosz: Broadly speaking, we all more or less formed a single group. Of course, at various times people drew closer or drifted apart. I became friends with Stomma at school, and then we drifted apart, but there was never any animosity between us, no recriminations. I was very close to Jędrychowski, but when he became an out-and-out Communist, we stopped seeing each other. That's all.

Michnik: Many years ago, I had the opportunity to talk with Father Meysztowicz, the author of wonderful memoirs, whom you mentioned, and I asked him about Henryk Dembiński. With tears in his eyes, he said, "He was like a son to me." He said this, knowing that

Dembiński was a Communist. I was greatly impressed that such a tone of warmth was possible.

Miłosz: That's a good illustration of the atmosphere in our group. Dembiński was charming, delightful, and passionate. He had an exceptional position in Vilnius, even after he became a Communist. Dembiński was a myth—a passionate speaker and so handsome.

Michnik: In your opinion, was he an honest person?

Miłosz: Dembiński was very emotional, impulsive, and probably often foolish, although very intelligent. I prefer this version to the picture of him as a cunning hypocrite.

Michnik: What about the young people associated with the *endecja*—Kazimierz Hałaburda, for example?

Miłosz: Hałaburda and I both belonged to the student club, the Wayfarers. He was probably the only member from the *endecja,* and people used to make fun of him a little. Poor Hałaburda, he died in a labor camp. But Jasienica, that's to say, Lech Beynar, was also a member of the Wayfarers; he had the nickname Bacchus.

Michnik: Was he attracted to the *endecja* at that time?

Miłosz: No, not at all. You could say that the main source of support for the *endecja* was the students' guild. And the Wayfarers Club was formed in opposition to the guild. In other words, we were looking for a different formula.

Michnik: I want to ask you about someone I've often discussed with friends: Teodor Bujnicki.

Miłosz: That's a big piece of my life. When I was at school, I heard about this fantastic poet who had appeared at the Lelewel gymnasium. Shortly afterward, I found myself with him in the [secret literary organization] Pet. The meetings at home, at Rudnicki's, looking through issues of *Skamander,* discussions about poetry—this was a sheer delight for me, a teenager, a budding poet, and it was all associated with Bujnicki. Later, at the university, in the Wayfarers Club and in the Żagary group, we were together all the time. I used to visit the Central European Institute, where he was secretary, not far from Rudnicki's café, and we used to sit for hours in Rudnicki's. We were together incessantly. Later, I realized that things were not going well with Bujnicki. He married, had children, and lived a comfortable, middle-class life. He came from a landowning family, and he used to spend his vacations at the country estate of relatives. But I was already horrified by what I read in his prewar poetry—that sense of being lost, of hopelessness, the image of slime, of living in the slime somewhere at the bottom of a lake, and so on. At the time, I interpreted all this as a metaphor for the impasse in his own life. It seemed to me that he was on the wrong path, that his life had taken a wrong turn, and he found himself in a trap.

During the so-called Lithuanian occupation, when Vilnius had been handed over to Lithuania [1939] and Józef Mackiewicz was publishing *Gazeta Codzienna,* Bujnicki was the paper's deputy editor. He was concerned mostly with the literary side of things, so we found ourselves cooperating once more in the same editorial group. Światopełk Karpiński was also involved, as was Janusz Minkiewicz, and God knows who else.

Then came the period of Soviet occupation. I was not a witness, because I escaped, across the "green frontier." My former girlfriend wrote to me about Bujnicki: "I can't imagine you writing the kind of horrors that Teodor has. He could have chosen an honorable way out, but he chose the worst one possible. He doesn't understand that the period of youthful foolishness is over, that serious things are going on here, and that one has to make a commitment." She seemed to interpret what had happened as the result of Dorek's eternal butterfly nature, of the fact that he remained a wunderkind.

When the Germans came, he hid with his relatives in Żmudza, where he met Franas Ancevicius, who was then a lawyer in Szawli. Together, they tried to decide what to do. When the Red Army was approaching, Ancewicz, of course, thought there was nothing to do but flee, and he fled by boat to Sweden with his wife and daughters. They were caught by the Germans and turned back. Then they escaped by the normal route, through eastern Prussia, during the bombing, and the whole family made it.

But Bujnicki didn't decide to flee. It was a difficult decision; he had a wife and small children. He returned to Vilnius. He didn't expect to be killed for having written pro-Soviet poetry. He never imagined they would have such a long memory.

For me, the chief explanation is his prewar impasse: nothing is happening, the slimy bottom, stagnation in his personal life and in everything else.

Michnik: In a review of an anthology that you wrote many years ago, you quoted extensively from the poem that Bujnicki wrote on the first anniversary of Lithuania's incorporation into the Soviet Union. If there was ever a crystal-clear example of collaboration with an occupying force, with an enemy, this is certainly it. What, in your opinion, did the Poles who read this poem have the right to expect from a poet writing in Polish, and what kind of punishment could be meted out to the poet? After all, if one can bestow awards, one can also bestow punishment. This is an absolutely fundamental question about the relationship between a writer and his readers, about responsibility for what one writes.

Miłosz: I'm not a moralist. I try to avoid passing judgment. If the best Polish poets, like Trembecki, wrote dreadful things, if they paid tribute to Catherine the Great and signed addresses to the czar in Vilnius . . . Nevertheless, I believe that the guilt of someone like Bujnicki is probably greater than that of those who collaborated quietly. It is very difficult to measure, but words really do have a force. Words are a serious business.

Michnik: Trembecki is a good example. Even bishops were hanged by Poles for similar offenses. Trembecki was lucky; nobody hanged him.

Miłosz: Of course, it's a fact that Polish history contains innumerable collaborators of various kinds, of varying—so to speak—degrees of involvement. Bujnicki is the only writer who was killed for it.

Michnik: This is why his biography constitutes a parable.

Miłosz: But he wrote other things afterward, after his disgraceful act of June 1941, when he was at his relatives' estate, and these show signs of enormous self-recrimination. He seems to have been examining his conscience. The disadvantage of death is that afterward you can no longer make amends for anything.

If someone considers himself blameless, he can pass judgment. I'm unable to pass judgment on Bujnicki because I myself have done some dirty things in my time. In 1945, I wrote some articles in Kraków which may have been the product of honest rage on my part, but they certainly won't bring me any honor.

Michnik: I think that's a different kind of situation. I'm unable to draw a moral equation between writing in 1945 in Kraków and writing in 1941 in Vilnius. Maybe it's a defect on my part, but I see a fundamental difference between the two.

Miłosz: Let's say it disqualifies me.

Michnik: Let's look at it not so much from a moralistic as a sociological perspective. Literature always involves a relationship between the writer and the reader. What does the reader have the right to expect of the writer?

Miłosz: It seems to me that Polish literature is in a different situation and has different traditions from that of French literature, for example. Throughout the entire German occupation, French literature functioned normally. When you read how the literary underground functioned, you can only envy the French. Of course, there were some who collaborated openly and who probably realized what they were doing. That's not the same as Bujnicki, who probably didn't realize, as my girlfriend wrote, that the days of that happy Vilnius, where everything was a bit of a joke, were now over. There was never any question of killing anyone in that charming city.

Michnik: The French sentenced to death Brasillach and Drieu la Rochelle after the war, when the occupation was over. What do you think of the fact that the Poles killed Bujnicki?

Miłosz: You know the affair of Józef Mackiewicz. He was sentenced to death, and Sergiusz Piasecki was supposed to carry out the sentence. But he didn't. Later, in Rome, he said that he had doubts that the sentence was justified.

Michnik: That's another issue. But is it permissible to kill a writer for even the most despicable poetry? This is a question that I myself am unable to answer. I'm glad that Brasillach was killed, not for his writings, but for other acts. If [Jerzy] Putrament had been killed, it would have been because he was a poet who was also a political officer. Bujnicki was no political officer. He was killed for his poetry, poetry of the most loathsome kind, but he was killed for his poetry. What do you think about this?

Miłosz: I don't know. Your question is the question of a moralist. Evidently, I'm not enough of a moralist; I've never thought about it. Some people think I'm moralistic in my writings, but no, I don't feel sufficiently blameless, or competent, to pass judgment on what is moral. I've always been guided by a kind of instinct, not consciousness.

Michnik: It seems to me that you are moralistic, but you're not a moralizer. These are two different things. You make great moral demands of yourself, not others.

Miłosz: Well, yes. I feel a little uncomfortable talking with you, because you have this moralistic bent, and I'm like someone who has been drowning all his life and can scarcely hold his chin above water. In a sense, my whole life has been filled with tragic events. So how am I to pass judgment if I found things so difficult?

Michnik: The point is not to pass judgment on anyone. The point is for us to consider how others pass judgment on all this. Look, for years no one said that Bujnicki, who had been executed, was a collaborator, but everyone said that Mackiewicz, who hadn't been executed, was a collaborator. Today, that situation is being reversed. Today, even the most outstanding critics in Poland are making Józef Mackiewicz into a kind of model.

Miłosz: A model in what sense?

Michnik: Well, that he was the only one who was right. How would you compare the case of Bujnicki with that of Mackiewicz?

Miłosz: These are two completely different cases, because Mackiewicz had his own point of view. He was deeply attached to the Grand Duchy of Lithuania; he understood the local nationalities, the Lithuanians, Byelorussians, and Poles; he understood their point of view, and he had this terrible hatred of communism.

   Mackiewicz found the Home Army unpalatable because it represented only one of the nationalities of the Grand Duchy. From this point of view he was correct: it did embody the line of a single nationality. Apart from this, he was concerned about something else: the struggle against the Soviet monster. This is a completely different viewpoint from that of Poland the homeland. He didn't care who fought against the Soviet Union, against communism, as long as somebody did. That's what he showed in his book *Nie trzeba głośno mówić* [One Must Not Talk Too Loudly].

Michnik: But did the Polish reader who lived under German occupation and who witnessed events popularly considered to be acts of collaboration really care? In Bujnicki's case, it was a matter of a certain lack of consciousness, lack of forethought, perhaps even a certain desire to avoid the inconvenient. In Mackiewicz's case, it was a question of a coherent point of view, a fanatical belief in a particular vision of the world. But the ordinary person couldn't care less. He knows that any policeman got it over the head for such things. He couldn't care less that Bujnicki was a butterfly and Mackiewicz had a coherent point of view.

Miłosz: Very well, but what exactly did Józef Mackiewicz do? What did he do?

Michnik: In his paper, which was nothing but a despicable rag, he published articles that were viewed as treasonous at the time.

Miłosz: That wasn't his paper. It was another Mackiewicz, Bohdan, who was the editor. Józef Mackiewicz published several articles in it at the time when everyone was breathing a sigh of relief that the Germans had come. After all, you have to take account of the completely different atmosphere of the region at that time. The entire local population welcomed the Germans after the experience of Soviet occupation. Carried along by this mood, Mackiewicz wrote a couple of pieces that were more or less identical to what he subsequently wrote in the story "Road to Nowhere." Nobody accuses him of anything more, except perhaps that he went to Katyń, but he went with the permission of the underground leadership. What else?

   In the summer of 1944, he came to Warsaw and talked with Minkiewicz and me. He said, "For God's sake, the Germans are losing. This is a perfect opportunity for us to have talks with them and to publish a journal that will warn people what to expect when the Bolsheviks get here." We just laughed in his face, because the atmosphere in Warsaw completely ruled out anything of this kind. But apparently he and his wife published a couple of issues of a journal in which he expounded the idea, probably while they were still in Vilnius. Nobody remembers this; they published perhaps only three copies of this journal. This was what his political plan actually amounted to in practice. He himself wrote about those who were genuine collaborators—Burdecki and Skiwski. In 1944 they published a pro-German periodical, *Przełom* [Breakthrough], and they were protected by the Germans. Anyone who wanted to meet with them had to give a password, because they were afraid that people from the Polish underground would do them in. So why is everyone after Mackiewicz? I don't understand.

Michnik: I think I understand. There are historical situations in which a dual morality is dominant.

Miłosz: Listen, Adam. I really feel uncomfortable in this conversation, because if you think about the wartime situation in this part of the world, the Vilnius region was one thing and the General Gouvernement another.

Michnik: And the difference is precisely one of perspective. In the Vilnius region, the Home Army leadership could have talks with the Germans, while in Warsaw it was out of the question.

Miłosz: But what was the situation in the East? The entire history of that period has been completely falsified, after all. It has been completely distorted; it was a system of dual standards, of dual collaboration—on the surface with one side and beneath the surface with the other. This system contained numerous jokers like Bierut, who worked in the Minsk city council as a Byelorussian and as an official of the German administration and who was actually a Bolshevik agent. That kind of thing was commonplace. In Poland, people still deluded themselves that the allies would come. But there, in the East, everyone was sober enough to know that no allies were coming; it would be either the Bolsheviks or the Germans, and one had to live with one or the other of them. It was a terrible situation.

Michnik: When you were talking about Mackiewicz, you referred to the political line of this—let's call it patriotic—group, which was dominated by supporters of the *endecja*. I share your antipathy toward everything in our culture associated with the *endecja* spirit and mentality. But if half the country was attracted to it, it must have spoken to some fundamental values. The *endecja* must have answered some basic needs within society. Hence the question: What kind of values, what kind of needs?

Miłosz: It seems to me that societies have a need for slogans, for simple explanations of complicated issues. I think that what we call the *endecja* could equally well be called a movement of opposition to outsiders, opposition to all forms of otherness. It involved group consolidation on the basis of nationality, a blind consolidation based on the exclusion of everything that in some way departed from collectively established values. It seems to me that it was an extremely primitive, tribal reaction.

This is one thing, but Dmowski's theory, based on biology and on Darwinism, is something else entirely. It is obvious that science has unforeseen consequences. All the indirect costs of Darwinism, all forms of social Darwinism, are the monstrous result of the vulgarization of science.

Michnik: Why were so many Polish intellectuals attracted to the *endecja*? Konopczyński, Chrzanowski, Grabski, Stroński, Nowaczyński—a whole legion of them. In the name of what? Why did they fail to understand what you understood? Why did you have such a sense of isolation under the Second Republic? Outside your small circle of friends, you felt an outsider, didn't you?

Miłosz: Yes. Here you are raising difficult issues. I still find myself asking what it was really like, and I don't have any clear answers. Where did my feeling of being threatened come from?

In school I was already different, although I was exactly like any other young person who came from the so-called gentry. So, where this feeling came from, I have no idea. This is a question of individual fate, perhaps related to the fact that when I started school I was very well read, already educated, and many pupils were way behind because of the war. I was one of the youngest in my class. Later, when I was under attack, from Father Kolbe's publication, for example, I had the feeling that it didn't matter that the "true Poles" were attacking me and wanted to destroy me. I don't know why it turned out that way.

Were there moments in my life when I felt a tribal instinct, when I was moved by tribal emotions or felt a tribal identity? Perhaps when there was a military parade—there were a few such parades in Vilnius—when the band was playing, and . . .

Michnik: And you felt a common fate with this beaten, downtrodden Polish nation, whose suffering was expressed, ineluctably, in your poetry?

Miłosz: I had very mixed feelings.

Michnik: Answer.

Miłosz: It's very difficult, very difficult.

Michnik: In his memoirs, Lednicki describes the following scene: he's sitting in a restaurant, in Russia, and nearby sit a father and son, Poles. And he suddenly sees in their faces a kind of defenselessness, a weakness, a softness.

Miłosz: I remember the scene. Weakness, defenselessness . . . these are complicated matters and so deeply rooted that they're impossible to understand. Folklore, for example. Perhaps folklore is a kind of bond. Language, of course, my Polish language. It is, as I once wrote, my homeland. Language was my homeland because it was the only one I had. I wasn't brought up within range of Polish folklore. All the songs I listened to were Lithuanian.

Whenever I go to Poland, I have a strange feeling: on the one hand, I feel a deep sense of identification, and on the other, I feel myself an outsider. I'm split in two. It's very bad to be a cripple. But perhaps if I weren't a cripple, I would write worse than I do. I don't know.

Michnik: Perhaps you wouldn't write at all.

Miłosz: Perhaps I wouldn't write at all. I want to add something, perhaps from a slightly different perspective: the question of identity. I've thought about this for a long time, but it's only now that I've begun writing about my social origin, my genteel parentage, which I tried to keep under my skirt, so to speak. This means that there were some kind of complexes that held me back.

I guess that a class complex interfered with my sense of belonging to a social group. I had a guilty conscience; I found it deeply shameful to think of myself as the young master. And I was the Polish—and Polish-speaking—young master of peasants who spoke Lithuanian. This situation was bound to leave its mark.

My early years in Vilnius were a bit like those of the students who belonged to the secret society at Vilnius University in the nineteenth century. The circle that I entered while still at the gymnasium and during my first years at the university was made up of warm friends. This was not isolation but integration into a particular intellectual milieu. I would say, first of all, that I was a poet writing in the Polish language—that's fundamental—and second, that basically the only place where I could feel at home was in a Polish intellectual milieu. I want to add this to avoid giving the impression that I'm some kind of oddity.

Michnik: I'd like to ask you now to comment on what you wrote in *Treatise on Poetry,* that "the party is the heir of the ONR." As a young man, you used to read *Prosto z Mostu.* Did it ever occur to you that there was a hidden relationship between the line espoused by this journal and Communist or Marxist thought? For a certain time, the very best writers wrote for *Prosto z Mostu.*

Miłosz: There was a brief moment when that was justified. Today, it's not so easy to understand this. But for our group in Vilnius, *Wiadomości Literackie* was not a journal that we read with any great enthusiasm. Of course, we were largely brought up on *Wiadomości Literackie* and *Skamander,* but we already felt ourselves opposed to the journal. It's interesting that this opposition to what was then termed the "superficiality" of *Wiadomości Literackie* came from both the left and the right. Apart from this, we read *The Magic Mountain* by Thomas Mann and we were fascinated by Naphta, not Settembrini. I never felt the slightest temptation to write for *Prosto z Mostu;* in other words, I had an aversion to this tendency very early on.

Michnik: But why did the *crème de la crème,* including Andrzejewski and Gałczyński, write for *Prosto z Mostu?*

Miłosz: Wiadomości was a rather snobbish publication that didn't tolerate any drivel. And this was a period in which there was plenty of drivel of all kinds. But this wasn't enough for us. We were looking for some kind of idea, some kind of weltanschauung. Here I must say something about my work for the radio. I'm not talking about Vilnius, because I was run out of there as a result of—let's be honest—the attacks of the press run by Father Maksymilian Kolbe.

Michnik: Namely?

Miłosz: They published articles denouncing me and Tadeusz Byrski—someone who had done an enormous amount for radio and theater—for having allowed Jews to take part in discussions about religion, for being, in a word, crypto-Communists. You could be the target of such an accusation for nothing more than simply displaying a slightly different attitude toward Byelorussians, Lithuanians, and Jews, as did my friend Byrski and I, his assistant. But that's not important.

When I moved to Warsaw, my boss at the radio was Hanna Sosnowska, a wonderful woman who deserves a monument. A young woman when the Polish state was created, she had been an enthusiastic supporter of Piłsudski and subsequently became a loyal follower. As deputy director of the radio, she tried to do what she could to hinder the right-wing shift toward the National Unity Camp. We had very frank conversations. I used to say, "There's nothing there, just a total vacuum. The only real structure, which is lurking under the surface, is Marxism."

Michnik: What about the ONR?

Miłosz: Of course, the ONR existed, but there was no need to discuss it; it was a vacuum, a nothingness, empty sloganeering. I used to say, "I can feel that Marxism is the only thing lying in wait for us. Tell me, what can we do to counteract it?" Truly, I believed at the time that it was an enormous threat, but the only likely future reality. I could feel this reality. That's by way of comment.

But various journals emerged at this time, not just *Prosto z Mostu.* There was *Pion,* edited by Józef Czechowicz, and there was Jerzy Braun's *Zet,* full of Hoehne-Wroński's confused ideas. There were numerous such attempts as a result of the superficiality and poverty that we found in *Wiadomości Literackie.* Poverty-stricken in terms of the ability to oppose *Wiadomości Literackie* was the Poland described by

Aleksander Wat as a house of cards, the Poland of the Ziemiańska Café on Mazowiecka Street.

Michnik: But if you look today at this liberal tendency that you accuse of shallowness, it appears to be the only attempt in Poland to think rationally about Poland. It was simultaneously anti-fascist and anti-Communist.

Miłosz: Of course. I agree with you to a large extent, but it's another thing to look from today's perspective. It's interesting what later happened to *Wiadomości,* when it moved to London; Grydzewski completely changed the journal's line. He was an editorial genius, closely in touch with his readers. Who read *Wiadomości Literackie* before the war? In large part, the Jewish intelligentsia. In any small town, subscriptions to *Wiadomości Literackie* were taken out by the Jewish lawyer, the Jewish doctor, and the pharmacist . . . well, no, actually most of the pharmacists weren't Jews.

Michnik: And the priest?

Miłosz: Never! The hairdresser, the Jewish hairdresser, also subscribed. In my gymnasium class in Vilnius, the only person who read *Wiadomości Literackie* apart from me was Stefan Zagórski, the cousin of Jerzy Zagórski. But that was a very special family, because his father, a lawyer, was an old SDKPiL [Social Democracy of the Polish Kingdom and Lithuania] activist and his mother was a Jew. So the journal was read by people in a completely different milieu, with a liberal, progressive orientation.

When this milieu was destroyed, Grydzewski found himself in London among an émigré community made up in large part of military people, former military people, and people who had found themselves in the military by accident. And he adapted to this new readership. In my opinion, we shouldn't forget the sociology of literature during this period.

Michnik: Explain to me why you never engaged in intellectual polemics with the ONR? Why didn't you ever try to see what real questions they were trying to answer? You always saw the movement as one of unenlightened imbeciles and you rejected it as a subject for serious consideration.

Miłosz: Yes, I did.

Michnik: But you did argue with the Communists.

Miłosz: Yes. Why? This is a far-reaching question. What was the source of this automatic antipathy? In my student dormitory in Vilnius, there were several supporters of the *endecja,* and I even became friends with some of them. But we never discussed any fundamental issues.

Michnik: I sometimes have the impression that, in the case of Marxism, you did something unprecedented. You used your powers of introspection to view the world from a Marxist perspective in order later to subject this view to analysis and reveal the evil of Marxism. Why didn't you ever make such an effort with nationalism? I'll go further. Why, in your opinion, does Polish literature not contain a single intellectual settlement of accounts with the *endecja* legacy? You could paper the walls of three apartments the size of yours with the writings of conscience-stricken Communists, but not the *endecja.* In Germany, this phenomenon exists; in France too. Why doesn't it exist in Poland?

Miłosz: I don't know that it does exist in Germany.

Michnik: Yes it does! There's that wonderful book by Hermann Rauschning, *The Revolution of Nihilism,* an analysis of the treachery of the German right that supported Hitler. He wrote this account from the perspective of someone on the right.

Miłosz: Again, I have a kind of sociological comment. The situation was such that anyone who wrote for a nationalist publication was excluded from literary circles. The only exception, of course, was *Prosto z Mostu,* and this was the big breakthrough achieved by its editor, Stanisław Piasecki. He managed to involve the intellectual elite in the journal because of his social contacts; social contacts were extremely important in this case.

Michnik: In your opinion, why did no one ever write the equivalent of *The Captive Mind* on this subject?

Miłosz: I was once invited by Stanisław Piasecki to a meeting to celebrate the publication of Miciński's book, *Podróże do piekeł* [Journeys to Hell]. This was in 1937 or 1938. The whole nationalist elite was there, the elite in all spheres, beginning with music and theater criticism — an elite that was preparing itself to take power in Poland, an elite that was on the ascendant, aware that it would replace the former liberal elite. From this point of view, the meeting was very interesting, but I didn't discuss fundamentals with any of them. Of course, Piasecki invited me to collaborate on *Prosto z Mostu.* I politely refused, and that was the end of it. I never had a discussion with him.

Michnik: Doesn't the totalitarian temptation lurking beneath these nationalistic ideologies deserve to be treated seriously? Why hasn't anyone done so? The Polish cultural elite has never seen nationalism as a serious partner. Why not?

Miłosz: This is an extremely important question. As I said, I was always fascinated by Naphta, not Settembrini, and this was typical. Being fascinated by Naphta, I ought to have been interested in this question; in the last analysis, Naphta was a totalitarian more of the right than the left.

Michnik: I think Mann's genius resides in the fact that in Naphta he portrayed totalitarianism as such, a totalitarianism made up of components from both the right and the left.

Miłosz: Of course. Naphta was actually modeled on Lukács, the Hungarian Marxist philosopher.

Michnik: That was the left-wing component, but all Naphta's thinking about the legacy of the Middle Ages belongs to the right.

Miłosz: Yes, but all our youthful rhetoric—before Dembiński became a Communist—was directed against demoliberalism, in other words, against Settembrini. This preceded Dembiński's conversion to communism; before that we used to make fun of demoliberalism.

In the spring of 1935, I was at an anti-fascist cultural congress in Paris. The congress was organized, of course, with the assistance of— or perhaps by—Soviet agents. I took an ironic view of the speeches. They seemed to be full of mumbled humanitarian slogans against some kind of dangerous force then gaining strength in Germany; they were imbued with a kind of humanitarian weakness; and all this was connected to the shrieks of laughter that demoliberalism used to evoke in Dembiński and us. Everything was thus extremely ambiguous. Now, we say, either fascist totalitarianism or Communist totalitarianism. It was different then; then, a large part of Settembrini was on the side of Marxism.

Michnik: What about Brzozowski?

Miłosz: Among the many people who influenced us, Brzozowski played a major role. [The writer] Karol Irzykowski once defined Brzozowski's ideas as "a dream about an idle whip." The cult of Naphta and the cult of Brzozowski were somehow connected to each other, although it's clear that Brzozowski was also appropriated by right-wing interpreters of his work.

Michnik: I think this is both a good and a bad example, because Brzozowski is perhaps the only Polish writer who polemicized seriously with nationalism. You never did so yourself. I don't understand why not.

Miłosz: I don't understand it either. It was probably connected with my complexes about my national identity.

Michnik: But we're not necessarily talking about Polish nationalism. After all, at that time the whole of Europe was inundated by a wave of nationalism. This was an intellectual project in which enormous numbers of ordinary people were swept up. Why didn't the elite engage it in debate? Either they succumbed to it or they rejected it, but they never entered into discussion with it. Later, the issue was never revisited, and this means that now we're virtually defenseless in the face of a similar threat.

Miłosz: You've raised an interesting point. Nobody ever discussed anything seriously with Dmowski. People poked fun at him, denounced him, or sneered at him, but no one ever initiated a serious discussion with him. We rejected some aspects of political thought simply because they were at such a low level. Brzozowski's thinking, for example, was rooted in literary analysis and criticism, in the intellectual trends of the time, in philosophy, but Dmowski was only interested in the Polish nation, this was his only topic. The question arises, why the Polish nation and not the Croat or Chinese nation? I don't know; he was only interested in local issues. I think we needed something more universal, a broader horizon of the kind to be found in the work of Brzozowski or Marian Zdziechowski. Can you imagine Zdziechowski as a supporter of Dmowski? It's simply inconceivable!

We mustn't forget that we were still under the influence of the former republic. Although everything became modified during the nineteenth century, vestiges remained in interwar Poland. When you read Brzozowski's *Sam wśród ludzi* [Alone in a Crowd], you see how much importance was attached to the Ukrainian question, the issue of the borderlands, relations between Poles and Russians; it has a broad sweep. But Dmowski was another matter, incredibly provincial, incredibly narrow and local in his concerns.

Michnik: Do you think it would be possible to do a comparative analysis on the susceptibility to communism and the susceptibility to fascism? Karol Irzykowski once wrote a marvelous essay, "Filozofia koralowców" [The Philosophy of Coral Reef], in which he argued that both Communists and fascists treat human beings as the moral equivalent of coral, which have no significance in their own right and acquire significance only when they join together to form a larger entity, a coral island. It doesn't matter whether this entity is based on class or nationality. This perspective is exceedingly rare in Poland. In fact, no one apart from Irzykowski has analyzed these phenomena from this perspective. Only you formulated the thought later, in *Treatise on Poetry,* that "the Party is the heir of the ONR, and apart from them, there was never anything but the rebellion of contemptible individuals." How did you arrive at this? Can you recall the way the idea developed? For many years, these lines were an embarrassment to the Communists, and now they're an embarrassment to the nationalists.

Miłosz: How did I arrive at this idea? From the very beginning, chauvinist propaganda was very strong in [Communist] People's Poland. This gave the impression of a masquerade, as though they were dressing themselves up in national costume, including the traditional four-cornered military cap. It was obvious to any observer. It was a satellite, puppet state, which dressed itself up in the garb of an independent state.

Michnik: But that's not the ONR. The ONR was more than this.

Miłosz: It was a hierarchical, totalitarian organization. You're asking me a lot of interesting questions that I haven't really thought about before. It seems to me that, in many cases, you're more interesting and unbiased than I ever was. Many of the things I wrote simply seemed to me incontrovertible, obvious.

Michnik: I understand perfectly, but it's just that a younger generation comes along and asks, Why exactly did things happen this way?

Miłosz: Don't forget that during the war I was in Warsaw, where I observed a great deal, including the strong totalitarian tendencies within the underground.

Michnik: After the war, what was your attitude toward *Kuźnica?*

Miłosz: I never wrote for *Kuźnica.* The role of *Kuźnica* was to try to incorporate Polish culture into communism. It was an attempt to subdue us. All those dramas or semidramas of its members, who were trying to practice a slightly unorthodox version of Marxism, were completely alien to me.

Michnik: To whom did you feel closest after the war? In your correspondence with Wańkowicz, you referred to a circle of people who thought along the same lines as yourself.

Miłosz: I became friends at that time with Andrzejewski.

Michnik: And you think he thought the same way that you did?

Miłosz: Yes, I think so. I became friends with Tadeusz Kroński and Irena Krońska, and there was Ryś Matuszewski and Tadeusz and Irena Byrski. And then there was Iwaszkiewicz and that whole group that used to visit Stawisko during the occupation. There was also Wanda Telakowska, about whom I want to write something, who later became head of the Institute of Design; Maciej Nowicki, the architect; and Stefan Kisielewski.

There was also Minkiewicz, who during the German occupation sometimes held literary evenings at which he drove everyone to fury because of the way in which he used to insult Polish orthodoxy. He used to read cruel stories, especially about our common friend, Leszek Bortkiewicz, who also appears in Józef Mackiewicz's book *Road to Nowhere* as the character who teaches Marxism to the workers. He was a landowner from Cisna. When the Germans came, he passed himself off as a Byelorussian, and his land was returned to him. He used to walk around holding a whip and telling the peasants, "Now I'll show you what communism really means." The partisans shot him through the window one day while he was eating supper. Minkiewicz used to tell this story as though it was the most amusing anecdote.

Michnik: Tell me about *Kultura*. Did you already know Giedroyc before you found yourself abroad?

Miłosz: I was supposed to meet him. Marek Eiger (Stefan Napierski) told me about this incredibly charming and talented young official in the Ministry of Agriculture who supported young writers and organized publications. Giedroyc was then publishing *Bunt Młodych*. But we never actually met before the war. I just heard a lot of good things about him. It's interesting in a way that I never felt the inclination to write for conservative publications such as *Bunt Młodych*. Evidently, my journalistic inclinations were underdeveloped; I was more interested in philosophical-literary questions.

When I was in Washington, I was visited by Józef Czapski. I'd got to know him before the war, and I knew his sister, Maria Czapska, very well. She was active in the Laski group. It was she who gave me the manuscript of Jacques Maritain's book *The Twilight of Civilization* [1943], which I translated. I later got word from France that the Polish underground edition of the book, in my translation, had appeared before the French version, published by Vercors. A great achievement, if I may say so.

So Czapski came to see me. He'd come to the United States in search of money for *Kultura*. He'd met with numerous long-standing émigrés, many of whom talked in peasant slang. One day, he'd been talking with a woman all decked out in diamonds and fur who suddenly said to him, "Get your butt out of here, old man."

I was anathema to the whole émigré community because I worked in the embassy, and all of a sudden Czapski appears. He provided a bridge, a certain incentive to further communication. I guess he did this at the prompting of Giedroyc.

Michnik: How did your conversation with Czapski go?

Miłosz: It was very frank, very warm; there was no attempt to pretend or conceal anything on my part. So when I was in Paris I simply telephoned *Kultura,* but I had to do it furtively, because I was being followed, I and Nela Micińska. Whenever we went into a café, the same characters would show up. I thought it was the Polish security service, but it was the French Sureté. So, having given them the slip, I called from the main post office to Maisons-Lafitte.

They invited me to come over, and I went. I was extremely nervous, a complete wreck. I was very unpleasant to them, extremely stubborn and sullen. But the kindhearted Zygmunt Hertz took me under his wing. For a long time he wouldn't let me go into town alone, because of the possibility that I might be kidnapped. At that time, the Communists did such things.

Michnik: Kultura was a new social and intellectual milieu for you. How did you feel in this environment?

Miłosz: I felt terrible, because I was an outsider, and they were linked by common experiences. I heard endless conversations about what it had been like in the Mari Republic, in Yangiyul, in Iraq. I behaved very badly toward them and imagined the worst possible things about them. This satisfied my sense of deep humiliation. I was prickly. I tried to compensate by telling myself they were all fascists. I used to tease them by asking, "What do you mean, labor camps? What labor camps?" although I knew perfectly well what they were talking about. I drove them to a frenzy. Trying to understand myself today, I just have to accept all these contradictions and stupidities.

At that time, I had much warmer contacts with Czapski than with Giedroyc. I had the warmest possible relationship with Zygmunt Hertz, full of friendship and kindness but not particularly intellectual.

I had more opportunities to talk with Czapski. Later, Kot Jeleński arrived, but for a long time we had a rather formal relationship.

Michnik: When did you get to know Gombrowicz?

Miłosz: Not until he came to Europe and settled in France.

Michnik: You didn't correspond with him before that?

Miłosz: Our correspondence consisted of friendly polemics on the pages of *Kultura*. I think we respected each other; my relationship with Gombrowicz was always very correct.

Michnik: Do you think that *Kultura* created a particular way of thinking about Polish culture, about Polish politics and society?

Miłosz: Certainly. The biggest dispute in which *Kultura* was ever involved was with Polish political émigrés, who accused the journal of being an agent of communism. *Kultura* published Gombrowicz and Miłosz at a time when they were both condemned by the prevailing émigré orthodoxy. The position of the political émigré community was as follows: The country is occupied. What happens when a country is occupied? Nothing but terror. And *Kultura* made an enormous effort to be interested in what was happening in Poland. Immediately after the war, several issues of the journal were devoted to People's Poland. In other words, the journal wanted to influence events in Poland. Lay the ground for change, that was the policy of *Kultura*.

Michnik: Didn't your instinctive dislike of the *endecja* also bring you closer to *Kultura*?

Miłosz: Absolutely. Giedroyc represented the continuing presence of the old republic. He was enormously interested in the question of Ukraine, Belarus, and Lithuania. Giedroyc actually published books in Ukrainian—for example, the anthology entitled *Rozstrzelane odrodzenie* [A Massacred Renaissance], dealing with the Stalinist terror and the destruction of the Ukrainian intelligentsia. I would say that Giedroyc was to a large extent the heir of Stanisław Stempowski, Maria Dąbrowska's lifelong companion. In fact, Stanisław Stempowski's son, Jerzy Stempowski (Paweł Hostowiec), worked closely with *Kultura*.

Michnik: What kind of relationship did you have with Maria Dąbrowska?

Miłosz: I knew them both, and I visited them on numerous occasions and with what I might call varying degrees of success. Sometimes they liked me, sometimes they didn't like me. I even think my wife and I spent our last night in Poland, before we left for the States, in Dąbrowska's apartment. Stempowski gave me a letter to some of the big shots in Washington, which I never used. I became much greater friends with Anna Kowalska, Dąbrowska's friend, than with Dąbrowska herself. I sometimes compared Dąbrowska with Eliza Orzeszkowa, which offended her mightily. I don't consider such a comparison offensive.

Michnik: You are fascinated by Russia. I once said that Miłosz has a kind of love-hate relationship with Russia, and someone replied, "Hate, maybe, but where's the love?" I, at any rate, have the impression that your studies of Dostoyevsky, Pasternak, and Brodsky betray a fascination with Russia.

Miłosz: As I've said many times, I love Russia, I love to talk with Russians, I love their language. They have a great literature. Polish literature doesn't come anywhere near it. I'm talking about Russian prose.

Another thing that's important for me is the incredible process that took place among the Russian intelligentsia during the nineteenth century. Whenever I tried to explain to my American students what happened at that time to the Russian intelligentsia, I used to say there were once villages in the Carpathians where the entire population was infected with endemic syphilis, but they had become resistant to it, and it no longer did them any harm. If outsiders became infected, however, they always died, so strong was the dose. The Russian intelligentsia began to absorb the West from the moment the Napoleonic wars drew young Russian officers to France. In the West, all the ideas that had led to the decay of the old system, especially atheistic ideas, had been assimilated gradually by a stable society. In Russia, by contrast, these ideas were absorbed much more rapidly. The effect was as though the intellectually unprepared organism of the Russian intelligentsia had been struck by a bolt of lightning. Moreover, the intelligentsia confronted a totally ossified social structure, with the result that the ensuing turmoil took place only in the mind, the mind of Ivan Karamazov.

From this point of view, the whole of nineteenth-century Russian literature, which is the literature of the Russian intelligentsia, is fantastic. The same can be said of all the ideas that take shape and come to maturity in this literature. These are Western ideas taken to the level of paroxysm. This is why I am fascinated by Russia and by Russian literature.

But I see a certain analogy here. Poland may now absorb the West with a similar result. The country may absorb various poisonous substances, because the West is decadent, it has a highly developed nihilism, which Nietzsche saw as European nihilism. However, in the West, this nihilism exists within the framework of a very stable society that knows precisely what to do and how it should be done and that thus functions perfectly well. Western society can also cope with enormous advances in science that will probably—I've said this before—depend on a process of constant social decomposition. Perhaps all this will now have the same effect on Poland as endemic syphilis once had on those who had no resistance to it.

Michnik: You have often referred to yourself as extremely anti-Western. You've lived in the West for forty years, surrounded by foreigners. Basically, you have never tried to become part of any culture other than Polish. Tell me something about your attitude toward the West.

Miłosz: I think I can be proud of the fact that I've lived so long in the West without succumbing to disintegration. This is a victory of a kind. I could have succumbed to disintegration by losing my sense of direction; I could also have fallen apart as a poet. It's very strange. As a friend of mine used to say, "How is it? Those Russian poets who emigrate can't stand it, they go crazy. How come you've managed to behave like a poet?"

I really didn't become integrated. In France this was because all intellectuals thought like Sartre: they saw Marxism as the last frontier of twentieth-century philosophy. Integration in France was therefore out of the question.

The same is true of the States, although there has been a certain exception, which I didn't anticipate. When my books of poetry began appearing in English and when I began to go around reading my poems, I became, to some extent, integrated into American poetry and literary circles. In the States I feel comfortable in the sense that I've achieved a certain standing; I'm not a total outsider; I get invitations to read my poems. In a certain sense, I'm an American poet, although it's clear that all my poems are translated from Polish.

In other respects, I haven't become integrated because my way of thinking has remained that of our circle in Poland. In addition, I have a particular resistance to, a wariness of, new vogues; a complete resistance to fashion. Perhaps I was influenced in this by Gombrowicz and his writing—in the sense of opposition to, even a certain arrogance toward, all kinds of intellectual and literary fashion. It's hard to say, though, what would have happened if I hadn't had a Catholic grounding, a Catholic education, and a strong sense of the sacred, and if I hadn't been influenced by Oskar Miłosz. He inoculated me against both France and America.

Michnik: Tell us something about how you experienced the student revolt of 1968. You were then here, in Berkeley, so you were at the center of events. In your book *Visions from San Francisco Bay,* I found an extremely ambivalent attitude toward this conflict.

Miłosz: I put a great deal of effort into writing *Visions from San Francisco Bay* as I wanted to achieve a distance that the events themselves did not evoke; in fact, they evoked an extremely intense reaction. When you stand at the window of a campus building with a professor of German origin, watching them burn the library, and she says "I remember," it's rather distressing. So I distanced myself, writing as though these were transient, short-lived events. In Berkeley, the young people worked themselves into a frenzy. At one time, I was giving a lift to some hippie or other, and he said, "Revolution, tomorrow there's going to be a revolution!" That was the atmosphere at the time.

There were also some humorous incidents. Once a crowd of students was barricading a path, and I went up to them and said in my best Slav accent, "Be gone, you spoiled children of the bourgeoisie." They were completely taken aback.

But these events were really very serious. This was an attempt to burst through the constraints imposed by the older generation, an attempt to disrupt the old order. These young people were inspired by the best intentions, which made it difficult for me to condemn them. Nevertheless, I was one of the few professors who dared to vote in the university senate against some of the absurd proposals presented—for example, a proposal to abolish the study of foreign languages. Most of the faculty behaved in an incredibly cowardly and conformist fashion.

Michnik: What's your reaction to the wave of neoconservatism now sweeping the States? A lot is being written about this in Poland, and many books by American neoconservatives are being published. The American right has become fashionable. Does this interest you?

Miłosz: No, not really. It's nothing remarkable.

Michnik: Suppose you had to situate yourself somewhere on the intellectual map of the States, who would be close to you?

Miłosz: I talk about this all the time at home with my wife, Carol. Carol supports the Democrats and strongly opposes the Republicans. But I usually say, "That's fine, I'm inclined to vote for the Democrats, I'm registered as a Democrat, but why are they so dull? They don't have a program, they don't have any personalities." I don't really have any need for the kind of politics specific to America.

Of course, this doesn't mean that I don't care about the dreadful aspects of both capitalism and life in the States—or about the total ignorance about the States that you find in Poland. When I read the Polish press or Polish literary journals, I have the impression that people take from America only the dregs of popular culture, nothing that is genuinely interesting and creative. There is enormous social injustice, there are horrifying ghettos. These are problems that cry out for vengeance, that demand solutions—hence my complaints about the Democratic party. So I see life in the States as part of the apocalypse of the twentieth century.

Michnik: What seem to you the most interesting things in American culture right now?

Miłosz: From the point of view of culture, America presents a rather strange spectacle, because it has been infiltrated by French intellectual fashion. Under the influence of such philosophers as Derrida, the deconstructionists have ensconced themselves in several universities and have begun to fight everyone whom they consider "old hat" and who doesn't recognize deconstruction. In English departments, you find contempt for science and philosophy, because the only thing that counts for deconstructionists is literary criticism; they treat it as humanity's most advanced outpost. This is a French disease. Marxism was a similar disease.

To a large extent, the atmosphere at American universities is also shaped by people who were revolutionaries in 1968. Now they have become professors, but they haven't made much progress in the meantime. Berkeley is full of these bizarre fossils. Together with the influx from France, they make for a very specific atmosphere. I don't know whether much is being written in Poland about "political correctness." These days, you have to be "politically correct," which means you have to be on the side of the blacks, against racism, for everything that's progressive.

Michnik: How does your religious sensibility react to this environment? In a letter you wrote to Thomas Merton in 1958, which was recently published in *Tygodnik Powszechny,* you wrote that you were not revealing your Catholic roots to your readers. You began to do this later. Tell us something about your relationship to Catholicism and how it has fluctuated over time.

Miłosz: It has been a constant process of rapprochement and withdrawal. This process of fluctuation began with my altercations with my catechist, Chomski, in middle school. Polish Catholicism was so totally Polish that I was repelled. There wasn't really anywhere in Poland where you could unburden yourself of your inner problems or the problems associated with independent religious thinking. Mysticism is still regarded as intellectually suspect, and the word *mystic* remains suspect, so I've taken great care to steer clear, to avoid having my writing classified as mystical. In all this, the work of Oskar Miłosz played a major role. But this is a separate, complicated matter.

Michnik: He wasn't a Catholic?

Miłosz: He was a practicing Catholic from 1927 until his death. And he was always seeking the advice of his confessor. Religious motives played a fairly major role in his opting for Lithuania. After a mystical experience in 1914, he wanted to serve people, and he found his goal in serving Lithuania, a small, downtrodden country that was trying to stand on its own feet. So for him, Catholicism meant actively serving humanity.

Michnik: What about your contacts with American religious life?

Miłosz: I had problems in the States also, because until Vatican II traditional Catholicism was extremely rigid and conservative. And after Vatican II, there was this craze to acknowledge the world, to adapt to it, so that the sermons one heard in church contained the most amazing heresies—it was quite incredible. But that was a human reaction.

Michnik: Have you always been a believer?

Miłosz: Not at all. A woman friend of mine, who's no longer living, once wrote to me, "Your whole life, you have always said both yes and no." This reminds me of Pascal's idea that "to believe, to err, to doubt are to man what running is to a horse."

Michnik: What changes in Polish Catholicism seem to you to be the most interesting and significant?

Miłosz: I was very pleased by what took place in Polish Catholicism after the war—the creation of an intellectual milieu, largely due to the efforts of Turowicz and those who continued, in some sense, the line of the prewar Verbum circle. And of course, the activity of the Catholic University in Lublin, where there were many brilliant minds, and the work of the *Éditions du Dialogue,* Father Sadzik's publishing house in Paris. All of this together led me to consider the possibility of working with the Church. Before the war, it would never have occurred to me to collaborate with a priest, but it was Father Sadzik who published my translations from the Bible.

Michnik: What does the Church mean to you today?

Miłosz: The Church is, above all, the sacrament. In other words, the Church is based on the mystery of the Eucharist, the mystery of transubstantiation and the Eucharist. In general, I find it hard to imagine Christianity outside of Catholicism or, perhaps, the Orthodox Church. I'm not the slightest bit attracted to Protestantism.

 The Church is important to me as a place where I can find myself in a community with others in the presence of the sacred. At the same time, respect is a fundamental consideration. I have no time for any philosophy that has no sense of respect. For me, the Church embodies respect for—we can call it by its general name—God.

Michnik: What kind of tendencies do you fear within the Church?

Miłosz: I realize that the kind of horizontal religiosity that I wrote about in a recent article, "A Confessional State?" which you published in *Gazeta Wyborcza,* is inevitable. This is related to the national characteristics that color Catholicism in many countries—in Spain, in Italy, in Ireland, in Poland. But I must admit that I'm allergic to the Polish-Catholic combination.

Michnik: Which tendencies do you feel close to in the West?

Miłosz: Here I'm rather torn, in the sense that I don't belong to the unequivocal enthusiasts of what has happened in the Church since Vatican II. At the same time, I don't share the schismatic views of Archbishop Lefèbvre. There were certain advantages to Latin as the language of worship, especially since prayer books that gave the text in both Latin and Polish, or French or English, compensated for any difficulties in understanding. This is a complicated question. I know someone who converted to Orthodoxy because of the liturgical reforms.

Michnik: How did you come across Simone Weil? Hers is a religiosity that is very intense, profound, and fervent, but free of dogma.

Miłosz: I think it was Czapski who lent me her first book. Then it occurred to me to put together a collection of her writings. I came to the conclusion that it would be worth doing this specially for Poland. Simone Weil became part of the mission I had set myself—to contribute to the revival of religious thought in Poland. It didn't matter if it was heretical thought, as long as it existed. My anthology of Simone Weil's writings was published by *Kultura* in 1958. Later, I had the satisfaction of being told by Bishop Kominek of Wrocław—he was in Paris in 1971, I think—that this book was compulsory reading in all the seminaries in his diocese. Maybe I helped indirectly to produce a few intelligent priests.

Michnik: You put your name to your translation of Simone Weil and wrote an introduction. You didn't put your name to your translation of Raymond Aron's book *The End of the Age of Ideology,* also published by *Kultura,* nor did you write an introduction. Why?

Miłosz: Because I didn't agree with the ideas set out in the book. Now I think that Aron was right, but he was twenty years too soon.

Michnik: In other words, it's dangerous to be right before your time; but that's a problem you're familiar with.

Miłosz: Yes, that's often the case. But I'm still adamantly opposed to a narrow interpretation of *The Captive Mind.* I don't agree with all those interpretations that now negate the historical role of Marxism, arguing that it was nothing more than ordinary human opportunism or simple terror.

A misunderstanding recently emerged in a conversation with young poets from the journal *NaGłos.* I said that Stalinism was a powerful intellectual force, and they accused me of still being a Marxist. But I had actually said that this force derived from the fact that Marxism was an integral part of European nihilism. Brzozowski was in some way right when he wrote about Hegel and Marx as the crowning achievement of philosophy, after which philosophy is doomed to find itself in a blind alley. Marxism really was a major ferment, a kind of insanity. But to say this does not imply that one is a Marxist. Today, Russia provides an example of the phenomenal role that ideology can play and what it means to lose an ideology.

Michnik: I would go further: anyone who says that Marxism was nothing more than terror renders himself incapable of understanding the experience of others, their life story, their sufferings.

Miłosz: If we apply this interpretation—which emphasizes opportunism above all else—to Germany, where does this lead us? The Germans became fascists simply out of opportunism?

Michnik: Precisely. Let's go back to a question I've already asked you. You managed to settle accounts with Marxism because you recognized that it had the power to fascinate; Marxism swayed millions of people in the Soviet Union, all over the world. Why didn't you settle accounts with nationalism in the same way? After all, the Germans are proof of the enormous resonance that nationalism possessed. We've also seen it in Poland.

Miłosz: Nazism was a German, not a universal, phenomenon . . .

Michnik: But nationalism was.

Miłosz: Do you really think so? In Polish intellectual circles in the interwar years? Ferdynand Goetz wrote a eulogy to fascism but not nationalism. He praised Italian fascism. In Poland, some people were attracted to Italian fascism, and to Salazar.

Michnik: But there weren't even any intellectual polemics with these tendencies. Bolesław Miciński was one exception. What he wrote about de Maistre constitutes an attempt to examine the right-wing roots of fascism. But you never wrote anything on the subject.

Miłosz: I was organically incapable of it.

Michnik: What about anti-Semitism? How come you were so resistant to anti-Semitism?

Miłosz: I think this dates from my school days. For a certain period when I was young, the atmosphere was such that you were supposed to beat up Jews on May 1, because May 1 was a Jewish holiday. Who marched through Vilnius on May 1? Mostly the Bund, a few members of the Polish Socialist party, and young Communists. It was a traumatic experience for me when I succumbed for a month or two to this idea. Since then, I've been immune.

Michnik: What, in your opinion, are the intellectual underpinnings of anti-Semitism? Why is it that, despite the fact that there is no longer a Jewish community in Poland, anti-Semitism lives on in the mind and in public life?

Miłosz: I think it's a question of accumulated cultural layers. The figure of the Jew that became fixed in Polish literature is a ridiculous stereotype, a hostile figure, because Jews were assigned a special place in the Polish economy during the eighteenth and nineteenth centuries. Moneylenders, innkeepers, and shopkeepers—nearly all trade was in the hands of Jews. These stereotypes undoubtedly have a very long life. Of course, you can analyze anti-Semitism as a psychological phenomenon, but I'm not going to do that.

I saw Lanzmann's film *Shoah*. It was disturbing, but I also found it distasteful. Of course, the Poles he shows are miserable creatures. Lanzmann's perspective is precisely one of Parisian intellectual contempt for these primitive people. It was very distressing, but he grasped some of their characteristics. Even in this film, you can see the contrast between them and the Jews, who belonged to another cultural world. Aleksander Wat used to say that Jewish tradition held that men should always be able to read. Of course, there were many poor Jews who couldn't read, but in general Wat was right. And then alongside the Jews you have this Polishness; in proto-Slav fashion it is slovenly, anti-intellectual, incapable of manipulating ideas, like in the poem by Jerzy Liebert: "Here, there is neither West nor East, it's as though I were standing on the threshold."

Apart from that, Jews had been in Poland for centuries, not because of a deliberate policy, but because of inertia. England expelled the Jews during the Middle Ages. Jews settled in Poland, after fleeing from the pogroms in Germany. They populated the small towns of Ukraine and Belarus, which became, essentially, ghettos. There, they lived in abject poverty, because there were simply too many of them. The relative size of any population is always important.

Michnik: What is the essence of the sin—if we can use this word—of anti-Semitism?

Miłosz: The sin of anti-Semitism? It's the idea that it's a question of oil and water, that if you mix the two, the Jews will always come to the top because they are smarter.

Michnik: But what does the sin consist of?

Miłosz: I think any attempt to explain anti-Semitism is a sin. Because, by explaining, you justify it.

Michnik: And there are no justifications?

Miłosz: The moment you start to justify it, you actually begin to defend it.

Michnik: I think we need to understand the origin of this phenomenon. I'm trying to get under the skin of an anti-Semite, to look at the world in his categories. If I succeed, I may write a book called *The Mind Held Captive by Anti-Semitism*.

Miłosz: I think anti-Semitism involves the same mechanism that you find in the people who now write that Miłosz is just pretending to be a Pole. It's the same mentality.

Michnik: That's simply stupidity and narrow-mindedness, and there's nothing to be done about it. I think the problem is more complicated. Anti-Semitism has played a major role in Polish culture, and it's playing a major role in the whole post-Communist debate. You have it in Hungary, in Romania, in Slovakia, and you have it in Russia. Marina Tsvetayeva once wrote that every poet is a Jew, because he carries within him the fate of the damned, the accursed. I think there's something in this.

Miłosz: My feeling of disconnection is very similar. I said that I only feel at home in a Polish intellectual environment. But I feel disconnected from the mass of Poles. When I get letters telling me that I'm bringing honor to our unhappy fatherland, when I look around in some places of worship, I feel ill at ease. I think Tsvetayeva was probably right.

Michnik: What does your past mean to you? After leaving Poland, you wrote an article for *Kultura* entitled "No" in which you said that you considered yourself an anti-Stalinist and on the left. Does the notion of the left have any meaning today?

Miłosz: It has a certain meaning. In the last analysis, for example, the notion of the separation of church and state can be considered a legacy of the left. But is it a legacy only of the left? After all, Jefferson can hardly be considered a leftist.

Michnik: One could say the same about de Gaulle or Giscard d'Estaing, who also supported the separation of church and state.

Miłosz: Of course, there are certain left-wing instincts, and I think I have such instincts.

Michnik: What instincts are they?

Miłosz: That one should not be indifferent to human suffering, because it cries out for vengeance from heaven. My friend Józef Czechowicz, who was neither on the left nor particularly involved in politics, once described a train station in Warsaw, full of hungry, homeless people, and he wrote: "From this, the walls of Jericho will come tumbling down." To be on the left is to want to do something to change this kind of situation.

For many years now, my poetry hasn't been directly concerned with social problems, but they're still there somewhere. In the book *A Year of the Hunter,* I described my stay in Hawaii. Hawaiian civilization was a feudal society based on a cruel religion involving human sacrifice. But because it had been destroyed, because it had lost its language, I felt a solidarity with it. This is also an expression of a left-wing instinct. I felt the same when I was young; when I read a book about the destruction of Milan by Barbarossa, I cried bitterly.

Michnik: What did the Nobel Prize mean to you? During the 1960s, you wrote a book, *A Man among Scorpions,* which many of us read—or at least the title—as an allusion to your own life history. And then this accursed poet suddenly receives the highest honors.

Miłosz: I was never one of those writers who aspire to the Nobel Prize. It's clear, after all, that some people wait their whole lives to receive this prize and most of them don't get it. It was really very strange. In any event, what I said—that it was a prize for Solidarity—wasn't actually true, because in May 1980, when the verdict was reached, Solidarity didn't yet exist. The Swedish Academy was extremely annoyed that it all looked so political when I accepted the prize in October. I tried not to be too political because I could sense they were uncomfortable. The Swedish Academy doesn't like to stick its neck out.

I'm convinced that I would never have received this prize if I'd stayed in France. How things would have turned out if I'd stayed in Poland, I have no idea. The fact is the English translations of my poems played an enormous role.

Michnik: But what did it mean to you? It's a unique moment for any writer, and it was yours, someone of whom it had been said he would never write again, that he'd spend his days in impotence, gazing at the frescoes in Ravenna. And suddenly, a miracle . . .

Miłosz: I can tell you one thing: it's one thing to look at this from the inside and another thing entirely to look at it from the outside. These are two completely different perspectives. From the outside, I was a poet unknown outside a fairly small circle.

Michnik: It wasn't until 1980 that teachers of Polish literature found out that there was a poet by the name of Miłosz.

Miłosz: Yes, it was really amazing to jump from this to the Nobel Prize. But I considered myself a distinguished poet, satisfied with a dozen or so readers. So from my point of view, it wasn't so remarkable. After all, I'd been published in American anthologies and I was esteemed as a poet. In Poland, I was unknown. So you have to take these two perspectives into account.

It's clear that the Nobel Prize can turn your head. Saul Bellow wrote that the Nobel Prize can be the "kiss of death." Here, I can say with some pride that ten years have passed since I was awarded the prize and that these have been creative years.

Michnik: How did you feel when Brodsky received the Nobel Prize?

Miłosz: Enormous satisfaction, great happiness, perhaps because it was going to yet another émigré poet. There's a whole string of us: Miłosz, Canetti, Singer, Nelly Sachs, and Brodsky.

Michnik: Do you feel close to Brodsky as a writer?

Miłosz: More so as an essayist than a poet, because our poetry is very different.

Michnik: Recently, you've spoken out frequently on the question of the Baltic states. This is a constant theme in your intellectual life; you wrote about the Baltics in *The Captive Mind* and you spoke about them in your Nobel acceptance speech.

Miłosz: When I spoke about the Baltic states and the Molotov-Ribbentrop pact in Stockholm, it was out of a sense of moral obligation. In my wildest dreams, I never imagined that I would see a time when the Molotov-Ribbentrop pact would be officially condemned and the Baltic states would regain their independence. It was all in the far distant future. As far as the chapter on the Baltics is concerned, I well remember hesitating about whether to include it in *The Captive Mind*.

Michnik: Why?

Miłosz: I didn't see myself as a warrior against the Kingdom of Evil. I wanted to confine myself to literature. Including the chapter on the Baltics meant going beyond this sphere and beyond Poland, which was the focus of the book. Anyway, I decided to include it. I'm still interested in the Baltic states; I'm friends with Tomas Venclova, and I've translated into Polish, via English, several poems by the Estonian poet Jaan Kaplinski.

Michnik: Today, you read me an elegy on the death of communism. What does the end of communism really mean to you? Your whole life, you had to deal with communism; Bolshevism constantly dogged your footsteps. How are we going to live now? How does one live without communism?

Miłosz: I personally am very happy to see the end of communism, but it may be that many people will begin to think that perhaps things were better under communism. There's going to be a period of terrible disorientation, when people take the leftovers of the West and imitate everything American, including mass culture.

To keep one's senses and equilibrium in this new post-Communist world, one needs a firm foundation, but people don't have it. What will remain? On the one hand, Catholicism; on the other, nationalism. This will provide a frame of reference of a kind. If belonging to a nation becomes the main organizing principle of the world, then people will hang on to this. This is nothing new. For a long time now, we've seen nationalism or Great Russian imperialism replacing Marxist doctrine everywhere. It looks as though this is likely to continue.

Michnik: You once wrote in a letter that you situate yourself at the end of the eighteenth century in Poland: you're strongly opposed to Sarmatism [Polish nationalism], but you're also strongly anti-Western . . .

Miłosz: I discussed this question with the editors of *Res Publica,* but they twisted my argument around. They came to the conclusion that I want Poland to become a kind of Skansen, a cultural museum, that I think we shouldn't write any new styles of prose, that we should stick to old-fashioned styles of storytelling. This is a complete misunderstanding. I don't want to create any museums. I simply hoped, in 1989, that the rich and dramatic experiences of the previous forty-five years would create an antitoxin that would immunize us against the desire to seize unselectively on all the idiocies coming from the West.

Today, I no longer hold out any such hope. I see very little sign of the awareness that suffering should bring. Today, nobody even wants to hear the words and slogans that were de rigueur during the time of Solidarity. People want to reject everything as though it no longer has any significance because it's already old and out of date.

I don't see any polemics with the West in the name of those values that were specific not only to Poland but to all the countries that went through the Communist experience and ought to be a little wiser for it. I don't see any polemics, I don't see any inclination to reject some of the tendencies prevalent in the West. After all, we must recognize that there are apocalyptic elements in the twentieth century. The collapse of communism doesn't mean the end of the apocalypse, because the apocalypse hinges on complete fluidity, on the absence of firm foundations. This was all foretold by Nietzsche.

Michnik: On what can we build a foundation?

Miłosz: This is really a problem for the schools and universities. Those who teach in the United States are themselves without any criteria, without any foundation. They just stagger from one day to the next. That's why I think it is so important to maintain the vertical dimension of Christianity.

Michnik: How did you perceive the past twenty-five years, when new writings and new names emerged in Poland?

Miłosz: I felt involved in the events taking place in Poland. This was symbolized by my meeting in 1981 with the people who had been printing my books. It was extremely moving. So my isolation was only relative. I felt most isolated during the years 1951–56. I followed the intellectual ferment in the country and then the appearance of *Zapis*. I translated many Polish poets, Herbert and others, into English. You can call me a "rootless cosmpolitan" or an "émigré," but I think I've done quite a lot.

Michnik: What is literature today? That's a simple question.

Miłosz: Simple, but at the same time very complicated. Very complicated, because today a new concept of literature is emerging. This is connected, in fact, with the revolution taking place in university English departments. Literature professors want to consider themselves the salt of the earth; philosophy is finished, and science doesn't deal with the fundamental issues. The boundary between the word and reality is becoming blurred, because everything is relative. There's no such thing as objective reality—in which case, language actually becomes everything.

I have to counterpose to this my old-fashioned understanding of objective reality. This is deeply rooted in my weltanschauung. I believe that an objective reality exists and that art consists in making contact with this reality, in the attempt to grasp it. Certain literary genres are undoubtedly going through a crisis and may die out.

Nevertheless, considering the de facto nonexistence of the novel in Polish literature, and considering the fact that this literature is now under fire, or is being subjected to Western influences in which the subjectivization of writing, the subjectivization of art, is so strong, I would propose the following: that Polish writers write using proper syntax, with punctuation, and without internal monologues; that they write decent novels to make up for the shortage thereof. Russia has a magnificent realist literature, going back to Dostoyevsky, Tolstoy, and Chekhov. Where can we find greater finesse than in the simplicity of Chekhov? But when I pick up Polish writings, I see nothing but innumerable attempts to make things unnecessarily complicated. It seems to me that Polish literature is in danger of succumbing to an excessive preoccupation with form.

I am very critical of today's literature. I read very little, and I read scarcely any novels. I ask myself how many years I have left, what I still need to do, what obligations remain. I read only those books that I have to read. I'm currently reading a history of Finland.

Michnik: I can highly recommend the history of Ireland also. It is simply fascinating and an invaluable guide to Joyce's *Ulysses*. Unless you know the history of Ireland, *Ulysses* is simply incomprehensible.

Miłosz: Yes, from those tangled Irish roots, Joyce managed to create world-class literature. A great achievement. I wonder if it would be possible to do something similar based on Polish-Lithuanian roots . . . I have tried to do something with them.

Michnik: How would you define lying in literature?

Miłosz: How would I define lying? It depends on whether a piece of literature is good, and if it is, then we don't apply the criterion. This question is related to the question of whether a really bad person can create good literature.

Michnik: That's another question. I'm interested in artistic lying.

Miłosz: One recognizes artistic lying in a nonrational way. You look at a page and you either see it or you don't, that's all.

Michnik: Does the word *betrayal* have any meaning in the sphere of culture? The artist has a calling. At what point can we say he has betrayed this calling?

Miłosz: It seems to me that the example of Joseph Conrad can provide an answer to this. Conrad was concerned, first and foremost, to make money from literature, but he sat over every book, crossing out every line several times, in torment. Why? He could have written quickly, he could have sought earnings by hiring himself out. But he couldn't bring himself to do this, he simply couldn't, even though he was constantly in dire financial straits. If he had abandoned these standards, he would have committed an act of betrayal. There's an imperative that commands us to sit and to create to the best of our ability.

Michnik: Have you ever felt, when writing, that you were committing an act of betrayal?

Miłosz: I'll say this. I wrote the novel *The Seizure of Power*. I had very little time, and I had to finish it in time for a competition. When Jeanne Hersch told me that it was very good and that I was a very good writer, I said to her, "But the novel is not a literary genre to which one should ascribe any artistic significance." That was a genuine betrayal, because I was writing in a genre whose artistic value I did not recognize.

Then I wrote another novel, *Issa Valley*. I wrote this novel because I was going through a crisis with poetry. I was having an internal crisis connected with nihilism, and to rid myself of it I had to write as I did in *Issa Valley*. So *Issa Valley* was in some sense a therapeutic exercise. This goes some way toward answering your question.

Michnik: Tell me, when you look back, what makes you most happy and what do you most regret?

Miłosz: As I once wrote in a poem, one part of me regrets and the other part does not regret that I never became a prominent citizen of the city of Vilnius and that we did not form an alliance with Ferrara or Modena. The only thing is that in order for me to have stayed there, history would have had to take a completely different course. I wonder, if things had turned out that way, whether I wouldn't have met the same fate as Bujnicki, before his political downfall, before 1939. You only have to read his poetry from that period to see he was at an impasse. But this is all theoretical.

Michnik: And what do you regret in your work?

Miłosz: Of course, there are things that I would prefer to have avoided. I think my beginnings were a little crazy. I was too concerned with ideology and politics, I tried too hard to be a political animal. I wrote idiotic articles to which one could really apply the term "condemned to the idleness of the whip," heavy-handed, Zhdanovite stuff without any real substance.

And I would have to add a number of poems that were a mistake. During the war, I was commissioned by Wierciński—in other words, by the underground theatrical council—to write a prologue for the opening of a theater. What was the basic assumption? Not belief, but assumption? That the war would end, that there would be a celebratory opening of a theater in Warsaw, and that for this opening Wierciński would commission a prologue from me. For this occasion, he also commissioned a translation of Shakespeare's *As You Like It,* because the play deals with banishment to the forest of Arden, and everything ends happily. So, I wrote this prologue, of which I am somewhat ashamed. Luckily, it was never performed, because it was very weak and artificial. Evidently, I didn't identify sufficiently with suffering Poland . . .

Michnik: To which of your books are you most attached?

Miłosz: I'm attached to my poetry, to the volume *Three Winters,* and I like the poems I wrote in emigration. I like the collection *Unattainable Earth,* because of the mixture of transpositions, aphorisms, and so on. Of all the poems that I wrote in Poland, I probably value "Świat poema naiwne" [The World] the most.

Michnik: What do you say to people who ask you how one should live?

Miłosz: In the nineteenth century, Vassily Rozanov wrote, "They ask me: What should we do? And I answer: What should you do? Go gather berries, make preserves, and eat them."

I can only answer on the basis of my own experience. Because of my psychological and physiological makeup, my restless disposition, I couldn't function at all if I weren't constantly under the sway of a kind of internal incantation. At night, when I'm unable to sleep, a line of poetry will suddenly come into my head, and then I'm able to fall asleep. So, in my experience, one has to rise early in the morning and try to write a few lines. Obviously, this isn't a recipe for everyone . . .

Michnik: Rise early and write, and then go gathering berries. So let's go gather some berries. Thank you for the conversation, and best wishes from everyone at *Gazeta Wyborcza.*

22

The Strange Epoch
of Post-Communism

A Conversation with Václav Havel

Václav Havel: Adam, it seems you want to interrogate me for three hours.

Adam Michnik: That's right.

Havel: But I don't know enough about anything to talk for three hours.

Michnik: But you have plenty of experience, because you've been interrogated so many times already. Three hours is nothing for an old felon like you.

It's two years since the "velvet revolution," since the celebrated year of 1989 when, two hundred years after the French Revolution, communism collapsed in our part of the world. I remember being in Prague in the summer of 1989 and visiting you in Hradeček and telling you that you'd become president. Do you think communism has been overthrown once and for all, or could it make a comeback? Is a Communist counterrevolution or restoration possible?

Havel: I think a global restoration of communism, a return to the times of Brezhnev or Stalin, is out of the question. This process is irreversible. However, local restorations are possible. I can imagine a new version of Communist rule might reemerge under a slightly different banner. Somewhere or other, for example in one of the Soviet re-

---

Translated by Jane Cave from *Gazeta Wyborcza*, November 30, 1991.

publics, the *nomenklatura* might be able to dress itself up in slightly more nationalistic colors and use the former party hierarchy to create something akin to the old system. Local restorations of this kind are feasible, but the empire or the bloc as a whole has gone forever; history can't be reversed.

Michnik: What do you think is happening, and what will happen, to everything that belongs to the ancien régime—the people and the institutions?

Havel: I think this is an enormous problem for the whole post-Communist world. Those people who directly contributed, to a greater or lesser extent, to the creation of this regime, those who tolerated it in silence, and all of us who subconsciously adapted ourselves to it—we're all here together. We are left with these huge, centralized, monopolistic state enterprises and with a state administration full of officials from the previous era. This is one source of the enormous problems and difficulties that the post-Communist world must now tackle. It isn't the only one, but it's one of the most important.

It's not a question of struggling against particular individuals associated with the old regime or its representatives. First and foremost, it's a question of struggling against the habits of ordinary citizens. They genuinely hated the totalitarian regime, but at the same time they lived their whole lives under it and, despite themselves, they got used to it. They got used to the fact that above them loomed the all-powerful state that took care of everything and was responsible for everything. They acquired a paternalistic attitude toward the state, and this won't disappear overnight. You can't eradicate in one fell swoop all the bad habits that the regime systematically inculcated in people over the course of years. This is a powerful and troublesome legacy, another source of the problems that the post-Communist world has to deal with.

Michnik: There are two symbolic terms used to define two different ways of approaching relations with Communists or members of the old regime. One such way is referred to in Poland as "the policy of the thick line." Tadeusz Mazowiecki used this term in his first speech as prime minister. He was concerned to draw a thick line between past and present and simultaneously to say that the only criterion to be used in assessing government officials would be their competence and loyalty to the new government. This provided a basis for some people to accuse him of wanting to use "the policy of the thick line"

President Václav Havel (left) visiting Adam Michnik at the offices of *Gazeta Wyborcza*, Warsaw, September 1992. (Photo: Sławomir Kamiński)

to protect Communist criminals and thieves, and so on. The second approach comes from the Czech and Slovak Federal Republic and is referred to as "lustration." These are two extreme approaches to this issue. What do you think of the philosophy proposed by Mazowiecki and that proposed by the advocates of lustration?

Havel: This is another major problem. You have to steer a course somehow between Scylla and Charybdis. I think both of these approaches are mistaken in their extreme form. Our history teaches us that we pay dearly whenever we take the approach that we should not concern ourselves with the past, that it is of no importance. It means we have failed to remove a kind of abscess that continues to fester and goes on to poison the whole body. It seems to me that the need to cut it out, to see that justice is done, is completely justified and natural.

At the same time, however, we mustn't open the door to lawless revenge and witch-hunts; this would simply be another version of what we've just left behind. This approach has also been tried several times in Czechoslovakia. I remember various postwar avengers, and the most energetic of them usually had the most skeletons in the closet. I think the demand that we make public the names of all those who in one way or another were associated with the police—regardless of when and why—is highly dangerous. It's a time bomb that could explode at any minute and poison the political atmosphere all over again with fanaticism, illegality, and injustice.

The point is to strike an appropriate balance. We have to adopt a cultured and civilized approach that doesn't flee from the past. We have to look our past in the face, we have to name it, draw conclusions from it, and render justice, but we have to do this honestly, with circumspection and tact, with magnanimity and imagination. When we're faced with confessions of guilt and expressions of repentance, there ought to be room for forgiveness.

So I'm in favor of a humanitarian approach, not a new wave of persecution and fear. People were afraid of the security service for forty years; they shouldn't have to be afraid for the next ten years that someone will dig up something from their past. After all, many people don't even know whether or not they got mixed up in something by accident. That's why I had reservations about our lustration law and publicly called on Parliament to amend it.

Michnik: Let's take a specific example. Yesterday in Prague I was told that the lustration process threatens the well-known philosopher Karel Kosík, who was persecuted and condemned to silence for years after the Prague Spring. He is about to be persecuted again for events that took place over twenty years ago, for the fact that in 1968 he was a member of the Central Committee of the Czechoslovak Communist party. How would you assess this fact?

Havel: Let me begin with a clarification. While the law is generally referred to as the lustration law, it is actually broader in scope and deals not only with lustration. The term "lustration" refers to checking whether someone is on file at the Ministry of Internal Affairs as a collaborator of the ministry. At the same time, the law prohibits a range of people from occupying public office for a period of five years. They include anyone who during the past forty years was a member of the People's Militia, the Communist verification commissions of 1948 and 1968, or who were party activists from the district committee level on up. There is one exception: people who were party officials during the period between January 1, 1968, and May 1, 1969, are excluded. I think Karel Kosík is included among those who are covered by this exception, although as a young man of twenty he was a member of the verification commissions that expelled people from the universities in 1948.

In general, I believe this law is very severe and unjust. For example, it's enough for someone to have been a member of the People's Militia for a single day thirty years ago to be prohibited from occupying certain positions. And this also applies to the militia who in 1968 [during the invasion of the Warsaw Pact armies] defended the Extraordinary Party Congress in Vysočany against attack by the Soviet occupying forces. I'm not saying that such people are in the majority, but they're certainly a substantial minority. But from the moral point of view, even if only one innocent person suffered as a result of this law, I would still consider it a bad law. It's precisely for this reason that one should never apply the principle of collective guilt and responsibility but should always judge only the specific acts of each individual.

The amendments that I proposed to the Federal Assembly envisage that anyone could take his case to court and the court could pronounce him fit to hold a given office because of the specific circumstances pertaining to his individual case. If, for example, someone subsequently waged a lengthy struggle for human rights, the court would have the right to proclaim that his positive contribution outweighed his guilt for having belonged for a time to this or that organization or agency. This would be the case with people who were coerced into collaborating or those members of underground organizations who were delegated to work with the regime—one can imagine many such cases during the fifties.

Michnik: There's another problem here. I've heard that the deputy speaker of the Slovak Parliament, Ivan Čarnogurský, has accused the former prime minister of Slovakia, Vladimír Mečiar, of having collaborated with the security service and that Mečiar has leveled the same accusation against Čarnogurský. The only competent arbiter in this dispute is someone who knows the facts, in other words, a colonel in the security service. It seems to me we're getting into an absurd situation if security service colonels start issuing certificates of morality.

Havel: Yes, that's true, and I pointed it out in my letter to Parliament. The supreme, absolute, and final indicator of people's suitability for certain posts in a democratic state is to be found in the internal documents of the security service. This is just crazy.

Michnik: The case of Ján Kavan has caused a stir outside the country. A former émigré who helped the Czechoslovak opposition, he was accused, after returning home, of having collaborated with the security service. I've heard that last week you ostentatiously went to a restaurant with Kavan so that everyone could see the two of you together.

Havel: Yes, I did meet with him in a restaurant, but it wasn't a question of making a point. I met with him because our common friend, Petr Uhl, asked me to talk to him and hear his side of the story. I couldn't see any reason not to do this, especially since I worked with Kavan during my dissident years. At that time, he helped the then opposition and did a great deal for us. His case is extremely controversial, so I had even less reason not to meet with him and talk about it. But it was no demonstration on my part.

Michnik: You say that we somehow have to steer between Scylla and Charybdis. Where do you think the boundary lies? Where does justice end and vengeance begin?

Havel: This boundary can be defined only by something vague, something that can't be subjected to legal norms, something like sensitivity, taste, forbearance, circumspection, wisdom—in other words, certain human characteristics. If we allowed ourselves to be guided by them, perhaps we could find the boundary. It's a vital problem, and the boundary is difficult to define, as evidenced by our lustration law, which I consider an abortive effort despite the fact that it is the product of two years' discussion. The law shows how difficult it is to define this boundary in legal terms, but at the same time it must be defined in legal terms because even worse than a rigid law is a state of lawlessness in which everyone can lustrate and publicly slander everyone else.

Michnik: In one of your interviews, you talked about how you sense that people are becoming afraid of the past. I've just been in Germany, where I talked with our friends from the dissident era, and all of them were talking about the Stasi [secret police]. I had the feeling they were obsessed by the subject. They said that, for them, the activities of the Stasi were equivalent to an Auschwitz of the soul. They said one had to view the whole problem from the perspective of the victims. If someone was wronged by the Stasi, he has the right to demand justice in the sense that he has the right to know who wronged him. This means he has the right to see his files to find out who informed on him.

On the other hand, when I talked not long ago to the Spanish writer Jorge Semprun, I asked him, "How did you deal with this in Spain?" After all, they too had a dictatorship, policemen who tortured people, informers, and so on. He replied, "If you want to live a normal life, you have to try to forget, otherwise all the wild snakes let out of the cage will poison public life for years to come."

For his part, the German writer Jürgen Fuchs said, "Listen, I'm no bloodsucker. I write poetry, but I won't be able to live with this. If we don't finish this once and for all, it will keep coming back, like Nazism. We didn't go through a process of denazification, and it weighed on us for years."

What's the opinion of a Czech writer who is also president?

Havel: I want to say that my personal opinion on this issue differs somewhat from the opinion that I have, and must have, as president. As president, I have to take account of the state of society and its wishes.

My personal attitude is best illustrated by one example. Shortly after I became president, I was given a list of all my colleagues who had ever written to the authorities denouncing me. That very day, I not only lost the list but forgot whose names were on it. This simply means that I personally am inclined to let things be. I can keep my distance from the whole business because I myself fell into their hands and I know how they were able to destroy people. I've written plays and essays about it, and I've somehow resolved the issue as far as I'm concerned. For this reason, I have no need to punish anyone for the fact that he didn't meet the test.

As president, however, I have to take account of the fact that society needs a dividing line, because people feel the revolution is unfinished. There are people whose entire lives, and the lives of their families, were destroyed by the regime, people who spent their whole youth in concentration camps and who are in no state to reconcile themselves to this. All the more so, as many of their former persecutors are now much better off than they are. There's no getting away from it. People have a need to review the past, to get rid of the people who terrorized the nation and who clearly violated human rights, to remove them from the positions they still occupy. As I said, there is probably a historical necessity to confront the past and to name it precisely. For this reason, I can't treat these issues with the same nonchalance as I treated the fact that I lost the piece of paper containing the names of "my" informers.

Sasha Vondra (Havel's adviser on international affairs): It's interesting that on these issues there seems to be a difference between societies that are Catholic and those that are Protestant. On the one hand, you have Spain, as well as Hungary and Poland, and on the other, you have the Germans and Czechs. . . .

Michnik: I think Sasha has exaggerated a kind of philosophical structuralism, because in Poland it turns out—I don't know why—that no one is more vociferous in demanding a settling of accounts than Catholic politicians. Only terrible, suspect people like Kuroń or me say that we shouldn't go overboard with this. On the other hand, politicians belonging to parties that have the word *Catholic* in their names are more inclined these days to say that God is merciful.

Havel: The fact is, there are two traditions within Catholicism that create particular, dialectical tensions. One is the tradition of sin, toward which Catholicism is more indulgent than Protestantism. Hence the emphasis on forgiveness and remission. The second Catholic tradition is that of inquisition.

Michal Žantovsky (Havel's press secretary): But remission of sins is always related to confession, to revealing one's guilt, while inquisition involves searching out sins that have been concealed, which are always regarded as the most dangerous.

Michnik: I think each of us is doomed to this specific dialectic. When I was still in prison, I swore two things to myself: first, I would never join a veterans' organization that hands out medals for service in the struggle against communism; second, I would never seek revenge. But I used to repeat a few lines from one of Herbert's poems: "Never forgive, because it is not in your power to forgive in the name of those who were betrayed at daybreak." I think we're doomed to such a dialectic, that we can forgive only the wrongs that have been done to us, while it is not in our power to forgive the wrongs done to others. We can try to persuade others to do likewise, but people have the right to demand justice.

Havel: This is precisely the dilemma that I just mentioned. In my position, I can't behave exactly as I would as a private person. I have no need to persecute "my" security officers or informers. I feel no need for revenge. But as a state official, I don't have the right to declare a general amnesty on behalf of everyone else.

Michnik: A minute ago you used a term that disturbed me, you referred to an unfinished revolution. What does this actually mean? When will you consider that the revolution is finished?

Havel: It's hard to say. The revolution won't finish on any given day, and there's no single indicator that can be used to determine that it's over. It's a process that gathers force and then dies away. Only when a new generation enters political life will we be able to say it's finally over.

But there's a sense in which this revolution really is unfinished. We should remember, for example, that our program calls for a market economy, and we still have 95 percent state ownership. It's the same with the legal system: 95 percent of the regulations date back to Communist times. The same can be said about the political system. It will take time for new people to replace the state officials we have now, but for the time being everything is still in a state of flux.

I agree with you, though, that it will be difficult to say now the revolution is finished. It is bound to be simply a symbolic moment, like the transfer of the largest steel mill to private ownership, for example.

Žantovsky: Forgive me, but I think we're dealing with an issue that you've always tried to avoid. It's true that people have adopted the term "revolution" because of its use by the press, but what took place in Czechoslovakia was not exactly a revolution. A revolution always involves violence. If it had been a revolution, the constitution would have been suspended and revolutionary courts established, for example. We didn't take that course, and I think it's now too late to do so.

Havel: But from the very beginning we called it a revolution . . .

Žantovsky: We didn't.

Havel: OK, so it became known as a revolution, and the word can mean whatever we want it to. Now, for example, there is a dispute about where a federation ends and a confederation begins. As writers, we know perfectly well that we don't simply read but we also create language. We know that every word gradually takes on the meaning we assign to it. What took place in Czechoslovakia was called a revolution, and, regardless of whether this was correct or not, it has become a fact.

Žantovsky: Here, I have to disagree. Your friend Tom Stoppard has stated that language only makes sense when each word signifies a specific thing. Otherwise, people would be unable to communicate with each other. Of course, journalists can write what they want, but it transpires from the definition of revolution that ours was not a revolution.

Havel: That's the academic in you speaking, not the poet.

Žantovsky: But I just cited a friend of yours, who's no academic . . .

Michnik: It seems to me, Michal, that the demonstrations that forced the totalitarian government to make concessions were a revolution. And subsequent events—what the journalists called the "velvet revolution"—took place within the framework of the rule of law.

Some people think that this is where we went wrong, that we shouldn't have followed the rule of law but should have resorted to revolutionary methods—in other words, lawlessness—to destroy communism once and for all. Revolution always involves discrimination—either against your enemies or against members of the previous regime—while the law upholds the principle of equality. This is not just an academic question: either the law is the same for everyone, or it doesn't exist.

I fear it's still possible that certain groups—former Communists, for example—will be denied any legal rights, as was the case with the kulaks and the bourgeoisie in Russia after the Bolshevik Revolution. When I ask, what do you mean by "unfinished revolution," I know what I'm afraid of: I'm afraid the revolution will enter its next phase. We have plenty of historical examples of revolutions that began as a struggle for freedom and ended in despotism, from Cromwell to Napoleon, from Khomeini to other recent examples.

Many years ago, Semprun wrote the screenplay for a film by Alain Resnais, *The War Is Over.* The Spanish civil war was over, so there was no longer any need for military equipment. When you talk about an "unfinished revolution," I find myself wondering whether there won't be people who'll say, "Look, even Havel—humanist, writer, and philosopher that he is—says we need to continue the revolution."

So what should we do? Are we going to continue the revolution, or are we going to say the revolution is over; there are Communists among us, but they have the same right to live as the rest of us. If they committed a crime, they will be punished just like other criminals, but if not, we can't discriminate against them just because at one time or another they belonged to the Communist party.

Havel: I think the essence of these changes—and we won't call them revolutionary if you don't want to—was the introduction of the rule of law, not the beginning of a new lawlessness. It's just that this social pressure is the product of lawlessness, which has not come to an end. But the aim of this pressure is not the introduction of a new lawlessness. Take one of my friends, for example, Standa Milota, who was persecuted for twenty years and was unable to work. Today, he has a pension of one thousand crowns because he couldn't be promoted, and his salary, which formed the basis for his pension, was very low. The person who persecuted him and prevented him from working normally now has a pension of five thousand crowns, his own house, and many fine possessions. People see this kind of situation and say that even though the people "at the top" have changed, even though censorship has been lifted and they can write what they like, all the real, material, everyday wrongdoings remain in effect.

It's precisely against this kind of thing that people are rebelling. Unlike a few extremist politicians, they're not motivated by the desire for vengeance but by the desire for justice; they want moral and material satisfaction. This has nothing to do with any kind of Jacobinism or permanent revolution. It's a question of completing the renewal of public life. At least, that's how I see it. If I see signs of vengeance or fanaticism, however, I always speak out firmly against them.

Michnik: Today, we can perceive a particularly amazing phenomenon. Not long ago, I was in Yugoslavia, if we can still call it that. Perhaps I'd better say I was in Serbia, Croatia, and Slovenia. I got the impression that the press, radio, and television in these countries are speaking the language of fifty years ago, that conflicts we thought had long been dead and buried have been revived. In Serbia, for example, you hear about the Croatian Ustashe; and in Croatia, about the Serbian Chetniks.

In other countries, too, you can see the revival of language, symbols, and ideologies that haven't been in circulation for fifty years. In Poland, the *endecja* is making a comeback; in Ukraine, they're erecting monuments to Bandera; in Slovakia, Father Tiso[1] is being rehabilitated; in Romania, the paper *Romania Mare,* which glorifies Antonescu, has a circulation of one million; and in Hungary, Horthy is being extolled. What does this revival of old demons mean?

Havel: I'm also a bit surprised by the revival of old demons. It shows, as I once wrote, that communism somehow brought history to a halt; it brought to a halt its natural development. Metaphorically speaking, communism was a kind of narcotic, and people are now waking up in

---

1. Josef Tiso (1887–1947), a Catholic priest and president of the puppet Slovak state during the Second World War, was sentenced and executed by the postwar Czechoslovak government. — ED.

their preexisting state. All the problems that were central to these societies before the narcosis are suddenly returning, and everyone is surprised by this.

I'm also surprised by the extent to which not only the bad traditions that you've mentioned have remained alive but also the good
ones. I'm especially surprised that this is true of the younger generation, which didn't pick up any of this in school and had no other way
of learning about such traditions. In every small town and district,
people are harking back to traditions that were destroyed more than
forty years ago. Regional consciousness is reviving, together with a
sense of the ties between regions, and so on. So it isn't only the bad
demons but also benign spirits that are returning. This is quite amazing.

Michnik: Which demons of Czech tradition do you fear most?

Havel: I guess the most serious development is the emergence of anti-
Semitism and nationalist intolerance, the xenophobia that you can
see in Slovakia and in a somewhat different form in the Czech lands
too.

For example, we have a journal called *Politika,* which is very widely
read and full of anti-Semitic articles of the crudest kind. It's the kind
of gutter journalism that we haven't seen since 1938, during the period
of the so-called Second Republic, between Munich and the German
occupation, when fascistic organizations such as Vlajka were formed
and when attacks on Karel Čapek were organized. It involves a particular combination of complexes—chauvinism, fascism, intolerance,
and hatred toward everyone who's different. Now this is taking the
form of hatred toward Vietnamese, Cubans, Romanians, and Gypsies. This has something of the cult of "racial purity" about it. It's a return to the phenomenon of Czech fascism, which differed from German fascism only in that it was Czech.

In Slovakia, on the other hand, there's a tradition of what the
Communists used to call clericofascism. Memories of the Slovak state
of 1939–45 are being revived, and there are signs of anti-Semitism.
All this is very dangerous.

There are, though, other dangerous demons that might find suste-
nance in this time of uncertainty. In comparison with the previous totalitarian system, democratic rule is bound, by definition, to appear
indecisive, unsure of itself, insufficiently strong and energetic. This is
only natural. It is inevitable that people who lived their whole lives

under totalitarian rule feel this way. But this perception provides fertile soil for those who long for rule by a strong hand. There is a desire among some people for a so-called strong man, for someone to come and restore order. They don't much care which banner he carries, whether he's on the right or the left. I think that this kind of danger exists in all the post-Communist countries.

Michnik: Doesn't it seem to you that all our thinking during the Communist period was dominated by the question, Where did communism come from? How is it that the traditions of the left, its language, rhetoric, and system of values, gave birth to barbarous dictatorship? During this time we somehow forgot that left-wing dictatorship is only one of the faces of dictatorship, that totalitarianism can also be based on right-wing rhetoric and ideology. Aren't you afraid that this danger isn't fully recognized by us or by the societies in which we live? Today, no one is going to fall for the slogans of left-wing totalitarianism; anything that smells of the left is associated with communism. Don't you think, though, that anti-communism, which resorts to right-wing rhetoric and appeals to national values, could constitute a new danger for which neither our societies nor we ourselves are prepared?

Havel: I have to confess that I don't sense any such danger. I'm not afraid of the lure of right-wing rhetoric espoused by any new proponents of authoritarianism. Of course, I can only speak for myself, but I think I'm immune to totalitarianism of all kinds, whether of the left or the right. Perhaps this why some people suspect me of being on the left. Of course, there are some signs that right-wing, authoritarian rule is a possibility in our society. I take note of them, but I don't let them influence my actions.

Michnik: It's obvious to me that you would never be susceptible to dictatorial or totalitarian right-wing ideology; you're descended from a different kind of ape, one that wouldn't fit in with any dictatorship. You've often said that you don't situate yourself on either the left or the right. I define myself in the same way. What's more, you have said—and this is something I can really identify with—that these categories don't explain the world to you. But why is it that in the Czech lands, in Slovakia, and in Poland, this issue is reemerging? Why is it that there are people who refer to themselves as being on the left or the right? And what is it that they're trying to say by this?

Havel: I'm also amused sometimes when I read in the papers that someone has formed a right-wing party, or an alliance of right-wing parties, and so on. I think it's probably bound up with the desire to have a pluralistic political spectrum. People know that in traditional democracies, political forces are polarized to the left and the right, so they try to define and situate themselves on this spectrum. It's now fashionable to define oneself as a supporter of the right, which is understandable for many reasons. What else could one expect after the collapse of communism, which had leftism inscribed all over its banner? It's a completely normal reaction.

But I think that, as long as nothing disrupts the normal course of developments, the political spectrum will eventually become stabilized and this excess of self-definition will largely die out. Practical political work and the implementation of specific political programs are beginning to count; it's gradually becoming obvious who belongs where, and it won't any longer be necessary for people to proclaim their allegiance in such declarative fashion. All this is specific to this strange epoch of post-communism. After all, the world has never experienced anything like this; it's a new phase in which the most unexpected and dramatic events can occur. I confess that every day something takes me by surprise. It's a period full of various kinds of danger, and finding one's way around in the politics of this time is a grueling business. Every politically minded person would prefer to wait five years, until this fermentation process has come to an end, before becoming involved in politics. We just have to struggle through this phase, whatever its paradoxes and absurdities.

Michnik: I want to ask you about something that amazes and baffles me. What is the reason for the renewed popularity of Father Tiso in Slovakia? Perhaps I'm just betraying my ignorance, but my picture of Slovak history suggests that this isn't a tradition that ought to be rehabilitated.

Havel: You're quite right. I completely agree with you, and I think it's both sad and dangerous. I must say, however, that the majority of people in Slovakia are not demanding Tiso's rehabilitation; only a small group of people are interested.

But you asked about the reasons for this. They are specific and essentially irrational. Since the eighth century, the Slovaks have been under foreign domination. The Czechoslovak Republic didn't satisfy their desire for their own state. While this republic saved them from Hungarian rule and freed them from Magyarizing pressures, they didn't feel themselves masters of their own state.

The only period in which there was an independent Slovak state was the period of the wartime Slovak Republic. The state was a puppet of Hitler; he caused it to be founded, and it tried to please him in every way possible. All the laws of this state were modeled on, or even anticipated, German law. Nevertheless, in comparison with other countries that collaborated with Hitler, Slovakia followed a relatively moderate line—if you ignore, of course, the deportation of the Jews, or rather the fact that they were literally sold to the Germans. While the country was surrounded by the turmoil of war, within the country it was less in evidence. Slovakia didn't experience the horrors of war in the way that Poland did. Some older people may well remember this time as the only period in which the Slovaks governed themselves, even though it was in reality a puppet state. In addition, the Slovaks don't like it when the Czechs reproach them for this Slovak state. They consider it a problem they have to resolve for themselves, and the Czechs have no right to interfere.

These are some of the nuances of a particular historical consciousness that is to be found in certain circles, although it is not—I repeat—a widespread phenomenon. The fact is, Tiso's execution was a rather controversial matter. In Slovakia, people believe that you shouldn't take the life of a priest—even though Catholics, unlike myself, do not consistently oppose the death penalty. The memory of this case hasn't faded over time. In addition, the trial was a fairly well planned affair, in which they calculated such things as what would be the best date on which to hang the condemned man, and so on.

Despite such nuances, I have publicly distanced myself more than once from all reminiscing about the wartime Slovak state and have said that a democratic Czechoslovak government can have no truck with it.

Michnik: You said some interesting things on the subject of the Slovak complex, so now I want to ask you about the Czech complex. I shall never forget a conversation I had in November 1989, after the Polish-Czechoslovak Solidarity Festival in Wrocław, when I met with Pavel Tigrid, Karl Schwarzenberg, Jiří Pelikan, and Vilém Prečan. I declared that communism in Czechoslovakia was already kaput, to which Tigrid replied, "You don't know the Czechs. The Czech spirit lives somewhere between Švejk and Kafka. The Czechs won't be able to overthrow the Communist dictatorship because they have a complex about the fact that they didn't defend themselves in 1938 or 1968."

I don't have to tell you how happy I was when it turned out that I knew more about the Czech spirit than our friend Tigrid and all the others who agreed with him.

Havel: The events of 1989 confirmed something that I'd sensed for a long time. During the 1970s and 1980s, various foreign journalists used to visit me and all the time they'd say that the dissidents were just a tiny group, isolated in a ghetto, that the rest of the country would never join up with them, that people would never rouse themselves because they were satisfied with—or had at least become reconciled to—the situation, and that we were simply madmen banging our heads against a wall, and so on. And I used to say to them, "What can you possibly know? There are numerous possibilities lying dormant in the soul of this society."

I've lived through so many astonishing events that I think anything is possible. For example, I lived through the euphoria of 1968 that culminated in the nationwide, universal, peaceful resistance to the Soviet invasion. I was completely astonished by this because apathy had reigned for so many years. I was amazed that people had it in them. Nevertheless, in less than a year this same society was once more overcome by apathy, and I was once again amazed. How was it possible that the very people who not long before had gone against tanks barehanded were now saying that it was pointless and we should all just cultivate our own gardens. I realized at the time that we are all both Švejk and the surveyor K., but we're also Ján Hus. These characteristics are to be found simultaneously in all of us.

Michnik: Communism was an ideology that was able to explain the complexity of the world, in the simplest of terms, to any idiot. You only needed to know a little terminology and you were cleverer than Plato, Heidegger, or Descartes. So communism collapsed, and this simple method of explaining the world collapsed with it. There's now a gap. Don't you think this gap is now being filled by a squalid, primitive nationalism, that the people who once explained the world with the aid of Communist categories are now explaining the world with the aid of nationalistic categories?

Havel: Physics tells us that nature abhors a vacuum, that it attempts to eliminate negative pressures. This is what is happening in this case. Nationalism is at the forefront of the simplistic, primitive ideologies that are now rushing to fill this vacuum, but it's by no means the only one.

Despite this, I think this vacuum actually presents the world with a great opportunity—an opportunity to understand that the era of ideology is over. I've just finished writing a book in which I say that in certain parts of the world at least, the opportunity exists to finish with the era of ideology and to begin the era of ideas. By this I mean the era of the open society, an era in which we are aware of global ties and global responsibilities. This would also be an era of nondoctrinaire thinking, in which not everything would have to fit neatly together.

The modern epoch has been characterized by a tendency that holds that one thing can't be in contradiction to another, that we have to have a closed, complete picture of the world. The notion of "worldview" came into being. I find this a highly questionable notion, and I don't know what it actually means. Is the world really so simple that one can have a single view of it? I have thousands of parallel views and thousands of different opinions, depending on the issue.

I think the modern epoch, with the rational constructs formed since the time of Descartes, will be followed by a new epoch, one that [the philosopher] Václav Bělohradský has called the postmodernist epoch, an epoch of nondoctrinaire, pluralist thinking. In general, I think human beings are better suited to thinking about each issue in a different manner than to using just one style of thinking. At the same time, such pluralistic thinking would enable us to avoid conflicts of all kinds. All conflicts—regardless of whether they're ideological, class, or national—are rooted in a unified view of the world. The other side, of course, has a different view of the world, and this becomes the source of conflict.

But getting back to the vacuum: it's not only a potential disaster but also a potential opportunity and a challenge.

Michnik: Is the era of ideology really coming to an end? Isn't this just wishful thinking on the part of humanist intellectuals? In all the post-Communist countries, nationalism is reviving; the utopia of the ethnically pure state is being resurrected, the utopia of the pure nation, free of foreign devils and evil spirits. Nationalism as a doctrine not only of the nation and the state but also of the xenophobic mentality, with its antipathy toward Gypsies, Jews, and so on, is something that fascinates me.

In Germany, this kind of nationalism is articulated even more radically. An anecdote I heard there provides an illustration. Two Germans—one from the East, an Ossie, and one from the West, a Wessie—meet each other. The Ossie says, "Welcome! Now we're a single nation!" To which the Wessie replies, "And so are we." How would you define nationalism as an ideology, as a way of perceiving the world?

Havel: That's a complicated question. But if you read about the history of the last thousand years, you can see that it's made up of a never-ending series of tribal or dynastic conflicts, in which the main issue was the otherness of one of the sides involved. This suggests that the sense of belonging to a nation is much more deeply rooted in people than their sense of belonging to a particular class. Most of the wars in modern times have been national wars.

Appeals to national issues will always find an echo, because this is the simplest criterion of self-identification: you only have to say one word for people to know whether you're a Pole, a Czech, or a Hungarian, for example. People are always looking for a way to identify themselves, for something that they have in common. The simplest thing is one's nationality: to be a Czech, you don't need to do anything; you don't have to be wise or good, you just have to be born here. This is probably the main reason why, despite all our experience, nationalist appeals will always find a response. Appeals to Marxists, or phenomenologists, or existentialists would have no resonance, because most people wouldn't know how to define themselves in these terms. But everyone knows what nationality he is. It's the simplest definition and therefore highly dangerous.

Communism had a strong tendency to uniformity, to render everything the same, from Vladivostok to Berlin: the same administrative and state structures, the same storefronts, the same housing developments, and so on. This means that it tried—sometimes in the cruelest way possible—to eradicate all differences between nations and nationalities. Could we really have expected that the vacuum that emerged in the wake of such pressures would be filled with anything other than nationalism? I think it will take a long time before we create a civil society that respects every component of the collective "I," a society that values nationality but doesn't elevate it above other nationalities and doesn't use it as the basis of an ideology or as a principle on which to organize the state.

Michnik: What about xenophobia? What is its origin? Why is it that in Czechoslovakia, where there are now no Jews, anti-Semitism suddenly rears its head on the pages of *Politika?* Why this aggression toward the Gypsies? This isn't something specific to Czechoslovakia; you find it in every post-Communist country. In Germany, it's reached the point where Nazi symbols are reappearing, something that hadn't happened before now.

Havel: I think there are at least two reasons for this xenophobia in post-Communist countries. One of them is the fact that for forty years we lived in a closed society. When you go to London, Paris, or New York, you meet people of different races, people who speak different languages, and everyone is used to this. From time to time there are problems—with the Turks in Germany, for example, or the Arabs in France—but in general people have become used to the fact that they live in a fairly cosmopolitan world, that you can move around and change your place of residence. We, on the other hand, lived in a kind of isolated ghetto, and in our society it's a surprise to meet people who are in some way different from us, who speak another language, for example.

The second reason, which is related to this, is that people are looking for someone to blame. They are in a state of shock brought about by their sudden freedom. They've lost their sense of security and their value system. This is a condition that I've often compared to being released from prison. When you're inside, you look forward to the moment when you'll be released, but when it actually happens, you're suddenly helpless. You don't know what you're supposed to do. You might even wish you could go back inside, because you know what to expect there and you haven't the faintest idea what to expect outside. It's the same with a society that is frustrated because it can't cope with its own freedom and is therefore looking for an enemy that can be blamed for everything. Of course, the easiest thing to do is to identify as the enemy someone who immediately stands out from the crowd—someone who speaks a different language or whose skin is a different color. It's precisely for this reason that people say the Vietnamese, or the Gypsies, or some other "they" are to blame for everything. People have a need to attribute all the misfortunes of the world and all their own frustrations to someone other than themselves, to an enemy of some kind, in order to escape from the hell that they carry within themselves. It's easier to point the finger at someone else and say there's the devil than to acknowledge one's own weaknesses.

Žantovsky: Despite what the president has said, I think Czech society isn't so xenophobic when compared with others. We didn't have a wave of anti-Soviet outbursts after the revolution. Despite discussions about our past relations with the Germans and problems relating to the Czechoslovak-German treaty, there haven't been any anti-German outbursts. Attacks on Gypsies are confined to small groups of young people who define themselves as skinheads and who don't have any support in the wider community. International public opinion surveys carried out in all the post-Communist countries show that Czech society is to a large extent an open society. This doesn't mean there's no intolerance or xenophobia, but they're on a relatively small scale compared with other countries. Of course, we condemn every such incident, regardless of its scale, because it is dangerous.

Michnik: I'm glad to see that here, as in Poland, the president's colleagues argue with him. I must say, though, that I'm more inclined to agree with the president's line of thought. As far as potential dangers are concerned, it's not so much a question of quantity as of dynamics. Xenophobia usually involves attitudes toward foreigners, but this isn't necessarily the case, as illustrated by the German anecdote I just recounted. The Germans really are, after all, one nation, but it turns out, nevertheless, that they are not.

From this perspective, I can't help but note two things. First, it seems to me that decommunization in Czechoslovakia also serves as an expression of such sentiments. The attitude toward Communists is also a question of the attitude toward people who are different, whose history and experience are different. The second example is the Republican party. It's not by chance that both Miroslav Sladek, the leader of this party, and Jerzy Giertych, leader of Poland's National party, model themselves on Jean-Marie Le Pen.

What I want to say is that we face, in embryonic form, something that may appear to be insignificant, ludicrous, and marginal. But we are people of our time; we mustn't forget that Hitler was initially a ludicrous figure, with fewer supporters than Sladek now has. It seemed inconceivable that an unsuccessful Austrian painter could become a significant figure in conservative Germany . . .

Havel: I think that in the situation we have now, when we've destroyed the barriers that used to constrain us and the previous value system has collapsed, people like Sladek are provoked into proposing their own, simplistic values. At the same time, he proposes a negative self-definition: he hasn't put forward a single positive program. Sladek would just like to sweep into the Vltava the entire government, in-

cluding the parliament and the president. This kind of negative self-
definition strikes a chord with some people because it's clear and simple. All their lives, people have been used to cursing the Communists,
and now they're disoriented because they no longer have anyone to
curse. Sladek comes along and tells them to curse those who are running the country today. He offers them an easy way out. The current
situation provides fertile soil for all kinds of aggression and xenophobia. This is by no means limited to nationalistic intolerance. Of
course, the need to defend "the purity of the Czech nation" is a theme
that runs through everything Sladek says, but he could have chosen
any one of a number of cheap ideas. I'm fully aware of how dangerous they are. The example of Hitler has occurred to me several times,
and I even said so in public once, at which Sladek immediately filed a
lawsuit against me.

The situation could become especially dangerous in some regions
of the Soviet Union, where things are much worse in many respects
than they are here. I believe our social organism will manage to cope
with this virus. After all, we've had some experience in this area. During the interwar period, there were several attempts—from both the
left and the right—to overthrow Masaryk, but none of them succeeded and they remained nothing more than grotesque, marginal
episodes. I believe this would be the case today too, although the situation is potentially dangerous, especially since our young democracy
hasn't yet learned how to cope with such threats. The police are disoriented and don't know if they are supposed to intervene. They are
afraid of being seen as continuators of the Communist police, so they
prefer to turn their backs or remain passive bystanders.

Michnik: You've often said that in a world in which political culture has
been so thoroughly destroyed, we need to return to spiritual values.
How do you see the role of religion in the post-Communist epoch?
Under Communist dictatorship, it was a source of strength for all of us,
orthodox and unorthodox alike. Religion constituted an appeal to natural law, to which we must all be faithful. What is the situation now?

Havel: I think there are two dimensions to religiosity in the post-
Communist world—at least in the case of Czechoslovakia, and I'll limit
my remarks to my own country. First, religion is of major significance
because it broadens one's vision; it directs our attention to something
above ourselves, it reminds us of the metaphysical roots of our conscience and our responsibilities, and it emphasizes unselfishness and

love of one's neighbor. Our demoralized society desperately needs to be reminded of these traditional Christian values.

There is, however, a second dimension, which may be more pronounced in Poland than here — the intrusion of religion, or the Church, into political life. In this secularized, profane world, religion — something that is deeply personal and spiritual — is again being turned into a doctrine or an ideology. And as I've already said, it seems to me the world now has an opportunity to turn its back on ideologies.

Muslim countries, with their fundamentalism, show us much more clearly than do Christian countries how dangerous it is when religion intrudes into politics. In Muslim countries, the state is supposedly based on religious principles, but these are essentially ideological-doctrinal principles. A state that takes such principles as its basis is by its very nature intolerant, because it reduces the individual to a single dimension; it constrains and manipulates him. I think a state based on religious principles is always just as dangerous as one based on ideological or nationalist principles.

Michnik: Let me ask you a question in your capacity as head of state. How is the Church behaving in Czechoslovakia? Is it pressing for the delegalization of abortion, for example? Is it demanding that a clause asserting that the state is based on Christian values be inserted into the constitution? Is it demanding legislative guarantees that such values will have pride of place in the education system? When the bishops meet with the president, do they argue that, since the Czechs and Slovaks are Christian nations, the republic ought to be a Christian state?

Havel: I haven't come across anything like that, especially in the Czech lands. In Slovakia, where Catholicism is stronger and where the Christian-Democratic movement is a major political group, the Church isn't demanding that the state be based on religious principles or that its role be guaranteed by the constitution, but there are signs that it is intruding into political life.

The Czech primate, Miroslav Vlk, epitomizes, in my opinion, the kind of religiosity that we so badly need. His program is one of spiritual and moral renewal, and I consider this to be of primary importance. There are absolutely no tendencies within the Czech Church to define our country as a Christian or Catholic state. The Church wants separation from the state, it wants guarantees that the state won't interfere in its normal work, and it is demanding restitution of some of the monasteries that were seized after 1948. But in neither the Czech lands nor Slovakia have there been any attempts to "nationalize" the Church, to replace the former leading role of the party with the leading role of the Church.

Michnik: Now I'll ask you in your capacity as a writer, an intellectual, and a citizen: How would you react to the demand that any woman who has an abortion, and any doctor who performs one, should go to jail?

Havel: This is an extremely complicated issue, on which I don't have a firm opinion. I feel instinctively that abortion is a bad thing. I think most people feel this way. But I have no idea how we should resolve this problem in an age of population explosion.

Our abortion laws are very liberal, and some Catholic parliamentary deputies would like to tighten them. They asked me to support them on this issue, but I didn't feel I could do so wholeheartedly. It's such a complicated matter, on which there's such a wealth of professional literature, that I don't feel competent to say what should be done. Our problem is not that the law is too severe for society; rather, it's the opposite.

Michnik: And how would you react—as a citizen, not as president—if a priest told his congregation which political party good Christians should vote for?

Havel: From what I've said, it's clear that I wouldn't think this a good thing. So far, we've only had a few isolated cases of this kind in Slovakia. I don't think this is the duty of the clergy. I can understand that when the Communist system was collapsing, the clergy came out in support of freedom, that they spoke out in favor of Solidarity in Poland or our Civic Forum. Cardinal Tomášek conducted a mass in St. Vitus's Cathedral in support of our "mutiny." This was quite acceptable because it was a public issue that affected us all. But if a priest told people which political party they should vote for today, I'd consider it most unfortunate, and I'd consider him a bad priest.

Vondra: I simply can't imagine a priest telling people which party they should vote for.

Michnik: There are, though, some very interesting borderline cases. Not long ago in Slovakia, *Kulturny Zivot* published a religiously provocative story by a writer named Martin Kasard. Our common friend, the Slovak prime minister Ján Čarnogurský, subsequently withheld the paper's government subsidy, and the deputy prime minister of the federal government asked the prosecutor to initiate an investigation. Here, I can't resist some analogies. In Poland, the bishops issued a pastoral letter dealing with the mass media, in which they stated what kind of issues the media should, and should not, cover. Another example is the case of Salman Rushdie, accused of blasphemy and sentenced to death. Of course, it's a long way from withholding a subsidy to imposing a death sentence, but the logic is similar. As far as I know, you've spoken about this on the radio. Could you tell me what you said?

Havel: I said that literature should never be hauled before a court of law. Literature always provokes someone, sometimes more, sometimes less. I realize that literature may offend some people or offend their religious feelings. I can imagine being irritated, infuriated, or offended by a story, but I can't imagine taking the author to court.

Michnik: When the Iranian revolution took place twelve years ago, it struck me as bizarre and incomprehensible; the creation of a religious state at the end of the twentieth century just seemed absurd. Now, however, when I look at what's going on around the world, when I see the growing influence of religious parties and Jewish fundamentalism in Israel, when I see the rise in Islamic fundamentalism in all the countries of Islam, when I see the growing fundamentalist tendencies within Protestantism—in America, for example—and within Catholicism in the post-Communist countries, I have to ask myself whether the revolution in Iran wasn't just the first indication of a new phenomenon. Perhaps our mutual friend André Glucksmann was right when he wrote that the greatest challenge currently facing us is that of new fundamentalisms—nationalist, ideological, and religious. He says we are confronting a new phenomenon that is already changing our view of communism. Glucksmann suggests that communism is not a *symptom* of fundamentalism but one of the faces that fundamentalism wears. What do you think?

Havel: Before I answer, I must point out that the most powerful of all the fundamentalisms we are now witnessing—Islamic fundamentalism—can be explained by the fact that Islam is a relative newcomer. Islam arose several hundred years after Christianity, and it now finds itself in a position similar to that of Christianity several hundred years ago; in a sense, it's a bit like Christianity during the Middle Ages. However, this doesn't answer your question.

I genuinely believe that the greatest danger facing us today, now that communism has collapsed, is the possibility of religious or nationalistic fundamentalism becoming a major force. At the same time, however, I think there's a countervailing force—this planet's sense of self-preservation—which will, I hope, predominate. Our planet as a whole is now threatened by a variety of factors: the economic and social gap between rich and poor countries, population increase, environmental problems, and so on. Together, they constitute a global danger. I believe, though, that at least a part of humanity will begin to realize the situation and will come to understand, among other things, that we can only hope to deal with the problems that are so visible from an individual, human perspective if we free ourselves from the bondage of all doctrines, ideologies, and fundamentalisms. Otherwise, the road we're now on will prove to be suicidal. I believe, however, that the instinct for self-preservation will prevail.

Look, when Saddam Hussein invaded Kuwait, it was the first time that the international community, including the Arab countries, with the blessing of the United Nations, united in opposition. This is a new situation that can be interpreted as a sign of these mechanisms of self-preservation. Kuwait itself is a small country with a few oil wells, but the point is that this invasion could have constituted a precedent for spreading this rabid fundamentalism, for threatening other countries, for waging a genocidal war against various ethnic groups, beginning with the Kurds. It looks as though humanity has already begun to realize the scale of the danger, because otherwise Bush and Baker—even if they had been a hundred times smarter—would never have achieved anything. In other words, I wouldn't take such a gloomy view and say that we're entering an era of fundamentalism; fundamentalism is a dangerous phenomenon, but there are forces capable of withstanding it.

Michnik: What are the Czechs and Slovaks really arguing about? What are the real divisions between them?

Havel: This dispute has two dimensions, the first of which is totally understandable and justified. Over the past thousand years, the Slovak experience has been quite different from that of the Czechs. Because they never had their own autonomous state, they are "less structured"; they have yet to experience some of the things that we have experienced, and it could be said that they are only now going through particular phases of their rebirth as a nation. As the smaller and less well known nation of Czechoslovakia, the Slovaks have always been in the shadow of the Czechs. Despite the fact that the Czechs have helped the Slovaks to stand on their own feet, this help has been viewed as yet another insulting demonstration of the Czech sense of superiority—which is perfectly understandable from the psychological point of view. The Slovaks feel themselves to be an entity, they feel they are creating a community, they want to stand on their own feet, and they want to be on an equal footing with their older brother, who continues to tutor and overshadow them. All this is perfectly understandable and reasonable. Actually, these feelings, although widespread, are by no means universal. Understandably, the Slovaks are somewhat wary and suspicious of the Czechs; they're on the lookout for any signs that the Czechs are up to new tricks intended to keep the Slovaks in line.

The second dimension of this dispute is a political one, and here things are far worse. Various politicians are taking advantage of the situation I've just described to play the nationalist card, because it's the simplest and easiest way to mobilize the crowd. Some of them are playing the nationalist card in a fairly civilized fashion while others are completely demagogic, but they all believe the time has come: countries are liberating themselves, new states are being created, so now is the time for the Slovak nation to stand on its own feet. This is what has caused the tensions that are now reaching their culmination, and we really do face the question of whether our state is going to survive as an integral whole. I still believe it will survive, although we shall certainly experience more than one crisis. You have to distinguish between these two dimensions: the political game, which is reflected in, among other things, the current negotiations between the parliaments of the two republics, and the desires of the people. These desires are often related to a particular complex, but they derive, first and foremost, from a different experience or a different way of perceiving the world.

Let me give you a fairly absurd example, which nevertheless illustrates the situation. Imagine a federation with a population of 120 million—40 million Poles and 80 million Germans. This is a federal state, in which the Germans are in a much better situation, economically and in many other respects, and in which, moreover, they outnumber the Poles by two to one. In this situation, the Poles would certainly start to feel the same way many Slovaks do. In a way, the relationship between the two is like that between two brothers, where the older brother constantly leads the younger one by the hand. Nobody likes this kind of relationship, even if they are being led in the right direction.

Michnik: What about internal divisions? What do the Czechs and Slovaks argue about among themselves? The Poles are now arguing about how to move to a market economy—with Balcerowicz or against him. They are arguing about the role of the Church; about whether they want a presidential or parliamentary political system; about agricultural policy—a firm line or subsidies, credits, price guarantees, and tariff barriers; about decommunization; about whether Poland should adopt the European model or whether there's a specifically Polish option because Europe equals pornography, abortion, consumerism, drugs, degeneration, and so on. What are the main issues that people argue about in the Czech lands and Slovakia?

Havel: There are several. Elections will be held next spring. Political parties were formed only recently, but they are already thinking about the elections, and this colors all their pronouncements. The political spectrum is crystallizing at the same time as we are searching for a model for the state and writing a new constitution.

In the Czech lands, then, one dispute centers on the Slovak question. Some politicians would like the strongest possible state and therefore don't want to give in to Slovak pressures. The subtext to this is that they are hoping, in this way, to endear themselves to those voters who support such a policy. The Czechs are saying with increasing frequency that the Slovaks are just complicating the issue so it would be better if they went off on their own. Some politicians are further stirring up such sentiments simply to achieve their own ends. There's a similar dispute in Slovakia, where you have federalists, confederalists, and advocates of total independence. On the Slovak question, then, you don't have a confrontation between two monolithic groups, the Czechs and the Slovaks.

Another dispute centers on economic policy. A fairly strong and vocal right wing is now emerging. This group wants the most rapid and radical reforms to bring about—to put it in simplified terms—full-fledged capitalism. They are opposed by a kind of left wing, made up of numerous factions. These two groups are constantly attacking each other; the right refers to all liberals as crypto-Communists, and the left is becoming radicalized and is criticizing the entire reform process.

There are also disagreements over the possibility of autonomy for Moravia and Silesia and over the lustration law. Finally, there's a covert conflict, of a more psychological kind, between the so-called dissidents who were in the anti-Communist opposition and the younger generation about whom little is known and who cooperated with neither the Communists nor the opposition. Today, the latter quote Eugene O'Neill: "For so long I struggled against something petty that I myself became petty," by which they mean that the opposition struggled against the Communists for so long that they themselves became tarnished in the process, and their role is now finished. In addition, they point out that some dissidents were once members of the Communist party—during the fifties or sixties—and maintain that all Communists are the same and that it makes no difference whether they were in the party during the sixties or the eighties. Public opinion tends to identify with the nondissident politicians for the simple reason that most people were themselves neither dissidents nor members of the *nomenklatura*. For most people, these younger politicians personify their own situation and are thus closer to them in mentality.

There are many other, narrower disputes, but they are all imbued with partisan politics.

Michnik: The marginalization of former dissidents is a problem in all our countries. It is interesting—as you have frequently pointed out—that the dissidents have come to represent the guilty conscience of people who used to be conformists and who now indulge in the rhetoric of decommunization.

But I want to ask you about something else. All our more or less velvet revolutions have given rise to charismatic leaders. You were such a leader. It is not by chance that the Georgian dissident who was democratically elected president wanted to be known as the Georgian Havel. This charismatic Georgian leader and former dissident soon began to lock up his opponents in prison. Are we to assume, then, that each of us faces the temptation to impose authoritarian rule, on the grounds that democracy is an impediment, that it's ineffective, that everything moves too slowly, and we need rapid and decisive action? In Georgia, the situation developed to the point of barricades in the streets and what is essentially a civil war, one that is far from over.

What do you think about the threat of authoritarianism during the post-Communist period, when democratic structures are still weak?

How did you feel when you heard that Zviad Konstantinovich Gamsakhurdia is called the Georgian Havel?

Havel: I don't think I'm in any danger of seizing power to the extent that I'd imprison my friends. On the contrary, people I meet in bars, on the street, or wherever constantly accuse me of being too soft. They say, "You should be stricter with them." When they say "them," they mean everyone: Communists, decommunizers, Slovaks, Czechs, politicians, parliament. So, I seem to have the opposite problem; I'm not authoritarian enough.

Nevertheless, in general I think that in our fragile, infant democracies, we need to strengthen democratic institutions, mechanisms, and rules of the game as quickly as possible, precisely to avoid the emergence of authoritarian forces advocating a populist program calling for a strong hand. Democracy must quickly acquire authority. If it doesn't do so, authoritarian leaders like Sladek will. It isn't Havel as Havel who must acquire authority but the president, the government, and parliament. We need to create a framework within which these institutions can interact with each other. We need to construct a system of constitutional safeguards against permanent political crises.

In our case, all this is in the process of being created and is linked to the creation of a new constitutional system and new constitutions. I have to say that I am in favor of broadening the powers of the president. I'm not talking about a presidential system in which a popularly elected president heads the executive branch, but I'm in favor of restoring some of the powers that the president used to possess in democratic Czechoslovakia. For example, the president should have the power to present legislation to the Federal Assembly, and if the government fails to win a vote of confidence in parliament, the president should be able to dissolve parliament and order an election. So I'm in favor of strengthening the powers of the president, not to strengthen my own power, but to strengthen the authority of the head of state. Because this is the most effective weapon against those who advance the notion of strong-arm government.

Michnik: You've said several times that, as president, you've come to appreciate the significance of politicians' personal characteristics. Could you say a little more? What kind of characteristics do you have in mind? What has made the greatest impression on you in this regard?

Havel: I don't think I should talk about specific heads of state, only about my observations. I've noticed that when I like a particular politician, or vice versa, when we're on the same wavelength and really communicate with each other, this is reflected in a good relationship with the country he represents. I'm sure that Sasha, who takes part in all international discussions, will confirm this.

I really was greatly surprised when I realized the significance of personal contacts between leading politicians and the extent to which they have an impact on political life. It's a trifle alarming and makes you nervous about your responsibilities. It's easy to imagine a situation where—I'm just making this up—I have a meeting at 7:00 A.M. with Iceland's foreign minister, say, and I'm tired and sleepy or don't feel well. Of course, the conversation doesn't really take off. Then we have to appear at a press conference and answer various questions, but we don't, obviously, have much to say. Then the press starts saying that the talks took place in a chilly atmosphere, that the visit was disappointing, and it soon becomes an established political fact that relations between Czechoslovakia and Iceland have cooled. Of course, this is an example that I've made up, but you understand what I'm getting at.

Michnik: Our democracy is having a difficult birth. More difficult than we anticipated. Everywhere, the political arena is Balkanized. We have ethnic conflicts. And on top of everything else we have what I call the infantile disorder of postcommunism—the belief in a utopian capitalism. Just as we once believed that a planned economy would solve all problems, many people now believe that all problems will be solved simply by setting market forces in motion. How do things look in Czechoslovakia from this point of view?

Havel: I personally don't agree with those who think that market forces constitute the magic wand that will resolve everything. Above all, I don't think the market provides a worldview or gives meaning to life. I differ in this respect from several right-wing columnists and politicians, with whom I'm carrying on a dispute on this issue.

It's obvious to me that all property should have a specific owner and that the law of supply and demand should function, but I don't treat this as an ideology, as the meaning of life, or as a utopia. It's simply an arrangement that has been proven over the centuries, that corresponds with human nature and functions naturally. You don't have to be a genius to figure out that when you call in a private plumber, he does a better job than an anonymous employee of a state enterprise. It's obvious, because the private plumber has a personal interest in the result of his work, which affects the payment he receives for his services. In this respect, I'm an advocate of the speediest possible restoration of normal property relations, pluralism, and competition between firms. I see market mechanisms as something obvious; they're a tried and tested economic principle, but that's all. They're not a religion.

Michnik: The language of populism, the language of empty promises, is enjoying enormous success in public life in Poland these days. Political struggle is coming to hinge increasingly on populist promises to perform miracles: if you vote for me, I'll give you everything you want. To what extent does this tendency exist in Czechoslovakia, and where does it come from?

Havel: It comes, I guess, from the immaturity of our political culture. Obviously, if someone has to defend himself and his program in successive elections for fifteen years, he can't limit himself to demagogic slogans. He has to back his words with action and prove that he's capable of achieving some results. In countries that have a long and still developing democratic tradition, demagoguery alone isn't enough. In situations where democracy is only just beginning to take shape, however, populists have plenty of opportunity to exploit the chaos and come up with cheap and easy political programs.

However, I must mention something that troubles me greatly. As a writer, I consider myself a creative person. This means that I hate to repeat myself and that I hate to simplify. At the same time, I am obliged, by reason of my function, to repeat myself a million times and to address my audience in terms of simplified appeals. When I have to give a speech, I'm aware that I can't use long, complex sentences, that I have to keep it simple and end up with a comprehensible appeal. I often find that I come up with an original sentence, but by the time I've paraphrased it three times, it seems totally banal. All my life I've been on my guard against this kind of thing, I've criticized a way of life made up of platitudes, I've analyzed the language of platitudes, and now I find myself facing the professional temptation to resort to platitudes.

My colleagues can testify to the fact that I don't like giving speeches. I don't want to write them anymore, because I know I'm going to repeat what I've already said and I'm going to come even closer to platitudes. But at the same time, I can't read something they've written for me, because I have my own style; even though they write well, it's in another style. When they write something for me, I get embarrassed and I blush. As a result, I try to write my speeches myself, but I hate doing so. You have no idea how loath I was yesterday to write the speech that I had to give today. When I speak without notes, I sometimes manage to come up with something that's a bit original, but when I have to get it down on paper, it's almost physically painful.

Žantovsky: I understand this. Yesterday I was going to suggest that I write the speech, but when I realized I'd be up all night painfully writing something that you would find painful to read, I decided it would be better if only one of us were in pain.

Michnik: Czechoslovakia is the only country where émigrés have returned home and are being put to good use: Karl Schwarzenberg is your chief of staff; Pavel Tigrid—the "Czech Giedroyc"—is one of your advisers; Jiří Gruša is ambassador in Bonn. How do you explain this? It's clear that the émigré community has played a major role in the life of all our countries. Without this community, it's hard to imagine the democratic opposition. Why is it that in all the other countries émigrés give lots of good advice, but here they've come back?

Žantovsky: What about Tymiński?[2]

Michnik: Do you have to use such vulgar language?!

Havel: It must be said that the return of émigrés is not a mass phenomenon in Czechoslovakia. Most of them have remained in their adopted countries; they've invested twenty or forty years there, they have children, and so on; returning would mean uprooting themselves all over again. But they visit frequently. Every time I walk through the castle grounds to the Vikarka restaurant, at least a hundred elderly ladies grab my hand and tell me they're visiting from Australia or Canada and thank me for making it possible for them to do so. It's only now that you see how many people were previously unable to come. They're actually the most loyal citizens, and it's a pity they don't live here.

There really aren't that many who have come back, although there are certainly more than Schwarzenberg and Tigrid. They're mostly intellectuals who treat the return home as a challenge and who enjoy being in on the birth of this democracy. Some of those who've come

2. Stanisław Tymiński returned to Poland and challenged Lech Wałęsa in the presidential elections of 1991. — ED.

back are people who were unhappy abroad or who want to go into private business here.

Michnik: Tell me, what has happened to us—the dissidents—during the past two years? Everything in our lives has changed. You have gone from being a felon to being president, and I could give many other examples. How do you see yourself? In what way have you changed? As someone who is both a president and a writer, you must often find yourself having to choose between your responsibility to the state and your loyalty to the truth. How do you cope with this conflict?

Havel: This is a difficult question that calls for some introspection. First and foremost, I have to say that no serious person—and I consider myself such—is able to explain himself in terms of a single simple formula. Each one of us is characterized by completely contradictory attributes and character traits.

For example, I'm someone who is sensitive to the ridiculous and I have a tendency to be astonished by everything. I often have moments when I can't believe I'm president, although I've been president for nearly two years. I'm standing in the bathroom early in the morning, still half-asleep, hurriedly brushing my teeth, when I ask myself why I'm in a hurry. I tell myself that I have to go to the presidential office to meet with some prime minister or other, and suddenly I don't believe it. It seems ridiculous and unreal.

On the other hand, though—and this is the paradox—life has taught me never to be too surprised at anything. It's taught me to sail through even the most absurd and unexpected situations that I haven't created myself but that I simply encounter and seem to attract, although I don't know why.

It often happens to writers that the world they create actually comes into being around them. Bohumil Hrabal has created the Hrabalian world that we find in his books. But he has also created this world in a literal sense: he is able to create his own world not just here, in Kocoura's Bar, but at New York's Kennedy Airport. In his presence, the world somehow acquires a distorted structure and takes on a Hrabalian outline.

The same kind of thing happens to me. I'm someone who likes peace and quiet and a modicum of comfort, and that's how I would most like to live; but somehow I seem to distort the space around me, provoking a succession of unanticipated situations. The fact that I've been to prison several times is just as absurd as the fact that I'm now president, and I haven't the faintest idea what absurdities will be lying in wait for me in the future, when I'm removed from this office, or I don't get renominated, or I end up in prison once more; anything is possible. But not because I chose my fate or I go looking for trouble; this is absolutely not the case. I'm just a quiet petit bourgeois.

So there are two contradictory tendencies: on the one hand, I'm amazed by everything; on the other, I know that anything is possible in my life. The fate of each individual is an aggregation of such contradictory ideas, and we're constantly amazed at ourselves. For example, we suddenly become jealous in our old age, and we're unable to understand it.

Žantovsky: Neither can we. You're actually jealous?

Havel: This was just a literary example. But enough about me. You asked about a more important issue: the conflict between loyalty and truth. This really is a problem on occasion. Again, as a writer, I probably have an inbuilt tendency to look for a formula—and my colleagues assist me in this—that will allow me to be true to myself, that will keep me from betraying something in which I believe, without—insofar as it's possible—giving rise to unnecessary political complications or destabilizing the political arena or causing me to be disloyal to democratic principles.

To a certain extent, this is a matter of taste and imagination. It's a question of how one weighs one's words. When do you speak in generalities, without naming names, but in such a way that the person you're addressing understands what you mean? And when do you speak more concretely, and how do you do this so as not to evoke unnecessary conflict and introduce further elements of chaos? To a large extent, this all depends on taste, intuition, and imagination; these are far more important than any education in political science.

Michnik: Have you ever been in a situation in which, as president, you signed a law knowing that you shouldn't do so but were unable to do otherwise?

Havel: I was in precisely this kind of situation not long ago, and I even wrote about it immediately afterward. I gave a speech on the subject at a university in New York when I received an honorary doctorate.

Our constitutional system obliges me to sign laws into effect. I simply have to sign; if I don't, the law still takes effect and all I do is complicate the situation by creating tensions between the president and parliament. I had just such a situation in relation to the law on lustration, and I extricated myself by signing the law while simultaneously proposing that it be amended. Parliament is obliged to take up my initiative, which means it is obliged to consider the proposed amendment; but, in order for this to happen, the law must first take effect. My friends were divided on this issue: one group said I shouldn't sign, which would have been a gesture devoid of practical consequences; the others said it would be more constructive to sign and then propose an amendment. In the end, I chose the latter solution. Time will show whether I made the right choice.

Of course, such situations are bound to occur, and when they do, I immediately try to set everything down in writing. I simply do what I've done all my life: whenever I've found myself in a hole, the easiest way out has always been for me to write about it. This is a literary way of resolving life's problems.

Michnik: You're not only a president but also a writer, playwright, and essayist—and the author of the only book to date that attempts to provide an intellectual synthesis of the events of the last two years. I want to ask, though, about your reading. Of all the things you've read in the last two years, what has made the most impression on you?

Žantovsky: You really think he has time to read? What an absurd question!

Michnik: But he's a writer of the absurd.

Havel: As a matter of fact, 95 percent of what I read consists of official documents and newspapers. I rarely have time to read an essay, and novels are out of the question. The last book I read that sticks in my mind was a memoir of Jan Masaryk—our minister of foreign affairs who died in mysterious circumstances after the war—by his friend Marcia Davenport.

It's not a particularly remarkable book, but reading it suddenly made me realize how lucky I am. I'm worried from morning to night, I get angry, I get depressed and want to give it all up because there's so much chaos all around, the state is collapsing, and so on. And then I suddenly read about the terrible moral dilemma that faced Masaryk when the Communists were preparing to take over. He had sworn to his father, Tomas, that he wouldn't desert Beneš—his father's successor—but meanwhile communism was infiltrating on all sides. It was clear the Communists were going to take over and destroy all their opponents. Beneš—an old man, ill and half-senile—had clearly given up and was signing everything they put in front of him. Jan Masaryk was deeply, physically, afraid, but he felt bound by the oath he'd sworn to his father; at the same time, he felt the situation was utterly hopeless. On top of this, he suffered constant humiliation at the hands of Stalin, Molotov, Zorin, and people like Gottwald, and when he went on an official visit to Washington to meet with Marshall, the foreign secretary, it turned out that no one had time to meet him. Neither Marshall nor Truman would meet with him, even though Masaryk was known in the Anglo-Saxon world: his mother was American, he'd lived there ten years, and he spoke the language perfectly—not just the language of literature but various regional dialects too. And now his friends suddenly don't have time for him, and this just one month before the Communists' February coup, when the fate of Europe is about to be decided. In addition, this happens to a politician with strong Anglo-American sympathies who has become a popular figure in that part of the world.

The things that this man, who was far from courageous, went through at the beginning of the cold war made an enormous impression on me. I suddenly realized that a person can find himself in such a terrible situation that the only solution is to jump out of a window. And I thought to myself that in comparison to Masaryk, I really don't have things so bad.

Michnik: Yesterday, Jiří Dienstbier showed me the window Jan Masaryk jumped from. The coincidence of you recounting this story and me seeing this very window yesterday suggests that metaphysics really exists.

We've known each other thirteen years. Now, after all this time, when people ask me about my political orientation, I reply: Havelian. I want to thank you for this. Today I've been talking to a friend and a president. Let me, then, end this conversation by saying Thank you, Vašek; Thank you, Mr. President!

23

We Can Talk without Hatred

A Conversation with Wojciech Jaruzelski

Wojciech Jaruzelski: I arrived at communism via a rather strange route. After a deeply religious and patriotic upbringing, I suddenly found myself in a completely different world. You, however, were born into a Communist family but chose to follow a different path. How did this come about? By the way, I can't resist pointing out that your father probably had a worse time than you did. When he opted for communism, he risked being relegated to the margins of society; he risked imprisonment, as you did, but without the social support that you could count on, without the support of the Church, and without the support of the West.

Do you remember the first time we met in the Sejm? I'd like you to say something about this as well.

Adam Michnik: At that time I had encountered few people whom I disliked and feared more than General Jaruzelski. I was absolutely convinced that nothing could change for the better as long as Jaruzelski remained in power. This belief dominated my political thinking at the time. I thought General Jaruzelski was the cornerstone of a particular political structure to which I was implacably opposed. I remember discussions with Solidarity colleagues who used to tell me, "When it comes to Jaruzelski, you don't engage in analysis; you simply give

Translated by Jane Cave from *Gazeta Wyborcza*, April 25–26, 1992.

vent to animosity and rage." Bronisław Geremek used to argue that you didn't want to go down in history as the person who imposed martial law, so you'd have to come up with something. I was convinced he was wrong. In addition, I couldn't stand the army; I'm a sworn civilian.

When I went to the first meeting in the Sejm in the spring of 1989, I was genuinely afraid. Then I saw that General Jaruzelski was a normal person. There was no sign of the wickedness that I'd imagined for years. Later, I became convinced that it's impossible to gain a correct impression of what kind of person General Jaruzelski is just by reading his speeches.

The public image of General Jaruzelski was a mass of enigmas. I've always been greatly interested in history, so I went looking for a similar biography, but nothing matched. A young boy from a landowning family who finds himself in Russia during the war, he begins his working life as a manual laborer and suddenly he's making a career for himself in the army. With no inborn aptitude for politics, he becomes a politician. Then he does things that I'm unable to explain. Why does he appoint as vice premier Mieczysław Rakowski, someone who was by no means regarded favorably within the party? So he appoints Rakowski, but before this, when he was head of the army's Chief Political Directorate, he controlled *Żołnierz Wolności* [Soldier of Freedom], a really despicable rag. He comes across as someone who's rather puritanical and unsociable. He relies frequently on the argument of force; his speeches, delivered in uniform, are peppered with such phrases as "We shall not allow it," or "We shall resist." I found all this quite appalling, and it never occurred to me that one day I might come to like the private General Jaruzelski.

I saw him as a politician whose chief point of reference was the military. This was something new for communism. Once again, I failed to understand the situation fully and all I could do was speculate. I came to the conclusion that one ought to believe whatever the general said. If he said he wasn't going to relinquish power, I took it seriously. It seemed absolutely out of the question that General Jaruzelski would ever be capable of initiating a rapprochement with Solidarity.

In 1984, a friend came to see me and said, "I've just met with a close associate of Jaruzelski who asks that you not attack Jaruzelski and Kiszczak by name." This was when Father Popiełuszko had just been abducted and murdered. I immediately gave interviews to the

Adam Michnik (left) interviewing General Wojciech Jaruzelski in Warsaw, January 1992. (Photo: Sławomir Sierzputowski)

BBC, *Le Monde,* and *Der Spiegel* in which I attacked Generals Jaruzelski and Kiszczak even more strongly than usual, because I saw them as obstacles that had to be removed before there could be any possibility of change for the better in Poland.

When I realized that I was mistaken, I said so out loud, at a mass meeting in Kraków in 1989 on the anniversary of the March events. I told the students who had previously been hurling bottles at the Soviet consulate that I'd changed my mind about General Jaruzelski. I subsequently said the same thing on television and in the press.

So you are talking with someone who used to be not only an anti-Communist extremist but also an anti-Jaruzelski extremist—with one exception, the assessment of martial law. In 1983 I wrote, "Perhaps it will turn out one day that those people whose names are now inscribed in blackest ink on the pages of Polish history actually saved Poland from Soviet intervention." In Victor Hugo's *Les Misérables,* there's a scene where the villain makes his way to the battlefield with the aim of robbing the corpses. He suddenly spots a gold stripe on a trouser leg, he pulls out the body, and in this way he saves the life of one of the book's heroes. So I wrote as follows: "In December 1981, there was a real threat of intervention, and a real threat of a conserva-

tive coup d'état in Poland. By defending Poland against both intervention and a conservative putsch from inside the party, Jaruzelski
and his group saved the country. But not because they were high-
minded patriots. They were defending their own positions and
power; they knew that the Russians would kick them out once they
arrived."

As for my history, it's both atypical and typical. An intelligentsia
family; my mother was a Communist before the war, as was my father, who came from a poor Jewish family.

Jaruzelski: Did he spend time in prison?

Michnik: Eight years. He was one of the chief defendants in the 1934
Łuck trial. This trial achieved notoriety because the prisoners were
tortured. I must say I never caught up with my father in this respect:
I spent six years in prison and got punched in the face a couple of
times at the most.

People used to be afraid of the Communists. I wasn't afraid, because I thought it was my system. And since it was mine, there was
nothing to be afraid of. I wasn't afraid to criticize the government, because it was my government and if it did something wrong, I could
criticize it. It never occurred to me that some people in Poland had an
even worse opinion of the government but were simply afraid to say
so. My courage resulted from lack of imagination.

The first time I landed in prison, in 1965, I was eighteen years old.
To say there was social support at that time for people like me is simply a figment of our heroic mythology. We were considered deviants,
madmen who were best kept at arms' length. People said we were either agents provocateurs or foolish people who didn't know what
they were doing but who were unleashing a process that was bound
to end in repression and further tightening of the screws.

Jaruzelski: I was called an agent of Moscow and you, an agent of imperialism. Given the situation in Poland, these were not empty labels.

Michnik: Really? In 1968, anti-German hysteria reached such a pitch that
there was an uproar when Tadeusz Mazowiecki gave a very restrained
interview to the German press, and even some of his associates asked
what he was doing talking to the Germans. In my time, no one took
the term "imperialist agent" seriously, but the German argument did
have an impact . . .

Let's not mythologize the role of the Church. The opposition
could count on the support of the Church only after December 13,

and this support was by no means absolute. The Church may have been anti-Communist, but it didn't believe that communism was about to collapse. On the contrary, communism was going to survive, and this required judicious adaptation on the part of the Church. I'm not blaming our bishops for behaving in this way; it was quite rational on their part. What I do object to is the fact that now, years later, the history of the Church is being presented as an unbroken wave of democratic opposition.

The same is true of earlier history. It's not really the case that before the war Polish Communists felt marginalized and saw themselves as the agents of a foreign power. In 1928, the Communists got nearly one million votes. But above all, they were convinced—at least, until the major show trials of 1936–38—that they had enlisted in the service of a noble cause. And history seemed to be proving them right. The most enlightened intellects of the West supported communism. Gustaw Herling-Grudziński published *A World Apart* in 1948, but no one read it.

Jaruzelski: It was translated into eleven languages.

Michnik: And so what? It was published by anti-Communist organizations, so it didn't count. In 1976, I was visiting a friend in Italy, a philosopher. I noticed he had a book about Katyń, and when I took it off the shelf, he said, "That's a fascist publication," to which I replied, "Why the hell shouldn't a left-wing publisher produce a book about Katyń?" This was exactly the kind of logic that was summed up in Jean-Paul Sartre's famous statement to the effect that one shouldn't deprive the Billancourt workers of hope. If you criticized the Soviet Union, they would lose hope.

My father's drama began in 1936, with the show trials in Moscow and what came after. He considered himself a Communist, but at the same time he hated everything that could be called the Soviet model of communism. He stayed in the party until 1968. He didn't believe resistance could ever be effective, and he considered me a Don Quixote. It was only when KOR was established that he came to see that I wasn't crazy.

It's impossible to compare our situations in terms of better or worse, because the experience of my father's generation simply has no equivalent. These people came out of the First World War, a dreadful, senseless war whose purpose was absolutely incomprehensible to ordinary people. And suddenly they were presented with a proposal to create a world without war, poverty, or oppression. It was a kind of faith.

I reject communism as an ideology, but I have never espoused the view that communism is nothing but a Soviet plot. I have always believed communism to be the great disaster of man in the twentieth century. It was a project conceived by human beings and endorsed by millions. Until 1936 my father truly believed in the possibility of creating a perfect society, whereas I always believed that a perfect society could be created only in a concentration camp.

Jaruzelski: Your evolution is quite clear to me. It's all clear to me until the emergence of KOR, which I treated in my time as an extremely suspect undertaking. I saw it as a subversive group serving alien interests—although it wasn't clear exactly whose. It seemed to threaten the pace of our development, which, despite the occasional setback, was proceeding in the only direction open to us. Subconsciously, I also felt a certain amount of respect, although this certainly didn't manifest itself at the time.

What I find unclear and even ethically murky is what happened afterward. Solidarity emerged as an all-embracing movement that—in simple terms—combined right-wing and, in a sense, even reactionary and parochial politics with populist, leftist socioeconomic demands. I want to provoke you because people who were deeply committed, like you, identified with this movement in the name of the struggle against communism. This means that anyone who attacks communism is an ally, and you end up with a coalition like that between Stalin, Churchill, and Roosevelt, in which there's room for everyone, from Jerzy Giertych to Jacek Kuroń, in the struggle against a greater evil. But this comes back to haunt you later, because the former ally who has now come to power may turn out to be just as much of a Communist, only even worse. You once referred to "communism without communism."

I want to ask you—in your capacity as a historian also—the following question: How can one deny the contribution made by people who were convinced that the framework established by Yalta would outlast us and perhaps our children and grandchildren also? It wasn't a question of marching on Moscow but of making a space for ourselves within this framework, of broadening it and bringing about a greater degree of autonomy. In this respect, Poland is better off than any other Communist country. I'm not referring only to the Church, but also to the countryside, to the bastions of private enterprise, as well as to science and culture and even the military, which has made a unique position for itself.

You refused to acknowledge this. You treated us as though we had all kinds of powers that we simply refused to use. Of course, we could discuss whether or not we paid enough attention to broadening the space within this framework. Here I'll just mention martial law, which was, after all, part of a struggle for greater sovereignty. After martial law, I felt myself in a much stronger position vis-à-vis our esteemed Leonid. Previously, I'd had to explain my actions; subsequently, I was able to speak to him somewhat differently.

When I look at the world around me, I'm reminded of a quotation from Alexis de Tocqueville: "If many conservatives defended the government only in order to retain various privileges and positions, then it must be said that many oppositionists seemed to attack it only in order to acquire them for themselves."

Michnik: It's still a complete mystery to me why the Communists had such a poor understanding of the opposition. The members of KOR were very anti-Communist, but they were also very realistic. They weren't rash, and they did not—most of them, at least—have any desire for revenge.

The question you have raised confronted KOR members: how to struggle for sovereignty in a world shaped by Yalta and the Brezhnev doctrine. The articles that I and other KOR members—Jacek Kuroń, Jan Lityński, and Zbigniew Romaszewski—wrote at the time provided an answer. But one had to read them in good faith and not with one's mind already made up on the basis of police reports, if I may say so.

Solidarity was a confederation against evil. Solidarity brought together three great political cultures: Catholic nationalism, working-class populism—in other words socioeconomic demands, including the demand for human dignity—and, third, the democratic culture of the intelligentsia, so deeply rooted in Poland.

There were people in Solidarity who proclaimed anti-Semitic views. I never concealed my opposition to this orientation. But for me Solidarity is an example of reason, like the anti-Hitler coalition. Churchill had no illusions—although Roosevelt may have had some—as to what kind of person Stalin was. But he thought Hitler was evil and welcomed any ally in the fight against him.

All this time we're talking about the elites, but Solidarity was a mass movement of millions of people with an inchoate political consciousness. They wanted to live better, to have less poverty, less fear, and more rights, but none of this added up to a political program. Solidarity had an ethos. Its program was, don't give in to the Commies, learn how to cultivate those areas of freedom that have opened up. Social issues were formulated largely in terms of demands for improvements in living and working conditions.

Jaruzelski: What Professor Szczepański called the "revolt of the consumers."

Michnik: If Professor Szczepański had lived for a moment like the Łódź textile workers, he might well have said that this was a revolt of the hungry and the poor. I thought they were right and that it was my duty to be with them, even though I knew that their struggle lacked direction.

If we're talking about the coalition that made up Solidarity, then I must say that from the very beginning, of course, there were people in the movement whom I couldn't stand. But I thought that since I was fighting for democracy, I ought to deal with them using democratic methods. And, of course, I was far more afraid of the Communists than of the "true Poles" or Marian Jurczyk. I was far more afraid of the Communists because they had power. Ever since the invasion of Czechoslovakia and the events of 1968, I'd had no illusions as to what an "invincible" Communist party was capable of. Many people thought I'd got cold feet, but I was simply being realistic.

There's a certain order of priorities. Some things you don't like, but you don't consider them the number one threat. As far as I was concerned, after December 13 the main division was between those who supported and those who opposed dictatorship. We could argue about Catholic social doctrine or the *endecja* at a later date.

During the period between the August agreements and the Bydgoszcz events [August 1980–March 1981], I believed that we shared responsibility for the state. I was in favor of seeking a genuine agreement, but when I heard the term "normalization" I shuddered. Normalization is a Communist propaganda term formulated after the intervention in Czechoslovakia which means a return to dictatorship. I feared that you wanted to turn Solidarity into something along the lines of PAX,[1] that you wanted to adapt it to a Communist dictatorship.

---

1. PAX was a licensed Catholic organization that collaborated with the government. — ED.

You have said, "We need both Traugutt, the insurrectionist, and Wielopolski, who came to an arrangement with Russia." This line of reasoning is close to my own. But why was it that this line of reasoning was actually absurd? Wielopolski declared, "We Poles must come to an agreement with Russia because we are too weak to stand up to them. Let us come to an agreement and within this framework build the best place for ourselves that we can." On the other hand, the Communists said, "We are building the most wonderful system on the face of the earth, and anyone who wants something else is anti-Polish."

Who, after December 13, 1981, declared that we could negotiate? Solidarity. And who said that negotiations were out of the question? The Communists. The only negotiations I was offered involved a choice between leaving for the Côte d'Azur and signing a declaration of loyalty or sitting quietly in prison and letting myself get fucked. Looking at things from this point of view, you can see why we became convinced that the system wasn't run by Poles, why we thought those in charge were an alien group, Sovietized Poles.

Why did my side reject the analogy between the Communists and Wielopolski? Wielopolski spoke the truth: "If we organize an uprising, we shall lose. If we cannot win, let us try to reach an agreement." The Communists said: "The USSR is a wonderful place, it's what we're all aiming for, it's the defender of progress and peace against wicked imperialism, whose agents you are, Mr. Kuroń and Mr. Michnik . . ."

You had this inscrutable demeanor and you spoke in newspeak. Whenever I actually understood anything, it made me shiver because it was the language of brute force and nothing else; ideological newspeak and the language of power. You didn't say anything about what needed to be done for Poland, only about how to defend yourselves against the oncoming wave of common proles.

This is why martial law only broadened the scope of your sovereignty as head of state and dealt a crushing blow to the autonomy of the rest of society. Until December 13, I used to analyze the dilemma facing the authorities in terms of the conflict between their convictions and their sense of responsibility. On December 13, this conflict was resolved.

Jaruzelski: I hope that what I say today won't be interpreted as the words of an embittered former politician. I accept my share of responsibility for what happened. I hope the current reforms are successful. I think many of the current setbacks and disappointments are due to the fact that people were too idealistic and thought that as soon as we found ourselves in our own home everything would change as though at the touch of a magic wand. That's why there is so much bitterness now.

About the early 1980s, it's possible to say nothing but the very worst. But I also have the right to say that during this time we began to reform the economy along lines that seemed feasible to us at the time. The previous system functioned in contravention of the laws of economics and despite human consciousness. But there is one thing that cannot be denied: there were certain social and moral principles—I'm not talking about various distortions and dirty tricks, let's leave those aside—that we considered more important. When I became prime minister, my first speech to Parliament identified the ten most important tasks for the government. Now, when I read this speech, I think to myself, You idiot! These ten points included guaranteeing the supply of food, supplies of medications, and all sorts of other things. I didn't renege on these commitments; I did my utmost to fulfill them. I won't allow this to be forgotten in relation to either me or the previous system.

The question is, should we take a shortcut of the kind that we're now taking, as a result of which we may end up like South America, or should we follow the path suggested by Karol Modzelewski from Labor Solidarity? This path would take us by a longer route but would allow us to salvage a certain minimum, to keep ourselves from falling off the wire, to protect people and retain the educational, cultural, and health care infrastructure.

Michnik: Perhaps my perspective is a little distorted, but I never said that the journey would be easy and pleasant. During the 1989 election campaign I was among those who said we should not put forward a program full of promises, but we should promise to defend our fellow citizens and their civil rights. At that point, it occurred to no one that we might take over the government. There may be a few people who now claim that they predicted it would happen, but I never came across them at the time. I did hear some critics say that "the pinkos have done a deal with the reds" and that this was "an attempt to salvage communism."

When I wrote the article "Your President, Our Prime Minister," in which I suggested that Solidarity and the Communists come to a particular arrangement, I was attacked by my colleagues, not yours. They said I was crazy. I remember a conversation I had with Tadeusz Mazowiecki. We walked around Warsaw while he patiently explained the

situation to me: "If we take power, we'll be left with all the old apparatus, which will devour us; we'll have to deal with an insoluble economic crisis."

One thing was clear to me: we had to set things moving in a
specific direction. I believed the Round Table agreement could be
transformed into a Spanish-style pact whereby the two sides agree
that the war is over and that they will try to work together to construct democratic institutions. The strong point of this argument was
people's belief in Solidarity's enormous strength, as a myth and a
movement deeply rooted in every region of the country, in all generations and social groups, together with the power of the Church and
the pope, whose authority could be used as a stabilizing influence
during the difficult transition period.

But this argument had enormous weaknesses, whichever way you
looked at it. It turned out that the majority of the Solidarity elite were
unwilling to endorse the philosophy of the Round Table. They preferred the rhetoric of decommunization. I emphasize that I'm referring to rhetoric rather than practice; this is the worst of all possibilities because it creates the illusion that decommunization will solve all
kinds of problems while, in fact, it solves nothing. The "philosophy of
unity" of Solidarity gave way to the "philosophy of schism," at least
for the duration of the reforms.

At this time the Catholic Church executed a change of course,
which I still don't fully comprehend. If I may paraphrase the title of a
well-known French theological work, *From the Syllabus to Vatican II,*
the Church shifted course from Vatican II to the Syllabus.

I don't think that—at the beginning, at least—we promised miracles. We really were afraid to take power.

Jaruzelski: I'm concerned with 1981 as well.

Michnik: Our strategy at that time was a controversial issue within Solidarity. I supported strikes in defense of the union, but I was against all
strikes on behalf of social and economic demands. But to say "I was
against" doesn't mean anything on its own. What I feared most was
the possible accusation that people like me treated the union in an instrumental fashion, that we needed it as a kind of political artillery,
and that we would block all initiatives aimed at improving the lives of
working people. I don't know of a single economic strike that was
supported by the union's central leadership.

But Solidarity was an uncontrollable force. The populist wing,
which articulated working-class social and economic grievances, was

unbelievably strong, all the more so because it met with a sympathetic response among working-class party circles. A Mrs. Nowakowska from Łódź was a member of the Central Committee; she took a pro-Solidarity line on all social issues but not on political issues. In the factories, there was enormous rivalry to see which organization could deliver the most. Solidarity gave way to this pressure.

The Solidarity leadership faced the following dilemma: to distance the union from economic demands and run the risk that they would be articulated by the official branch unions or by Albin Siwak,[2] or to try to coexist with this tendency within the framework of a single union? And of course there were people who really believed that the authorities were refusing to give in to their demands simply because they didn't want to. Within Solidarity, all official policy was interpreted as having the aim of destroying the union. The authorities were always singling out some groups as "extremists" and "anti-socialist elements" in the attempt to divide Solidarity. Everyone was afraid where discussion of this might lead, so the response to such blackmail was often retreat.

Politics provided the key to the situation. But on political issues any kind of agreement turned out to be impossible. The whole time, one sensed the political game being played by the other side, as well as Soviet pressure and manipulation. It is extremely difficult to say unpopular things to your grassroots supporters in a situation in which you have nothing to propose in exchange. This rebounds in the sense that anti-Communist propaganda always claimed that everyone would have it better after communism; that's the nature of all propaganda.

People find it extremely difficult to get used to having something taken away from them, but they easily get used to being given something. On one occasion during the fall of 1981, I took the early morning train from Łódź to Warsaw. It was still dark when I walked to the station, but people were already standing in line outside the butchers' shops, which didn't open until eleven o'clock. People got up at 5:00 to exchange their ration card for a piece of meat at 11:00. We have now gotten used to being able to buy meat without standing in line. And to the fact that we can have a passport, that we don't need a visa to travel in Europe, you just buy a ticket and off you go. And to the fact that there's no longer any point in listening to Radio Free Eu-

2. Albin Siwak represented the most obtuse opposition within the party against the Solidarity movement. — ED.

rope, because the press isn't censored anymore. But people can't get used to the fact—and I understand them—that summer camps for their kids are falling into ruin.

You referred to the moral underpinnings of communism. When someone sits in prison he curses his fate, but in prison he knows where he'll sleep and what he'll eat; he knows that once a week he'll get a bath, every two weeks he'll be able to buy something at the prison store, and twice a week he'll get a shave. All at once, he's released from prison and he revels in his freedom. But he doesn't know where he'll sleep, what he'll eat, or where he'll be able to bathe. Life under communism was a life without responsibility.

The example you gave, of when the prime minister says it is his business to concern himself with the supply of medication, with libraries, and so on, is totally typical. I didn't vote for this prime minister; he was imposed on me. Now he's promising me something, and I'll keep score to see if he delivers. On the other hand, this system assigns me no obligation to look after myself. As a result, an interesting psychological mechanism emerges: one abandons all sense of responsibility. A system that deprives people of responsibility is a system without creativity.

The Communist state concerned itself with libraries, schools, and so on, but I can't ignore the issue of which books were to be found in these libraries and which were not, what was taught in these schools and what was not. This was a paternalistic model of the state. By contrast, the state that is being born right now, for all its offensive aspects, involves a mighty conflict between the paternalistic model—in other words, a state organized according to the same principles as a nursery school, with its small children and teachers—and the model of a state designed for adults.

Jaruzelski: Even so, as the primate has said, our vision at that time far transcended the situation that existed among our neighbors. It didn't go far enough for you, but we were, nevertheless, an island of heresy in the old system. In one interview, I said, "You went too fast, and we went too slow. But those were the realities of the time."

Michnik: When the brother of Czar Alexander II, Prince Konstantin, wanted to come to an agreement with the Poles, he met with a leading authority of the Polish elite, Andrzej Zamoyski, and asked him, "What can I do for you Poles?" Zamoyski replied, "Withdraw from this place." To which, Konstantin responded, "That is the one thing we cannot do for you." If we accept that Poland's most basic aspiration at that time was for a sovereign state, then this was a situation worthy of Shakespearean drama.

But if we take Poland's aspirations of 1980 – 81—for a social minimum, for genuine pluralism or a minimum of national autonomy— did they really exceed the possibilities of the state and party leadership? I know for certain that Solidarity could not have asked for anything less. I believe that, after the Bydgoszcz events, the authorities had an enormous opportunity to seize the political initiative . . .

Jaruzelski: . . . while the military maneuvers were in full swing, and Kuligov and Kryuchkov were sitting here? Absolutely impossible. If there had been a general strike following Bydgoszcz, it would have been far more dangerous than in December, because at that time Solidarity was functioning as a crowd. Our allies would probably have reacted with greater severity. Martial law—even though you insist on viewing it in the most negative possible light—was actually a controlled process; it was not without direction.

Strategically, you were all hawks, by which I mean you believed that, in the long run, the system had to be overthrown. But tactically you were all doves, although some of you, like Kuroń, sometimes twittered too loudly.

Michnik: That's a fairly accurate analysis.

Jaruzelski: Kuroń has the habit of saying things that should remain unsaid. Whenever we watched or heard you all speaking, Kuroń reminded us of a mutinous Kronstadt sailor—except that he would have done the hanging.

Michnik: He wouldn't hurt a fly.

Jaruzelski: And you were like a cross between a lizard and a tiger. The lizard signified cunning and shrewdness, and the tiger was going to bite us.

Michnik: We believed that—as the Holy Scriptures say—there is a time to sow and a time to reap. Our intentions were bloodthirsty when it came to institutions but never when it came to people.

Jaruzelski: In my opinion, your movement was dominated by hawks, tactical and strategic, or rather by tactical hawks and strategic asses.

Michnik: Well, but there was still Wałęsa and . . .

Jaruzelski: He was really difficult to work out. If someone says one thing in the morning and something completely different in the evening, and if you don't know him well, it's hard to know what he means.

We warned everyone about the economic situation; we produced statistics. Coal was a classic example, because everything else depended on it. Both the Soviets and the East Germans gave us the most trouble over coal; we were losing contracts that had taken us decades to build up. This really was a disaster for us. When I look at my notes from that period, all I see is "coal, coal, coal."

I confess that after the introduction of martial law we lacked the courage to begin talks. Undoubtedly, we should have done more and done it sooner. On the other hand, in 1981 the situation was the other way around. We frequently issued official proposals to set up a commission made up of trade union and government representatives. But you refused to sit at the same table with the branch and autonomous unions. Where's the democracy here? Maybe you didn't like them because of their shady origins. Today, I could talk at length about the meeting of all three unions, at my initiative, on November 4, 1981, and why nothing came of it subsequently. We genuinely wanted to create a Front of National Understanding.

Michnik: This was an anti-Solidarity front. The proposal that a trade union with nine million members sit down to talks with the branch unions on an equal footing is like me proposing that you, as first secretary of the party, sit down with Moczulski, chairman of the KPN [Confederacy for Independent Poland, a political party]. You would have been enraged by such insolence.

Jaruzelski: If there's a genuine desire for dialogue, then people will talk to each other even, if I may say so, in the john—because they don't want to shoot or beat each other up.

Michnik: For a couple of years after the imposition of martial law, I used to talk to you almost every day in my mind. I used to say, "General, none of this is worth shit. You can't keep a whole society in a state of fear and apathy for long. Let's get together." Then I'd pick up the newspaper, read your reply, General, and remind myself of everything that had gone before.

Jaruzelski: But you're talking about martial law.

Michnik: I looked back and interpreted everything as the logic of communism. Communism is capable of tactical retreat, but it will never tolerate a nontotalitarian vision of the state. At that time, you were all writing articles saying, "We have to imagine ourselves back in 1947 and open up some room for maneuver," which meant, of course, that you intended to advance once more, but more efficiently and effectively. You wanted to talk about cabbages and coal but not about politics. As long as you were unwilling to talk about politics, you had no credibility as far as I was concerned. It seemed to me that the dispute in the party, which turned out to be serious, was about how best to deal with Solidarity. What might be called the reformist wing never once tried seriously to talk to us about politics.

Jaruzelski: Solidarity made the fewest promises, at least in public, about freedom and democracy and the most promises about greater justice in the future. But, to a great extent, the prewar Communists fulfilled the promises they had made. Who eradicated misery in the countryside? Who provided an escape route for the millions who were vegetating there? I lived in a manor house, but I was surrounded by a sea of people who lived in farmworkers' dwellings, with dirt floors, in filth and squalor. I visited them only once, since further visits would have seemed inappropriate in those days. Today I live in a house of the kind inhabited by hundreds and thousands of peasants in the countryside. This is a measure of the changes that have taken place. I have been a general for nearly forty years, for fifteen years I was minister of defense, and for ten years the most important person in the state. I am not, by the way, complaining about my situation.

Michnik: How does the first secretary of the party committee in Bytom live, or his deputy, for that matter?

Jaruzelski: We were talking earlier about generals and colonels in the armed forces of the partitioning powers, and you skipped to another subject entirely. Please don't make us out to be worse than they were, because they would have served their commanders loyally if Poland hadn't exploded.

Michnik: But Sierakowski and Traugutt rebelled.

Jaruzelski: Let's not talk about a few exceptions who paid for their actions with their lives.

Michnik: Agreed, but my chief accusation against you is that you never talked to us as adults but always treated us like nursery school kids: "Don't touch the roses, Andy, you'll prick yourself." Never once, except for a brief period in 1956, did we have a normal conversation. Nothing but newspeak and double-talk. At one point, I began to think that the only constant factor within the ruling group was the desire to rule.

Jaruzelski: The movement that we're discussing has a major sin on its conscience: a tendency to idealize society and attribute all its negative characteristics to the influence of communism. By implication, everything was wonderful during the Second Republic. But intellectuals and politicians have to say, "Beloved Poles, you are admirable and worthy of respect for this and that reason, but remember that an ominous shadow has been following you not just for 45 years but for 450." One shouldn't indulge any old philistine who considers himself a true Pole.

You said that the strikes died down before martial law. That's not true. Young people were on strike. All the colleges and universities were on strike, and in Lublin, even some of the secondary schools. At the time, an association with the Warsaw Uprising came to my mind: those who instigated the uprising subsequently argued that they had had no choice because the young people were so worked up that they would have attacked the Germans on their own.

Michnik: I guess that in ten years or so we shall hear the following kind of explanation from our current president: "The nation is wanting, it has defects; the president had problems; he could not cope any more than King Władysław or Piłsudski could have." I'm the last person to pander to my fellow countrymen. After December 13, I went through a short period of total solidarity with the national mythology. You will not, however, find any mythologizing of the Second Republic in anything I wrote after the lifting of martial law or in the paper I'm now editing.

To put it bluntly, modern-day Poland has its origin also in the murder of President Narutowicz, the scandal about Żeromski's *Before the Spring,* and the 1926 May Coup d'État. But for forty years you served up an exceptionally mendacious account of the interwar period. It is dangerous to idealize a nation. On the other hand, I am basically opposed to any analysis of Polish history in terms of national defects. One has to analyze institutions and ways in which Poles perceived the world. To talk about national defects leads us into the realm of mysticism or genes, which I don't understand. The Germans have a history completely different from that of the Poles, but if you want to see a real *polnische Wirtschaft* ["Polish way of doing business"—a derogatory German expression], you should visit the former GDR.

As far as my generation is concerned, the Second Republic constituted a brief interval during which we were masters of our own dunghill, when all the rottenness that went on this country was rottenness committed by sovereign Poles and directed against sovereign Poles.

Of course, there is a syndrome running through Polish history in which the emotions of the young come to dominate certain key moments. In this sense, I understand that what I saw as a source of Solidarity's strength—the fact that it attracted the younger generation—you saw as a threat. It's interesting that Jan Józef Lipski said exactly the same thing at the time: "I'm horrified when I look at these young people, because I was here during the Warsaw Uprising and I know how badly things can end here." But now I'm talking in clichés. It's a fact of life that where the wise see danger, the young see opportunity.

Jaruzelski: What do you think would have happened if we hadn't imposed martial law? Is there any real basis for saying it was the lesser of two evils, or is such a statement a distortion based on the desire to defend a particular decision? I know that opinions about martial law vary enormously. It seems to me that Solidarity, or post-Solidarity, still views it in rather subjective, martyr-heroic terms, which is quite understandable, of course. After all, the more diabolical was martial law, the more elevated the picture we can paint of ourselves.

We don't know what form the future dispute over martial law will take, whether it will be constructive or destructive. You referred to the experience of Spain. There people are working together constructively and accept that there should be no further disputes about the past, regardless of who was right. Once again, I want to emphasize that when I say this, I'm aware that I was an oppressor and you were oppressed, and I don't want to approach these issues in moral terms but in political terms.

Sometimes I wonder why I didn't jump on a plane and fly to Gdańsk after the meeting of Solidarity's National Commission in Radom, at which Wałęsa shocked us all by talking about "beating up the Communists." I could have said, "Gentlemen, please, I beg you, I insist—do something!" But I could also ask why Wałęsa or his associates didn't send us a signal to the effect that Radom was just talk and they weren't in favor of confrontation? Nevertheless, I can't imagine that I could have gone to Gdańsk or that it would have had much impact. I understand that Wałęsa's position in the union was already weakened—he writes about this in his autobiography—and that he couldn't actually have behaved any differently.

Michnik: Why did you all attribute such importance to Radom? It was just a show.

Jaruzelski: It was followed by Wałęsa's meeting in the Radoskór factory, where he said there would be no agreement because there was no one with whom to reach an agreement.

Michnik: But General Kiszczak has said in one of his interviews that the decision to impose martial law had been made two months earlier.

Jaruzelski: We were technically prepared, but not to the extent that all we had to do was press the button. The temperature was rising, abroad as well as at home. We had decided that we would try to push through legislation on emergency powers, including, for example, a ban on all strikes during the coming winter. If this didn't work, and a general strike took place, we'd decided we would have to introduce martial law. Some people argued that we shouldn't wait for a strike but should seize the initiative and impose order using the emergency legislation, which did not, by the way, include measures to dissolve Solidarity. I realize that your side found this legislation totally unacceptable, but you must understand that we saw this as the only way to survive the winter. I have a handwritten note that Stanisław Ciosek wrote as early as November: "In order to avert a biological catastrophe, I propose that in large cities people from several city districts be evacuated to a single district and that only this district receive central heating." He was absolutely serious. We couldn't help having such ideas at that time. And, of course, there was also Moscow.

Only when you add all these factors together can you get an idea of the pressure we were under and the weight of the responsibility we felt. There was complete agreement among us—from Kubiak to Siwak [i.e., from reformers to the most intransigent wing of the party], despite their differences. When I finally pressed the button, I felt so relieved that the decision was behind me.

Look at it from two points of view. First, could it have been avoided, and if so, how? Second, how was it implemented, and with what results? While I would argue that I chose the lesser of two evils, I have to criticize what happened afterward.

Michnik: It could be said that if the May Coup [1926] hadn't taken place, the *endecja* would have introduced an authoritarian order—and we would have had Polish fascism. But I learned from Marxism that there's no such thing as historical necessity. There's a framework, but within this framework various courses of action are possible. If you

compare Gomułka with Imre Nagy, you see how much room for maneuver there was.

You said there came a point at which you were all in agreement,
from Kubiak to Siwak. We can be reproached—to some extent correctly—for having generated this agreement ourselves. I could put it
differently and say that, essentially, the authorities differed among
themselves on tactics but were united on strategy: self-defense. The
interests of the *nomenklatura* outweighed all else. From Rakowski to
Barcikowski, there was no sign of any willingness to talk about a new
political order. And if the political will had existed, someone could
have given us such a sign.

You ask about where to assign blame. I have various answers to
this question. I gave my first answer publicly in what I wrote after
December 13: the Communists are guilty because they're a bunch of
gangsters who from the very beginning just wanted to put us all behind bars.

My second answer, which I gave privately, to Kuroń for example,
was that we too were to blame. Both of us had misjudged the situation. Kuroń had argued that free elections were possible right then, in
the fall of 1981; I had said a compromise was possible in the form of a
bicameral legislature, with one chamber elected along Communist
principles and the second according to principles endorsed by Solidarity.

I gave my third answer in the spring of 1991 in Moscow. I told the
Russian democrats, "At all costs, you must seek an agreement with
Gorbachev, because if it comes to martial law in Russia, he'll have the
support of the West. You must stop thinking in terms of how right
you are and how determined you are to defend your position." And
then I said something I'd never said before—that my side shared responsibility for the imposition of martial law in Poland, because we
had failed to create a language of dialogue. If there is a compromise
that breaks down, everyone is responsible.

My political position during the Round Table had its origin in the
memory of the collapse of the compromise of 1980–81 and in the
feeling that it was now my obligation to make compromise possible
and to remember why it had previously failed.

This is why I have no simple answer to the question of what would
have happened if martial law had not been imposed. Where should I
begin my argument? In my opinion, an opportunity for compromise
existed during the first half of 1981. Subsequently, a confrontational

dynamic was unleashed, and neither side believed compromise was possible. In my opinion, the major part of the blame for this lies with your side.

For me, the real end of martial law was the Round Table. This means that I'm inconsistent in my reasoning. We would have judged martial law and its instigators differently if Poland's Communists had relinquished power in the same way as their brethren in Romania or even Czechoslovakia. At the Round Table, I accepted responsibility for an agreement with specific individuals—Kiszczak, for instance, to whom I had previously written an abusive letter.[3] It would be despicable of me if I were to say now something different from what I said then just because circumstances have changed in the interim. I knew perfectly well what Kiszczak had been responsible for. But if I didn't tell Kiszczak at the Round Table that he would be brought to trial for martial law if I ever came to power, it would be contemptible of me to demand it now. One pays for everything in politics. There's no such thing as total justice.

Somewhere in Poland there may be people who say that the Round Table was a mistake, that we should not have accorded the Communists legitimacy, that we should have done everything to achieve justice. But we don't know how many people would have lost their lives had it not been for the Round Table. I'm happy that I was able to contribute to a situation in which not a single drop of blood has been spilled during this transformation, and it would be most unseemly on my part if I refused to acknowledge the contribution of our former rulers.

Of course, there are some things that people of my generation will never forget. I shall always remember the Wujek mine,[4] because I feel responsible for what happened to those people. But I don't think in terms of a lesser evil. A lesser evil is not a concept that I could possibly endorse in the context of December 13.

What would have happened if martial law had not been imposed? Either there is no answer to this question or there are several. There is a negative and a positive scenario. If we were to analyze, one by one, all the events of the weeks leading up to martial law, it would be ap-

3. See "A Letter to General Kiszczak, 1983," in Adam Michnik, *Letters from Prison and Other Essays* (Berkeley: University of California Press, 1985), 64–70.—ED.

4. On December 16, 1981, while breaking the strike at the Wujek mine in Silesia, the armored police units (ZOMO) killed nine miners. It was the most violent episode of the imposition of martial law.—ED.

parent that the situation was not conducive to an agreement. Time was working against it. But it must still be said that at that time no one asked what the real problem was. It wasn't a question of whether or not Jaruzelski went to Gdańsk, because whatever he talked about there—the threat of Russian intervention, the situation with coal output—it would probably have been interpreted as yet another installment of trickery. The main point is that there was no attempt at a serious discussion about politics.

Since we're talking about the lesser of two evils, the lesser evil would have been for the Communists to relinquish some of their power rather than impose martial law.

Those who said that Solidarity had gone too far were wrong. They took as their starting point the fact that Solidarity could rightly be accused of wanting too much while ignoring all the accusations that could have been justifiably levied against the Communists. But they were also right in that Solidarity's political thinking was dominated by emotion, rhetoric, feelings, and phobias, with no distinction between strategy, policy, and program. I think it's quite probable that, on the eve of martial law, Solidarity was ready to endorse a particular stereotype, what I call "systemic anti-communism." I'm thinking of Marian Jurczyk, who threatened Communists with the scaffold and said that Poland was governed by Jews in the Politburo and that he knew which of them had changed his name to conceal his origin.

I remember [Politburo member] Stefan Olszowski's response to Jurczyk's speech. He didn't say that Jurczyk had indulged in anti-Semitism but that he was simply wrong because neither Olszowski nor Jaruzelski nor Kiszczak was a Jew. Thus the formula that I used in one of my letters from Białołęka to define martial law—a bunch of gangsters attacking a lunatic asylum—although somewhat frivolous, because it could have been used against Solidarity, wasn't completely fanciful.

Finally, the question of responsibility, to which I don't have an answer. I have no idea, for example, how I would have behaved if I'd had the feeling that my decision would result in a hundred deaths and that weakness on my part might send a hundred thousand people to their graves. At that time this kind of calculation was permissible.

One can always present the counterargument that Jaruzelski and his associates weren't actually thinking along these lines but were simply defending their own power. This kind of argument has been readily accepted in the case of similar events elsewhere, in relation to General Pinochet, for example. It is not by chance that the people who are ready to praise General Jaruzelski for martial law are the same people who accuse Pinochet of being a fascist, while those who praise Pinochet for having saved Chile from communism condemn martial law as a criminal act. Neither point of view appeals to me. I can't forget that both Chile and Poland avoided civil war, that both Chile and Poland emerged from dictatorship with the agreement of the very generals who had imposed martial law.

In the case of both Chile and Poland I was unambiguously opposed to dictatorship, and I know how I should behave now. It's time to cease all discussion of the subject in terms of possible criminal proceedings. Martial law is now a subject for historians, journalists, and writers; for priests, moralists, and confessors. It is no longer a subject for the public prosecutor.

Jaruzelski: Each of these themes raises questions. That's why this was the most dramatic decision of my entire life. I said I felt relieved, but I didn't mean this in the literal sense. I no longer confronted a dilemma. Weighing all the factors involved brought me to the notion of the lesser evil. One shouldn't misuse this term, but it offers a concise illustration of the situation as it appeared to me and my associates.

Solidarity adopted a certain grandiose tone. Actually, Solidarity wasn't the only one. In our time, we used to say that "society believes, expects, demands" one thing or another. Even the most powerful political force has no right to speak in such terms. Society is never monolithic.

Michnik: Do you think the majority of Poles wanted martial law?

Jaruzelski: I'd rather not talk in terms of the majority or minority.

Michnik: The overwhelming majority didn't want martial law; they wanted an agreement.

Jaruzelski: They wanted an agreement, but if agreement didn't materialize, they wanted peace. People were none too fond of us. But it's possible to be none too fond of someone, and even to regard him as a total scoundrel, but if I'm drowning and this scoundrel leaps into the water and pulls me out, I'll say, "I consider you a scoundrel, but thank you for rescuing me."

Michnik: The only thing I'm prepared to accept—although I have to admit defeat because of ignorance—is that it was a question of a choice between the following: martial law—just as it was, with all its nastiness, altogether one hundred dead, thousands wronged and humiliated, but with Poland surviving—or Soviet intervention. At this point, my imagination breaks down, because we would have had Budapest on a Polish scale. At the same time, all other arguments are without foundation.

Jaruzelski: Those who were in power at the time believed it was necessary to defend the system.

Michnik: This is precisely the crux of the matter.

Jaruzelski: But if you compare any other year in Poland with 1981, during which pluralism did not exist de jure but we had de facto dual power . . . everyone then had the feeling that they were governing on credit, that they were actually in a state of suspended animation.

Michnik: Why didn't you try to institutionalize this dual power?

Jaruzelski: And why didn't you . . .

Michnik: We tried, perhaps ineffectively and unskillfully, but you bear the greater responsibility because you had power. If coal was really so important, why didn't you once agree to talk to us about coal and the leading role of the party?

Jaruzelski: I don't think you can deny that between August 1980 and December 1981 our power was greatly weakened while Solidarity grew in strength. All the movement was in one direction.

Michnik: No, please listen to me now calmly and with goodwill. In 1956 and 1970 there were two great upheavals, and each time it seemed that there could be no return to the status quo ante.

Jaruzelski: And there wasn't.

Michnik: Not completely, but there was always a return to a formal monopoly of political power. There was no return to terror, and in this sense October proved to be irreversible. But there was a return to political prisoners. Gomułka locked up Kuroń and Modzelewski for having written a letter to the university party committee.

Jaruzelski: This was completely idiotic.

Michnik: It wasn't idiotic. It was quite logical. We considered it an example of the infamous law of Communist homeostasis: everything always returns to equilibrium.

Jaruzelski: A colorful but inexact comparison. At that time, we were dealing with spontaneous movements without any real political force behind them. In 1980 we faced a qualitatively new entity—a powerful movement that was actually stronger than the party.

Michnik: But you wanted to dismantle it from within using your network of spies. You should ask General Kiszczak how many agents he had inside Solidarity's governing bodies before December 13.

Jaruzelski: If he had any, it was only to find out what was going on.

Michnik: Not to find out what was going on, to create policy. Whenever I asked myself how the Communists could derail us without martial law, I used to recall the case of Mikołajczyk and how so many agents were let into the Peasant party that they finally got rid of him. I had absolutely no doubt as to what was going on. Rákosi used the term "salami tactics" to describe the process of finishing off your enemy one slice at a time. That's exactly what you wanted to do. First of all Moczulski, then Kuroń and Michnik. At the same time, you planted your agents throughout the movement. I saw this for myself in the Mazowsze region; there came a point when they were almost in the majority. Ask Zbyszek Bujak. These people nearly succeeded in throwing him out. How do I know they were all agents? Because when you imposed martial law, they stood at attention and we never heard from them again.

Jaruzelski: If we're going to talk specifics again, I was extremely disappointed by the outcome of the meeting between Solidarity and the other unions in November 1981. This opening should not have been rejected. Your side broke off the talks only because you wanted to have three of the seven seats on the proposed working body, the Consultative Council.

Michnik: Are you really saying that martial law was introduced to defend the branch unions? This isn't a serious argument.

Jaruzelski: No. But you have said that we didn't take a single step in the right direction, and I'm saying that you didn't respond to the step we did take. The primate was able to sit down with us, but not you. All of a sudden, you were all so concerned to keep your hands clean.

Michnik: You haven't answered my main point. The whole time, you only wanted to talk about cabbage, never about politics.

Jaruzelski: Not so. A new order was precisely what we wanted to talk about. The Council of National Understanding was intended to be a forum where we could discuss important issues. I must say—because I have the right to defend myself—that subsequent developments showed that we were right. After all, everyone sat down to the Round Table. But how could we have ignored Radom?

Michnik: You interpreted it incorrectly. After the imposition of martial law, it turned out that Solidarity had been totally unprepared for confrontation of any kind. We didn't have a single handgun, not a single grenade, not a single bottle filled with gasoline. So what are we actually talking about? Radom was simply a signal that we wouldn't back down, nothing more. Now I understand your position: you received a transcript of the meeting in which the "healthy tendency" in Solidarity talked about beating up the Communists, so you had a right to be angry. I, on the other hand, thought to myself, Lech is simply afraid that he's going to be isolated, so he's going for broke. But in reality it didn't mean anything.

* * *

Michnik: The maturity of nations, societies, and individuals is measured in terms of the way in which they live with their own history and their own life story. It's highly probable that if the guards at Białołęka had caught me trying to escape, they would have shot me dead. If I had been in the vicinity of you, General Kiszczak, or Premier Rakowski on December 13—a moment of national upheaval—and if I'd been armed, I'm quite certain I would have taken aim.

But at the same time, I think it of great significance—and in some ways I count it a victory for both of us—that today we are able to talk about all this without hatred, without hostility, and with mutual respect while remaining true to our own past. If Poland has a chance— and I believe that she does—it lies in people's ability to talk to each other without hatred and hostility.

Jaruzelski: The lesser or greater evil—this has preoccupied me the whole time. I remain convinced that what happened then was inevitable. Today, though, I know that one has to respect the arguments of others. It's not a question of black versus white but of trying to understand the other side. This doesn't mean that one can reach agreement on every point or identify completely with the other side, but we can understand each other. This is the most important thing.

24

I Am a Polish Intellectual

*Adam Michnik Talks to Adam Krzemiński
and Wiesław Władyka, Editors of* Polityka

Polityka: Adam, what will you be doing ten years from now?

Adam Michnik: You're joking, right? I haven't the faintest idea. One thing that's typical of my circle is that we've never asked ourselves this question; we've never tried to plan our lives. Ten years ago I was sitting in prison. If anyone had asked me this question then, I would probably have given a stupid answer. And ten years before that, I was in Poznań, finishing my undergraduate studies—which had been interrupted by the events of 1968—and working as Słonimski's secretary. It's hard enough to imagine what will happen in four years time, let alone ten.

Polityka: We were asking about your public life. Do you hope you'll still be an editor, or would you rather be a politician or even a writer?

Michnik: If I had to choose one of these, then I'd do something between editing *Gazeta Wyborcza* and writing. I've never considered myself a politician, and I've never really felt comfortable in that role. It was quite a relief to leave the Sejm.

Polityka: Perhaps the Sejm would have followed a different course if you had stayed.

Translated by Jane Cave from *Polityka,* February 6, 1993.

Michnik: I doubt it. I think certain social groups eventually exhaust their historical potential. This was true of those associated with the Home Army, which played such a major role during the war; this was true of the 1956 "revisionists" and it's true of us, the 1968 generation. Our time stretched from March 1968 through Solidarity, martial law, and the Round Table to the formation of the Mazowiecki government.

Polityka: Are you saying there's no room for this generation in Parliament?

Michnik: For this generation, yes, but not for this particular group [of political activists]. It has simply collapsed: Bugaj is in one place and Bujak in another, while Macierewicz and Naimski, Aleksander Hall and Jan Lityński are somewhere else entirely. I don't think the '68 generation has much political significance anymore. It may have more significance in relation to culture. I think you could find some interconnections there. What remains of the atmosphere of the Theater of the Eighth Day or the Lublin theaters? What have we inherited from the cinema of moral disquiet? From the climate created by the poetry of Barańczak, Krynicki, and Zagajewski? From the criticism of Tomasz Burek and Andrzej Werner? What provided the basis for subsequent ideological divisions? Over what issues did these people part company with each other?

Polityka: Are you saying that conspirators don't make good politicians?

Michnik: One becomes a conspirator for completely different reasons than one becomes a politician. Becoming a conspirator involves a moral choice, it involves choosing one's fate, whereas becoming a politician involves choosing one's profession. There's nothing unusual about this. As long as communism survived, we were at war. The war came to an end, and that particular coalition was demobilized. Of course, some of them stayed in the trenches, but the war is over.

Polityka: But they still have a certain obligation. Biology is forcing this generation to assume a parental role. In other words, they no longer need to stand on the barricades, but they do have to send out intellectual and moral signals; they have to formulate a purpose and goals. At the same time, the "March generation"—and you in particular—is viewed with hostility by some twenty-year-olds, those associated with the journal *brulion* [notebook], for example.

Michnik: I don't want to blow my own trumpet, so perhaps I should focus on my own shortcomings. But I don't take *brulion* too seriously.

Adam Michnik, May 1995. (Photo: Jerzy Gumowski)

I just want to say that all my life I've struggled for them to have the right to attack whomever they wanted, me included. But I'm unable to say anything much about them at this point. It's only three years since the end of communism, and they're still looking for their voice. They're not the only ones; we're all in the same situation.

Polityka: Is that why you want to be both an editor and a writer?

Michnik: Yes. It's easy to succumb to megalomania, but I don't think I'm mistaken when I say that *Gazeta Wyborcza* is playing a major role in creating a new language in which to discuss and evaluate the world around us. For us, *Gazeta* is not just a newspaper, it's an institution of civil society, an institution of Polish democracy.

Polityka: How would you define *Gazeta*'s system of values?

Michnik: I tried to deal with this in our New Year issue, where I identified four themes. First, we have a strong antipathy toward all populist tendencies while remaining sensitive to poverty and injustice. A second issue is our attitude toward the Church. We're strongly opposed to what we might call the forced evangelization of state laws . . .

Polityka: Which is why the primate referred to you as "a mongrel" . . .

Michnik: That's immaterial. Heinrich Böll and Günter Grass used to be referred to as "doberman pinchers," so I'm in good company. The third issue is our attitude toward decommunization. We have no Communist sympathies whatsoever. We're happy that we lived to see the end of People's Poland, and we think the changes that have taken place are positive. On the other hand, we have no sympathy for the kind of absolute hostility and aggressive—and essentially Bolshevik—mentality displayed by many so-called decommunizers. We don't advocate collective amnesia, but neither do we advocate blind hatred. On this issue, our position is clear, but people accuse me of exaggerating. Finally, we are extremely sensitive to issues of national dignity. We don't try to compensate for our own grudges by humiliating others.

Polityka: It's interesting that your list doesn't include the modernization or "Europeanization" of Poland.

Michnik: This always used to be *Polityka*'s specialty. In one sense, modernization is included in the fourth point. But modernization on its own is a cliché; everyone is in favor of modernization. In 1989, I myself said, Let us return to Europe. Only later did I realize that this is just a slogan. We have to define precisely what value system we're talking about. Europe includes de Gaulle and Mendès-France, Le Pen and primitive *gauchiste* militants, as well as Adenauer, Willy Brandt, and the fascist republicans in Germany. Europe itself is not a value. What *is* a value is that we can contribute something to Europe. And what can we contribute? Our experience of having lived under actually existing socialism, in the grip of the police and the censors, in a system of totalitarian fear but also totalitarian social security.

Polityka: When we refer to Europe, are we really thinking about a Poland that is open to outsiders?

Michnik: It's much more complicated than that. I see two dangers here. On the one hand, in all the post-Communist countries you find this syndrome of insularity, parochialism, and xenophobia; it's by no means specific to Poland.

But there's another issue, too. I was recently on the jury at the Polish Film Festival in Gdynia. I saw thirty-two films in the course of a week. I have to say that I'm horrified by the things that are reaching us from Europe—nothing but garbage, someone else's leftovers. I was strongly opposed to all the ranting and raving on the part of our bishops against depravity and pornography in Polish culture. But as I watched those thirty-two films, I realized that the bishops hadn't invented this pornography, that there really is something in our consciousness that is sickening. Pornography is treated in the most instrumental fashion. In any film, no matter what the hero is talking about, the heroine has to take her clothes off and walk around with bare breasts, because otherwise it's not cinema. The attitude toward women is absolutely outrageous; they have become tools for copulation. To me, this is nihilism. This is why I avoid the slogan of Europeanization; we have to spell out exactly what we mean by this.

Polityka: Europeanization involves more than just sex shops and Mercedes. It also means an enlightened legal culture, rational education, and a host of new issues: feminism, the environment, and so on. Is there a common theme running through these four points of the *Gazeta* program?

Michnik: Of course I realize this. Of course Europe isn't just about sex shops. But it's easy to caricature Europe or America, and I've seen such caricatures in many of our films and in the way many of us think. I think the common thread in *Gazeta*'s program is to keep asking what is the purpose and nature of democracy. If we look at the world around us, we can see that democracy is under attack from three sources: populism, ethnic fervor, and religious fundamentalism.

Polityka: In the rest of the world, or in Poland also?

Michnik: After visiting Morocco, I returned to Poland feeling quite fond of the Christian National Union. In Tangiers I came across some Islamic fundamentalists who make Stefan Niesiołowski seem quite harmless.

Polityka: But Niesiołowski will take Khomeini's side against Salman Rushdie. He wouldn't kill Rushdie himself, but he'll argue that one can't forbid it. And when they finally get Rushdie, Niesiołowski will wash his hands of the whole thing, like Pontius Pilate.

Michnik: All the same, Niesiołowski is a soft-hearted follower of Voltaire, a liberal Freemason in comparison to the Islamic fundamentalists I met. One of these days, someone in Poland will emerge to accuse Niesiołowski of being a member of the Catholic left and a representative of Jewish interests.

Polityka: This suggests that of the three threats to democracy you are least afraid of religious fundamentalism.

Michnik: I'd put it differently. One reaction to the crisis of the modern world, to chaos and instability, is the attempt to make a home for oneself, to root oneself in something that seems permanent and unchanging. Hence the turn to the nation, to a social group, and to religion. This is the basis of all kinds of fundamentalism, including religious fundamentalism. Religious fundamentalism—which in Poland might better be called integrism—involves the attempt to construct a state based on religious norms, to eradicate the boundary between religious norms and state norms, and to replace the philosophy of pluralism and tolerance with a doctrine that emerged in an ideological ghetto, the doctrine of the Catholic state of the Polish nation. Integrism is one form of religiosity but is not itself religion. I think that integrism is a form of religion that has become a political instrument, that has been interpreted in a populist fashion. Populism is to be found within both Polish Catholicism and Polish anti-clericalism. For example, the weekly *Nie,* which I'm ready to defend in the event of any attempt to harass it, is addressed to a populist readership, the kind of people who like the language of the KPN [Confederation for an Independent Poland] or Tymiński.

Polityka: But these two kinds of populism will never come together.

Michnik: These two, no, but others, for sure. It's not by chance that we're suddenly presented with a coalition in which Messrs. Miodowicz and Jurczyk join forces against Balcerowicz.

Polityka: So who is going to defend democracy, and in what way, if the populists and nationalists take to the streets? Will fine-sounding words of wisdom be enough?

Michnik: I prefer to stick with an example that can easily be verified. I don't know who would defend democracy if it were endangered. I do know, however, who buys which newspapers. Words have a force of their own; it is they that create the world in which we live, the intellectual climate and spiritual air that we breathe. Each of us chooses the language that suits us. For various reasons, hundreds of thousands of people in this country prefer to read *Gazeta Wyborcza* over *Nowy Świat* or *Słowo Powszechne,* prefer *Polityka* to *Ład,* or *Wprost* to *Spotkania.* I wouldn't underestimate the significance of their preferences. I realize, of course, that one could advance the counterargument that the potential for populism lies with people who have little contact with the printed word.

Polityka: One can also put it differently. The cultural sterility of the populists, fundamentalists, and nationalists shows that they're not on a rising tide. This is no longer the twenties, when the right had its intellectual torch-bearers. Today's nationalists couldn't find anyone with even a quarter of [the nationalist historian] Zbigniew Załuski's talent to provide them with an ideology in the way that Załuski provided an ideology to Moczar and his supporters. This is a sign that they're on the way out rather than the way in.

Michnik: It's not so clear. On the one hand, it seems that this may actually be the case, that present-day Polish nationalism has no cultural expression. But isn't it the case that the whole post-Communist epoch has not yet found its artistic language? It seems that the traditional language in which we described the world and its conflicts has lost its utility and that we're feeling our way, trying to construct a new picture of the world in which we live. We all face the same problem, but it's something we have to resolve for ourselves. I am not convinced that everything has already been decided. Nowhere has it been decreed, for example, that post-Communist societies are bound to follow a democratic path. In what language can we describe this? Slobodan Milosevic transformed himself from a Communist to a Great Serbian chauvinist, and thanks to nationalism managed to legitimate his power democratically. Gamsakhurdia provides another eloquent example. Poet, political prisoner, and defender of human rights, when he came to power . . . we all know what happened. These examples—and we can find similar cases here—show the strange combination of postcommunism with a fascist face and anti-communism with a Bolshevik face. But the language of nineteenth-century uprisings and liberal democracy is inadequate to describe them.

Polityka: So do you have your own, private, criteria against which you evaluate people?

Michnik: It seems to me that a person should always try to be better than he is. Kurt Vonnegut said that the moral of his story *Mother Night* is to be found in the opening sentence: "We are what we pretend to be, so we must be careful what we pretend to be." It's probable that I too am pretending, ineffectively, to be someone else.

Polityka: Why?

Michnik: Because it seems to me that it's better to pretend to be an ordinary, decent person than a post-Communist Rambo the Avenger. Poland needs ordinary, decent, rational people, and even if I'm not very good at pretending to be such a person, I think there's some value in such a person.

Polityka: But young people accuse you of being too lenient toward former Communists and too hard on your former colleagues from KOR, on Antoni Macierewicz, for example.

Michnik: Because my former friends now have a more decisive role to play. Macierewicz? I remember the hours he spent, in this very apartment, arguing on the side of Che Guevara and in support of the terrorist acts of Black September. I remember when he collected money in support of MIR, the radical left organization that attacked Allende, and when he collected signatures on a petition protesting against Nixon's visit to Poland because of the bombing of Vietnam. Macierewicz has always been extremely radical, single-minded, and bold in his thinking. No matter which way he was headed, he always developed his ideas to their logical conclusion. He was a very courageous person. But whether these are the qualities one needs in a minister of internal affairs at this time, I'm not so sure. I must confess that I find it easy to criticize Antek, but I don't know what I would have done in his place. I suppose that if I'd considered lustration necessary, I would have carried it out even worse than he did. Thank God, I had a different opinion; from the very beginning I considered lustration an unhealthy and foolish idea. It's not difficult to disqualify a person ethically, but intellectually and morally it's an easy way out. One has to opt for a much more difficult solution. My ideal, an example I shall never be able to follow, is Thomas Mann's essay "Adolf Hitler—My Brother." Mann's greatness consists in the fact that he was able to say that Hitler's supporters were not some kind of other Germans; no, they were the same Germans among whom he grew up and whom he loved, these were the Germans who took a "wrong turn" and followed Hitler. The context is different, but I'm convinced that Antek

Macierewicz represents the other side of my life story; he's where I would be if I'd taken a wrong turn.

Polityka: Is this why you are more forgiving toward General Jaruzelski? The generosity of the victor toward the vanquished?

Michnik: Not many people have written such dreadful things about General Jaruzelski as I have. I used to regard him as a totally negative figure. I was his prisoner and political enemy. This was when he was ruling Poland via martial law. Later there was the Round Table and the great opening to democracy. And then I began to analyze all the circumstances and possible motives in a more dispassionate manner. Of course, Jaruzelski presents me with a great challenge. Am I, someone who was Jaruzelski's prisoner for so many years, capable of transcending the limits of my own grievances? Am I capable of avoiding the sins that I accused him and other Communists of having committed over the years? They rejected the principle of a Poland that belonged to all of us. Essentially, they wanted a Poland in which there was no place for anti-Communists like me. I used to write about the need for a common Poland. I used to say, We only have one Poland, and we have to learn to live in it together. So this is my moment of truth. It's not difficult to argue the need for tolerance in relation to oneself. That is no moral achievement whatsoever, but try to proclaim tolerance for your enemy.

Polityka: This all began at the Round Table?

Michnik: At the Round Table, I said to myself, The war's over. We have to learn to live like people who've survived a war. At that point, I had enormous doubts as to whether I should participate in the negotiations. The main argument of those who were opposed to the Round Table was that it was not the Communists who were legalizing Solidarity but Solidarity that was legalizing the Communists. But that was absolutely not the case—the Round Table marked the beginning of a peaceful, evolutionary road to democracy. Along this road, General Jaruzelski played a major role. As president, he was completely loyal to the process of democratization. I wouldn't like any of the Communists to be able to say, "Michnik isn't any different from the rest of us. When we had power, we trampled them underfoot; now that Michnik's friends are in power, they are trampling us underfoot." You're a swine, I'm a swine, and he's a swine. Universal swinery, as Andrzej Osęka once put it, nothing but swine. This doesn't appeal to me at all. My response to this is that it isn't true. There are certain principles that we have to defend, regardless of the circumstances. That's why I sometimes find myself swimming against the tide. Years ago, when Pope John Paul declared that we must show mercy before we demand justice, I took him seriously.

Polityka: Does this mean you find the trials of Zhivkov and Honecker distasteful?

Michnik: The law is the law, and if Zhivkov actually embezzled some money, as they allege, then he should be held accountable. Honecker really isn't one of my favorite characters, but if he's going to stand trial, Kohl should be standing right next to him. After all, Kohl rolled out the red carpet for Honecker, he treated him like a head of state, even though he knew they were shooting people who tried to cross the Berlin wall.

On the other hand, to accuse Jaruzelski of imposing martial law simply to enrich himself is to insult Poland and to ridicule the tremendous drama in which we were fated to participate. Of course, I'm opposed to amnesia, and people who were on the other side shouldn't now pretend that they spent the last forty years at Monte Cassino acting as couriers for General Anders. *Polityka* has published plenty of this kind of writing. We need to talk and write about the past, we need to discuss it calmly. We also need to bear in mind that if you work for ten years in a brothel, it's unseemly to pass yourself off as a virgin. If you were able to accept martial law, perhaps you should show a little more humility before criticizing our young democracy. Nevertheless, there is no justification whatsoever for efforts to introduce legal discrimination against people associated with the old regime in the name of decommunization or lustration.

We must never forget that we have only one Poland and that it's our common home that cannot be divided into separate cantons for Communists and decommunizers, or for the proponents and opponents of abortion. We have to find a language that will help us live together in our common Poland. That's how I see it. Apart from anything else, egoism plays a strong role in my case. While I was in prison, I wrote General Kiszczak an insolent letter that ended more or less as follows: When the inevitable moment comes, and the crowd throws itself on you, I hope that once more I'll have the courage to come to your defense.

Polityka: And now you have to be true to your word. But it's not just a question of our attitude toward current developments, is it? It's also a question of evaluating the past, both the past of People's Poland and the more distant past, of perceiving the historical processes that have been taking place for the last hundred, two hundred years.

Michnik: We are deeply rooted in history. Each successive political class is deluding itself when it comes on the scene declaring that we have to break with the past and that Poland can't be ruled by the ghosts of Piłsudski and Dmowski. This is just nonsense. Nor do I believe [Professor] Maria Janion's argument that we've reached the end of a kind of "code" in Polish culture derived from the interwar years. The problem is precisely that history exerts an exceptionally strong influence in Poland. This is how we experience our identity. I think Polish reality is incomprehensible unless we examine closely the last two hundred years. The more deeply I look, the more fascinated I am by seeing our problems and ourselves. All the questions about "the end of the world of the light cavalry," the world of Count Wielopolski, about the point of the national uprisings, including the Warsaw Uprising, are questions about our origins, our identity, and the beginnings of modern-day Poland.

Polityka: Does this perspective give one a clearer picture of People's Poland?

Michnik: The balance sheet on People's Poland is closed. Of course, one might try to evaluate it from a certain distance, free of the immediate political context. There was a particular reality, and the problem was how to organize Poland in those particular circumstances. There wasn't any other Poland. Naturally, I believe that the anti-Communist opposition, to which I belonged, was historically correct. But one must be fair to those who labored on behalf of Poland but who had different ideas. I find it incomprehensible that the people who are attacked most virulently and passionately are those who tried to construct a more civilized, sober, and benign form of communism. You had the Grunwald Patriotic Association, you had the Moczarites, and you had Mieczysław Rakowski, who was fiercely attacked by both of them. Again, people tell me I'm crazy to defend Rakowski, because he got what he deserves. Of course, he's got a lot to answer for, but he also deserves to be judged fairly. Rakowski has the right to be judged by his achievements at *Polityka* also. On this point, we ought to state clearly that without *Polityka*, the intellectual life of my generation would have been significantly poorer. I consider Rakowski a political opponent, but I think he is being judged unfairly. People remember only his faults and mistakes and forget his achievements. I want to be clearly understood on this.

Polityka: Do you believe in historical justice?

Michnik: One pays a terrible price for injustice. And the time will come for a just assessment of the past forty-five years, which weren't one long Auschwitz or Katyń but something far more complex. And then woe to those who are now lying to the nation. Their lies will rebound on them in the same way as history always metes out punishment for injustice and spits in the face of liars, whether Communists or anti-Communists.

Let me repeat: I am for open debate about the past and against any attempt to blur the picture. I am for the clear identification of good and evil. But the Communists didn't have a monopoly on wicked deeds, and the rest of us weren't all paragons of virtue. We have to examine our history in its entirety. There were various kinds of Communists and they made various contributions to Polish history. Something distinguished Kazimierz Mijal from Władysław Bieńkowski and Mieczysław Moczar from Stefan Żółkiewski. To ignore these distinctions is pure simple-mindedness.

We should not, in my opinion, blur the boundary between good and evil during that period, but can anyone claim to be entirely without guilt? Can anyone claim to be the bearer of Historical Good?

Polityka: A delicate issue: Our generation, the 1968 generation, has always had difficulties with the word *nation,* which was appropriated by the Moczarites. We always preferred *society.* These days, you use the word *nation* quite frequently.

Michnik: I remember a conversation I had with Jan Józef Lipski in September 1969, after I'd gotten out of prison. We were walking along the Vistula and I told him that I'd come to understand something I hadn't previously understood, that we were just like the nineteenth-century conspirators who plotted so ineffectually against Moscow's despotism. I had an almost physical sense of the continuity of national tradition and of our plight. The year 1968 really was a "Forefathers' Eve," a great theatrical presentation on the national stage. And ever since then I've been trying to find the right language in which to write about it. Let me recall, somewhat immodestly, the essay on Piłsudski, "Shadows of Our Forgotten Ancestors," that I wrote nearly twenty years ago.

I think it's clear that at *Gazeta Wyborcza* the word *nation* signifies a major idea but one that is far removed from the nationalism of the KPN or Christian National Union.

Polityka: What kind of book would you like to write today to provoke a deeper debate?

Michnik: I'm just finishing a book whose working title is *Life after Life under Communism*. It's not a collection of previously published pieces but a new work. An extract, "Conversation with an Integrist," was published in *Gazeta*. It's a book about populism.

In addition, I'd like to write a longer essay about Polish literature, and I'm thinking hard about how to do it. I want to reinterpret two books. First, Konwicki's *Bohiń Manor*, which I consider a masterpiece. It's a kind of Polish folk story, a reconstruction of the Polish ethos, with which we bade farewell to communism and entered the Third Republic. The second book is Milosz's *Szukanie ojczyzny* [In Search of the Fatherland], which deals with the essence of our national identity. I'm also working on an essay entitled "The Return of Cezary Baryka," which deals not with the march on Belvedere but with the origins of modern Poland.[1] In my opinion, they are to be found in the murder of Narutowicz and the scandal surrounding Żeromski's book, *Before the Spring*.

Polityka: What about the Church, to which you devote so much attention in *Gazeta*?

Michnik: The Church now finds itself at a dramatic turning point. I consider myself a friend of the Church. The Church fascinates me, and I find much in it that appeals to me. I'm not interested in the kind of jeering that Boy [-Żeleński] went in for. The issues are too important. But my generation, which learned to read the Gospels anew, should also read Boy anew without just repeating his words parrot fashion. After Auschwitz, this kind of prewar discourse is no longer possible. It's impossible to have Boy's lighthearted, frivolous, and limitless faith in the power of common sense. In the same way that Adorno asked himself how it was possible, after Auschwitz, to educate . . .

---

1. Cezary Baryka is the protagonist of Stefan Żeromski's 1924 book, *Przedwiośnie* (Before the Spring). The final scene of the novel—known as the march on Belvedere—depicted a revolutionary event. The book expressed Żeromski's worries about the state of the newly independent Poland. It was criticized violently in conservative circles and caused a prolonged controversy.—ED.

Polityka: . . . and write poetry . . .

Michnik: . . . we have to ask what Boy's system of values signifies after Auschwitz. These are two major questions. The first question concerns the nature of the state. There's no point in pretending that Polish Catholicism doesn't present the temptation to create a religious state. What is the nature of this temptation, and how can we defend ourselves against it? The second question concerns the source of the phenomenon that emerged during the nineteenth century under the slogan "A Pole is a Catholic." This notion wasn't imposed from above; it was deliberately adopted as a way of separating oneself from the Orthodox Russians and Protestant Prussians. This is where I would look for the roots of the phenomenon that we are still unable to deal with intellectually, the phenomenon called Father Maksymilian Kolbe. We must find the courage to ask: Who really was Maksymilian Kolbe? He was undoubtedly a saint.

Polityka: Because he gave his life for someone else?

Michnik: More than that; because he has been accepted in this role by the Church and by Polish society. But at the same time, he was also the founder of *Rycerz Niepokalanej* [Knight of the Virgin] and *Mały Dziennik* [Little Daily], publications that symbolize the ignorant and obscurantist side of Polish Catholicism, primitive publications promulgating religious intolerance and ethnic hatred. I can think of only one attempt to take the measure of this phenomenon and that's Jan Józef Szczepański's splendid essay about Father Kolbe. Szczepański gives us an extraordinarily bold and penetrating examination of this fascinating duality, this strange combination of heroism and sainthood, and parochialism, primitivism, and venomous hatred cloaked in the authority of the Catholic Church and the sign of the Cross. Outside of this, we are left with one-sided accounts that either stress the saintliness or dwell on the anti-Semitism and obscurantism. But in fact, these two things are somehow closely intertwined with each other. Perhaps this constitutes a hitherto untold secret of our Polish heritage, something we are reluctant to talk about because it evokes in us a sense of real pride together with unease. What is the source of this syndrome in which extraordinary heroism coexists alongside barbaric intolerance? Father Kolbe is admired by those who personify all that is best in Polish Catholicism. But he is also admired by those who express all that is most repugnant. Cardinal Wyszyński is another example of both saintliness and anachronism. Perhaps this is why there's no honest biography of the primate, and we're condemned to hagiography.

Polityka: Nobody wants to make fun of saintliness, but the anachronism fills one with fear. It constitutes an obstacle to the reforms that Poland needs; it hinders the "reformation" of the Polish Church.

Michnik: My friend Bronisław Geremek once said in an interview that the Church ought to support political and economic reform. I don't actually think this is necessary. The Church ought to find a place for itself as teacher, educator, and witness but not as instigator of political events. Another thing: I'm afraid that opposition to some of the crazy ideas espoused by some Catholic groups will lead not to reformation but to nihilism. No one who is outraged by the stupidities he hears in church is going to follow in the footsteps of Martin Luther and nail his ninety-five theses to the door of the monastery in Częstochowa; he's going to make for the nearest bar or disco. In other words, he's going to opt for intellectual befuddlement. In other words, he's not going to reform the Polish Church.

Jarosław Kaczyński is right: a government based on the Christian National Union is the best way to de-Christianize Poland. The fundamentalism of some of the clergy who spout the theology of the *endecja* contributes to this process. In terms of Christian values, nothing good can come of this. And this is something I fear. This is why I have no desire to see the Church compromised and marginalized. I want the Church to be strong but also a different, more evangelical Church than that of the Christian National Union.

Polityka: Whom do you blame for this situation, the idiots out there or also your friends?

Michnik: In recent years, the circles associated with *Tygodnik Powszechny, Znak,* and *Więź* have become a major force within Catholicism. They have done much to create a Catholicism in tune with the Second Vatican Council, one that is open to the outside world. That's why they now bear an enormous responsibility. I think an enormous responsibility rests with such people as Tadeusz Mazowiecki, who at one point was one of the leaders of that Catholic coalition which took note of the existence of Auschwitz and rejected the *endecja* tradition. In my opinion, this coalition—and it pains me to say this, because I admire Tadeusz highly and owe him a great deal—has relinquished too much of its identity, has compromised too much in the name of political responsibility for the state. I think our Catholicism needs people who, guided by the Christian notion of circumspection, are capable of openly taking issue with fundamentalist tendencies, which are also expressed by some of our bishops. It needs people who, like Erasmus of Rotterdam and unlike Luther, will stay in the Church to defend the truth of the Gospels against the truth of political convenience. One such person is Father Józef Tischner. I preferred Tadeusz Mazowiecki when he was writing his wonderful essay about anti-Semitism, about Bonhoeffer, and about the need for dialogue than when he immersed himself up to the neck in a politics that I don't fully understand. How long can one keep silent when faced with arrant nonsense? The time has come when—to use the words of St. Matthew's Gospel—one has to know how to say clearly on some issues, yes, on others, no. We should no longer behave as though silence is a virtue. In my opinion, Tadeusz too often remains silent when he ought to speak out on the most important issues within a church that finds itself in a strange relationship with repugnant emotions and traditions and that, because of this, is coming into conflict with ever-broader segments of society. One should speak out with humility, because we are dealing with the Church. One shouldn't refer to the bishops in the same language that one uses to refer to the leadership of the Christian National Union. It creates some tensions within my editorial group when I sometimes behave like a censor on this issue. But we can afford to talk about Jaruzelski, Kiszczak, and Communists in general with a certain level of culture, so it shouldn't be difficult to do so in the case of the bishops when we recall their enormous contribution to our history. In this case, we should show not only tolerance but also great respect. Even when, and perhaps especially when, we can't count on its being reciprocated. I find it difficult to speak critically about our bishops, but I realize it's necessary. Sometimes it's better to keep quiet about one's own grudges.

Cardinal Glemp has recently directed numerous criticisms at *Gazeta* and at me personally. I'm sometimes tempted to reply. Nevertheless, I remind myself that mercy must come before justice and I bite my tongue.

Polityka: You avoided giving a straight answer to the question we asked you at the beginning, about "Europeanization." Do you believe that, several years from now, we'll be living in an integrated Europe, with all the consequences thereof, including the kind of problems that the

Germans are currently facing, or do you think this unlikely, given the explosion of nationalism all around us?

Michnik: The institutional integration of Europe is possible, but various ethnic-separatist scenarios are also possible; Belgium and Spain might follow the example of Czechoslovakia. When I was in France, I spoke in favor of Maastricht [unification of Europe], but I know that critics of the treaty are justified in many of their arguments against it. Of course, I can imagine a situation in which Poland is faced with an influx of several million people from other countries, with different languages, cultures, and customs. We have to use our imagination and understand the hostile reaction this might evoke. In the end, politics is the art of foreseeing and implementing the possible. Minister Goryszewski . . .

Polityka: . . . says that he won't join a Europe dominated by Germany. And the only people who appreciated this statement were those in the West who don't want us there anyway.

Michnik: Minister Goryszewski is another story. He says many things that are incomprehensible, but his party, the Christian National Union, has so far shown itself to be a credible and responsible member of the governing coalition. In the long run, this party will have to choose between the logic of its own narrow, provincial doctrine and integration into Europe. I believe that our national interest will best be served if we become part of the world around us rather than some kind of godforsaken Slav enclave in the middle of Europe. But this will require some effort on our part.

Polityka: Let's end with the eternal question—the intelligentsia and the Polish cause. The ethos of the intelligentsia as the leader of society survived during People's Poland. In the final analysis, it was the intelligentsia—both the old and the new, postwar intelligentsia—who, together with the striking workers, buried communism.

Michnik: Communism was buried by Solidarity, whose uniqueness lay in the fact that it made intellectuals out of electricians and drivers— Frasyniuk and Bujak, for example.

Polityka: OK, so what possibilities will workers have for social mobility now that the Communists no longer recruit them into the universities like they did in the fifties and Solidarity no longer encourages self-education? The level of education is falling, and the same can be said of newspapers, television, even church sermons. Who is going to defend, not the ethos of the intelligentsia, but its level of thinking? Who will identify with it? Maybe it will leave the stage and give way to the arrivistes?

Michnik: What nonsense. People will create their own social mobility, once it appears worth the effort, once it yields moral and material satisfaction. There won't be any more artificial mechanisms for changing over elites. Who will identify with the ethos of the intelligentsia? I, Adam Michnik, am a Polish intellectual belonging to the tradition to be found in the writings of Żeromski, Strug, Brzozowski, Słonimski, Irzykowski, Kotarbiński, the Ossowskis, and Dąbrowska. These are great role models, and role models for me. I'm allowed to say this because I'm not talking only about myself. For example, the whole of *Gazeta Wyborcza* is made up of intelligentsia. We try to translate our solidaristic system of values into the language of today. That's what we want to do. It's so obvious to all of us that there's no need to spell it out at editorial meetings. We want to do something useful. We mustn't allow ourselves to become isolated but must find the things that unite us, bearing in mind the words of Słowacki: "I beseech you—let the living not abandon hope, let them hand on the torch before the nation; and when necessary, let them go to their deaths, one after the other, like stones hurled at the ramparts by God." Essentially, this is my credo; it defines who I am much more than any ideological, ethnic, or other factor.

Polityka: Does anyone outside Poland understand this?

Michnik: They do in Russia, and in Hungary and Serbia. My Serbian friend Nebojša Popov gave me a wonderful title for an article: "Can the Geese Save Rome?" It is precisely the duty, fate, or ethos of the Polish intellectual to save Rome—in other words, Poland—by his squawking. Of course, we need to think again about the nature of the Polish intelligentsia. It includes people as varied as Boy-Żeleński, Ludwik Koniński, and Jerzy Turowicz and Mieczysław F. Rakowski. It does not, however, include anyone who ever belonged to the ONR.

Polityka: Why not?

Michnik: For the same reason that it doesn't include any Bolsheviks—because they served a different set of values. An intellectual can get caught up in the ambiguities of historical processes; he may succumb to the totalitarian temptation, but he ought to know how to escape it.

In essence, the ethos of the Polish intellectual—whether secular or Catholic—is the ethos of someone who fights for freedom and is on the side of the weak. The ethos of the ONR or the Bolsheviks, in contrast, involves siding with power and hierarchy, with a movement that aims to subject everyone to its will. Nobody did Doctor Judym's thinking for him.[2] He was like a tree cleaved in two; he had the starry sky above him and moral law within him. A little of Kant, a little of Konwicki, and a little of Brzozowski and Turowicz. The Polish intellectual is a bit of a sniveler, but that's because he inhabits a world of values in which there's a place for tears. Shedding tears over the misery of the world has acquired fundamental significance in our culture, and may our tears not dry too quickly. We must follow our own path, otherwise we'll get lost. Let's not pretend that we're not descended from Żeromski.

Polityka: And not from Mickiewicz?

Michnik: Mickiewicz has nothing to with the state of the intelligentsia but with the state of the nation and its collective memory. The intelligentsia is descended from Żeromski, from all those terrible stories, from those "homeless people." Don't pretend that we're about to create America here, as my friend Ernest Skalski likes to think. It's impossible. We have to define our friends and our enemies here, because this is where they are.

Polityka: But isn't it time to transcend the horizons defined by our "intellectual masters," as another friend of yours, André Glucksmann, has written? Isn't it time to "murder our fathers"?

Michnik: If you're waiting for me to attack Leszek Kołakowski or Czeslaw Miłosz simply because you have some stupid Freudian dream of murdering your father, I can tell you that I have no such need. If I come to the conclusion that we need to transcend their horizons at some point, I shall try to do so.

There are some stone tablets that should not be smashed but simply translated into current language. Of course, I've crossed certain horizons because I've changed during the course of my life. And I'm glad that I crossed these horizons in the company of Leszek Kołakowski, Jacek Kuroń, and Jan Lityński. I have no desire to struggle

2. Doctor Judym is the protagonist of another novel by Stefan Żeromski, *Ludzie bez-domni* (Homeless People, 1899).—ED.

with my "intellectual masters." I have no desire to murder anyone. In this country, because everything is—as Norwid said—so rickety and fragile, someone is always murdering someone else. I place great value on continuity and long-term perspective—in relation to both the past and the future.

Polityka: Thank you for talking with us.

25

The Velvet Restoration

A Summing-Up

When I read in the Polish press about "the return of communism," I sometimes think it would be good to imagine an actual restoration of the Communist system. The banging on the door at dawn. The declaration of martial law, the dissolution of Parliament, the liquidation of political parties, the confiscation of newspapers, censorship, closed borders, thousands imprisoned, trials, and sentences. And over and over again on the radio a speech by the Leader on the need for "law, order, and discipline."

For a year now a coalition of post-Communist parties has governed in Poland. A similar coalition governs in Lithuania. And in Hungary a post-Communist party recently won the elections. Nowhere, however, did the Communist system return. What, then, do these "returns" mean?

In Poland, and other countries of the region, a revolution had taken place: the system of totalitarian dictatorships in the realm of politics, economics, and international order was overthrown. Fortunately, this was carried out—in Poland thanks to the Round Table agreements—without barricades and guillotines. It was—as Václav Havel so aptly put it—a velvet revolution.

Reprinted by permission from *East and Central Europe Program Bulletin,* New School for Social Research, October 1994. Translated by Elżbieta Matynia. Also published in *Grappling with Democracy: Deliberations on Post-Communist Societies (1990–1995),* edited by Elżbieta Matynia (Prague: SLON, 1996).

However, every revolution—even the velvet one—has its own logic. It releases expectations and hopes that it can never satisfy. Therefore it has to radicalize its own language, devour its own children, eliminate the moderates from its ranks, decree successive "accelerations," lustrations, purges. The revolution is forever unfinished. That is why it causes frustration and bitterness. Somebody must be held responsible for the fact that manna has not fallen from heaven. The revolution finds the guilty ones. First the people of the old regime, then their defenders, and finally its own leaders.

The revolutionary camp always has its own "moderates" and "rabid ones." The former want to defend freedom in the name of the rule of the constitution and of the state of law; the latter believe that defending freedom means annihilating the enemies of freedom—that is, the people of the old regime. This is their only way of showing their concern for the well-being of the wronged and humiliated who started the revolution. After all, the liberation from dictatorship brought freedom and joy only to a few. The majority, left in poverty and despair, did not enjoy the fruits of victory. According to this majority, the revolution was betrayed by the "moderates"—the majority has to liberate itself once again. This is why "acceleration" and "completion of the revolution" are necessities. For these to happen, it is necessary to stop playing "the state of law game." Clear and firm decisions are needed: with regard to the people of the old regime, revolutionary justice should be applied, since no other justice is relevant.

Bourbon was tried ostensibly for collusion with the enemy, but in fact it was because he was a king. The execution of Louis XVI was a sentence on the monarchy, "this imperishable crime," as Saint-Just defined it. In the name of this logic, Constitution was losing to Revolution.

"Measured against the immense sufferings of the immense majority of the people"—as Hannah Arendt characterizes Robespierre's thought— "the impartiality of justice and law, the application of the same rules to those who sleep in palaces and those who sleep under the bridges of Paris, was like a mockery."

Before, the goal was the constitutionally guaranteed freedom of citizens; now justice and the welfare of the people have become the goal. A goal so defined divides the revolutionary camp in an obvious way: the "moderates" and the "rabid ones" begin to perceive each other as enemies. This conflict tears apart and exhausts the revolution. Can anything still save it? Yes—a savior who, liquidating both camps, reaches for his armor and the language of the diktat.

But would the masses follow this leader? Or would they rather choose restoration? The same guillotine cut off the heads of Bourbon, Danton, and finally Robespierre. Revolution may give birth to terror. It can also avoid it, but then it has to give birth to restoration. Every revolution either culminates in dictatorship or brings about a restoration.

Poland's velvet revolution gave birth to the velvet restoration.

A restoration is never the return of the old regime and the old order. The restoration is a reaction to the revolution, a paroxysm of old-timers' comebacks, of former symbols, traditions, customs. Revolution feeds on the promise of a Big Change; restoration promises the return of the "good old days."

But the restoration—like the revolution—must bring disappointment. First there is joy. Humiliated by the revolution, the people of the old regime live a moment of relief and glory. Justice has been done. The self-proclaimed revolutionaries are handing over power. Loyal crowds joyfully greet the legitimate monarch and his retinue. The royalists strive to outdo one another in right-thinking declarations. The "ultras" get ready to fill the posts. However, it soon becomes apparent that among the senators praising the House of Stuart or of Bourbon, there are many who once voted to execute Charles I or Louis XVI. Therefore the "ultras" demand purges, restitution of property, punishment and humiliation for the people of the revolution.

The legitimate monarch, returning from exile to assume the throne, utters the memorable words, "Gentlemen, nothing has changed. We just have one Frenchman more." As a witness of the period observes, "The easygoing manner, the worldly tone, the friendly dignity, in such contrast to the domineering attitude and the proud and overbearing responses of Napoleon, made the biggest impression on those present. We felt transported into some new world. We were coming back to a fatherly rule."

Nevertheless, the very same witness—Talleyrand—noted that "soon denunciations began, feigned zeal, resentments, forced displays of devotion. . . . A crowd of firebrands and plotters of all shades were jammed into his palace. Each of them had reinstated the monarchy. Each demanded to be rewarded for his devotion and for his services. All posts needed new people. Originally the king himself was not a partisan of a settling of accounts: 'Gentlemen,' he would say to the 'ultras,' 'I urge and oblige you to find as few people guilty as possible.' " But this did not satisfy everyone. Soon there appeared criticism of the moderate approach. The "ultras" demanded more radical action and just punishment of the revolutionary malefactors. The restoration kept losing supporters, and the defenders of the lost revolution were winning them back. Because, just as the revolution failed to keep its promises earlier, the restoration did not keep them later: the peace and order of the good old days did not come back.

For a large number of those who voted for the SLD [Alliance of the Democratic Left] and the PSL [Polish Peasant party], this year of coalition rule has calmed things down. Fear from the craze for decommunization and lustration has ended, along with fear of the contempt and discrimination of those who called the PZPR [Polish United Workers party] "paid traitors" and "lackeys of Russia," and who compared it to the NSDAP [the German Nazi party] and the Volksdeutsche population that had supported it in the occupied countries. Now, prior membership in the PZPR has ceased to be something shameful. This has happened thanks to the hard work of the most "rabid" zealots in the Solidarity camp.

The fear of change that brought success to the SLD and the PSL resulted in a slowing down of privatization and the reform of local self-government, the reintroduction of centralization and state monopoly, the raising of protective tariffs, subsidies for enterprises going bankrupt, credits for weak farms. The decision of the parliamentary majority concerning the concordat with the Vatican and abortion dealt a blow to the prestige of the Catholic Church.

Nevertheless, for a decisive majority of the SLD and PSL electorate, the last year has brought disappointment. The good old days have not returned: the welfare state, an economy without unemployment, free vacation resorts for employees, free education and health services. The time of that peculiar egalitarianism did not return, when poor work was rewarded with a poor wage and even the very thought of personal wealth was eradicated as a harmful relic of capitalism.

The restoration—just like the revolution—has its moderate wing and its "rabid ones" or "ultras." The moderates want to change the logic of the democratic state of law and the market economy in such a way as to become its beneficiaries. They do not want, however, execution squads, massive purges, censorship, and closed borders, dictatorship, and the nationalization of enterprises. The "ultras," on the other hand, desire revenge and a turn back from reform. The "ultras," taking advantage of the rise of an anti-clerical climate, desire the humiliation of the Church. The "ultras" are dangerous—it is not difficult to see this.

Nevertheless, none of these observations justifies the thesis on recommunization and the return of the Polish People's Republic.

A theorist of the moderate restoration, Talleyrand characterized his point of view in "Memorial for a Monarch":

When religious feelings were strongly etched in people's hearts and strongly influenced their minds, people could believe that the might of a ruler was an emanation of divinity. . . . In times, however, when those feelings leave slight traces, when the religious bond, if not broken, is at least significantly loosened, one does not want to recognize this as a source of legitimacy.

Popular opinion today . . . says that governments exist exclusively for the people. From this opinion comes the unavoidable conclusion that legitimate power is the one which best guarantees peace and prosperity for the people. Therefore it turns out that the only legitimate power is the one which has already existed for many years. . . . But if by some misfortune the thought arises that abuses of this power are outweighing its benefits, the result is such that its legitimacy is perceived as a chimera. It may suffice—but it is also necessary—to constitute it in such a way that all the reasons for anxiety which it could provoke will be eliminated. To constitute it in such a way is equally in the interest of the ruler and his subjects; because today absolute power would be just as heavy a burden for the one who wields it as for those he rules.

Talleyrand was right, but he had to submit his resignation. Other people had won, those with more radical views. The French restoration was taking the path of revenge and repression. These people led France to a new revolution.

The mark of a restoration is its sterility. Sterility of government, lack of ideas, lack of courage, intellectual ossification, cynicism, and opportunism. Revolution had grandeur, hope, and danger. It was an epoch of liberation, risk, great dreams, and lowly passions. The restoration is the calm of a dead pond, a marketplace of petty intrigues, and the ugliness of the bribe.

François René, the viscount of Chateaubriand, was the enemy of the revolution and of Napoleon. He longed fervently for the restoration and did a great deal for it. At the same time, however, he called the people of the revolution "giants, in comparison with the small vermin who have hatched from us." He noted: "To fall from Bonaparte and the Imperium to what happened afterwards was to fall from being into nothingness, from the mountaintop into a chasm. . . . Generations that are crippled, without faith, dedicated to a nothingness which they love, are not able to grant immortality; they do not have the power to bring glory; if you put your ear to their lips, you will hear nothing; no sound comes from the heart of the dead." He had contempt for the epoch of the restoration and its people: how to "cite Louis XVIII after the Emperor"? Of the

Chamber of Peers he wrote: "For those assembled old men, dried out remnants of the old Monarchy, the Revolution, and the Empire, anything beyond platitudes looked like madness."

One does not have to like the Solidarity revolution anymore, and it is easy to criticize it. There is a great deal of criticism of Wałęsa and Mazowiecki, Bielecki and Suchocka, Gieremek and Kuroń. Balcerowicz and Lewandowski, Skubiszewski and Rokita, are not spared either. I have been collecting the whole repertoire of attacks on *Gazeta Wyborcza,* and I myself do not spare the Kaczyński brothers, Olszewski, or Macierewicz. Many of these criticisms are well founded. Nevertheless, it was all those people, amid errors, inconsistencies, ill-considered decisions, and demoralizing arguments, who carried out the historic task of the anti-Communist revolution in Poland.

With this revolution, the time of Solidarity and Wałęsa had passed. The great myth turned into a caricature. The movement toward freedom degenerated into noisy arrogance and greed. Soon after its victory it lost its instinct for self-preservation. This is why the post-Solidarity formations lost the last elections to Parliament. Let us emphasize this: it is not so much that the post-Communist parties won as that the post-Solidarity parties lost. They were unable to build an elementary preelectoral coalition—a necessity obvious to anyone who has read the electoral law—because it was blocked by pettiness and a lack of imagination. Thanks to that, the party that received 20 percent of the votes won a stunning victory.

Now—in the face of the crawling, though velvet, restoration—the parties of the anti-Communist opposition who lost ought to undertake a critical accounting. There is nothing, however, to suggest that such a process is taking place. Aside from a few exceptions, we still hear the speech of tired words and worn-out phrases—a song that no one wants to hear anymore.

The people of Communist Poland returned to power. How do they differ from the people of Solidarity?

The people of Solidarity were of all kinds: wise and stupid, courageous and cautious, modest and boastful. What they shared, however, was the sense that some time ago they had made the decision to choose a more difficult life path. The memory of that decision gave them a sense of dignity and pride, the ability to act in uncompromising and nonopportunistic ways. They usually lacked experience, which could lead either to amateurishness or to a freedom of the imagination. Yet politics was for them not only a game but also a choice entailing real risk—even though, later on, many of them were to become players of the sleaziest kind.

The people of Communist Poland also come in all kinds: wise and stupid, modest and boastful. But their whole experience was different, built on their being at the disposal of others, on obedience, on the capacity for conformist adaptation. The people of Solidarity had both the good and the bad features of revolutionaries, or of reformers revolutionizing their own times. The people of Communist Poland have all the features of routinized bureaucrats. The people of Solidarity frequently made decisions that were risky and faulty; the people of Communist Poland would like best of all to make no decisions except those regarding personnel. In accordance with the rule that "the cadres decide everything" (Lenin), the people of Communist Poland consistently awarded all posts according to internal party ranking. It is only a few steps from this to handing out perks and privileges.

The people of Solidarity pushed the Wheel of History forward; the people of Communist Poland have not turned the Wheel back, but they are stubbornly putting the brakes on it.

Poland today is like a casserole prepared from various ingredients, each of which contributes to the flavor of Polish democracy.

Democracy needs the conservative factor; it needs a strong voice from the world of hired labor; and it also needs a liberal-humanist strain. The conservative factor represents that which is organic, rooted in the collective memory, constant and resistant to fashion, guaranteeing continuity, and determining the limits of change in accordance with loyalty to customs. But how to be a conservative in a world of communism? What's to conserve, since the changes made by the totalitarian revolution over several decades are totally rejected?

For the conservative factor, the elementary frame of reference is the Catholic Church. I regard the question of the place of the Catholic Church in a democratic state as one of the most dramatic.

Will the Church become the conscience of the Polish state or a powerful pressure group on the political stage? The more the episcopate and the clergy try to intervene in the political game, the more they lose the capacity to exert political pressure and influence public opinion; the more they use the rhetoric of war and the besieged fortress, the more they bypass the sensibilities of society.

The conservative element, invoking the teachings of the Church, national rhetoric, the traditional family, and stern morals, is entangled in a peculiar paradox. Even though it voices conservative values, it uses the language of revolution; even though it proclaims a religion of mercy, it demands revenge and discrimination; even though it states on its banners a radical anti-communism, it was developed in the conflict with the liberal-humanist current of the anti-totalitarian opposition. After all, for the people of the Christian National Union [ZChN] or the people of the Center Alliance [PC], the pink devil of the left—the "Catholeft"—was hidden not in the Polish United Workers party but among the supporters of Mazowiecki's candidacy for president. The Polish right is closer to the thought and method of Le Pen than of de Gaulle; to the German republicans than to Adenauer. It is more populist than conservative, more vindictive than Christian.

The conservative wing of the Polish political scene faces a dilemma today; either it will take the path of aggressive anti-Communist and clerical rhetoric, to the point of a political instrumentalization of the Church, or it will choose the language of peace, compromise, responsibility for the state, and a civilized defense of traditional values. Unfortunately, everything today indicates that temperate conservative thought, in the manner of Aleksander Hall, is losing in the circles of the so-called right.

Lech Wałęsa and Waldemar Pawlak. These two people are the symbols of two epochs: the revolution and the restoration. Wałęsa will remain forever a symbol of a great Poland, creative and heroic but also unleavened, primitive, and cocky. Pawlak is today a symbol of a gray and ordinary Poland that does not want heroism but normality.

The Solidarity governments were under the pressure of their own history: they were handed an invoice by all those who had attached to them their hope for a miracle. And of those there were many. This legion—internally differentiated, deafened and frightened by the dynamics of change—saw itself as the victor over communism but soon began to perceive itself as the victim of anti-Communist reform. Bitterness and helplessness were being transformed into the aggressiveness of people who have been cheated. That is why the Solidarity governments were stuck in a certain schizophrenia, whether to give up to their former colleagues from the movement or to take care of the economic interests of the state. Pawlak's government is not perceived that way anymore. Along with a slowing down of the reforms, it is bringing about a calming down and an end to the schizophrenia.

Whence comes the political strength and popularity of Waldemar Pawlak, about whom one can say many critical things except one: certainly he is neither a heroic man nor one of that new breed of political loonies.

Poles have had enough of that peculiar syndrome: honest heroism associated with the megalomania of the power mad. They have had enough of appreciating someone else's—real or imagined—deeds and sacrifices; they have had enough of listening to the boastfulness of yesterday's—real or imagined—conspirators from the anti-Communist underground. They sense intuitively that deeds and sacrifices become devalued, are converted into cash and high positions in the state administration. They want to live normally, and they have a right to do so. They want calm. They want the right to respect their own biographies—no matter whether they were the biographies of the Polish People's Republic and the Polish United Workers party or those of the anti-Communists and the opposition.

Those who do not understand this understand little about today's Poland.

I do not like restoration. I do not like its ethics or aesthetics, its shallowness or boorishness. Nevertheless, one cannot simply reject this velvet restoration. One has to domesticate it. One has to negotiate with it as with an adversary and/or partner. One has to permeate it with the values of the velvet democratic revolution. Even though it is bad, the logic of the restoration is better, after all, than the logic of a Jacobin-Bolshevik purge, revenge, or guillotine. A consistent restoration is gray with boredom; a consistent revolution is red with blood.

Restorations, too, are sometimes bloody, but their shape depends on the strategy of their opponents. If the people of the revolution reach for violence and announce revenge, restorations will use the same weapons. This is why one has to look carefully at the hands of the restoration and not turn one's back on it. Brauzauskas, Horn, and Pawlak are better, after all, than anti-Communists with a Bolshevik face.

One must not forget that although restorations do not bring back the old order, they can cause gangrene in a democracy. After all, neither a return to communism nor a return to Solidarity is possible. We are entering a new epoch, a world of new conflicts and new divisions. Wałęsa and Pawlak are signs of a nostalgia for the past, whether for the Polish People's Republic or for Solidarity. Who today is a sign of the future?

Somewhat timidly, I think of certain distinguished politicians of the anti-Communist opposition, people of the Church, and people of the post-Communist formation, who were once divided by everything and are still divided by many things today. But they nevertheless share a certain perspective on reality: they all look to the future. In the face of the ominous temptations of the contemporary world, in the face of class, ethnic, and religious wars and hatreds, these people are proposing a conversation about an ordinary Poland in an ordinary Europe.

This project is free of the utopianism that has usually accompanied great turning points. Yet this very project has been the utopian dream of several generations of Poles.

Gray Is Beautiful

A Letter to Ira Katznelson

I

People from Central Europe like to tell jokes. For years, jokes offered them asylum. In the world of jokes, they not only felt free and sovereign, within captivity and Soviet domination, but they also laughed.

So, two people, with the experience that comes with age, were playing tennis. The tennis ball ended up in the bushes. Looking for the ball, one of the players saw a frog. The frog spoke to him with a human voice: "I'm a beautiful princess, turned into a frog by a mischievous wizard. If you kiss me, I will become a princess once again. I will marry you, you will be a prince, and we will live happily ever after." The player put the frog into his pocket, found the ball, and continued the game. After a while, the frog again spoke to him, this time from his pocket: "Sir, did you forget about me? I am this beautiful princess, turned into a frog. If you kiss me, I will become a princess again. We will get married and live happily ever after!" And then she heard his answer: "Dear lady frog, I

Written in November 1996 in response to Ira Katznelson's *Liberalism's Crooked Circle: Letters to Adam Michnik* (Princeton, N.J.: Princeton University Press, 1996). This essay was translated by Elżbieta Matynia.

will be completely honest with you. I have reached the age at which I would rather have a talking frog than a new wife."

This frog is Central Europe, knocking at the gates of NATO and the European Union. NATO and the European Union have not yet made up their minds to kiss. They don't yet know whether they prefer to have a talking frog or a new wife.

II

Let us skip the controversies about defining the borders of Central Europe. Let's remind ourselves, however, of the statement by the Hungarian writer György Konrád: "It is we, who live in Central Europe, who began the two great World Wars." Put differently, this multi-national mosaic, conquered by German, Austro-Hungarian, Russian, and Ottoman empires, was and still is a source of conflict and destabilization. Today, seven years after the collapse of the Berlin wall, the nations of Central Europe are facing new opportunities and new challenges. How will things turn out for them?

More than ten years ago, through the works of its artists, philosophers, and writers, Central Europe came to be thought of as a realm of spiritual freedom, diversity, and tolerance. Milan Kundera was creating this myth against the fact of Soviet domination: in the place of the Anglo-Saxon formula "the countries of the Soviet bloc," an image appeared of Central Europe as a home of equal nations with abundant, colorful culture, nurtured by a diversity of languages, religions, traditions, and personalities.

It was not an absurd idea, and it was not a false image. Kundera as well as Havel, Konrád, and others were fully justified in rereading and presenting to the world the cultural heritage of this region of borderlands—where nations, religions, and cultures rub up against one another. They were fully justified in presenting it as the realization of a multicultural ideal of society—a miniature Europe of Nations—founded on the principle of maximum diversity in minimum space. These writers also had a wise idea concerning spiritual-political strategy: these nations, strikingly weak and powerless in confronting the imperial appetites of their neighbors, are transforming this powerlessness into power. Here we have a land of small nations, conquered, subjected, and enslaved for generations, transforming itself into the fertile soil that gave birth to

Robert Musil and Franz Kafka, Thomas Masaryk and Karel Čapek, Mickiewicz and Conrad, Singer and Einstein, Krleža and Tatarka, Miłosz and Seifert, Canetti and Levinas, Ionesco and Lukács.

The trump card of these small nations was their very nonimperial character, which made them natural allies of freedom and tolerance. Decades and centuries of existence in an environment of oppression and repression produced a specific culture, characterized by honor and self-irony, the stubbornness to stand by values, and the courage to believe in romantic ideals. Here, national and civic consciousness developed as a result of human bonds—and not by the order of state institutions; here, it was easier to devise the idea of civil society, precisely because the sovereign national state remained largely in the realm of dreams. The great cultural diversity of this region was to be—and frequently was—the best weapon of self-defense against the claims of ethnic or ideological powers.

"The Eastern European," wrote Barbara Toruńczyk in 1987, "already has his own kingdom. It emerges in the place where he lives. It is a realm of the spirit, but firmly rooted in reality. Today the East European of the post-Yalta generation can do without a cult of the West. . . . He gives new names to Europe and does it from right here at home."

What remains of this vision seven years after the fall of communism?

III

Communism was like a freezer. Within it a diverse world of tensions and values, emotions and conflicts, was covered with a thick layer of ice. The defrosting process was a gradual one—so first we saw beautiful flowers and only later, the rot. First came the grandiloquence of the peaceful fall of the Berlin wall and of the velvet revolution in Czechoslovakia. Later, a wave of xenophobic rage that took over Germany in 1992–93 and the breakup of Czechoslovakia. First was the memorable "Autumn of the Nations" in 1989. Freedom returned to Central Europe, and Central Europe returned to history. It returned as a messenger not only of freedom and tolerance but also of hatred and intolerance, both ethnic and religious. Conflicts—difficult to understand for people who perceive this territory simply as the Soviet bloc—came to life once more. But these conflicts were understood all too well by the inhabitants of those lands. They were understood because this world of many nations and cultures had experienced the deep ambiguity of the right of nations to sovereign existence: the right of one nation usually endangered the right of another nation, and this would bring about ethnic cleansing. Grillparzer, a great Austrian writer of the nineteenth century, warned prophetically against the road that leads "from humanism, through nationality, to bestiality."

IV

Dear Ira,

I suppose, for the American public, these meanderings of Central European democratic thought may appear a bit exotic. This thought was put to a double test: the test of captivity and the test of freedom. Hence certainly some statements will appear unclear; others, perfectly banal. However, it seems to me that this thought was born out of a common inspiration: a passionate dream, about freedom and democratic order.

Democracy is not identical to freedom. Democracy is freedom written into the rule of law. Freedom in itself, without the limits imposed on it by law and tradition, is a road to anarchy and chaos—where the right of the strongest rules. For my generation the road to freedom began in 1968. It was in that year that tens of thousands of students filled the streets to demonstrate their protest against the establishment. Was there any common denominator in the rebellions of students in Berkeley, Paris, and West Berlin and those on the streets of Warsaw and Prague? At first glance these were completely different phenomena. The students of Berkeley and Paris rejected the order of bourgeois democracy. The students of Prague and Warsaw were fighting for the freedom that bourgeois democracy guaranteed. Moreover, the students of Berkeley and Paris were fascinated by the Communist project, and by the revolutionary rhetoric of Mao Zedong—of which the students of Warsaw and Prague had had enough.

Nevertheless, I think there were also some common threads: the anti-authoritarian spirit, a sense of emancipation, and the conviction that "to be a realist means to demand the impossible." And finally the need for rebellion, rooted in the conviction that "as long as the world is as it is, it is not worth it to die quietly in your own bed." "The world as it is" meant an unjust world.

So there we are! At the root of the rebellion of 1968 was a need for justice: a need to have access to freedom and to bread, to truth and to power. There was something wonderfully uplifting in this rebellion, which transformed not just the collective consciousness of one generation. But there was also something frightening in it: the vandalized universities, destroyed libraries, barbarian slogans that substituted for intellectual reflection; and finally, violence, terrorism, and political killings. All of this also belongs to the heritage of 1968.

At that time we defined ourselves as socialists and people of the left. Why today does this formula cause in me an internal protest? Why do I not want to subscribe to any of the great ideologies? Here, I believe, lies the source of many arguments with my American friends. But possibly, this is more often an argument about language than about ideas. I once asked Jürgen Habermas, "What do we have left of the idealistic faith in the freedom-oriented socialism of the sixties?" His answer was, "Radical democracy." Since this formula is close to me, I will try to decipher it in my own way.

V

The system of parliamentary democracy and market economy has had fierce adversaries since its inception. Let's give them the symbolic names "conservative" and "socialist." For the conservative, the democratic order was a negation of tradition—the defeat of the Christian spirit by a rapacious nihilism; the total victory of relativism over the world of tested and absolute values. For the socialist, it was a system that generated, disguised, and perpetuated inequality and injustice. The conservative saw in man a wild being, which cannot be domesticated by calls to reason. Only strong institutions can achieve this. The socialist, by contrast, saw in man a good being, forced by inhuman social conditions into animal behavior. Both conservative and socialist rejected the order of a freedom based on the free play of political and economic forces, on the specific domination of property and money.

The conservative held that this order liberates in man an animal rapaciousness, whereas the socialist was of the opinion that this order virtually requires an animal aggression. This is how the two great utopias were established: one retrospective and the other prospective, a utopia of conservative, hierarchical harmony and a utopia of egalitarian, socialist harmony. One can debate the relations of both these utopias with the two totalitarianisms of the twentieth century. One can argue whether bolshevism was preying on the socialist idea, or whether the socialist idea provided bolshevism with its intellectual and political arguments. One can also try to explore whether fascism used the anti-liberal arguments of conservatives and the conservative dream of returning to a world of preindustrial values, or whether the conservatives saw in fascism a way to defend themselves against demoliberal destruction. But there is no doubt that such connections existed, even though we can find conservatives among the anti-fascist opposition, and we can find socialists among the most consistent adversaries of bolshevism. The crown for both anti-liberal utopias became the totalitarian systems. I lived in one of them for forty years; but I learned to distrust both.

VI

Why did we rebel against communism? Why did we prefer to become a small repressed minority, rather than to join the majority that lived and made careers in the world of totalitarian dictatorship?

Well, we rejected communism for several different reasons: it was a lie, and we were searching for truth; communism meant conformity, and we desired authenticity; communism was enslavement, fear, and censorship, and we desired freedom; it was an ongoing attack on tradition and national identity that we held to be ours; it was social inequality and injustice, and we believed in equality and justice; communism was a grotesquely deficient economy, and we sought rationality, efficiency, and affluence; communism meant the suppression of religion, and we held freedom of conscience to be a fundamental human right. So we rejected communism for reasons equally dear to a conservative, a socialist, and a liberal. In this way, a peculiar coalition of ideas emerged, which Leszek Kolakowski noted in his well-known essay "How to Be a Conservative-Liberal Socialist?" This coalition collapsed along with communism. But before it collapsed, the coalition had marked public debate with a specific tone of moral absolutism.

The moral absolutism of the anti-Communist opposition required us to believe that communism is inherently evil, the evil empire, the devil of our times, and that resistance to communism and Communists is something naturally good, noble, and beautiful. The democratic opposition demonized Communists and made itself angelic. I know what I am writing about because this moral absolutism was to a certain degree also my experience. I don't regret this experience, nor do I think I need to be ashamed of it. Standing up to the world of totalitarian dictatorship was to risk, or even to sacrifice, not only one's own safety but also that of one's friends and family. One had to believe that "human life is a serious game," as a Church historian of the Communist period wrote. Each day one had to make a choice that could have costly consequences. Those decisions were not the result of academic debates but were moral acts frequently paid for with imprisonment, or ruined careers. For active dissidents, this situation created a climate favorable to harsh and demanding valuations. One professed humanistic values but lived within heroic values, with their fundamental principle of loyalty to one's own identity and loyalty to one's friends from the democratic opposition; loyalty to values that were betrayed and mocked; loyalty to the nation, to the Church, and to tradition. "The weak side," wrote Bogdan Cywiński, "was always under siege." The most outstanding witnesses of resistance in those years—Solzhenitsyn, Havel, Herbert—defended absolute values. Herbert wrote, "Let your sister Scorn not leave you for the informers executioners cowards—they will win."[1]

And in the end it was we who won. But woe to those moral absolutists who emerge victorious in political struggles—even if only for a while.

VII

Moral absolutism is a great strength for individuals and groups struggling against dictatorship; but it is a weakness for individuals and groups active in a world in which democratic procedures are being built on the rubble of totalitarian dictatorships. There is no more room there either for the utopias of a just, harmonious, and perfect world or for moral absolutism. Both of these come down to anachronism or hypocrisy; both of these threaten the democratic order. Because a democratic world is a chronically imperfect one. It's a world of freedom (sinful, corrupt, and fragile) that came after the collapse of the world of totalitarian necessity (also, luckily, imperfect).

This world not only forced the collapse of the coalition of antitotalitarian ideas but also revealed their contradictory character. Egali-

1. Zbigniew Herbert, "The Envoy of Mr. Cogito," in *Mr. Cogito* (Hopewell, N.J.: Ecco Press, 1993), 61. Translated from Polish by John Carpenter and Bogdana Carpenter.

tarianism found itself in conflict with the principles of liberal economy; conservatism challenged the spirit of liberal tolerance. Dilemmas appeared which the socialist, the conservative, and the liberal resolved in different ways. Let's mention some of them: the ways of dealing with the Communist past, the shape of the market, the fundamental principles of the state, the place of the Church and religious values in the new reality.

For the socialist, the central issue will be to give a human face to a rapacious market economy; to defend the poorest sectors in society, the secular character of the state, and tolerance toward people of different faiths and nationalities.

The conservative would bring back the continuity of national symbols; he would fight for a Christian reshaping of the constitution and institutions; he would warn against the dangers coming from liberalism and relativism; he would demand harsh treatment for people of the old regime.

The liberal will say, the economy first: economic growth, clear rules of the market, stable system of taxation, privatization, exchangeable currency. He would be a careful defender of the idea of a tolerant state—with regard to the Church, to national minorities, to neighboring countries, and to the past. The point is that each of them will be formulating his ideas in a new context, the context of a new, populist, and still unnamed ideology. There is a bit of fascism in it, and a bit of communism; a bit of egalitarianism, and a bit of clericalism. These slogans will be accompanied by a radical criticism of the ideology of Enlightenment and by the harsh language of moral absolutism. At the same time, a nostalgia will appear, surprising for all—for the socialist, the liberal, and the conservative. A nostalgia for the security of the "good old Communist days," when, as they said, "the state pretended to pay the people, and the people pretended to work."

One must know this context to understand the dilemmas of the new post-Communist democracies. Dealing with the Communist past has divided the participants of the debate into spokesmen for justice and spokesmen for reconciliation. The first demanded the methodical punishment of the guilty parties. The second proposed a process of national reconciliation in the name of future challenges. Both those attitudes at times took on a grotesque form: the first went so far as to demand discrimination against the members of the Communist apparatus; the second behaved as if they had forgotten that the dictatorship ever existed. The formula for which I was a spokesman—"Amnesty, yes; amnesia, no"—turned out to be too difficult for the people of the democratic opposition.

The dispute over the shape of the market economy took on the form of a social conflict, in which the arguments of the socialist and of the conservative came together in a criticism of the policies of liberal transformation. Unemployment, social contrasts, the frustration of employees, all of that resulted in a slowing of the pace of reform. The dispute over the shape of the state—should it be national or civil?—turned out to be fundamental, especially in multinational countries, which had just regained independence after their long enslavement.

Conservative partisans of national principle emphasized the need to reconstruct the ethnic fabric destroyed through the years of official denationalization; the partisans of the civil principle were defending the fundamental tenets of democracy against an invasion of intolerant chauvinism. And finally, the Church. After years of repression, the Church reasserted its claim to a place in the public debate. In communities where national identity was frequently accompanied by a religious identity, there appears a natural temptation to endow those new states with a religious identity. The Church called for a constitution and criminal code that would be in accordance with the moral norms of religion. The debate over the penalization of abortion was a classic illustration of the argument about the axiological foundation of the state. Does the admissibility of abortion imply approval of the murder of unborn children? Does the criminalization of abortion constitute an attack on the fundamental right of a woman to decide about her own maternity? Each of those arguments was accompanied by extreme emotional tensions: there was a constant appeal to moral arguments; the language of war propaganda was used. Two opposing worlds of values confronted one another: the pragmatic, often saturated with corruption and with the cynicism of people of the old regime, versus the chronic patriotism of people of the world of conservative values, which in the recent past had resisted communism. The former heroism of the world resistant to repression showed its second face: intolerant, fanatical, and resistant to new, modernizing ideas. This is a natural turn of events in the world of post-Communist democracies.

VIII

None of these disputes is fatal for democracy, which after all is a permanent debate. Fatal, indeed, would be such an intensification of conflicts in which all sides, while absolutizing their positions, become incapable of compromise. Then it will already be easy to undermine the procedures of the democratic state. Because radical movements— whether under black or red banners—gladly use the procedures and institutions of democracy to obliterate it. In the meantime, democracy is neither black nor red. Democracy is gray, it is established only with difficulty, and its quality and flavor can be recognized best when it loses under the pressure of advancing red or black radical ideas. Democracy is not infallible, because in its debates all are equal. This is why it lends itself to manipulation, and may be helpless against corruption. This is why, frequently, it chooses banality over excellence, shrewdness over nobility, empty promise over true competence. Democracy is a continuous articulation of particular interests, a diligent search for compromise among them, a marketplace of passions, emotions, hatreds, and hopes; it is eternal imperfection, a mixture of sinfulness, saintliness, and monkey business. This is why the seekers of a moral state and of a perfectly just society do not like democracy. Yet only democracy—having the capacity to question itself—also has the capacity to correct its own mistakes. Dictatorships, whether red or black, destroy the human capacity for creation; they kill the taste for human life, and eventually, life itself. Only gray democracy, with its human rights and institutions of civil society, can replace weapons with arguments. Parliamentarianism became an alternative to civil wars even though a conservative would argue with a liberal and with a social democrat whether that was the result of common sense or the wisdom that comes from misfortune.

IX

The subject of democracy is people, not ideas. And this is why, in the framework of democratic institutions, citizens can meet and collaborate independently of their faith, nationality, or ideology. Today the classic ideological positions, like liberalism, conservatism, or socialism, do not dominate public debate about taxes, health reform, or insurance. Yet in each of those debates, there is a need for the presence of a socialist care for the poorest, a conservative defense of tradition, and a liberal reflection on efficiency and growth. Each of those values is needed in democratic politics. It is these that give color and diversity to our life; it is these that equip us with the capacity to choose; it is thanks to their mutual contradictions that we can afford inconsistency, experimentation, changes of opinion, and changes of government. In opposition to so-called corrupt demoliberalism, the fanaticism of ideological inquisitors offers again and again new projects for a "promised land." Fundamentalists of different varieties condemn the moral relativism of democracy, as though it were the state that should be the guardian of moral virtue. We, however, the defenders of gray democracy, do not grant the state this right. We want human virtues to be guarded by the human conscience. That is why we say, gray is beautiful.

And all of this has been told to you by a frog from Central Europe.

Guide to Events and People

Anders, General Władysław (1892–1970)   Commanding officer of the army formed in Russia by Polish prisoners released as a result of the Soviet-Polish pact of 1941. After the war, commander of the Polish armed forces in exile.

Andrzejewski, Jerzy (1909–83)   Eminent writer and friend of Czesław Miłosz during World War II.

Bereza   Concentration camp for political prisoners set up by the Polish government in 1934.

Black Hundreds   Monarchist paramilitary units in czarist Russia at the beginning of this century. Renowned for attacks on workers and Jews.

Boy-Żeleński, Tadeusz (1874–1941)   Writer, satirical poet, prolific translator of French literature. "Boy" was an ironic commentator on the pomposity and clericalism of Polish political life. Executed by the Nazis.

Brześć   In September 1930, at Józef Piłsudski's orders, several leaders of the Center-Left Coalition were detained in military prison in the Brześć fortress.

Brzozowski, Stanisław (1878–1911)   Influential philosopher and writer, accused of collaborating with czarist police.

Bujak, Zbigniew (Zbyszek) (b. 1954)   Legendary Solidarity leader from the Warsaw region, who managed to stay underground for three and a half years after the imposition of martial law on December 13, 1981.

Bujnicki, Teodor (1907–44)   Poet from the Żagary group in Vilnius. Executed by a Polish underground organization for his support of Soviet authorities.

Bydgoszcz Events   Political crisis provoked by a police attack, on March 19, 1981, against Solidarity activists holding a meeting in the city of Bydgoszcz.

Dąbrowska, Maria (1889–1965)   Writer, author of several novels and collections of short stories. Posthumous publication of fragments of her diary was an intellectual event.

December 13   On December 13, 1981, martial law was imposed by the government of General Wojciech Jaruzelski.

Dembiński, Henryk (1908 – 41)   Left-wing political writer and activist. Member of the Communist youth organization. Executed by the Nazis.

Dmowski, Roman (1864 – 1939)   Founder and ideologue of the National Democratic party (SN-*endecja*), the main current of the Polish right.

Endecja See *Dmowski, Roman.*

Frasyniuk, Władysław (b. 1954)   Solidarity leader from Wrocław.

Gałczyński, Konstanty Ildefons (1905 – 53)   Popular poet.

Geremek, Bronisław (b. 1932)   Historian of medieval France and politician. One of the main protagonists of the Round Table negotiations and, at that time, a close adviser of Lech Wałęsa's.

Gierek, Edward (b. 1913)   First secretary of the Polish Communist party, 1970 – 80.

Gombrowicz, Witold (1904 – 69)   An irreverent and revered writer, whose work mocks the inauthenticity and rituals of public life. In exile from 1939 on, he published in *Kultura.* He is the author of, among others, *Ferdydurke, Transatlantic,* and *Diary.*

Gomułka, Władysław (1905 – 82)   One of the leaders of the Polish Communist movement. First secretary of the Polish Communist party, 1943 – 48 and 1956 – 70.

Grunwald Patriotic Association   An "independent" group created in the 1960s and affiliated with the nationalistic and anti-Semitic wing of the party.

Herbert, Zbigniew (b. 1924)   Eminent poet, author of the volume of poetry *Mister Cogito* and of the volume of essays *A Barbarian in the Garden.*

Home Army (AK)   Underground Polish military forces of the Second World War.

Katyń   Name of a forest in which much of the systematic killing by the Soviets of Polish officers, prisoners of war, took place in 1940.

Kisielewski, Stefan (1911 – 91)   Witty, irreverent, and provocative writer, essayist, novelist, and composer. Collaborated with *Tygodnik Powszechny* and *Kultura.*

Kołakowski, Leszek (b. 1927)   Philosopher, historian, and writer, the most influential teacher of his generation. In exile since 1968 in Great Britain and the United States. Author of, among others, *Main Currents of Marxism.*

Kolbe, Saint Maksymilian (1894 – 1943)   Franciscan monk who volunteered to enter the starvation bunker at Auschwitz to save the life of another prisoner. Before World War II he edited anti-Semitic Church publications.

Konwicki, Tadeusz (b. 1926)   Novelist and filmmaker, originally from Vilnius. Author of, among other books, *A Minor Apocalypse* and *The Polish Complex.*

KOR   See *Workers' Defense Committee.*

Kultura Founded in 1947 and subsequently based in Paris, the foremost émigré political and literary monthly. Its editor-in-chief is Jerzy Giedroyć, whose Institut Littéraire also publishes a historical quarterly as well as fiction, poetry, and political literature.

Kuroń, Jacek (b. 1934) Dissident and politician who spent nine years in Communist prisons. Author (with Karol Modzelewski) of the *Open Letter to the Workers' Party.* Founder of Workers' Defense Committee (KOR). Later minister of labor in the first two post-Communist governments.

Letter of the 59 An open letter signed by intellectuals, artists, and writers protesting amendments to the Polish constitution (1976). The amendments constitutionalized the one-party system of government and Poland's limited sovereignty.

Lipski, Jan Józef (1926–91) Essayist, historian of Polish literature, and political activist. Member of Workers' Defense Committee (KOR).

Mazowiecki, Tadeusz (b. 1927) Catholic writer and politician, founder of the Catholic periodical *Więź,* adviser to Solidarity, later prime minister of the first post-Communist government. Founder of Democratic Union party.

Miłosz, Czesław (b. 1911) Poet, novelist, and essayist; Nobel Prize laureate, 1980. While in exile in France and later in the United States, he wrote, among other books, *The History of Polish Literature* and *The Captive Mind* as well as several volumes of poetry.

Moczar, Mieczysław (1913–86) Representative of the nationalistic wing within the Communist party, minister of security in the 1960s. Inspired anti-intelligentsia and anti-Semitic purges of 1968.

Modzelewski, Karol (b. 1937) Historian of the Middle Ages, political activist, author (with Jacek Kuroń) of the Open Letter to the Workers' Party. In 1980, spokesman for Solidarity. Spent several years in prison.

ONR (National Radical Camp) Extreme nationalistic, anti-Communist, and anti-Semitic organization founded in 1934.

Open Letter to the Workers' Party Manifesto written by Jacek Kuroń and Karol Modzelewski in 1965.

Piłsudski, Józef (1867–1935) Socialist in his youth, Piłsudski was the restorer of Polish independence in 1918 and the dominant figure of Polish politics in the interwar period.

Polityka A weekly created in 1956. It served the party's liberal wing.

Popiełuszko, Reverend Jerzy (1947–84) Catholic priest who actively supported the then-delegalized Solidarity. Kidnapped and murdered by police in 1984.

Po Prostu Periodical founded by liberal activists of the party in 1956. Its closing a year later caused riots and protests and signified the retreat of the party leadership from promises of liberalization.

Putrament, Jerzy (1910–86) Writer from the Żagary group. Political officer in the Polish division of the Soviet army during World War II.

Radom and Ursus   In 1976, after a price hike, workers went on strike in the city of Radom and in the Ursus factory near Warsaw. The strikes were subdued by the police and followed by massive repression. Michnik refers to these events as well as to a meeting of Solidarity's Presidium on December 3, 1981. Parts of the edited tape of that meeting were played on the radio and used as a justification for the military coup of that year.

Rakowski, Mieczysław F. (b. 1926)   Founder and first editor-in-chief of the weekly *Polityka*. He was one of the main architects of the December 13, 1981, military coup against Solidarity.

Round Table Agreements   The 1989 negotiations between representatives of the opposition and representatives of the authorities, which led to the gradual transfer of state power from the Communist party to Solidarity.

Sanacja   Political group governing Poland after the 1926 May Coup d'État by Józef Piłsudzki.

Second Republic   Poland between the two world wars.

Sienkiewicz, Henryk (1846–1916)   Writer, revered author of historical novels written "to comfort the heart." The most popular is his trilogy *With Fire and the Sword, The Deluge,* and *Pan Michael* (1884–88). His novel *Quo Vadis* (1896), for which he was awarded the Nobel Prize in literature (1905), was later filmed in Hollywood.

Skamander   Literary group of poets and writers in Warsaw in the 1920s and 1930s.

Słonimski, Antoni (1895–1976)   Poet and essayist, member of the Skamander group. Renowned for his cutting wit. Michnik was his secretary in the early seventies.

Solzhenitsyn, Alexandr I. (b. 1918)   Prisoner in a Soviet gulag, Nobel Prize laureate for literature (1970), author of *One Day in the Life of Ivan Denisovich, Cancer Ward,* and *The Gulag Archipelago.*

Tischner, Reverend Józef (b. 1931)   Philosopher, essayist, collaborator of *Tygodnik Powszechny.*

Tygodnik Powszechny (Universal Weekly)   Publication of the open, ecumenist Catholic intelligentsia. Founded in Kraków by Jerzy Turowicz. Pope John Paul II collaborated with this periodical and was on very friendly terms with its editors.

Tymiński, Stanisław (b. 1947)   Exiled businessman and unexpected runner-up in the 1990 presidential elections against Lech Wałęsa.

Ursus   See *Radom and Ursus.*

Wałęsa, Lech (b. 1943)   Legendary leader of the Solidarity movement, later president of the Polish Republic.

Więź   Catholic monthly, founded in 1958 by Tadeusz Mazowiecki.

Workers' Defense Committee (KOR)   Oppositional organization founded in 1976. The first "anti-political" institution of East European dissidents, its members represented many political persuasions. KOR dissolved itself during the Solidarity period (1981).

Wujek mine   On December 16, 1981, during martial law, while breaking the strike in the Wujek mine (Silesia), armored police units killed nine miners.

Wyszyński, Cardinal Stefan (1901–81)   From 1948 until his death, primate of Poland. A staunch defender of the Catholic Church against communism, he was nevertheless relatively open to dialogue with the authorities. Under house arrest 1953–56.

Żeromski, Stefan (1864–1925)   Eminent writer, called "the conscience of Polish literature." Author of novels (*Homeless People, Ashes, Before the Spring* [Przedwiośnie]) promoting social responsibility and patriotic values.

Index

Printed in the United Kingdom
by Lightning Source UK Ltd.
108036UKS00001B/187-189